MILLEDGEVILLE

MILLEDGEVILLE

GEORGIA'S ANTEBELLUM CAPITAL

James C. Bonner

The University of Georgia Press
ATHENS

Copyright © 1978 by the University of Georgia Press
Athens 30602

All rights reserved

Set in 10 on 13 point Monticello type
Printed in the United States of America

Library of Congress Cataloging in Publication Data

Bonner, James Calvin, 1904–
    Milledgeville, Georgia's antebellum Capital.
    Bibliography.
    Includes index.
    1. Milledgeville, Ga.—History.   2. Georgia—
Capital and capital.   I. Title.

F294.M6B63   975.8′573   77–6667
            ISBN 0–8203–0424–7

TO PATRICIA,
SHANNON, AND
MARIAN

Contents

Illustrations and Maps

Preface

Research on this book began in 1944 when I came to Milledgeville to teach history at what was then known as the Georgia State College for Women. Several articles and an edited work have appeared as by-products of this research. They are quoted here only sparingly and are listed in the bibliography. They may serve to illustrate the rich possibilities of research in local history, a field generally ignored by scholars and inadequately treated by home-grown historians.

When I began writing this story, I had already assembled three times the number of note-cards needed to produce a book which would fall within acceptable limits of space. The problem of selecting and organizing material was therefore an agonizing one. I have run not only the usual risks of authorship but also that of faulty judgment in my choice of the more appropriate topics and supporting facts from such a vast wilderness of stocked material.

Thomas Fuller, in speaking of history in 1638, called it "a velvet study and Recreational Work," and then he added: "History maketh a young man to be old without either wrinkles or gray hairs; privileging him *with* the experience of age *without* either the infirmities or inconveniences thereof." Likewise it can be said that research on this study has been a highly rewarding exercise. It has given me the rare opportunity of living for more than a century in a relatively small community and to know a wide range of interesting people. The activities and diverse relationships of these people as they shared a common space through a constantly moving span of time have produced what I hope may prove to be a palatable capsule of nineteenth-century Southern history.

Milledgeville lies at the fall line of the Oconee River near the heart of the old plantation cotton belt. It is at the approximate geographic center of Georgia. From 1807 to 1868 it was the seat of state government. It therefore possesses unusual significance for the type of in-depth study which I have attempted. By probing into its entire range of social, political, and economic developments, I have attempted to elevate a local history to a level of much broader significance.

After the removal of the capital, Milledgeville lapsed briefly into the role of an agricultural trade center and it was without distinguishing characteristics other than that afforded by the presence of the Georgia Lunatic Asylum. By 1890, however, it had become the seat of two colleges. It was not until the twentieth century that Milledgeville completed its transition to a modern industrial city. Since the latter development was not unusual for this period, no effort has been made to treat in a comprehensive manner the more recent history of the community.

In the preparation of this book I have been assisted by a grant from the American Association for State and Local History which eased the burden of travel to research centers. For this generous aid I am deeply grateful. Donald H. MacMahon and Rosa Lee Walston have read the entire manuscript and offered valuable suggestions. Parts of the manuscript were read by Professor William I. Hair and Professor Salvatore Mangiafico of Georgia College. Each has made a contribution to whatever merit this book may possess. Also I wish to express my gratitude to President James Whitney Bunting and his administrative associates at Georgia College for providing me with office space after my retirement from teaching. Without this gesture of hospitality this book would have been difficult if not impossible to produce.

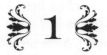

1

Expansion into the
Trans-Oconee Region
1790–1807

The establishment of a town on the west bank of the Oconee to serve as Georgia's capital was a result of historical trends well under way by the end of the Revolution. The war had not prevented thousands of Virginians and Carolinians from settling in Georgia's newly opened lands in the upcountry of Wilkes County, where they became staunch supporters of the Whigs' struggle against the Crown. With Savannah having fallen under control of the King's troops early in the war and the coastal area becoming strongly affected by Toryism, Augusta was made the new capital in 1786. Later, in 1795, upcountry members of the constitutional convention obtained the removal of the seat of government to Louisville, which at that time was near the outer perimeter of white settlements. Before the capital could be moved farther into the interior, additional land had to be ceded by the Creek Indians.

Land policy had become the most important single issue to be decided and would determine the future of the state's development. Public land claimed by Georgia at this time amounted to almost 100 million acres, but because of Indian ownership not more than 10 percent of this area was subject to immediate acquisition by private owners. No other state at this time could boast so large a public domain.

In 1783 a group of Creek chiefs reluctantly ceded nearly 3 million acres between the Ogeechee and Oconee rivers, stretching for nearly 170 miles across the length of the state. In the following year this area was organized as Washington County and opened for immediate settlement by whites. One of the largest ever settled in Georgia, this county began a few miles south of the future site of Athens and ran southward to a point several miles below what was to become Reidsville. The total effect was to move Georgia's Indian boundary westward from the Ogeechee to the Oconee.

Despite the fact that the sprawling new county was rapidly becoming settled, the Creek leader, Alexander McGillivray, and a large number of his subordinate chiefs did not recognize the legality of the 1783 cession, claiming that it and a subsequent treaty at Shoulderbone Creek were consummated through shameful intimidation of the chiefs who had signed. The central government under the Articles of Confederation appeared to side with the Indians against Georgia by declaring the controversial treaties void. This tended to embolden the Creeks, whose warriors now crossed the Oconee in small bands to harass the settlers. They committed murder, carried off livestock and food, and burned some houses. Georgia resisted by sending out militia patrols which had a number of minor skirmishes with the Indians. This fighting became known as the Oconee War.

One of the earliest acts of President George Washington's administration in 1789 was an attempt to settle this controversy between Georgia and the Creeks. In that year the president sent a commission to Georgia headed by no less a figure than General Benjamin Lincoln, formerly the secretary of war under the old Articles of Confederation. The commission met McGillivray with 2,000 of his warriors and lesser chiefs at Rock Landing on the Oconee, a short distance south of the future site of Milledgeville. Dissatisfied with the terms proposed and apparently incensed by the presence of guns and soldiers, McGillivray quietly left the treaty ground in the night and returned to the Ocmulgee; he later explained that the west bank of the Oconee provided insufficient grazing for his horses.

During the following year McGillivray was induced to bring a small delegation of Creeks to New York, then the capital of the United States. Late in July, thirty-five Creeks, including twenty-three chiefs, met President Washington face to face amid considerable pomp and ceremony, including the firing of a military salute. Later McGillivray was granted the rank of a brigadier general in the American army, with a pension of $1,200 a year. Special medals were struck for his chiefs, six of whom were given an annuity of one hundred dollars each.

The treaty itself must have pleased the Creeks greatly, but it was wholly unsatisfactory to most Georgians. While it confirmed the state's possession of land between the Ogeechee and the Oconee rivers, it also recognized, at least by implication, the Oconee as the permanent western boundary of white settlements. Any Georgian who crossed that river from Washington County without a passport would do so at the risk of being treated as an outlaw and could be shot on sight. He was not allowed to hunt or fish on

Creek lands. But what incensed Georgians most was the tone of finality they found in the agreement. It appeared to many that the Creeks on the west side of the Oconee were to be transformed into farmers and husbandmen and eventually to come into individual possession of their former tribal lands. Toward this end, the United States government was to provide free seed grain, animals, and "implements of husbandry" and, further, to send trained experts to reside among the Creeks to teach them the arts of the white man's civilization.[1] Later, in 1795, Congress authorized the establishment of a "factory," or trading house, at frontier military outposts where certain goods could be furnished at cost to the Indians and where skins and pelts might be received in partial payment.[2] This is one of our country's earliest examples of aid to underdeveloped nations.

Georgians had no intention of permitting the Indians to occupy permanently millions of acres of rich cotton land west of the Oconee. Completely ignoring the Treaty of New York, they continued to carry on the war with the Creeks. President Washington remonstrated, but to little avail. Finally, small forts were built at intervals along the Oconee and garrisoned by federal soldiers who were charged with maintaining peace in this troublesome frontier. But it was a tenuous and uncertain peace.

The first of these forts was at Rock Landing, near which appeared the settlement of Federaltown on the east side of the river, eight miles below the future site of Milledgeville. The earliest settlement in this section, Federaltown contained fifteen houses and a tobacco inspection station. One observer, noting its activity, suggested that it might some day "become the grand Warehouse for the riches of the Western Frontiers, and that trade from Tennessee will pass to the Atlantic by boats . . . which now navigate the river."[3]

Because of sickness at Rock Landing the garrison was moved in April 1793 to a new stockade known as Fort Fidius, farther up the river and two miles below the mouth of Fishing Creek where later appeared the east landing of Holt's Ferry.[4] Within a half mile of Fort Fidius, still farther up the river, appeared a new settlement known as Montpelier (Mount Pelier), and as this town grew Federaltown rapidly disintegrated. Montpelier became the most populous community of a wide area along the east side of the river. It was surveyed and platted before settlement and, like its predecessor, it had a public warehouse mainly for the storage and inspection of tobacco. Fort Wilkinson came into existence in 1797, supplanting Fort Fidius. It was the first of these garrisons to be placed on the west side of the river, where the Indians could visit without trespassing on lands already ceded to the whites.[5]

In addition to the federal garrisons, a number of blockhouses were constructed along the frontier by order of Governor Edward Telfair in April 1793. These were to be occupied by state militiamen.[6] Since these militiamen represented the local interests of Georgia frontiersmen, they often were in conflict with soldiers from the federal garrison whose purpose was to pacify the Indians by scrupulously enforcing the terms of the New York treaty of 1790. The settlers were particularly critical of federal officers for enforcing the law forbidding white men from crossing the Oconee River. Governor James Jackson wrote the Secretary of War complaining of the arrest of a citizen "for merely being in a canoe" on the river. The man was confined in a "Military Dungeon [and then] marched to Louisville as a criminal," he wrote. "The situation of the River Oconee in Summer [is such] that the waters get so low as to render it impossible for the inhabitants on its banks to prevent their horses, Cattle, or Hogs from crossing it. A few days since a lad . . . followed his father's Hogs over a Shoal to the other side . . . and was instantly seized and carried to the Garrison and paraded as a criminal." Jackson mentioned the case of one Williams caught asleep in a boat on the boundary line (the Oconee) and who as punishment was handcuffed and chained to a stump for six or eight days in very cold weather, all at the mandate of Colonel Henry Gaither. Afterwards "he was dragged to Savannah where Judge Clay on examination declared he had been guilty of no offense." These alleged misdemeanors were taking place "whilst the Indians were roaming at large through all frontier counties, painted in a warlike manner, and take what they please from the Inhabitants," he stated. He concluded that Colonel Gaither, commander of the garrison, had by such actions rendered himself "disgusting and obnoxious" to the frontiersmen.[7]

Creek depredations upon white settlements continued and, more often than not, the perpetrators went unpunished. Nicholas Vines was shot dead by a group of Indians who fired upon him from ambush while he was walking with women and children on the east bank of the river. A Creek named Tuskeegee Tustonegau, charged with committing rape on one Mrs. Hilton, was placed in jail and later released by the Inferior Court of Oglethorpe County on the excuse that such leniency was necessary to prevent Indian depredations.[8]

Under these conditions the Indians soon learned that federal troops could be trusted, and they sought their protection at the garrison. However, neither the Creeks nor the federal authorities could place much trust in the state militiamen and their commanders. In September 1793 James Seagrove, the federal Superintendent of Indian Affairs, was sent to the Ocmulgee to negotiate with the Indians, a move which the Georgia settlers strongly opposed. To guarantee Seagrove's safety on the journey from his headquarters at Augusta, he was met near Louisville by a body of federal troops under Captain Joseph Dickinson who accompanied him to Fort Fidius. In a letter to the Secretary of War, Seagrove reported that "parties of Georgians, mostly volunteer brigands" were crossing the Oconee and making depredations on their Creek neighbors between that line and the Ocmulgee.[9] In May of the following year a party of Indians carried off some horses near Sparks Station. This theft occurred during a peaceful visit of some chiefs, in company with Seagrove, to Governor Telfair in Augusta. The horse thieves were pursued by fifteen militiamen under Lieutenant Hay, who fell into an ambuscade at the High Shoals of the Appalachee, where Hay and two others were killed.[10] The survivors of this ambuscade, augmented by more than 135 additional militiamen, now sought revenge on a group of Indians encamped on the Oconee near Fort Fidius awaiting the return of their chiefs from Augusta. This group of 150 mounted men under Major David Adams launched a surprise attack on the Indians as they rested on the west bank of the river. The Indians fled in wild confusion, but ten of them managed to cross the river and take refuge inside Fort Fidius, where twenty others had already found safety. Here they sought the protection of federal soldiers. The Georgians now demanded of Major Brooke Roberts, commander of the fort, that he surrender all the refugees. If Roberts complied, he would violate the faith of the United States; yet in affording the Indians protection he would run the risk of an attack on his fort by state militiamen. Roberts arranged for the Indians to escape from the fort and to cross the river to safety. Later Major Adams refused to turn over to the garrison commander the horses, rifles, and skins which his men had taken from the Indians.[11]

The chiefs visiting Augusta were now in great danger. It was necessary to provide them with a federal military escort to assure them a safe return to their nation. In order to avoid the Georgia militia they were compelled to cross the Oconee some fifteen miles south of Rock Landing.[12]

Because of these incidents, Major Roberts reported to the authorities in Washington on May 10, 1794, that the Indian war had actually begun.

"The Indians and Georgians seem now mutually roused and there is not a doubt that war will break out in all its horrows [sic]," he reported. He requested the immediate strengthening of Fort Fidius, which he characterized as "totally defenceless." Its effective military strength at this time was about seventy men. The fort's water supply came from springs some 300 yards away and could easily be cut off by attackers. Thus he believed that the fort was vulnerable at all times, and in such a condition it could afford no protection.[13]

The predicted full-scale Indian war, however, did not materialize. This was partly a result of a spectacular event which occurred elsewhere. Early in May, Elijah Clarke and a rag-tag collection of adventurous followers emerged from the wilderness of coastal Georgia and took a stance along the west bank of the Oconee, in complete defiance of laws prohibiting such trespass upon Creek territory. Clarke originally had recruited his little army for the purpose of invading Spanish Florida, where his followers had been promised land, wealth, and immunity from both state and federal laws. His expedition having failed for lack of French support, this old hero of the Revolution now found employment as well as adventure in the troublesome trans-Oconee region of central Georgia. Here his army was augmented by new recruits, most of whom were veterans of the Revolution who had come in from Wilkes, Washington, and adjoining counties.

Clarke mapped out a buffer state running 120 miles along the western bank of the Oconee and erected forts at intervals along the entire length of its border. While he claimed to be protecting the interests of Georgia, his performance possessed many characteristics of a large-scale land-grabbing venture. Each of his followers was promised 640 acres of land as soon as it could be surveyed and an additional 500 acres later. Fort Advance was constructed by Clarke's men on high ground on the west side of the river opposite the federal post at Fort Fidius. Here also a town was laid out which, though then nameless, became rapidly settled. Six miles above Fort Fidius, on the opposite side of the river, they erected Fort Defiance. Within the outer limits of what later became Milledgeville appeared Fort Winston.[14]

During June and July a constitution for this "Trans-Oconee Republic" supposedly was framed and a Council of Safety inaugurated. Before the end of the summer President George Washington issued a proclamation calling for Clarke's arrest and trial. One of the state's most beloved war heroes, Clarke was certain that most Georgians would support him in his enterprise, so he returned to his home in Wilkes County and surrendered himself to the custody of old friends. True to his expectations, the four justices-of-the-peace who conducted his trial discharged him by unanimous vote, stating that he had violated no law known to them. Clarke's settlement now began to take on an air of permanence.

At this point, however, the fall session of the superior court was in progress at Augusta, and Judge George Walton now issued a legal opinion on Clarke's venture. He pointed out the dual dangers of federal intervention and civil war among Georgians which the enterprise might engender. But what appealed most to the logic of the masses was his clever statement that the rich lands of the Trans-Oconee belonged to all the people and not to a group of scheming adventurers.

An urgent message from the Department of War now stirred Governor George Mathews to action. Reenforced by a decision from the state's attorney general, he ordered the militia to destroy Clarke's forts and his settlement. Finally, the old war-horse, now sixty-one years old, was forced to surrender to the state's forces under Jared Irwin. Many of the settlers, their houses and stockades burned, had already left with their families. Efforts to have Clarke tried for treason failed, however, and these efforts even brought unfavorable reaction upon the governor.[15]

Georgians remained unrelenting in their efforts to obtain additional cessions from the Creeks. None of these was successful until 1802, when the treaty made at New York in 1790 was abrogated and a new basis laid for the transfer of additional Creek territory. This treaty, which will be discussed below, was made at Fort Wilkinson near the future site of Milledgeville.

As already noted, the federal garrison abandoned Fort Fidius in 1797 and moved into the newly constructed Fort Wilkinson on the west side of the river just within Creek territory. It was situated on a bluff between a creek called Itchco wam otchco (Camp Creek) and one, farther up the river, called Thlock-laoso. The latter was valuable for fishing, particularly for spring shad, and hence came to be called Fishing Creek. The area between these two streams was quite fertile, with numerous canebrakes for the winter grazing of livestock. The Indians, apparently wishing to conduct their affairs with garrison officials without having to enter the white settlements at Rock Landing, recommended this location "as the fittest place for a military post."[16]

The area in the vicinity of Fort Wilkinson has a peculiar significance in the early development of the trans-Oconee region. The river itself received its name from old Oconee Town, once located a short distance below Rock

Landing. When William Bartram crossed the river at this point in 1777, he pitched his camp on the site of this old Indian town which already had been abandoned for more than sixty years and which he described as a pleasant and beautiful spot. The Yamassee war of 1715 caused the Oconees to move to the Chattahoochee River, where part of the group remained until 1799. Others went to Florida, where their new town was named Cuscovilla. There they became the nucleus of the Seminole Nation with whom they became amalgamated. But the dominant composition of the Florida Indians remained Muscogean, or Creek. The Oconees spoke the Hitchiti language, and they are said to have provided most of the head chiefs of the Seminoles.[17]

Rock Landing had been the principal crossing point on the river for more than a century before its east bank was settled. Converging at this point were several Indian trails which fanned out across the wilderness. Two of the most important were the Old Horse Path and the Lower Creek Trading Path, both having their origin at Augusta. The latter path was one of the most historical aboriginal routes in North America. From Augusta it followed the fall line to reach the present vicinity of Columbus, where its connections extended southward and westward beyond the Tallapoosa and the Coosa and on to the Gulf of Mexico.[18] There was also an Upper Creek Trading Path which ran from Augusta to the Creek villages on the upper Coosa and Tallapoosa rivers in Alabama. This path crossed the Oconee some twenty miles north of Rock Landing, passed through Indian Springs, and kept well above the fall line.

Since Rock Landing provided a ford at most seasons of the year and was the actual head of navigation on the river, it retained its importance long after Milledgeville was settled, yet it never became an important river port or the center of extensive trade as some had predicted. A large warehouse was built there on a high bluff overlooking the river and "the Landing" grew into a sizeable village, its area enclosed by a fence.[19] When the botanist William Bartram broke camp here in 1777 he joined a caravan of Augusta Indian traders comprising twenty men and sixty pack horses. It was the custom of such travelers to cross streams in canoes while swimming their animals. Bartram carried with him an inflatable rubber boat for this purpose.[20]

By 1807 a ferry boat had been established at the landing. In March of that year Aaron Burr, a former vice-president of the United States, was brought here under arrest on a charge of treason. One of his guards reported that this was the first ferry boat they had seen since leaving Natchez. When Burr and his seven guards stopped for breakfast at the house of William Bivins, they ate their meal under the first roof they had encountered on their long journey from Mississippi.[21] Apparently Burr's party abandoned the Lower Path after leaving Rock Landing and took the Old Horse Path to Augusta, following a more northern route.

Burr and his escort had spent the night at Fort Wilkinson, which even then was in the final process of abandonment in favor of a new stockade on the Ocmulgee known as Fort Hawkins. Fort Wilkinson's history spanned less than a decade.[22] After it supplanted Fort Fidius in 1797, the trading house, or "factory" as it was then called, was moved there from Colerain in southeastern Georgia. Edward Price, the factor, arrived on July 5, 1797, and goods for the Indian trade were sent by boat to Augusta and thence by wagon to the post on the Oconee River. Price was succeeded by Edward Wright, who in turn was replaced by Jonathan Halsted. Two of Fort Wilkinson's military commanders were Colonel Henry Gaither and Colonel William R. Boot.[23]

The day-to-day operation of this fort suggests that its garrison never exceeded thirty or forty men. While their principal function of patrolling the frontier was a drab one, their routine was sometimes relieved by noteworthy events. A general court martial in August 1801 convicted Lieutenant James K. Love of the Fourth Infantry of abandoning his post without leave, and he was dismissed from the service. A private found guilty of murdering a man caught in the act of robbing the soldier's fish trap was turned over to civil authorities, who sentenced him to death. He was perhaps the first man ever hanged in what later became Baldwin County.[24] During Colonel Boot's tour of duty at the post he sent to the east side of the river several hundred women, apparently the families of soldiers doing garrison duty there and elsewhere along the frontier.[25] This, together with regulations concerning shaving and personal grooming, suggests that the post may not have been entirely lacking in social life.[26]

Fort Wilkinson has been described as a small post but one having its entire grounds cleared and improved. Soldiers with families were permitted to build cabins and live outside the walls and to cultivate gardens and fruit trees. Colonel Boot had the bank of the river transformed into a beautiful garden and vineyard, using French vines sent to him by General Lafayette. Nearby was a well-stocked fish pond.[27]

With the easing of frontier tensions after 1794 the policing duties of the garrison declined, but the trading house took on increasing importance. Deer skins were the principal commodity the Indians brought in, and the price was 25 cents for each skin. Small furs brought half this price, but raw cow hides commanded a price ranging from 75 cents to more than a dollar each. Bear skins, beaver, and otter varied in price from one to three dollars. It is doubtful that the government realized any gain from these purchases. The hides had to be beaten once a week to prevent rotting or infestation by worms. Great care was essential in packing for shipment, despite which many losses were sustained in transit. Transportation by water down the Oconee to Darien and thence to Savannah was 50 cents per hundredweight, while the return trip was 75 cents. Sometimes furs and pelts were sent overland to Augusta, and from there to Savannah by river boat, all at a cost of one dollar per hundredweight. From Savannah the skins were shipped to Philadelphia or New York, where they were further processed and sold.[28]

The long water voyage by Darien came to be the favorite route, both for outgoing freight and incoming supplies. Suggesting that frontiersmen in the area were also using the Oconee as a trade outlet, Henry Harford wrote from Darien in 1803 that "there is [sic] now 16 large Boats employed in bringing down from the neighborhood of the Garrison, corn, cotton, and tobacco. In the winter and Spring months boats pass with facility and ease, in the summer and fall months the waters are generally low." The schooner, Seahorse, owned by Harford and the firm of Keen and Stillmore in Darien, was plying regularly between that little port and Philadelphia.[29]

The upstream traffic in supplies apparently exceeded that going downstream. This was largely because the Indians bought more goods than the value of their credit in skins and furs, a fact which did not discourage them. Actually, the Indians' great desire for the basic accoutrements of the white man's civilization, combined with their willingness to go into debt to acquire them, were important factors in their undoing. In the end the Indians were required to pay their debts with cessions of land, the only other commodity they possessed which the white man coveted. Debts owed by the Creeks to the factory at Fort Wilkinson in November 1801 amounted to $23,874. In a treaty made there the following year, the United States agreed to cancel almost half this amount in return for a new cession west of the Oconee.[30]

This treaty, signed at Fort Wilkinson on June 16, 1802, resulted in the first land cession made by the Creeks since 1790. While the passport system was continued, the treaty finally brought tranquility along both banks of the

Oconee. It moved the boundary westward from that river about 12 miles to a line where Commissioner Creek crossed the Lower Creek Trading Path. It also included an area on the extreme northern part of the Oconee-Ocmulgee region, and another in the extreme south, later organized as Wayne County.[31]

Later, in 1806, the boundary was extended to the Ocmulgee. Both treaties involved payment of considerable sums of money to the Creeks, partly in the form of credit for goods which they might obtain from the factory and for the payment of debts already incurred.[32] By similar agreements Indian claims to wild lands all the way to the line of the Chattahoochee River had been extinguished by 1826. The frontier garrison and trading house had moved westward with each important land cession. After 1813 the trading post was located at Fort Mitchell on the west bank of the Chattahoochee, near Coweta Falls and the future site of Columbus.

A significant feature of the cession of 1806 was the stipulation that the federal government be permitted to cut a horse path through Creek territory from the Ocmulgee River to Mobile. Opened almost immediately, this "Federal Road" soon became an important wagon road. It followed in general the course of the Lower Path through Georgia, crossing the streams at the fall line. The section of this road between Fort Wilkinson and Fort Hawkins now became known variously as the Garrison Road and the Hawkins Trail. This road and its western arteries became the principal route of travel for Indian traders and later for thousands of farmers who settled the Southwest. Because this road brought the white man into more intimate contact with the Creeks, it increased the former's greed for additional land cessions, and antagonized the Indians.

Somewhat unknown but of some importance was another trading path which passed through what became the northern limits of Milledgeville. Known as "Tom's Path" and later as "Old Tom's Path," this trail appears to have been in existence as early as 1757 when a trader, William Tobler, in defiance of Colonial regulations, was engaged in selling whisky to the Indians. Tobler, who appears to have fathered several Indian children, lived at the mouth of Tobler's Creek, which flows into the Savannah just south of Augusta. Here the trail known as Tom's Path appears to have originated. It ran westward to Old Town below Louisville and crossed the Ogeechee at a ford where another Tobler's Creek enters that stream. Some distance westward the path veered northward, crossed the Lower Path, and reached the Oconee at the McKinley plantation near Milledgeville. At this point it crossed the Oconee a few hundred yards north of where a third Tobler's Creek enters that river. Thence it ran westward along the route which later would be called Dunlap Road and followed the higher ridges to a point on the Ocmulgee just below Pope's Ferry (on what became Georgia Highway 87). Here still another Tobler's Creek enters that river. Finally, the path reached the Flint River at the place (on U.S. Highway 90-80 in 1976) where a fifth Tobler's Creek empties into that stream. The path crossed all these rivers at shallow fall-line fords, three of which also bore the name of Tobler.[33] Tom's Path, which linked these fords, marked a surreptitious rum-running route from the Savannah to the heart of the Creek country. Licensed Indian traders and those who did not shun observation by others used the Lower Path, except in extremely wet weather, during which they would follow the Upper Path lying some twenty miles to the north. Thus Tom's Path became identified with the earliest bootlegging enterprise in upper Georgia.[34]

In early nineteenth-century records Tom's Path frequently appears as "Old Tom's Path." Old Tom was a slave on the Barrow plantation who often guided early travelers to the ford on the Oconee at the mouth of Tobler's Creek. However, the name also may have derived from a Cusseta Indian named Tom who was a courier for Benjamin Hawkins. At any rate, Tom's Path or Old Tom's Path is the earliest English placename associated with the area which became Milledgeville.[35]

Many old trails and similar landmarks appear on the early land maps of the region, being required as part of the new land system of orderly surveys before distribution and settlement. The first of these followed the land cession of 1802 at Fort Wilkinson. After an orderly, rectilinear survey into farm-sized lots, the land was later distributed through the lottery. The details of this new land system were outlined in an act of the Georgia legislature on May 11, 1803, in which Baldwin, Wilkinson, and Wayne counties were created.

Originally Baldwin County extended to the High Shoals on the Appalachee River a few miles south of Athens. The southern boundary, which separated Baldwin from Wilkinson, was a line beginning on the Oconee at Fort Wilkinson and running south forty-five degrees west to the new Indian boundary. In 1807, when Baldwin County was enlarged at the expense of Wilkinson, this line was moved southward a few miles. At the same time parts of Washington and Hancock counties were also added to Baldwin.[36]

The surveyors of Baldwin County were ordered to lay out five land districts with their lines running parallel to the Baldwin-Wilkinson dividing line. Then they were required to lay out tracts forty-five chains square (each containing 202½ acres). These lines were to run "parallel with the district lines, in regular progression, and leaving a space of 45 chains between each line, and these lines crossing others at right angles."[37] The instructions help to explain why the original land lines in this region all run from northwest to southeast and from northeast to southwest. Elsewhere west of the Oconee these lines run from north to south and east to west. One precedent for this unique exception to the rule is found in adjacent Washington County, where

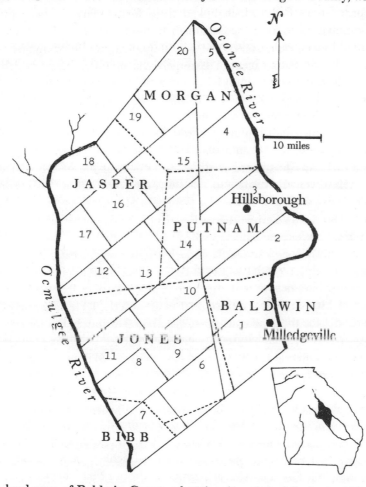

The land map of Baldwin County showing its original limits in 1805

Dotted lines show the boundaries of succession counties

district lines under the old system of indiscriminate surveys were originally run perpendicular to the Ogeechee and Oconee rivers which flow in a southeasterly direction.[38]

The five surveyors appointed—one for each land district—were James Lamar, Levin Wales, Reuben DeJarnette, D. Creswell, and Abner Franklin. Appointed by the legislature, they were provided compensation at the rate of $2.75 per mile out of which they were to pay an axe-man, two chain-bearers, and any other expenses which might be incurred.[39] The surveys were made during the spring and summer of 1804. After they were completed, a plat was provided showing the number and location of each lot in the district.

Minute and quite detailed instructions were issued by the surveyor general, Daniel Sturges. The manner of marking lines differed from that used previously anywhere in the state. Trees standing exactly on the county line were to be marked at every quarter mile with four notches and the letters *CL* and with the letter *B* (Baldwin) on the north side and *W* (Wilkinson) on the south side. All "elbow trees" received two chops, and all trees on the course of district lines were marked with four notches and the letters *DL*, fore and aft. All corners were marked both with chops and blazes. Fractional lots, created where river boundaries intervened to prevent the creation of a full lot, were dealt with in special instructions. Surveyors were required to note all water courses, Indian paths, lakes, swamps, and ponds.[40] While each of the various surveys conducted in subsequent years might differ in precise details, the instructions formulated by Sturges set the general pattern for all of the state's rectilinear surveys which followed.

District Number Two of Baldwin County, which begins a few miles north of Milledgeville, received one of the most meticulous surveys ever recorded in the surveyor general's office. Its precision is a result of the skill of Levin Wales and his nephew and chain-bearer, William Lloyd Thomas. Wales's early plats show not only the Indian trails but a number of grist mills already operating on the west side of the Oconee, such as Reed's, Lowe's, and Purifry's. He also marked the path of a hurricane which occurred on April 5, 1804 and which ravaged a large area in his district. In 1807 Wales moved to Mississippi, where he became a distinguished surveyor in that state. Thomas continued his work in Georgia and became equally notable in western Georgia where his most celebrated achievement was the skillful running of the Georgia-Alabama boundary from Miller's Bend on the Chattahoochee to Nicajack in Tennessee.[41]

The act providing for the distribution of the land by lottery was incorporated in the law of 1803 setting up the survey. This lottery was held at Louisville in 1805, being the only one of seven lotteries not held at Milledgeville. Tickets were printed which equalled in number all persons in the state eligible for a draw. (These included unmarried white men twenty-one years old who had resided one year in the state, one draw; a minor orphan or a family of orphans, one draw; married males with wife or child, two draws; and a widow with minor child, two draws). Tickets were prepared representing each of the lots surveyed, and these constituted prizes. The number of blanks was determined by subtracting the number of prizes from the total number of persons eligible for a draw. On each prize ticket was written the number of the lot which it represented and the number of the district wherein it lay. All of these tickets were then placed in a box from which the drawing was made. In subsequent lotteries two hollow-rimmed wheels, made at the penitentiary, were used to facilitate shuffling of the tickets.[42] Tickets were drawn from the "prizewheel" and placed to the credit of a name similarly drawn from a large wheel containing names of all eligible drawers.

While the lottery system had its origin in colonial history, none of the older lotteries were so comprehensive in design as that described above. The law of 1803 provided for an appraiser to determine the quality of the land and to place it into one of six categories, each with a value classification. The price of the land was to vary from 6¼ cents to one dollar an acre.[43] Before this regulation was put into effect, however, this section of the law was repealed, and only a flat charge of $16, called a "grant fee," was made to recipients of fortunate tickets. Thus the state finally adopted the principal of free land.

White men trespassing and settling on land west of the line of Commissioner Creek hastened an additional cession, in 1805, which moved the limits of white occupation westward to the Ocmulgee River. A second lottery, held in 1807, extended the settlements of Baldwin County to this river.[44]

This was accompanied by the organization of a county government, the last of three stages outlined in the new land policy. The first act of organization came in December 1805 when five justices of the inferior court were appointed. In the following year the county was divided into five militia districts, each with a justice-of-the-peace; provisions were made for the election of clerks of the superior court and the inferior court, a sheriff, coroner, and county surveyor. The county was made part of the second brigade of the third division of the state militia and was placed in the western district of the superior court. The Ocmulgee circuit, of which Baldwin and all of its succession counties became a part, was not formed until 1807.[45]

The first election of local officials held in the county took place in July 1806 at the house of George Hill in the settlement "commonly called Hillsborough," which was six miles east of the future site of Eatonton and approximately in the geographic center of the county's original limits.[46] After one election there and one session of the superior court, Hillsborough gave way to Milledgeville as the county seat when, in December 1807, an act of the legislature provided for the holding of Baldwin County elections in the statehouse at Milledgeville. This act was repealed in the following year when authorization was given for a special tax levy to construct a county courthouse and jail; in the meantime courts were held in rented houses. The new courthouse was completed in 1814 at a cost of $3,875. Eight years later a new jail, built of stone, was constructed on a spot near the courthouse.[47]

Hillsborough, incidentally, had meanwhile become the first seat of Putnam County, which was created from Baldwin County in 1807 along with Jones, Morgan, and Randolph (later Jasper) counties. However, the town never had more than four dwelling houses in addition to a jail and a courthouse—all built of logs—and a saloon, and within a few years after Eatonton took over in 1809 as the seat of Putnam County, Hillsborough fell into rapid decay and soon disappeared. Before long it could be identified only by the graves of two federal soldiers from Fort Wilkinson who were buried near the town.[48]

By its fourth year Baldwin County had already experienced considerable changes in its boundaries and had known two county seats. It had come into existence at a time when troublesome Indian hostilities had barely subsided and when rampant land speculation had been brought under control through the state's inauguration of a liberal and democratic system of land distribution. The creation of Baldwin, Wilkinson, and Wayne counties in 1803 thus helped to set the pattern for future expansion of white settlements to the line of the Chattahoochee River.

Frontier Capital: 1807–1830

The act of 1803 that outlined the new land system and created Baldwin, Wilkinson, and Wayne counties also provided for the location and survey of a town which was to be called Milledgeville. This town—named in honor of John Milledge, who was then governor (1802–1806)—was to contain sixteen lots, each of 202½ acres, for a total of 3,240 acres, only a small part of which was designated as residential. Each residence lot was to be one acre in size. These were later sold by the state and the money applied to the construction of the Statehouse and other public facilities.[1] In December 1804 Milledgeville was declared by legislature to be the seat of government—an action which immediately increased the value of land within the town.[2]

The first town plat, surveyed in July 1804 by John Ragan, contained only 500 acres. This plat comprised eighty-four squares of four acres each, so that each residential lot was on a corner in juxtaposition to three other lots. There were also four public squares of twenty acres each. The streets, which interlaced the pattern in checkerboard fashion, were 100 feet wide—except for Jefferson and Washington streets, each of which had parkways and a total width of 120 feet. The streets accounted for an additional eighty-four acres. Because the streets ran from east to west and north to south, they were a variance by forty-five degrees with lines on the land map upon which the town plat was imposed. A later map of the town, made in 1808 by Daniel Sturges, shows an additional 3,290 acres in the north commons and approximately the same acreage in the south commons.[3] The commons lay outside of the area reserved for residential use, providing grazing for livestock and free fuel for the use of early residents.

Town plats with one or more public squares and streets intersecting at right angles were common to Georgia town planning, having originated at Savannah in the early colonial period. Unique, however, was the system of corner residential lots initiated by the plan for Milledgeville. This influenced the town's residential pattern throughout the entire nineteenth century, when houses tended to be constructed nearest street intersections. Thus the structures were placed relatively close together in clumps of four, one house on each of four corners, an arrangement not only promoting sociability but also giving each household easy access to a common well or spring. The houses were set close to the street, some actually encroaching on the public right-of-way. This pattern eliminated the problem of keeping a front lawn in that age of wild undergrowth, and it also left ample room in the rear for garden, stable, orchard, a small pasture, poultry house, and sometimes a family burial lot, all of which might be squeezed into an acre lot. Some residents owned two adjacent lots, which was the maximum permitted to early purchasers.

These early houses, all of frame construction, had the appearance of typical plantation groups, or messuages, as indeed they were sometimes called in the literature of this period.[4] Many early residents acquired agricultural land in the county and still others left their plantations to the care of overseers in order to enjoy the social life of the capital. The presence of so many absentee farmers helped to impart to the town the appearance of rural simplicity. Buildings constructed in the early period were without much elegance or style. They were likely to be without porches or columns and to have dormer windows in the roof so as to utilize all available space within. Since there was little stone in the vicinity, chimneys often were constructed of brick made from local clay. In the least pretentious houses chimney stems often were constructed of wood daubed with clay.

Milledgeville's location might well have been fixed at any point on the Oconee River from Rock Landing to Furman Shoals, seven miles northward. It was doubtless the presence of an abundant supply of excellent drinking water which finally determined its site. No fewer than eight bold springs were found in the small area just north of Fishing Creek.[5] The best known of these were Commissioners Spring (later called Jarretts Spring) and Hawkins Spring. The latter, located at the southwest corner of what was to become Liberty and Franklin streets, was where the five commissioners appointed by the legislature to dispose of lots in the town met on March 1, 1805, to name the streets and to begin the sale of lots.[6] (Streets took their names from existing Georgia counties, most of which had been named for Revolutionary War generals.)

The former spring was even more famous, for it was at Commissioners Spring, according to tradition, that the original commissioners who were seeking the best location for the town came to rest after many wearisome hours of walking. There they found a large oak fifteen feet in circumference and ground carpeted with grass. Someone in the group produced some whisky, which was tempered with water from the spring before it was served. In his enthusiasm for the excellent drink which resulted, one of the commissioners thrust his cane into the ground and announced, "This is it!"[7] The entire area at that time was covered with hickory, oak, and other hardwoods, indicative of the high fertility of the soil.

One of these original commissioners, John Clark, had found his work extremely troublesome and exhausting, but he felt a sense of pride in his accomplishment when his task was completed. He thought well of the final design of the town, and its site gave him assurance that it would be free of sickness—an assumption which later was found to be only wishful thinking.[8]

One of the early lots sold for $4,000, which was perhaps the highest price that had ever been paid in Georgia for an acre of wild land. Some of the cheaper lots sold for as little as $190. Speculation was discouraged by limiting each purchaser to two lots. In order to make the land available to more people, two and a half years were given in which to complete payment, at the end of which period the purchaser was required to have made certain improvements on his property. This period later was extended.[9]

The organization of a municipal government for Milledgeville began on December 8, 1806, with the appointment by the legislature of a new commission of five members who were required to appoint a town clerk, marshal, and vendue master. On the first Monday of 1808 and in every subsequent year thereafter, the ruling commission was to be chosen by the citizens of the town.[10] A year later, in 1809, and again in 1810 extensive new powers were granted to the commissioners. In order that they might "secure the welfare and convenience of the community," they were empowered to make rules, by-laws, and ordinances relating to streets, public buildings, markets, conveyances, fire protection, the regulation of conduct, levying of fines, assessment of taxes, and maintenance of the public springs. No person would be eligible for election to the board of commissioners until he had been a resident of the town for one year, and he was further required to have been a freeholder or a leaseholder for at least four years.[11]

In 1810 another act divided the town into four wards whose boundaries were formed by the intersection of Washington and Jefferson streets. Each ward now elected its own commissioner, who in turn met with his colleagues at the Statehouse and chose an intendant "not of their own body."

John Milledge,
governor of Georgia from 1802 to 1806

Three additional commissioners were appointed by the legislature in 1816, bringing the total number to seven.[12] The act further expanded the powers of the commissioners and the indendant, specifically charging them to "compel due observance of the Sabbath," to rent that part of the town common "opposite James Rousseau's Ferry," and to prevent illicit traffic between slaves and shopkeepers.[13]

While these laws were amended from time to time, they remained the basic pattern of the town's municipal government until 1836, at which time an act of legislature replaced the commission form with one incorporating the town as a city with an elected mayor and council.[14] Throughout the existence of the commission there were a total of twenty-five elections for the office of intendant. Twelve of these officials served only a single term.

William Y. Hansell served three terms as intendant and later was twice elected mayor.

In December 1805 a special commission was empowered to contract for the construction of a statehouse, to be completed by October 1807 and not to exceed $60,000 in cost.[15] An old Indian burial mound stood on the hill chosen as the site for the Statehouse, and the southeast corner of the building was laid only a few yards from that reminder of an earlier civilization.

By November of 1807 the Statehouse was far enough toward completion that the legislature could meet there. The treasury and the public records had already been removed from Louisville in October, transported to Milledgeville in fifteen wagons and guarded by twenty horsemen. The arsenal, however, would remain in the former capital for several more years. The Statehouse was at this time in the form of a rectangle, with neither porticoes nor wings; yet its pointed arched windows and its battlements proclaimed its Gothic Revival style. It is said that this was the first use of this style in a public building in America.[16]

The enlargement of the building progressed slowly over the next twenty years. It was not until 1811 that the first stage of the structure finally was completed by the builders, Jett Thomas and William Scott. The addition of the north and south wings was authorized in 1827.[17] Six years later the older portion of the structure underwent extensive repair. Its outer walls received two coats of paint, and a copper roof replaced the original one of wooden shingles. Not until 1836, however, did the building assume its final form, when a wing was added to the south end to complement the one already completed on the north end. A new well was sunk near the building, which by now was surrounded by a picket fence.[18] Throughout its entire history as a governmental building the Statehouse was heated by numerous open fireplaces, which consumed approximately seventy cords of hardwood annually. (A fireplace was built into each of the four walls which enclosed the Senate and House chambers.)[19]

The original furnishings of the Statehouse were crude and primitive. The 1810 legislature authorized the replacement of the old church-style pews by carpenter-made writing desks containing drawers with locks, and the seating in the House and Senate chambers was then rearranged into a half circle. The old seats were sent to the Baptist Church, where they remained in use for many years. The new desks later were painted an umber color and "varnished in the best copal varnish." They were also supplied with "ink glasses sunk in holes bored in the desk." Still another replacement of desks was made in 1836.[20] Authorization was given in 1810 for the purchase of carpeting to reduce the noise made by lawmakers walking the floors, but only the aisles and the area in front of the presiding officer's table were finally carpeted.[21]

At this time Few's (later Fluker's) Ferry had just been established near the Statehouse. Holt's Ferry was downstream below Fort Wilkinson, and the boatyard was just above the fort. Milledgeville was located slightly above the head of navigation on the river, and five small shoals lay between it and Rock Landing.[22]

On the southwest corner of Statehouse Square stood the market house, while the dwelling of Isaiah Eilands stood on its northeast corner. Other structures, used both for lawyers' offices and for private homes, had arisen on this square, apparently through leasing permits from the state. On the hillside east of the capitol, between that building and the ferry, were the public toilets.[23] Daniel Mulford's map of Milledgeville, sketched in 1809, labels these as "Public Depositories," but elsewhere he uses far less delicacy: one dwelling, on Franklin Street some four blocks west of the Statehouse, he names simply "A Whorehouse" and then adds, "These are plenty and make money out of the venturous old bachelors of the town."[24]

The governor's residence originally was a double-log house on the east side of South Jefferson Street, overlooking Fishing Creek. It was here that the first of the Milledgeville governors, Jared Irwin, a former brigadier general in the state militia, unpacked his saddle bags in the fall of 1807. A few days later his wife, who had recently been injured in an accident, arrived in an ox-drawn cart.[25] Two years later, in 1809, the second governor's house was purchased by the state from John Scott for the sum of $4,599. This plain two-story house with hand-riven clapboards stood on the east side of South Wayne Street, halfway between Baldwin and Franklin Streets.[26] By 1820 the state had acquired a two-acre double lot on Clarke Street between Hancock and Greene on which there was a two-story frame house facing the latter street. Known as Government House, this building served as the residence of the chief executive until 1838 when the Executive Mansion was completed, facing Clarke Street, on the same two-acre lot.

While the Executive Mansion has become the most-photographed house in Georgia and has been described in minute detail by admiring architects, very little is known about its immediate predecessor, Government House. The few extant verbal descriptions of this structure and its furnishings

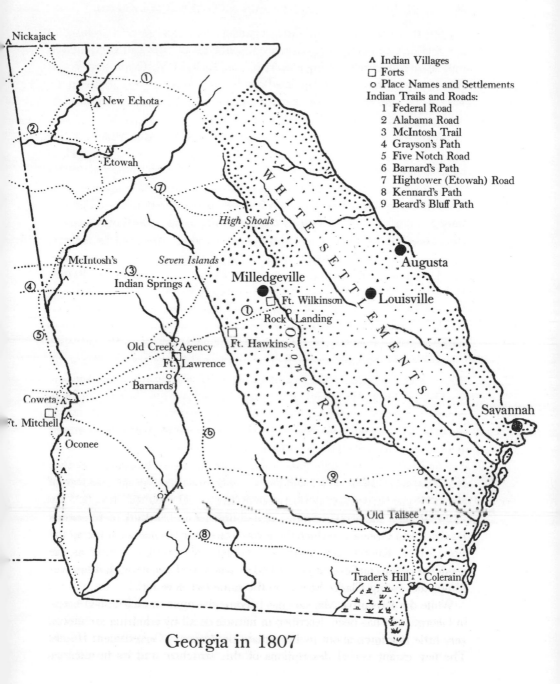

Nickajack

Indian Villages
Forts
Place Names and Settlements
Indian Trails and Roads:
1 Federal Road
2 Alabama Road
3 McIntosh Trail
4 Grayson's Path
5 Five Notch Road
6 Barnard's Path
7 Hightower (Etowah) Road
8 Kennard's Path
9 Beard's Bluff Path

New Echota
Etowah

WHITE SETTLEMENTS

High Shoals

McIntosh's   Seven Islands

Augusta

Indian Springs

Milledgeville

Louisville

Ft. Wilkinson

Rock Landing

Ft. Hawkins

Old Creek Agency

Ft. Lawrence

Barnards

Coweta

Savannah

Ft. Mitchell

Oconee

Oconee R.

Old Talisee

Trader's Hill   Colerain

Georgia in 1807

suggest that it was a house of little elegance; in fact, one governor refused to live there. A contemporary observer described it as "not half as commodious" as the residences of Peter J. Williams, Richard M. Orme, and W. H. Armstrong.[27] It was the dilapidated condition of Government House in the late 1820s and early 1830s that prompted the legislature to appropriate funds for a new mansion.[28]

Three more public squares comprised the rest of early Milledgeville's public property. The square on the north side of the town, between Hancock and Montgomery streets, was known as Penitentiary Square as early as 1807, for already there were plans to construct a state prison upon it. This institution was opened in 1817 with fewer than a hundred inmates. Penitentiary Square was also the site of the Baldwin County courthouse and jail (mentioned in chapter 1). A third square, lying three blocks west of Statehouse Square and connected to it by Washington Street, was never developed for governmental use. Known originally as Government Square and later as Nesbit Woods, its terrain was unusually rough and uneven. Once it had been envisioned as the site of the governor's mansion, which would have faced the Statehouse at the opposite end of Washington Street. This street had therefore been laid out in a manner similar to Pennsylvania Avenue in the nation's capital.[29] The fourth public square was the south one, nearest Fishing Creek. Beginning in 1807 any church that wished to could apply for a one-acre lot on this square; land was also earmarked for an academy. Later known as Cemetery Square, these twenty acres were deeded in 1819 to the commissioners of Milledgeville, along with an additional twenty acres on the square's north side.[30]

The Methodists were the first of the religious groups to avail themselves of a building lot in the south square. The area assigned to them was toward the center of the square, near Hawkins Spring. The church was founded about 1809 with approximately 100 members, and the building was in use by the summer of that year.[31] The structure was described as "a mere barn ... [with] no glass in the windows or sufficient security to keep out the cold." When the Methodist Conference met in Milledgeville in 1814, the church building was still in such condition that the assemblies were ordered to be held in private homes. (At that time tree stumps and a few uncut trees still stood in the streets of the town.) Yet a New England visitor concluded that its congregation was the most fashionable and popular one in the community. Indeed, it was in their building that General Lafayette attended services during his visit to Georgia's capital in 1825.[32]

The Baptists were not behind the Methodists in their zeal for organization. On the east side of the Oconee, in what originally was Washington County, Baptist churches had been organized in the 1790s at Montpelier and at Island Creek. Already identified with these communities were the families of Ennis, Boykin, Shinholster, McDonald, and Barrow.[33] James Barrow and his wife, the former Nancy Hardwick, were members of the Island Creek Baptist Church until 1806, after which they enthusiastically affiliated with the newly formed Baptist congregation at Milledgeville. Many members of the Montpelier church also were absorbed into the Milledgeville church, originally called Mount Zion.[34]

In July 1809 the Baptists were assigned their building lot, which was on an eminence near Fishing Creek, about five blocks south of the Statehouse and near the more settled part of town.[35] The lot on which their building later was constructed, however, was in the north commons at the intersection of Montgomery and Liberty streets. This site apparently was chosen because of its proximity to a fine spring (despite the fact that its water also supplied a distillery operated by Horatio Gates).[36] The Baptists' building bore a close resemblance to that of the Methodists. Only one of its windows was glazed; the rest were merely equipped with wooden shutters to keep out the winter wind, which no doubt made its presence felt through the many chinks in the siding, since the building had no inner wall and was without either fireplace or chimney. The church could, however, boast a larger capacity than any other meeting house in the town, and it was there that Governor Troup delivered a patriotic address on July 4, 1827, to an unusually large audience. Despite the size of the building, many people could not get inside, and at first it seemed that they would miss the governor's speech. The problem was easily solved, however, when a large section of the weatherboarding was removed from one end of the building.[37]

All churches in the town eventually were rebuilt on the Statehouse Square, where in 1822 a new half-acre lot had been provided for each of them by the legislature. It was here that in 1828 the Presbyterians, who had organized just two years earlier, built their first place of worship in the town. To help finance construction they started the practice—later copied by the Episcopalians—of renting pews to members, after designating a suitable number for visitors. By 1830 there were three churches on the square, to be joined by the Episcopal sanctuary ten years later.[38] The fence which surrounded the Statehouse now was extended to enclose the churchyards. In the meantime the three-story armory, called the State Arsenal, had been erected a few yards west of the capitol building. The magazine was soon to occupy the east side of the square facing Elbert Street.[39]

In moving to their new location the religious organizations were following the shifting center of the town's population. The earliest business and residential area had developed south of the Statehouse, centering on South Wayne and South Jefferson streets. The town's first building, constructed of logs, appeared in 1804 on the corner of Franklin and Elbert. A year later the first frame house appeared in the same area.[40] One visitor to the town in 1818 referred to South Wayne as "Main Street," noting that a great majority of all business houses lay between the Statehouse and Fishing Creek. Coming from Sandersville, he had crossed the river at Holt's Ferry near the mouth of Fishing Creek and entered Milledgeville at "Buffington's Corner," where he encountered the first of many taverns.

Samuel Buffington advertised his tavern fare of "big corn, fat hogs and long peas" at prices in keeping with the depressed economic conditions of the times. Because the kitchen under his house had inconvenienced guests with smoke-filled rooms, he had moved this appurtenance to a separate structure on the edge of the yard. In a newspaper advertisement he notified the public of these changes and also informed them that the bridge over Fishing Creek was again in good repair and that one could find his house "without going all around town."[41]

At this time a large commercial building, with the names *Crenshaw and Cunningham* in large golden letters over the door, stood on the corner opposite the market house. Nichols and Demming were early grocers, operating on the corner of Hancock and Wayne. At their warehouse on the river below the town they unloaded supplies which came by boat from Darien and Savannah.[42] Clustered around Statehouse Square were offices of lawyers and county officials, as well as taverns and a few private residences. The town's first newspaper was *The Milledgeville Intelligencer*, published during 1808 by A. McMillan on Franklin Street. It was replaced in 1809 by *The Georgia Journal*, published by Seaton Grantland, whose shop was on Jefferson Street north of the capitol. Just opposite this newspaper office was the house of Enoch Lunceford, "where the courts were being held." This house was soon to become a tavern operated by Henry Darnell.[43]

Tavern-keeping was a popular if not a lucrative business in early Milledgeville, particularly in November and December, when legislative sessions brought several hundred visitors to town. (On such occasions many private homes also were opened for the accommodation of these visitors.)

Among the community's earliest taverns was that of Roger Olmsted and David Fluker, located on Liberty Street facing the Statehouse, where twenty to thirty members of the legislature were accommodated during the 1810 session.[44] At this time there were also a number of other taverns in the town. Thomas G. Collier advertised that he had taken a house—recently erected by Captain Jett Thomas and fronting the capitol square—which he offered for public entertainment, promising to furnish the house with handsome furniture from New York; he also promised choice liquors. Moreover, a dancing academy would be held in his assembly rooms on Fridays and Saturdays.[45] A double-story house belonging to Philip Cook on South Wayne Street opposite the market and rented to Peter Jaillett entertained ten boarders. William D. Jarrett opened a house on the north end of Wayne Street near the spring which later came to bear his name.[46] Also opposite the market, Peter Gent rented the house "lately occupied by Zachariah Lamar," where he promised "to keep a good table, the best liquors and an orderly house." In 1820 John Lucas opened a new tavern on the corner of Greene and Wilkinson streets.[47]

Perhaps the most enterprising of these early tavern-keepers was John Downer. He operated in several locations from time to time, but finally, in 1812, he purchased the house of Captain Jett Thomas on the east side of Statehouse Square and converted it into a tavern renowned for its good wines and other spirits, as well as for its clean beds, warm fires, and good stables.[48] Later he was able to offer legislators "large rooms in clubs with fireplaces attached to them [and,] having a farm within a mile of town, excellent pasturage for horses." He also promised to build a gravel walk from his door to the Statehouse to avoid the inconvenience of red mud.[49] Soon Downer was able to expand his establishment to accommodate as many as sixty guests. He called his tavern the Coffee House, which may have been an oblique way of renouncing his well-known addiction to strong drink. (He had earlier promised potential guests "that a frailty peculiar to himself shall not occur.") He now advertised private family rooms separate from the main house, but he continued to promise "a good bar and plenty provender for animals."[50]

Downer's talents as a hosteler doubtless were challenged in October 1824 with the opening of Lafayette Hall by William F. Scott. Located on the northwest corner of Hancock and Jefferson streets, it was just one block from the Statehouse. Until a short time before its destruction by fire in 1858 this triple-story house (including the basement) remained the largest tavern in Milledgeville and the only one of masonry construction. It boasted thirty-seven fireplaces—one in each of its thirty-odd guest rooms—"a large and airy Stable, convenient Carriage House and a well of water equal to any in the town." It had a separate kitchen, smokehouse, and other appurtenances. Its stable could accommodate eighty horses. Its dining room was eighty by twenty-six feet. All stage lines operating through Milledgeville used it as headquarters, and its permanent guests included a large number of state officials. Some seventy to eighty members of the legislature were boarding there when it burned in November 1858. Among its succession of proprietors were ex-Governor David B. Mitchell, Peter J. Williams, and former Comptroller General Ezekiel S. Candler, who was an uncle of Asa G. Candler, a founder of the Coca Cola Company.[51]

Tavern expenses in this period averaged approximately one dollar a day, which covered both food and lodging. Robert McComb, who operated the Eagle Tavern on the west side of South Wayne Street (between Greene and Hancock), published the following rates in 1828: Lodging, 12½ cents; breakfast and supper each 37½ cents; dinner (which came at noon), 50 cents. A horse could be fed for 25 cents, while a man and his horse could be lodged for a day and a night for $1.75.[52]

Most of these taverns were transitory. They changed hands frequently and with these changes new names were acquired. By 1830 the principal establishments, in addition to those already named, included five other taverns, one of which was the Mansion House, on the northeast corner of Elbert and Hancock, where George M. Troup was a boarder during his second term as governor. Three blocks south on Elbert Street was Jackson Hall—formerly the Coffee House—now operated by Samuel Buffington. The Farmers Hotel stood on South Wayne facing the market house. Owned by Mark D. Huson, it boasted "a large and convenient supply of water . . . expressly for Drovers." Huson also owned the Planters Hotel on the southeast corner of Hancock and Wilkinson, near the courthouse. This establishment offered a reading room "with ample selections of journals, critiques, and reviews." Directly across Hancock Street, on the "Sanford lot," was the tavern known simply as "Mrs. [Eliza] Allen's."[53] The latter two were somewhat removed from the center of the town but were convenient for those attending sessions of the superior court.

Georgia taverns and roadside inns during this period were far below the standards of those in Europe and in the northern United States. Even as late as 1840 the English traveler James Silk Buckingham, en route by stage from Augusta to Columbus, found the roads unusually rough and tavern fare even more so. Arriving at Sparta early in the afternoon, he expected a warm meal to offer some respite from the freezing rain through which he had been riding. The fare consisted of boiled pork, corn bread, and rancid butter, all served in broken china with rusty knives and forks on a filthy table cloth. He turned away in disgust to continue his journey toward Milledgeville. At the state capital he expected to find a good hotel, but in this too he was disappointed. "The inn at which the coach stopped," he wrote, "was a wretched one, and though all we desired was a cup of tea and some cold meat . . . we had the greatest difficulty in getting them." The dirty Negro maid who prepared the tea brought the small quantity of leaves to the bedroom in the hollow of her hand, together with some milk in a broken glass. "When a slop basin was asked for, the thing was unknown," he wrote, "and a large salad bowl was brought for that purpose."[54]

Garnett Andrews, in his reminiscences about Georgia taverns in this period, stated that the general rule was to change table cloths and towels once a week and to change bed sheets "when very much soiled and without reference to the previous number of occupants." He recalled finding one servant sniffing the bed linen, and on asking why, he learned that the bed had just been vacated by a sick man and the proprietor was interested to know if the sheets smelled of turpentine.[55] While Milledgeville's taverns may have been slightly more profitable than the average, there is no reason to suspect that they were any less primitive. All were overcrowded during legislative sessions, when two and sometimes three guests occupied the same bed—and these occupants may have been total strangers to each other. Guests frequently complained of incessant talking and moving around throughout the night. Despite the presence of numerous "spit boxes," tobacco stains blemished the walls and floors. Alcoholic spirits were always in evidence. It is not surprising then, that the more sophisticated and affluent visitors sought lodging in private homes.

While tavern life was crude and unpleasant, a journey by stagecoach was even more so. Travelers in this period were never wished a pleasant journey but always a safe one. The coaches, generally painted red or yellow, were equipped with three seats, the middle one having broad leather straps to lean back on. The maximum capacity was nine people, but an additional passenger might sit on the outside with the coachman, who drove four to six horses. Runaway horses presented a hazard, and under such circumstances passengers were cautioned to remain inside the coach. James Resseau was killed near Milledgeville in 1824 when he violated this rule and jumped from the stage. In the same year an attempt was made by three men to rob the Augusta stage as it approached Milledgeville. An obstacle was placed across the road to halt the vehicle, and a rifle was fired at the driver. However, the ball passed through his clothing, and the hold-up was thwarted when he rushed his horses over the obstacle.[56]

Throughout the antebellum period travelers were unanimous in agreeing on the wretched condition of the roads and the difficulties in crossing streams, most of which had to be forded or crossed in a ferry boat. Roads avoided swamps and flatlands if possible and traversed higher ground, but this meant the traveler had to deal with rain-washed gullies along the thoroughfare. Passengers might be called upon to throw their weight first to the right and then to the left to prevent an upset when one wheel was sinking into a deep rut. Worse still, they might be ordered outside to walk through the mud while the driver rushed his steeds over a fallen tree or up a sharp incline.[57] For all this trouble the traveler was charged ten cents a mile, and his rate of travel was five miles an hour. Each driver went approximately twelve miles with the same set of horses. Until 1850 the legislature licensed all ferries and bridges across streams and fixed toll charges. The average ferry toll for a loaded vehicle was 75 cents, but a man on horseback was charged 12½ cents.[58] It was not until 1820 that a bridge spanned the river at Milledgeville. Poorly constructed, it soon collapsed under the weight of a heavily loaded wagon, resulting in the loss of its freight and several horses. After the bridge was repaired, a ferry boat was again set up to accommodate the heavier traffic.[59]

As already noted, the earliest connection the Milledgeville area had with the outside world was the old Garrison Road leading from Rock Landing to Fort Hawkins. In 1805 this road was linked to the town when a new road was opened from the Montpelier Ferry to Statehouse Square.[60] An early map indicates that this road began at what later was Holt's Ferry, ran northwestward, and then crossed the Statehouse Square diagonally to the northeastern corner, from which it continued in the same general direction, ignoring all street plans and veering westward.[61] Two miles northwest of the town this road divided, the northern branch going to Indian Springs, where it picked up the McIntosh Trail leading westward to the Creek village of Senoia in what later became Coweta County. It was from this village that the northern branch took its name, though much later it would be known as the Monticello Road. The lower branch eventually was extended to Clinton in Jones County. At the junction of these two roads a tavern, which later was operated by William R. Hill, was established in 1816. By this time the Senoia Road had been intersected by a road leading to Eatonton.[62]

A road was opened to Sparta which crossed the Oconee at Bolan's Ferry several miles north of Milledgeville. Just east of the Statehouse in 1810 was Fluker's Ferry by which travelers might go to Salem and Sandersville. In time this route came to be greatly preferred over all others leading eastward from the capital. Soon after 1820 new roads to Sparta and Island Creek connected with the road leading to the new bridge over the Oconee. The Fort Hawkins road was again linked to the west side of Milledgeville by the extension of Franklin Street. This roadway left the town in a southwesterly direction and crossed a new bridge over Fishing Creek. Early known as Shakegut road, this thoroughfare must have been well named.

Streets within the town at this period were likely to be in no better condition than the rural roads which now began to thread the countryside. It was not until 1810 that all streets in the town began to be cleared of roots, stumps, and holes and the surfaces made firm so they would be "fit for carriages 15 feet wide."[63] Hills and ravines within the limits of the town were obstacles to well-kept streets whose location had been determined by a checkerboard design rather than by terrain. One ravine began in the heart of the town, at the intersection of Hancock and Wayne streets, running north down Wayne to Tanyard Branch. At this intersection the gorge was so deep that the Augusta stagecoach disappeared from view when crossing it.[64]

Improvements on the federal road from Fort Hawkins to Mobile were completed in 1811, allowing for the first time the passage of carriages of every description. Four years later overseers of roads in Baldwin County were required to erect mile posts showing the distance from Milledgeville and to locate place-markers at crossroads indicating the next point to which each road led.[65] The town's communication with the outside world was greatly improved with the completion of the federal road. The New Orleans-to-Washington mail route, which formerly went by Athens, was now routed through Milledgeville.[66] One of the longest mail routes in the nation, it greatly enhanced both mail and travel service to Georgia's frontier capital.

Mail service at Milledgeville began on October 1, 1806, with the establishment of a post office at the house of postmaster Thompson Bird. This office was moved frequently, and when not in a postmaster's house it was likely to be in a very humble building, often a mere shed. At times it was even located in a confectionery where liquor was sold. Postmasters were known to accommodate patrons by keeping "credit accounts" for letter postage due them. The accumulation of unclaimed mail was considerable—often in excess of 200 letters.[67]

Until the 1820s the delivery of mail was expensive and highly uncertain. "We have mail but once a week," wrote a Milledgeville lawyer in 1809. "The packages are made up previous to its arrival . . . [and the stage] stops but a few minutes in the town, so that we can never answer a letter until the successive week."[68] Up to 1845 postage costs were excessive, even on the Washington–New Orleans route. Ten cents was required to send a letter to Macon, just thirty miles away; and the cost increased with distance. Private carriers operating between the capital and points north and south had their own problems—on one August day in 1810 the "northern mail" arrived fifteen hours late with the carrier riding an exhausted horse. This north-south mail service remained inadequate until the railroad era. As late as 1836 there was no direct mail service from the state capital to such places as Monticello, Decatur, Rome, and Chattanooga. It required ten days to send a letter from the capital to Rossville in Walker County, a distance of only 200 miles; a letter to the nation's capital took much less time. In 1827, however, a new mail route was established from Milledgeville to Tallahassee which passed through Hartford (Hawkinsville) and Bainbridge. Similar lines were added during the following decade.[69]

The mail stages also carried passengers, although such travelers were severely inconvenienced. Foot space was frequently usurped by mail bags, and the coach stopped at numerous rural postal stations, where the bags were opened and searched for letters directed to them.[70] One stage from Columbus to Augusta carried mail only as far as Milledgeville, from which point the mail was carried by another contractor; the former then became an "accommodation stage." Passengers who bought through tickets to Augusta were often delayed at Milledgeville, since they were not given preference for seats from that point onward. The same situation existed at Augusta, where through passengers might lose preference on stages west of that place.[71]

After 1830 travelers from Milledgeville to points in the northern states had available to them one of the most popular routes in the southern stageline network. This was the Piedmont Mail Route to the nation's capital, flanked on the west by the beautiful Blue Ridge mountains for much of the total distance of 654 miles. Beginning at Milledgeville, it passed through Eatonton, Greensboro, Washington, and Petersburg in Georgia; then through Abbeville, Laurens, Union, and York districts in South Carolina. In North Carolina it touched Charlotte, Salisbury, and Lexington, and entered Virginia near Danville. Among its stops in that state were Lynchburg, Charlottesville, Orange, Culpeper, and Warrenton. While the scenery on this route was unequalled, travelers had to spend much of their time riding through darkness. To make the required eighty miles each day, the stage had to start at three or four o'clock in the morning and stop for the night at eight in the evening. On the eighth and final day of the journey the trip began at 2:00 A.M. and ended at 9:00 P.M.. This stage departed from Milledgeville on Tuesdays, Thursdays, and Saturdays, and the full fare was $45, an exceptionally low rate for that period. However, the stage assumed no responsibility for parcels and luggage.[72]

Freight to and from Milledgeville remained a problem throughout most of the town's antebellum history. Most of the early freight was hauled by wagons overland from the river port of Augusta and sometimes all the distance from Savannah. Such products as unprocessed tobacco, skins, and cotton were sent on the return journey. This overland freight was inefficient and expensive. Once a merchant lost his entire supply of coffee and pickled pork when the owner of a freight wagon took off for other points and never showed up in Milledgeville.[73] The problem is further illustrated by the experience of Thomas Fitch, a Milledgeville lawyer. In 1810 he ordered from Savannah forty window glasses, a book case with sliding doors, and a mahogany dining table capable of seating twenty people. He sent the description to a cabinet-maker, asking him to let him know the cost "as soon as a pigeon can fly from you to me." While the waggoner was given explicit instructions about handling the glass, it arrived "well broken and robbed of seven lights."[74]

The most obvious solution to early problems of transportation was the improvement of the Oconee River to provide cheap water traffic to and from Darien and Savannah. In 1805 the Oconee Navigation Company received a charter which was amended several times thereafter. Its principal effort was expended in an attempt to make the river navigable from Milledgeville northward to Barnett Shoals near Athens. This was to be accomplished by removing obstacles and building locks at the shoals. From 1805 to 1820 the company used every known form of financing, including private subscriptions, a lottery, and outright state subsidy, but failure resulted in all instances.[75] In the meantime pole boats plied the river between Milledgeville and Darien, and the actual head of navigation remained at Rock Landing. In 1827 contracts were let for the construction of two locks immediately below Milledgeville. Because of poor construction and damage from freshets, these facilities were almost constantly being repaired and never produced the results contemplated.[76]

The first steamboat (the *Williamson*) to reach Milledgeville from Darien arrived on April 13, 1819. While the engineer gave a pessimistic report on the river's navigability, citizens of the town appeared to be convinced that a new era had arrived in their quest for cheaper transportation. In the following year they prepared an anniversary dinner and celebration for the boat's engineer, including fireworks and a balloon ascension, although they had difficulty in mustering the skill and technology for the latter.[77]

In March 1820 the steamboat *Samuel Howard* arrived with freighting boats in tow after a thirteen-day voyage from Darien. Owners of boats who held the charter to navigate the Oconee apparently were finding business on that river unprofitable and were fulfilling only the minimum stipulations of their charter. Consequently they sent a boat to Milledgeville only in the late spring, when business elsewhere was dull and also when seasonal rains had brought the river to a favorable water level. By this time most of the cotton had already been carried off by pole boats and wagons. The company now cited the unprofitability of the trip to justify infrequent voyages. They also recognized the high risk of cotton being destroyed by fire when towed behind steamboats over a narrow and circuitous channel. (Such an accident had destroyed 200 bales of cotton at the Milledgeville boatyard in February of that year.)[78]

At this time cotton sold in Milledgeville at twelve to thirteen cents per pound and in Darien at one cent per pound more, freight and storage accounting for the difference in price.[79] Apparently convinced that the situation could be improved through local enterprise, Farish Carter and John T. Roland in 1824 announced their intention of running several boats between Milledgeville and Darien regularly "during the boating season." The latter owned two new boats capable of carrying 400 bales of cotton each, and they would be ready to start by the middle of November. All these apparently were pole boats "commanded by careful and well experienced Patroons." They announced freight charges to Darien would be 50 cents per 100 pounds of cotton and freight would be brought from that point at the same price. Unfortunately the enterprise of Carter and Roland was short-lived. For the next dozen years or more, steamboat traffic on the Oconee was practically nonexistent until the *Wave*, owned by Nichols and Demming, was propelled to Milledgeville in 1836. It required a full week to ascend from Darien. At this time freight from New York to Darien cost $2.39 per hundred pounds, and from the latter point to Milledgeville the cost was upwards from one dollar per hundred pounds.[80]

Milledgeville's unfavorable location with regard to transportation and communication was the principal reason for its slow growth. This problem continued even after the building of railroads. In fact, it was the town's relative isolation which provided the decisive argument against its continuation as the seat of government after the Civil War. By that time Georgia's five fall-line cities had grown in size at an approximate ratio to the size and navigability of the streams on which they were located.

The earliest census of the town was made in 1810 when it had a population of 1,256 and ranked as the third largest center in Georgia. By 1828 the population had increased to only 1,599, of which 49 percent were slaves; there were also twenty-seven free Negroes.[81] During the same period the whole county's population increased by only 321, from 6,968 to 7,289. The black population now comprised more than 62 percent of this total. Nineteen planters held more than fifty slaves each.[82] There was a heavy migration outward to new cotton lands which had been opened west of the Ocmulgee, and this resulted in the concentration of landholdings in the older area.

The first wave of westward migration was well under way by 1815, at which time one observer reported seeing in a single day a caravan of 150 persons on their journey to new lands in Alabama. Other migrants were stopping on the west side of the Ocmulgee to settle on Indian lands soon to be ceded to the state.[83] This avalanche of emigration was joined by many early settlers of Baldwin County or by their older sons. Among these were John H. Horne and his brother. The former by 1860 became perhaps the largest slave-holder in Mississippi and one of the state's larger landowners. Eli S. Shorter, a lawyer and later a superior court judge, left Milledgeville in 1814, going first to Eatonton and later to Columbus where he abandoned law and engaged in land speculation. He later amassed a great fortune in Alabama lands vacated by the Creek Indians.[84] Representatives of early Milledgeville families could be found all the way to Texas and included the families of Seaborn Jones, Alston, Troutman, Lamar, Blount, Michlejohn, deGraffenreid, and many others. A large number of emigrants from the old capital found new homes in Macon and Columbus. The latter city, the youngest in the Georgia trans-Ocmulgee region, was well under way and thriving by 1830.[85]

Very few of these emigrants ever returned to live near their ancestral hearthstones. Among those who did was Arthur I. Butts, who became disenchanted with Alabama and returned to Baldwin County in 1828. He settled at the crossroads made by the Senoia and the Flat Shoals roads, where he built the first house in the community later known as Meriwether.[86]

Milledgeville as well as the county continued to receive some settlers from the Carolinas and Virginia, but this ingression was a modest one which barely enabled the community to hold its own—a third of the dwellings in the town were reported vacant in 1813. However, all houses were occupied two years later, when a population in excess of 1,500 was reported. The penitentiary, now nearing completion, together with the enclosure of Statehouse Square with avenues of newly planted trees, had added greatly to the town's appearance. The editor of the *Georgia Journal* suggested that homeowners plant ornamental flowers and paint their houses to give the town an appearance of durability and permanence.[87]

Like all frontier communities Baldwin County in this period had a greater percentage of residents under eighteen years old than did the state as a whole, and the number of males was large. Almost all of its farmers were small landowners, and collectively they owned few slaves. However, the size of the average holding in this type of property increased with the growing concentration of landownership. John Rutherford, James Barrow, John Howard, William Lewis, Thomas Moughon, Farish Carter, John Lucas, Zachariah Lamar, and Jesse Sanford were among the larger slaveholders in 1820; their holdings averaged sixty-four in number. Perhaps the most impressive of these was Jesse Sanford, who at the time of his death in 1827 possessed twenty-five domestic servants and 228 field hands distributed among six plantations. His personal wealth included fine mahogany furniture, silver plate, and cut glass decanters.[88]

Such elegance was quite exceptional in this raw and new community. Livestock had free range, even in the town, where local ordinances failed to end the problem. Picket or rail fences were erected around houses as barriers to roving animals, and stiles rather than gates adorned the entrances. A few alligators could still be seen in the Oconee River, and bears abounded along the Little River swamps. Deer were plentiful, as was a great variety of wild turkeys and small game.[89]

The new capital attracted people of varied talents from all walks of life. In the early years of the town's history, lawyers, innkeepers, printers, government officials, and artisans comprised the great majority of its residents. As a class, the innkeepers were the largest slaveholders, possessing an average of thirteen. The artisans comprised the largest single group, many of whom were foreign-born. Edmund Wadlow and John Marlow (Marlor) were Englishmen who constructed a number of early houses. Those built by Marlow which have survived suggest that he may have been more an architect than artisan. Construction work on his houses was performed by slaves, of which he owned seven in 1825; all of these were listed as carpenters.[90] John Speich, a watchmaker by trade and a native of Switzerland, died in November 1814. Because he had no known heirs, his property was advertised for sale in the following year by Abner Locke the county escheator. In addition to the tools and equipment necessary to his trade, his personal property included fine paintings, engravings, maps, drawings, and books written in seven different languages.[91]

The new town also had an unusually large number of Revolutionary War veterans, many of whom moved in from the adjacent county of Washington, where they earlier had received bounty grants. A total of twenty-six veterans in Baldwin County drew prizes in the land lottery of 1827, and twelve other fortunate draws went to war widows.[92] One of these was "old Mrs. Clarke," who had been scalped by the Indians and wore a silver plate in her skull. Among the Revolutionary veterans who moved to the area in the first two decades of the century were Allen Tapley, S. B. Clark, Oaty Prosser, John Cone, Philemon Franklin, William Hand, Uriah and William Brown, Samuel Beckham (Beckcom), William D. Evans, John and Thomas Miles, George Searcy, James Thomas, John Morris, Jacob Gumm, Edward Brown, Henry Meacham, William Spurlock, Anderson Redding, John Fuller, John Scott, Toliver Davis, William Ackridge, James Barrow, Peter Fair, and Abner Hammond. Also among these veterans was Jim Thomas, who was at Braddock's defeat in 1755. A slave of James Thomas, Jim lived to be more than 100 years old.[93]

These veterans seemed to enjoy some political preference in the community. Abner Hammond was secretary of state from 1811 to 1823, and he held other offices in both local and state government.[94] Peter Fair was a former French soldier who remained in America after the war. Governor Jared Irwin brought Fair to Milledgeville with him in 1807 and gave him employment as executive messenger and later as doorkeeper to the senate.

He had various other titles from time to time, one of them "Keeper of the Capitol Clock," and he was also charged with the responsibility of maintaining the statehouse in good repair between legislative sessions.[95] When Governor Irwin vacated his residence on South Wayne Street, Peter Fair moved into his house and remained there for the duration of his life.

Many of these early families deserve more than passing notice. Their stories illustrate the peculiar fabric of the Milledgeville community, where the warp and woof of marriage alliances extended relationships to families in many other parts of the state and represented a wide diversity in geographic origins, interests, and talents—a set of conditions quite unusual for that period of limited travel. James Barrow (1757–1828), a survivor of Valley Forge and the battles of Germantown and Brandywine, came to Georgia from North Carolina. In 1802 he purchased a large tract of land on the east side of the Oconee near the future site of Milledgeville (where some of his descendants are still residing). His first wife, Nancy Hardwick, died in 1814 just twelve years after her marriage. His second wife, Patience Crenshaw (b. 1799), bore him two children, David Crenshaw and Patience. The former attended Harvard College and the University of Georgia at Athens, where he later married Sara Pope. From this union was born David Crenshaw Barrow II, who became chancellor of the state university. His sister, Lucy Pope, married John A. Cobb, son of Governor Howell Cobb. Lucy's aunt, Patience Barrow, became the wife of William McKinley (1809–1878), a lawyer and a member of the legislature from Oglethorpe County.[96] It was through this marriage that the Barrow house and plantation became identified with the McKinley family. James Barrow's house, "Beulah," was long famous for its hospitality. His magnificent library was said to have held the finest collection of books to be found anywhere between Savannah and Athens.[97]

Archibald Carlisle McKinley was the son of William and Patience Barrow McKinley. Archibald married Sallie Spalding of Sapelo Island, while his sister (Sarah) married Sallie's brother Thomas. Sallie and Thomas were the children of Randolph Spalding. William McKinley's second marriage was to Mrs. Anne Sims of New Haven, Connecticut, whose father, E. A. Andrews, had been headmaster of a girl's school where McKinley's mother had been a student. Three sons resulted from this marriage—William, Guy Cummins, and Andrews.[98]

Another of Milledgeville's early settlers was Thomas Holmes Kenan (1744–1837), whose father Michael Johnston Kenan (b. 1746) came to

Georgia from Duplin County, North Carolina, where he had married Anne Holmes, sister of Governor Gabriel Holmes of that state. Thomas Holmes Kenan held many offices of public trust in Baldwin County and was once federal marshal for the district. His two sons were Michael Johnston II and Augustus. The former married Catherine Ann Spalding of the famous Sapelo Island family, which also became allied through marriage with the families of Horne, Alston, Livingston, White, Gignilliatt, and Lamar.[99]

Progenitors of the Lamar family in Milledgeville were the brothers John and Zachariah, who moved from Warren County in 1810 and settled on the Putnam side of Little River, ten miles north of Milledgeville. John's son, Lucius Quintus Cincinnatus, studied law in the capital under the tutelage of Joel Crawford, later becoming his partner, and eventually was named judge of the Ocmulgee circuit. In this capacity it once became his duty to sentence to death a Methodist minister at Milledgeville after his conviction for the murder of his wife's fifteen year-old sister. The minister's wife was the principal witness against him, yet the evidence was circumstantial. Apparently Lamar developed his own doubts about the guilt of the condemned man, and later, after the minister was hanged, a man in Mississippi confessed to the deed from the gallows. In a fit of melancholia, Lamar came into his house, quietly kissed his wife and children, then walked into the garden and shot himself.[100] This was on July 4, 1834, when he was thirty-seven years old.

Judge Lamar's wife Sarah, the daughter of Dr. Thompson Bird, had borne him eight children, the most famous of whom was L.Q.C., Jr. (1825–1893). After moving to Mississippi, he became a distinguished politician. A brother of the elder L.Q.C. Lamar was Mirabeau Buonaparte (1798–1859), who served as Governor Troup's executive secretary from 1823 to 1826 and then moved to Columbus, where he edited the Columbus Enquirer. In 1835 he went to Texas, where he joined the revolutionary army and rose to high rank. He later became the second president of the Republic of Texas.[101]

Zachariah Lamar, the somewhat eccentric brother of John, was a self-taught man with exceptional literary interests. He was an avid reader of history, and in his Methodist prayers he often gave thanks for the heroic examples of greatness which both ancient and modern history afforded. It is said that he was responsible for the classical names given to his brother's children and grandchildren.[102] Zachariah also possessed a singularly acquisitive nature. His tax returns for 1832, the year of his death, listed 220 slaves and more than 15,000 acres of land in Baldwin and four adjacent counties and in various other counties throughout the state. His property in Milledgeville was valued at $5,000, and he owned considerable bank stock.[103] Only three of his children survived him—John Basil, Mary Ann, and Andrew Jackson. John Basil never married, and Andrew Jackson died at an early age. The great bulk of his estate eventually passed to his daughter, Mary Ann. This affluent daughter became the wife of Howell Cobb, whence came Cobb's general reputation for wealth and high living during a long political career which included a term as governor in the early 1850s.[104] In 1860 Cobb was recognized as one of Georgia's larger slaveholders.

Other families of Milledgeville also had a close relationship with the struggle for Texas independence. One of these was that of John Troutman, who built and operated the first grist mill on the Oconee River near the ferry. On the southwest corner of Hancock and Clarke streets stood the Troutman house, where Mrs. Troutman, the former Joanna Bainbridge, died in 1818. Her two children were Joanna (b. May 30, 1794), who married Jeremiah Lamar, and a son Hiram Bainbridge Troutman, who later settled in Crawford County. It was here that Hiram's daughter Joanna (born in Milledgeville February 19, 1820) designed and wrought the first Lone Star Flag and presented it to a company of volunteers on their march to join the Texas Revolution.[105]

The Texas revolutionary hero best known in Georgia was James W. Fannin. The detailed accounts of the massacre of Fannin and his men at Goliad in 1836 were received in Milledgeville with unusual interest, for a number of his men came from the Milledgeville area, and Fannin himself was born within twenty miles of the capital. He was a cousin of Martha Low Fort, the wife of Tomlinson Fort (1787–1859), in whose home he had once been a frequent visitor.[106]

Tomlinson Fort was with little doubt the most prominent of Milledgeville's early citizens. The son of Arthur Fort (1750–1833) and the former Susanna Tomlinson, he became not only one of the more distinguished physicians of the state but also a leading figure in politics, banking, and educational development. When Fort returned from Washington in 1829, after serving a term in Congress, the old Troup-Clark factionalism (see chapter 3) was dying out. This factionalism which had resulted in a long and bitter political feud for more than two decades, was based largely on personal and family loyalties. Because no newspaper in the state capital was now supporting the old Clark faction, Fort purchased the *Federal Union* and made Clarkite John Polhill its editor. It became a leading Jacksonian and Unionist newspaper and opposed the states rights doctrine which had become the trademark of the old Troup faction.[107]

Newspaper editors and printers were relatively numerous and formed an important and highly respected segment of the town's early society. Among the first families who achieved leadership and financial success in this work were the Grantlands, the Grieves, and the Ormes. Seaton Grantland (b. 1783) and his brother Fleming (b. 1790) came to Milledgeville in 1809 from Virginia, where they had followed the printer's trade. In the same year they opened *The Georgia Journal*, and in 1810 they bought new presses in Philadelphia and were awarded the lucrative job of state printing. Fleming died in 1819; but the talent and worth of his brother continued to be recognized, and in 1820 Seaton began publication of the *Southern Recorder* with Richard M. Orme. He saved his earnings, acquired slaves, and eventually purchased the plantation and former home of ex-Governor Clark a few miles south of Milledgeville near Scottsboro, where he pursued the role of planter and political functionary.[108] His daughter, Ann Virginia Grantland, was born in 1823, shortly before her mother's death at age thirty. In 1844 Ann Virginia married Charles DuBignon of Jekyll Island, with whom she had become acquainted when he was a member of the legislature from Glynn County.[109]

Miller Grieve, Sr. (1801–1878), came from Scotland and settled in Lexington, where in 1822 he entered a law partnership with his brother-in-law, Joseph Henry Lumpkin. In 1829 Governor Gilmer brought him to Milledgeville as his executive secretary. Here he remained and later married Sarah Caroline Grantland, daughter of Fleming and Agnes Jones Grantland. In 1831 he became editor of *The Georgia Journal*, which had been founded by the Grantlands. A friend and supporter of President Taylor, he was appointed chargé d'affaires to Denmark, in which post he served from 1849 to 1853.[110] Grieve's daughter, Eliza Grantland Grieve, married Captain William A. Williams during the Civil War. Captain Williams was the scion of another early local family of considerable importance, that of Peter J. and Lucinda Parke Williams, who came to Milledgeville in 1817 and built a twenty-two-room mansion at the corner of Liberty and Washington streets, two blocks west of the Statehouse. Here he entertained members of the legislature and engaged in extensive speculation in lands newly distributed in the land lotteries. A daughter, Frances Way Williams, married

New York newspaper editor David Ferguson. The house remained in the hands of their descendants in 1976.[111]

The print shop at *The Georgia Journal* produced yet another prominent early Milledgeville editor. Richard McAllister Orme (b. 1797) was a Marylander who settled first in McIntosh County and then came to Milledgeville in 1811 to learn the printer's trade from the Grantland brothers. In 1819 he established *The Southern Recorder* with Henry Denison, a twenty-three-year-old schoolteacher and son of a prominent Vermont family. Denison died before the presses arrived, and Seaton Grantland took his place in the partnership. Like Grantland, Orme saved his earnings, invested carefully in land and slaves, and amassed a modest fortune.[112] Under the principal guidance of Orme *The Southern Recorder* became one of the most influential papers in the South. While he often ignored party labels and followed political principles instead, he leaned toward the Troup–States Rights–Whig leadership.

Orme's first marriage was to Jean Moncure Paine of Richmond, Virginia, who bore him several children. Among these was Richard M. Orme, Jr., who became his father's partner but who later went to Savannah, where he continued in newspaper work. The elder Orme's second marriage was to the former Abby Adams (1797–1869), daughter of John Adams, headmaster of Phillips Academy of Andover, Massachusetts. From this marriage there were five children. One daughter, Mary Elizabeth, married Dr. William Flinn, a prominent Presbyterian clergyman; another daughter, Ann Ripley, became the wife of Captain Charles P. Crawford. The Orme house, built in 1820 by John Williams and acquired by Orme in 1836, was still in the possession of the latter's descendants in 1976.[113]

One of the most far-reaching and fascinating webs of eighteenth-century genealogy to be found in early Georgia is suggested by the Milledgeville family of Iverson Louis Harris. Born in 1805, he came to the Georgia capital at an early age and in 1826 married Mary Euphemia Davies; from this marriage there sprang an imposing list of prominent local citizens. Harris was descended from a line of prominent Virginia families, including the Laniers and the Iversons, while Mary Euphemia was the daughter of Federal Judge William Davies of Savannah and his wife, the former Mary Ann Bailie, the daughter of Robert McIntosh Bailie. The Bailie-McIntosh genealogy can be traced to the nobility of Scotland and even very close to the steps of the royal House of Stuart.[114] A study of the American descendants of this clan produces a saga of unparalleled diversity and fascination.

John McIntosh came to Georgia during Oglethorpe's administration, received a Crown grant in what is now Alabama, and became a loyal colonial official. One of his six children was Captain William McIntosh, who fought with the Tories during the Revolution. It was during this struggle that Captain McIntosh formed a liason with a Creek woman named Senoya (Senoia), who bore him a son who took his father's name and in time became the chief of the Cowetas. Chief McIntosh (Tustuneegee Hutkee) had a half-brother who, like himself, was of mixed blood, another who was a full Indian, and still another who was a full white man and a member of the Georgia legislature in 1817. By virtue of the fact that the chief's father was a brother of Barbara McIntosh, he was a first cousin of George McIntosh Troup, governor of Georgia from 1823 to 1827. In addition, through his Creek mother he could lay claim to the highest degree of wilderness aristocracy. His mother was a member of the privileged Wind clan, and two of her brothers were Indians of considerable standing and influence. One of these was a mixed-blood named Howard, who was chief of Chehehaw Town on the Flint River; the other, Tomoc Micco, was a subordinate chief known as a law-mender who lived on the Chattahoochee. Chief McIntosh's genealogy became further distinguished by his own polygamous marriages and by those of his children. One of his wives was Eliza, the white daughter of Stephen Hawkins. McIntosh and Hawkins must have made some kind of matrimonial bargain, for Hawkins's brother (Sam) took to wife McIntosh's oldest daughter, whose name was Jane. Jane and her brother Chilly had been sent to school in Milledgeville and could speak and write fairly good English. Before her marriage to Sam Hawkins, Jane had been the wife of William Mitchell, son of Governor David B. Mitchell.

The youngest of Chief McIntosh's daughters was Croesy. In 1825, when her father was assassinated by a group of disaffected Upper Creeks on the west bank of the Chattahoochee, Croesy fled to the white settlements and took refuge at the house of Richmond Bridges near Senoia. There she remained while other members of her family moved to Arkansas. Her brothers became leading political functionaries among the Creeks in Oklahoma, and one of the McIntosh boys became the highest ranking Creek officer in the Confederate army. In contrast, the unfortunate Croesy was given menial employment on the Bridges plantation and finally married a Negro slave belonging to Richmond Bridges. She and her son Chilly, who had served briefly in the Confederate army, died of smallpox in a pest house at Senoia during the Civil War. Thus the strange peregrinations of this family reached all the way from Government House at Milledgeville to a humble slave cabin in Coweta County.[115]

The town's business community during this period did not produce such prominent leaders as did its agricultural and professional groups. However, two of its early business leaders, Issac Newell and Farish Carter, deserve more than passing notice. Newell came to Milledgeville from Southington, Connecticut, and built a large commercial house known as Newell Hall. As his business prospered, he established branches at Eatonton and at Gordon; this is said to have been the earliest example of a chain store in Georgia. He was married to Parmelia Duncan of Eatonton in 1826. The youngest of their six children was Tomlinson Fort Newell, who married Ann Lane Colquitt, daughter of General Alfred H. Colquitt, who later became governor and United States senator. The Newell house, built in 1838 near the Executive Mansion, remains in the hands of Newell's descendants.

Farish Carter (1780–1861), a native of South Carolina, moved from Washington County to the vicinity of Milledgeville in 1811 soon after his marriage to Elizabeth McDonald of Hancock County. (Elizabeth's father, Charles J. McDonald, became governor in 1839.) Carter became interested in various early projects connected with the navigation of the Oconee and once constructed locks on that river just below the town. He became a government contractor during the War of 1812 and finally amassed a fortune through acquisition of valuable Cherokee lands in North Georgia.[116] One of Carter's daughters married Dr. John H. Furman, grandson of the prominent Baptist clergyman for whom a university in South Carolina is named, and it was this family which inherited the Carter plantation at Scottsboro. Perhaps the best known of the Furman descendants is Farish Carter Furman (b. 1846), who married the oldest daughter of Dr. Joseph Le Conte (who for a brief period was a professor at Oglethorpe University at Midway and who, along with his brother John, had a distinguished career at the University of California after the Civil War). Furman's early death in 1883 ended a promising career in law and politics.[117]

Many of the family names found in Milledgeville's history are also associated with the village of Scottsboro, which was located on a high plateau overlooking the Oconee some four miles south of the capital. The site was noted for its promise of a healthy environment, free of the usual summer ailments. The village underwent development in the late 1820s, partly as a result of Milledgeville's reputation for "insalubriety of climate [ascribed to] miasma from the river and the putrid exhalations of adjacent pools of stag-

nant water."[118] (The town had experienced some mortality from malaria
and similar illnesses during the summer of 1823, at which time an alarming
degree of sickness was reported in other areas from Virginia to Louisiana.
At Natchez deaths from yellow fever were so high that only 200 inhabitants
remained there.)[119] By 1829 all of Scottsboro's one- and two-acre lots had
been disposed of. The village at this time was described as the "gayest,
happiest, brightest community in Georgia." The seat of one of the best-
known girls' schools in the area, it was known for the variety and excellence
of its fruits and was the gathering place of affluent and refined people, some
of whom were summer refugees from the coast. Among those identified
with the village were the Barneses, Turks, Grantlands, Carters, Furmans,
DuBignons, Buckners, and Thomases. Also, Hamilton Fulton, civil engineer, lived there in 1828.[120]

While Scottsboro was experiencing rapid development and growth during the 1820s, Milledgeville again went into decline. As we have already
noted, depressed economic conditions, the beginning of the exhaustion of
cotton lands in the area, and the renewed westward migration were the
principal causes of this problem. By 1830 the town's white inhabitants
occupied only 170 houses which was approximately the total number of
white families in the community. The town had twenty-six carpenters, five
blacksmiths, six shoemakers, four silversmiths, eight tailors, and twenty-one
printers, plus a few artisans of other categories. There were fifteen lawyers,
five doctors, and nearly a dozen innkeepers. Twenty of the town's thirty-four
merchants sold groceries, which in that era included hard liquor often dispensed by the drink. Of the total number of white families, 75 percent
owned slaves, most of which were in small single-family holdings; only
thirteen people held more than ten each. There were only about 700 voters
in the entire county.[121]

Most of the town's deserted houses were on the south and east sides,
where neglect and rapid deterioration were evident. South Wayne Street,
once the center of the community, was the first area to feel the impact of
change as the community's center of gravity shifted westward and northward. That part of town between Fishing Creek and the Statehouse now
came to be known as "Dogsboro."[122] Mrs. Anne Royall, a well-known
author, was a visitor to the town in 1831, arriving early one morning on the
Washington–New Orleans mail stage. Bumping over poor roads and eating
food to which she apparently was unaccustomed, she probably viewed Milledgeville and its people with an even more prejudiced eye than her vitu-

perative nature normally would have dictated. In her customary sharp rhetoric, she wrote that the place "was entirely deserted by men of business" and that she believed the town would never rise from its doldrums. "The massy State House and Penitentiary" were the only structures she thought worthy of notice, and the people she termed as unpleasant rabble—"the refuse of all nations, runaway convicts from other states, wooden nutmeg Yankees," all poor and unmannerly. The statehouse officers were described as "a vulgar set of men as ever disgraced a seat of government"—although she did exempt Secretary of State Everard Hamilton from this category. She also thought well of William A. Mott, the town constable, and Major Ambrose Day, a Revolutionary veteran and former newspaper editor. Passing the test of her feminine appraisal with unusual ease was one Nathan McGehee, whom she characterized as "quite an Adonis," describing him as a young man with a round face, fine complexion, black hair and eyes, and a handsome figure.[123]

The first rumblings of discontent with Milledgeville as the seat of government appeared toward the end of the 1820s. This question reappeared at various times until 1877, when it was finally put to rest in the confusion of Reconstruction politics. A Milledgeville editor in 1827 admitted that the town had seen better days, "but now [lawmakers] seek another place to forge out the laws, and her glory is going with the feet of empire and she to the weeds." He recalled that the site of the town had been chosen because of the excellence and purity of water from its many springs and because its seven hills gave it a similarity to ancient Rome. Unrealized, however, was the dream that these hills "would one day be covered with Theatres, Colosiuses [sic], Temples, and superb private edifices fit to lodge the leaders and rulers of a great republic." He recounted with nostalgic fervor the days when the community had been recognized for the beauty of the women who gathered there during legislative sessions. He spoke of these occasions as "a continual carnival where one could enjoy both the cotillion and the country dance." He predicted that one day "some Volney will sit upon these ruins and take up his brush to paint worlds which are passed."[124]

Milledgeville was Georgia's fourth capital. It was the only capital in the state's history—and one of the few in America—which was laid out and designated specifically as a seat of government. Carved from the wilderness, its growth was slow and uncertain in that era of expansion to the Southwest. The precarious navigability of the Oconee River limited the town's chances for expected growth. The arrangement of its streets, ignoring natural terrain, helped to give the town an unattractive appearance consistent with the rawness of the surrounding countryside. Yet the character of its people always remained high and earned for the community a reputation for social attractiveness.

3

Early Political and Commercial Life

Banking services were not available to people in the Georgia upcountry until after 1815. Although the Savannah branch of the Bank of the United States opened in 1802, it was another eight years before banks were chartered under state regulations. At that time there appeared the Bank of Augusta and the Planters Bank of Savannah, both of which were strictly commercial banks designed for the older areas in which they were placed. These banks avoided the cheap money policies desired by most farmers in the upcountry who later became strong backers of John Clark's party and, later still, Jacksonian Democrats.

This group believed that the only effective way to ease the pressure of debt and to aid in the development of new agricultural land was for banks to issue notes which people would accept in lieu of gold or silver coins. Milledgeville had already been introduced to this phase of banking when certain merchants such as R. J. Nichols and Company (later Nichols and Demming), began accepting deposits (which were placed in an iron vault), making discounts on notes and mortgages, and issuing their own notes, script, and change bills, all for the convenience of their customers. This script circulated as money wherever the standing of the issuing firms was recognized. D. B. Sanford was perhaps the first merchant to issue change bills in the Georgia upcountry. These notes, which might be called a form of private currency, appeared in denominations of 6¼, 12½, and 25 cents, with engravings on them respectively of a hog, a cow, and a horse.[1]

In response to a long-felt need for better regulation of credit practices, a group of Milledgeville people in 1815 formed a committee to raise by subscription $150,000 to be used in opening a bank in the town. On this committee were Zachariah Lamar, Fleming Grantland, Myles Green, William Y. Hansel, and the Yankee lawyer, Thomas Fitch. Within two weeks most of the shares had been subscribed, and plans were laid to petition the legislature for a charter.[2]

This was the first bank movement in the interior of Georgia where the capital had already become the state's largest upcountry cotton market, with the exception of Augusta. The older communities along the coast and the Savannah River, whose leaders were hard-money advocates opposed this extension of banking into the upcountry. Accordingly, the legislature worked out a compromise whereby it chartered a new bank known as the Bank of the State of Georgia, having the principal office in Savannah, with branches in Augusta and Milledgeville. It was to be capitalized at one and a half million dollars with 40 percent of its 15,000 shares reserved to the state.[3] The institution retained the characteristics of a commercial bank.

This bank went into operation in October 1816, and throughout the antebellum period it remained the largest banking operation in the state. With the growth of the upcountry it later opened additional branches in Eatonton, Macon, Greensboro, Athens, and Washington. Milledgeville merchants hoped that its presence in the town would increase the business of local factors in their purchase of cotton, which otherwise would "go by tedious land carriage" to distant markets where farmers in turn would be compelled to buy their supplies. With undue optimism it was pointed out that cotton could be shipped from Milledgeville to Savannah by water at a third of the cost by land, and even less than wagon freight to Augusta.[4]

The high cost of upstream freight on supplies, however, discouraged the appearance of large cotton factors on the Oconee. Also, the new bank in Milledgeville was not designed to meet farmers' needs for long-term credit at reasonable rates of interest. This problem was accentuated by the rapid growth and settlement of a large area west of the Oconee, and it continued to receive the attention of upcountry legislators, whose efforts were intensified by the high price of cotton following the outbreak of the War of 1812.

The result of these efforts was a compromise between the coastal area and the interior which led to the chartering in 1818 of a bank at the little port of Darien at the mouth of the Altamaha River. This bank was to have branches at Milledgeville on the fall line of the Oconee and at Marion (later at Macon) on the Ocmulgee. Since these two streams joined to form the Altamaha, the system's geographic pattern appeared designed to funnel the cotton trade of central Georgia into the port of Darien. At the same time a state law ended private banking, which was a concession to conservative banking interests at Savannah and Augusta. This law forbade any individual from issuing or circulating change bills or notes, or from keeping offices of deposit and discount "in any room, house, shop, or office."[5] It did not apply to change bills that might be issued by counties and municipalities.

The Darien branch opened in Milledgeville in 1819, on the southeast corner of Greene and Wilkinson streets. It was housed in a double-story masonry building which survived until 1956. Like all of its forebears, the Darien Bank was a commercial one, dealing in short-term loans and thus not ideally suited to the plantation economy of the region which it served. The bank's opening coincided with the depression of 1819, during which the older banks reduced their loans and discounts and called in their notes. The Darien Bank, however, having no backlog of such paper, began to increase its loans and discounts, partly because it served an area undergoing development. As a result of these circumstances, Darien bank notes became the principal circulating medium in Georgia throughout the early 1820s.[6]

By 1825 the value of Darien notes had dropped considerably and the bank found itself unable to redeem them in specie. Since Darien notes formed the principal circulating medium, the state began to suffer a depleted paper currency reminiscent of the period following the Revolution. People now paid their taxes and other obligations to the state in depreciated Darien notes which the state was obligated to accept, and soon the state treasury was surfeited with more than a half million dollars of this devalued currency. Since half of the capital stock of the Darien Bank had been purchased by the state and since many private subscribers had become indebted to the bank,

The Milledgeville branch of the Bank of Darien (built 1819)
before its demolition in 1957

they now transferred back to it some $231,000 of its own shares in payment. This not only reduced the bank's capital but increased the state's ownership of the institution to 80 percent of the total. Under these circumstances the state was faced with a dilemma. If it liquidated the bank it would be taking action against itself as the principal owner and operator. The state not only would lose the bank's notes which it held but it would also have to assume the greater portion of the bank's additional liabilities. State authorities simply left the bank alone to work out its difficulties. In this it fortunately was successful. By 1830 public confidence had been restored and, when its charter expired in 1835, it was renewed for another twenty years.[7]

In the meantime, in 1828, the state took a most significant step in establishing at Milledgeville a "unit bank," the first of its type ever located in the interior of the state. This was the Central Bank of the State of Georgia. It was unique in that it was owned and operated entirely by the state, its principal office being located in the Statehouse. It was to serve as the state's fiscal agent and to receive all deposits of public funds. In additon, it was to discount paper and make loans "on more favorable terms than heretofore customary."[8] It differed from previous banks in that it would make loans of the state's existing capital funds rather than convert credit to capital. Its rates of interest were moderate, and loans were made on longer terms than were possible under previous arrangements. It clearly was a departure from the old commercial bank format, being designed to serve the needs of farmers and planters. Governor John Clark and his party of upcountry farmers had long advocated such a bank.

By 1839 Georgia again was in the doldrums of a depression, and the Darien Bank again found itself in deep trouble. In that year it ended specie payments and stopped discounting. The bank also suffered the embarrassment of having some $23,000 of its notes stolen. This circumstance necessitated the withdrawal from circulation of all old notes and the issuing of new ones signed by the new president, Anson Kimberly.[9]

The problems of the Darien Bank were attributed largely to the fact that its directors, appointed by the state, often had limited ability and little interest in the bank's profitable management. Governor Charles J. McDonald suggested either that its charter be forfeited or that the state dispose of most of its stock in the institution. As a result, in 1841 the bank's assets were transferred to the Central Bank for liquidation, a process which extended over a period of several years.[10]

In the meantime the Central Bank came under heavy fire from the hard-money group, who believed that the 1839 panic was largely a result of this bank's easy credit policies. While the bank had never violated any provision of its charter, its powers of active operation were ended in 1842 when its fiscal business was transferred back to the state treasury. Its operations were declared ended in 1856 when its remaining indebtedness of more than a half million dollars became an obligation of the state. Thus the Central Bank, whose office building now stood on the north side of Greene Street near the Presbyterian Church, closed its doors.[11] The Bank of the State, which stood near by, remained for a time the only banking institution in the capital. The Bank of Milledgeville had been organized in 1836 under a charter granted the previous year to a group of the town's leading business men, but not a single private bank was incorporated in Georgia for the next fourteen years. In 1848 this bank too, ceased to do business, although it continued its organization in the hope of disposing of lands it held in Mississippi and of collecting what it could from a large number of insolvent debtors.[12]

The struggle between hard-money advocates and those who favored cheap money, which characterized early banking issues, was closely related to a series of stay laws which the legislature originally enacted in 1808, and which were reenacted by every subsequent legislature through 1814. Since these laws, called "alleviating laws," postponed the execution date of contracts which creditors had with debtors, they greatly favored the latter group but penalized and hence greatly incensed the former. When Governor Peter Early vetoed the stay law of November 1814, a regiment of militiamen were in Milledgeville for their annual muster. The colonel in command marched his regiment around the Statehouse in an apparent move to intimidate the governor and members of the legislature who opposed the alleviating law. Governor Early reprimanded the colonel sharply for his threat of treason and ordered him to march his regiment forthwith to Fort Hawkins, threatening to have him shot in the presence of his men if he disobeyed. The officer complied, but he was later tried and dismissed from service.[13]

This incident was one of many occurring in Milledgeville which reflected the bitter differences over political issues during the first quarter of the nineteenth century. While almost all Georgians were Republicans (Jeffersonians) on national issues, politics within the state sharply divided the people. One faction was headed by George M. Troup, William H. Crawford, and

David B. Mitchell many of whose followers belonged to the more affluent and aristocratic element. The opposition, known as the Clark party, found its strength in the upcountry among the farmers and frontiersmen. Personal and family loyalties rather than principles often formed the unifying ingredient of both groups, and physical violence was a frequent occurrence. Of the early Milledgeville governors, Clark, Troup, George W. Crawford, and David B. Mitchell all fought duels with political adversaries, as did an even greater number of less important leaders. Once Clark ran into difficulties with Judge Charles Tait, a crippled leader of the Crawford-Troup party, after Tait had been involved in charges against Clark for Negro-stealing. Believing that it was a political conspiracy against him, Clark waylaid the judge as he rode in an open sulky on Jefferson Street and soundly horse-whipped him from his vantage position on horseback. For this outrage on judicial dignity Clark was fined $2,000, but the fine was later lifted by a friendly judge.

Clark's gubernatorial contest with Troup in 1819 was a bitter one. Largely as a result of the depression of that period, people were beginning to think in terms of principles and to judge each candidate on his position on basic economic issues. In a close legislative poll, Clark won with a margin of thirteen votes. In the next election, that of November 1821, Clark received only a two-vote majority over Troup.[14]

The last regular election in Georgia in which the legislature chose the governor was that of 1823, in which eighty-four of the 166 ballots were required to elect. On this occasion Matthew Talbot, a Clarkite, was Troup's opponent. The house chamber was packed with people, and the excitement was intense as the votes were tallied. In the final minute of the tally the count reached eighty-two for each candidate, and when only one vote remained to determine the winner, the clerk called out the name of Troup. Bedlam broke out and continued for some time. Daniel Duffy, an ardent Methodist and an equally ardent Troupite, ran across the Statehouse Square shouting that "the state of Georgia has been redeemed from the devil and John Clark!" Jesse Mercer, the Baptist divine, was seen running down the street, waving his hat above his bald head, and shouting "Glory, Glory!" until he grew hoarse and disappeared from view over the rugged terrain of Statehouse Square. General David Blackshear, holding his hands in prayer, was heard to say: "Now, Lord, I am ready to die." The feeling during this election had been so intense that even husbands and wives of different political backgrounds had become divided on the issues. In one instance it caused the separation of a couple who were of high social standing and the parents of eight married children.[15]

Troup's success was a victory for the conservative planting and commercial classes over the small farmers and frontiersmen. The general pattern of this schism was to reappear during the Populist Movement of the 1890s.

Those who achieved high political office provided whatever preferment they could to their supporters. During the opening months of Clark's second term he became embroiled in an effort to oust Abner Hammond from his position as secretary of state, an office to which the legislature had elected him. In July Hammond left Milledgeville for a prolonged visit to the coast, where he hoped to improve his health. He left a power-of-attorney to Thomas H. Crawford so that the office could function during his absence. Clark now issued a proclamation declaring the office vacant and announced the appointment of Simon Whitaker to the post. When Crawford refused to vacate, the governor had the lock on his office changed and threatened to throw him out of the Statehouse. A judicial hearing resulted in the decision that Hammond had not vacated the office, and Judge Christopher Strong issued a writ of mandamus forcing Whitaker to return the office to Hammond.[16]

Another controversy in which Governor Clark was engaged was that centering around the Georgia Penitentiary. The penitentiary system had been established in Georgia in 1811 under Governor Mitchell, although it was not until February 1817, during his second term, that the facility was ready for use. It occupied the center of the north square in Milledgeville (which later became the main campus of Georgia College.) Prior to this time all punishment of criminals had been administered by the sheriff of the county in which the crime was committed (the hanging of criminals continued to be a function of county sheriffs until 1924). The methods of punishment were relics of a barbaric age: convicted persons were subject to public hanging, branding, ear-cropping, whipping, or confinement in the stocks, the pillory, or the dungeon of the county jail. Highway robbery, second-time horse-stealing, counterfeiting, and murder all drew the death penalty. Since such executions were public throughout most of the nineteenth century, they drew large crowds, and newspapers reported every gruesome detail of the proceedings.[17]

With no court of appeals and no state supreme court during the early period, punishment was unusually swift. In 1815 Noyle Nelms was convicted of passing a five-dollar counterfeit note in Milledgeville and was hanged five days later. Despite the fact that he was sixty years old and that the new criminal code about to take effect would have substituted penitentiary confinement for hanging in his particular case, Governor Mitchell refused to intervene.[18] Not so unfortunate was a horse thief who received a pardon. Earlier Judge Peter Early passed sentence on a Milledgeville woman who had been convicted of being a common scold. The judge ordered Sheriff Philip Cook to duck her three times in the Oconee River. The sentence was executed by tying the convicted woman to the rear of an old sulky which was successively pushed into the water and then withdrawn, while a large crowd of people looked on from the banks of the river.[19]

The establishment of the penitentiary brought its own problems. At no time before 1830 did the penitentiary have more than 100 inmates. Three years after it opened there were only sixty-four prisoners, whose actual upkeep was costing the state less than twenty cents a day per person. Each convict was lodged with four or five others in a dirty, unswept, and unscrubbed cell. Blankets and pillows were piled together in one corner. Prisoners slept on straw mattresses placed indiscriminately on the floor.[20] In contrast to the $4,000 annual cost of food was an administrative cost of $10,000. Administrative and staff personnel totaled twenty-eight employees—or approximately one for every three convicts. The transporting of prisoners to Milledgeville was a significant item in the institution's budget. Sheriff Abraham De Lyon of Savannah received a compensation of $642 for two trips to Milledgeville early in 1822. In operation at this time were prison shops for making wagons, saddles, and shoes, and also tailoring and blacksmith shops. With the passage of time other shops were added, and by 1830 the inmates were engaged in twenty different crafts.[21]

When John Clark held the office of governor, he realigned positions at the penitentiary, thus setting a pattern of patronage at this institution which long weakened its usefulness. Yet public criticism of the penitentiary was headed by the governor himself, who claimed that it was not serving the purpose for which it was intended and threatened to have it abolished. Local citizens described it as "both a curse and an eyesore to the town." Milledgeville's artisans were particularly resentful of the practice of maintaining a penitentiary store outside the walls where products of the shops were sold, for this depressed the market for work done by professional craftsmen. Moreover, prison enterprises were often conducted in a loose, unbusinesslike fashion and showed annual deficits. Those responsible attributed the losses to the comparative smallness of the Milledgeville community and its remoteness from commercial centers and adequate sources of raw materials.[22]

Other problems plagued the penitentiary during its first decade. Too often the principal keeper was a political hack without interest or experience in penalogy. In 1828 the legislature sought to improve the situation with a law which, in effect, made the governor the principal official of the prison (this in spite of the fact that throughout the penitentiary's history the governors had often been at the center of petty intrigues revolving about that institution).

In May 1827 the prisoners managed to set fire to the wooden buildings, and although no one escaped during the confusion which followed, nearly everything in the compound was destroyed. Partly as a result, the legislature abolished the penitentiary in December and set aside the new criminal code. However, the law to abolish the penitentiary was repealed in the following year, and money was appropriated to replace the buildings with granite, fire-proof structures. While arson continued to remain a problem, the penitentiary was not again threatened with extinction until after the Civil War.[23]

The editors and publishers of Milledgeville's newspapers thrived under all controversial developments and were particularly devisive on all issues involving Troup-Clark politics. They were playing for high stakes, for the state printing contract was a lucrative one. The *Georgia Journal* and the *Georgia Patriot* were pro-Clark and inclined to be critical of Troup and his ally, David B. Mitchell. The latter, who had been born in Scotland, was referred to as a foreigner by the *Patriot*. Its editor apparently was delighted to publish accusations against him of smuggling Africans into the state contrary to both state and federal law. This charge later resulted in Mitchell's dismissal from his post as Indian agent, for which he had resigned the governorship in 1817.[24] The *Southern Recorder* and the *Georgia Argus*, on the other hand, were strongly pro-Troup. The former stated in 1823 that Clark's administration was "a blot on the history of the state which all the talents and virtues of his predecessors and successors [could] not obliterate." In contrast, Troup was described as "a man of talent, dignity, patriotism, and magnanimity."[25]

Troup faced Clark again in the 1825 election, the first in Georgia to be decided by popular vote. Issues this time were quite real, being highlighted by Troup's ardent stand for Indian removal and for state rights.[26] Troup won by a slim margin of 727 votes. As the state moved out of its earlier frontier stage of development, Clark's popularity began to wane. Troup continued to represent the more settled farmer and the rising plantation master.

Born of a Tory father on the Tombigbee River in Alabama, Troup had been tutored by a Catholic priest in Savannah and reared in the tradition of an urbane gentleman. He later acquired a plantation in Laurens County, where he built a house of logs on an eminence overlooking the Oconee River. To this house he gave the name Val d'Aosta (Valdosta). Although he was the owner of many slaves, Troup's furniture, dress, and social habits were quite simple—and he was indifferent to etiquette. As Georgia's foremost champion of state rights, he became an excellent orator on this subject. It was his habit to speak briefly in sharp sentences, never using an unnecessary word. His arguments were cogent, graceful, and conclusive. Troup has been described as short in stature "but compactly built and straight as an Indian's arrow." Fond of horseback riding, he was often seen on the streets of the town. While at the capital he lived alone in a single room at Mrs. Jenkins tavern on East Hancock Street near the Statehouse, although he did use Government House for rare social occasions.[27]

The legislature with which Troup worked in 1825 was a remarkable one. Still divided into Troup and Clark factions, it was one of the last in Georgia in which frontier traditions were to be so predominant. Its membership included such notables as Duncan G. Campbell, William H. Sparks, Stephen Upson, Joseph Lumpkin, William Law, Charles Doughtery, Robert A. Beall, Henry Branham, John Abercrombie, and Thomas Stocks. The most colorful of these was the Troupite Abercrombie, who was noted for his unusual size and bulk (although he was only five feet, six inches, in height, his weight exceeded 330 pounds).

A scene from the activities of the 1825 legislature might serve to illustrate its character. Among the five counties which were to be created that year was one embracing the Indian Springs resort. Abercrombie was eager to have the new county named for Samuel Butts of Hancock County, who was killed in the War of 1812. At the third reading of the bill, the name of the county was still unresolved. Now at this time Abercrombie was serving as speaker of the house, and William C. Dawson was clerk. The latter frequently served temporarily as speaker when an inexperienced member was in the chair. When the bill came up for approval, Abercrombie called Representative Burnside of Columbia County to the chair and assumed the latter's seat on the floor beside Baldwin County representative John Polhill, who was a Clarkite and a man of slight physical proportions. When Dawson, reading the bill, came to the blank space and asked what the name of the county should be, Abercrombie sprang to his feet. He moved that the new county be named in honor of Samuel Butts. "He deserved this honor," continued Abercrombie. "I knew him well from the cradle to the saddle. He was brave before he could walk." Then bursting into tears, he concluded: "Whilst many who are now enjoying the honors and emoluments of high office were hiding behind stumps and trees, he stood boldly out, facing the enemy and was shot through the belly and died, by God, without a grunt." Abercrombie's grotesque figure and excited language and mannerisms convulsed the House, but Polhill only managed a torpid grin. The heavyweight wiped his steaming brow with his coat sleeve, then turned on the fragile Polhill like a hyena and said, "Go to hell you damn fise! [sic]." The speaker never even put the question to a vote but simply announced the organization of Butts County.

Representative Burnside, incidentally, was later killed in a duel, and Abercrombie, shortly after his performance on behalf of Samuel Butts, succumbed to a ruptured blood vessel while laughing at a story told by Daniel Brailsford. When this stroke occurred, Abercrombie sent for Dr. Samuel Boykin, who in turn requested the counsel of Dr. Henry Branham, then rooming at Boykin's house. Despite a feud between the stricken man and Branham, the latter gave his consent. When the doctor entered the room, Abercrombie merely asked him to be truthful and sincere for once in his life. After a brief examination Branham informed the patient that he was dying and suggested that he make his peace with his Maker. "By God, I never was at war with *him*," replied Abercrombie, and then he expired.[28]

During Troup's second term in office the legislature received a visit from Karl Bernhard, Duke of Saxe-Weimar-Eisenach. Being the first nobleman that had ever honored the General Assembly with a visit, Bernhard was accorded rare civilities both by legislators and by citizens of the town. He was escorted everywhere by two of the governor's aides, Daniel Brailsford and Seaborn Jones. The latter had never bothered to acquire a military uniform, but he was able to borrow one for this occasion from Adjutant General Thomas Dawson, a much larger man than he. Jones had little difficulty getting into Dawson's baggy uniform, but he balked at wearing Dawson's military hat and finally settled for a plain civilian headpiece.

Bernhard was found to be as plain and unostentatious as any Georgia Republican. Informally dressed, he waived all ceremony. He preferred to walk everywhere he went throughout the town. Some members of the legislature, however, were determined to show him all the courtesies commensurate with his rank and title. One suggested that the duke be welcomed with three standing cheers given by the legislators. Another suggested that he be introduced to the speaker and the president, both of whom should give a speech of welcome. It was finally decided that the visitor should be received with members merely standing, and then he would be invited to a seat where he could witness legislative proceedings. Bernhard observed with great interest each legislator who spoke. Later he wrote that each was characterized by great individuality, "all attesting the fact that they had been reared separately and apart from the civilized world."

From the Statehouse Jones and Brailsford escorted the nobleman to the governor's plain room at Mrs. Jenkins equally plain boarding house. They found the governor seated tailor-fashion in the middle of his bed, wearing a weather-beaten hat and reading a book of Akenside's poems. When introduced to his foreign guest, the governor merely nodded his head but did not remove his hat. When invited to be seated the duke placed his own hat on the unkempt floor, but after a slight gesture of invitation from his host, he quickly placed it back on his head. After a brief conversation the duke rose to leave, at which time Troup offered him some brandy which one of his aides was asked to produce from a closet. The governor then rose in his stocking feet and joined the other three in a drink. Without again touching his hat the duke bowed himself from the room.[29]

Apparently Bernhard was less than thrilled with his visit to the frontier capital. "We were constrained to remain in Milledgeville on the day after Christmas, how unpleasant soever it might be," wrote the duke. Perhaps he found some consolation in the fact that he was able to observe some genuine American Indians—Creek men and women—on the streets of the town, not only buying certain goods and trinkets but also selling their own wares, such as woven baskets and even bows and arrows. "Some were well dressed," he observed. "They wore moccasins and leggings of leather; broad knee bands ornamented with white glass beads, a sort of coat of striped cotton, and upon the head a striped cotton cloth . . . like a turban. . . . They were all wrapt up in woolen blankets."[30]

The Creek Indian boundary had been moved westward to the Chattahoochee by the time Troup left office in the fall of 1827. Moreover, the political factionalism which had been so keen in the early part of that decade had so much diminished that Judge Owen H. Kenan took note of it in his charge to a Baldwin County grand jury. He congratulated the community on the return of the day "when men can meet and part in good feelings" and thus announced the end of a long and unhappy strife.[31] However, the judge's optimism was ill-founded, for the basis of new strife was already being laid. Almost all Clarkites joined the new Union party (later the Democratic party), while Troupites generally found a home in the State Rights party (later the Whig party).

National issues such as the tariff, nullification, and the abolitionist movement were coming to the fore in 1827, and Milledgeville newspapers realigned themselves accordingly. In that year Elijah H. Burritt, a New England native and a strong Union sympathizer, became the sole owner of the *Georgia Statesman* and at the same time bought the *Georgia Patriot* from Cosam E. Bartlett. The two papers were now combined to form the *Statesman and Patriot*, under the editorship of John G. Polhill. In 1830, however, Polhill—who by that time had become editor of the newly formed *Federal Union*—accused his former partner of distributing copies of an incendiary pamphlet written by the Negro abolitionist, David Walker. When a true bill was returned against Burritt, he fled North to avoid trial. While Burritt may have been innocent of all the charges against him, the fact that he was a known liberal and a brother of the reformer Elihu Burritt, whose abolitionist sympathies he shared, made it extremely doubtful that he could have received a fair trial in Milledgeville. Consequently he never returned; within a few weeks after his departure his property was sold by the sheriff.[32]

Before the Burritt affair had quieted down, the press war broke out on a new front, this time involving a bitter personal feud between the state rights editor Seaton Grantland of the *Southern Recorder* and the Unionist editor John A. Cuthbert. The latter, who had served in a term in Congress, had joined Polhill in May as editor of the *Federal Union*, and the two also conducted a law partnership in the commissioner's hall of the market house.[33] Their paper had given strong support to the candidacy of Wilson Lumpkin for governor, to which office he later was elected by a considerable majority. As a reward for his loyal support, Cuthbert became Lumpkin's executive secretary in December 1831. Grantland, despite his politics, was elected president of the branch Bank of the State, to which announcement Cuthbert laconically stated, "Thereby hangs a tale."[34] The editorial columns of each paper began to fill with statements and innuendoes critical of

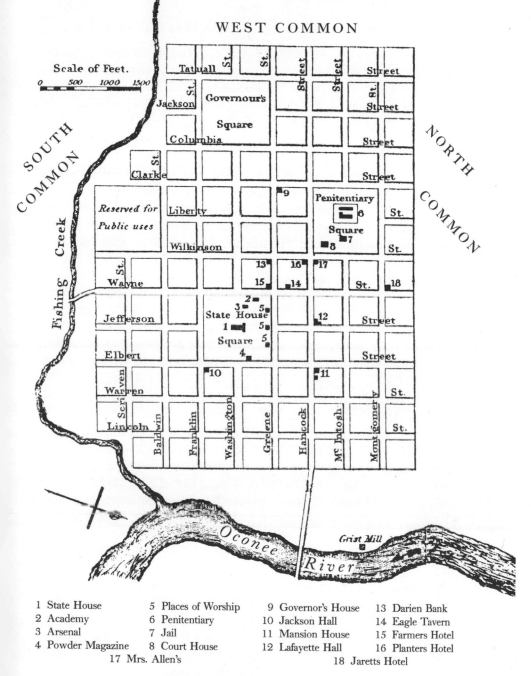

Milledgeville in 1830

1 State House	5 Places of Worship	9 Governor's House	13 Darien Bank
2 Academy	6 Penitentiary	10 Jackson Hall	14 Eagle Tavern
3 Arsenal	7 Jail	11 Mansion House	15 Farmers Hotel
4 Powder Magazine	8 Court House	12 Lafayette Hall	16 Planters Hotel

17 Mrs. Allen's   18 Jaretts Hotel

the other editor. In the contest of barb-throwing Grantland was perhaps the superior of the two—he frequently described his adversary's actions as comic opera, with Cuthbert as the leading buffoon.

One episode occurred during the early part of December when a report reached Milledgeville of a slave uprising in nearby Jones County reminiscent of the one led by Nat Turner in Virginia earlier that year. The Turner uprising, which had resulted in the massacre of sixty-five innocent people, had greatly alarmed the people and caused Southern state legislatures to strengthen their laws on slave control. Consequently, when the Jones County rumor hit Milledgeville, a special volunteer guard was created and placed under the command of Cuthbert. By virtue of this captaincy, Governor Gilmer named Cuthbert "the Military Commander of Milledgeville."

In the end the report of an uprising in Jones County proved false, but Cuthbert reacted to it with his usual vigor and was determined to take all necessary precautions against a local uprising. The town was alarmed by the ringing of bells and, according to Grantland, "Cuthbert did run, halloo, and sever the air with his sword for a great distance through the town of Milledgeville, more like a maniac than a man of cool, deliberate courage, crying out as he thus ran and flourished his weapon, 'To your Arms! To your Arms!!'" A group of men in the courthouse were reported to have seen him running past that building to the western limits of the town as if to meet single-handedly the on-marching insurrectionists.

Cuthbert's response to this reporting was an explanation that, on the contrary, he had been busy all the while in posting guards and in collecting women and children at the Statehouse. Then he accused Grantland of not even having been present at the scene because he had been seen fleeing the town in the direction of his plantation near Scottsboro. Somewhat subdued, Grantland admitted going to Woodville, where his aged mother and his children were living on the plantation with fifty slaves and without the supervision of an overseer. His purpose, said he, was to quiet their alarm and to provide them aid.[35]

The climax of this quarrel was a physical encounter between the two men near the south door of the Statehouse. Cuthbert claimed that Grantland came to his office armed with a stick, a pistol, and a sword. After an exchange of words, during the course of which Grantland was called "a skulking coward," Cuthbert was struck in the face with a blow from Grantland. Cuthbert wrested the stick from his adversary and forced him to retreat, whereupon Grantland drew his pistol and Cuthbert went for a dirk in his pocket. At this point several members of the legislature interceded, as did Governor Lumpkin, who ordered the two men taken into custody. Cuthbert lost both his hat and his wig in the fracas, if not a sizable portion of his dignity.[36]

Cuthbert soon resigned from his post as the governor's secretary and devoted more time to his editorial functions and his legal practice. When John G. Park acquired the *Federal Union* in 1837, however, Cuthbert ended his editorship of that Union party paper. He later moved to Mobile, where he continued to practice law and where he became judge of the circuit court, but later he fell upon unhappy times. At the end of the Civil War his fortune was gone, and in 1867 he lost his position as assistant clerk of the federal district court at Mobile. At the age of ninety-one he was again attempting to practice law. He died two years later, in 1881.[37]

Cuthbert's old Milledgeville antagonist, Seaton Grantland, fared little better. In 1835 he was elected to Congress, where he served two terms; later he became an active and prominent Whig in politics. However, while performing political errands in the nation's capital in 1852, he suffered a mental collapse from which he never recovered. He died twelve years later at Woodville. John G. Polhill was more fortunate. After serving briefly as postmaster in 1834, he became judge of the superior court, replacing the deceased L. Q. C. Lamar.[38]

The careers of Cuthbert, Grantland, and Polhill illustrate the strong addiction to politics which possessed many of the town's early settlers. While nearly all sooner or later became victims of political vicissitudes, the greatest sufferer was the town itself. Characterized as "a political community," its people were peculiarly vulnerable to the sharp divisions of political issues which engaged their energies and divided them. Frequently these issues developed into family feuds which survived long after the original issues were forgotten. Homocides involving prominent residents were a frequent occurrence for many decades, and more often than not these carried political overtones. Robert McComb was attacked by William Ward and Henry Byron armed with dirks, a gun, and a sword at the Eagle Tavern in December 1833. One assailant was killed and the other seriously wounded in the affray. Earlier, two of Milledgeville's young men had met in a formal duel on the South Carolina side of the Savannah River, where shots were fired without fatal effects. Then friends intervened and their differences were settled. Eighteen-year-old Jackson Mahon was sentenced to life in the penitentiary for shooting to death Martin P. Smith in a Fourth of July brawl in 1835. Two years later Robert Darnell was stabbed to death with a bowie knife by an antagonist who had followed him to Alabama.[39] Such incidents prompted a Baldwin County grand jury to urge a more effective law against dueling. It suggested forming an association which functioned very much as "Alcoholics Anonymous" was to do in a later age.[40]

One of the most dramatic feuds involved the Alston family who lived near Milledgeville in the late 1820s and the 1830s. The most violent effects of the Alston affair were felt as far away as Tallahassee and reached all the way to Texas. For reasons which are difficult to explain, the Alstons had long been at odds with the Ingram family of Hancock County. When the Seminole War began in 1835, Augustus Alston was made colonel and placed in command of a regiment which went to Florida. There Augustus fought a duel near Tallahassee with the brother of one Lieutenant Ward, who had been fatally shot by another officer and for whose death Colonel Alston was being held responsible. General Leigh Reed now became involved in the controversy, and Reed and Alston fought a duel in which the latter was killed. Alston's sister removed the fatal bullet from the body, remoulded it, and sent it to Willis Alston in Texas, asking him to hurry to Tallahassee and avenge their brother's death. When Willis arrived in Tallahassee he found General Reed eating dinner at a hotel. He promptly shot him through the hips, stabbed him in the stomach with a bowie knife, and then fled. Back in Texas Willis Alston shot to death another person, for which he was seized by a mob, taken out on the prairie, and lynched.[41] The last of the Alstons to meet a violent death was Robert A. Alston (b. 1832), son of Willis. He was killed in a pistol duel with Edward Cox in March 1879, in the office of the state treasurer in Atlanta. Their quarrel grew out of the convict lease system, of which Cox was a sublessee.[42]

The strife which revolved around the Statehouse, and the political climate which engendered it, appeared greatly magnified by the relatively small number of permanent inhabitants of the town. This caused Milledgeville's commercial life to seem dwarfed by comparison, yet it possessed certain peculiar aspects. Its Indian trade was of some importance in the early period, as that of Augusta had been previously. Goods advertised for this trade included "Gila Handkerchiefs, Sooty Rowall, Pulty Putty, Madras, Indian Checks, Blue Strouds, . . . Calico, Green and Blue Grounded Shawls [with] rich borders, Small Beads, . . . Blankets, Scarlet Cloth, etc."[43]

Newspaper advertisements of this period reflect the primitive character of the town's economy. For example, in January 1815 Adna Rowe announced that he would pay the highest prices throughout the season for "Beaver, Otter, Mink, Mooserat and Rabit [sic] furs." Others offered to buy seed cotton and shelled corn. Jacob Mordecai offered to buy homespun cloth and pay part cash and the rest in goods.[44] Jabez Roberts wanted 200 pounds of new feathers. Another venturer offered liberal wages to a good distiller of whisky and also sought the construction of a grain mill, to be powered by horses on a treadmill. Henry Darnell, a tailor operating in a room at the Eagle Tavern, would accept produce for his work.[45] Blacksmiths, of whom there were a large number, advertised such items as mill irons, gin saws, screws, castings, nails, Swedish iron, German steel, plow moulds, horse-shoes, and branding irons.[46]

The town had a number of artisans who called themselves "whitesmiths"; they worked in silver and also repaired guns, umbrellas, locks, printing presses, cotton gins, and surveyor's instruments. There also was an occasional clock-maker. Frequently one man followed as many as three trades in the same shop, or in successive stages of his career. One of the more noted of Milledgeville's highly skilled artisans was Templeton Reed (1789–1851), who came to the capital in 1812 from Putnam County, where he had been engaged in repairing watches and clocks and in making jewelry. In 1824 he began the manufacture of rifles. Later, when gold was discovered at Dahlonega, he went there and operated a private mint, stamping gold into $2.50, $5, and $10 coins.[47] By 1832 Reed was back in Milledgeville, where he resumed gunmaking. Eight years later he moved to Columbus and settled down as a specialist in this craft.[48]

Specialization was extremely rare in the field of merchandizing. Peter Menard, for example, offered for sale the widest variety of goods, ranging from staple foods and dried fish and fruit to candies and an assortment of imported wines. At the office of the *Southern Recorder* one might renew his subscription and at the same time purchase such drugs as laudanum, paregoric, Tarter emetic, camphor, and pills for billious fever. At the "areated water establishment" on the west side of Statehouse Square one might quench his thirst with un-iced soda water "prepared on correct chemical principles."[49] While bathing was considered a quaint French custom in early Milledgeville, much prejudice against its practice must have disappeared by 1825 when Henry Darnell announced the opening of "the Milledgeville Baths." He sold single tickets for twenty-five cents and season tickets for five dollars. Another note of advancing refinement is seen in the announcement of one Leslie, who informed the public of the opening of a dancing academy "to be held in Mr. Buren's Long Room ... until the Legislature rises and then will remove to Mrs. Huson's."[50]

At his apothecary shop next to the Eagle Tavern, Dr. Wilson sold paints and dyes as well as patent medicines, and he offered to pay the highest prices for beeswax, black snakeroot, and senega.[51] His advertised list of drugs, many of them addictive, a few actually poisonous, and all sold without prescription, would astonish the modern druggist.

Near the Eagle Tavern also was the office of Dr. Childers, who advertised his skills in medicine, surgery, and midwifery. He announced that he would attend gratis those who were unable to pay, a procedure which might bewilder the modern medical practitioner. A. B. Hayden, an itinerant dentist, offered to make house calls and "to set natural and artificial teeth in all the variety of ways, as well as ligatures, springs, pivots, and on plates of gold and in a manner both useful and ornamental."[52]

Nearly all grocery stores also sold hard liquor and wines; hence barrooms as such were slow to multiply. Barkeepers usually were merely vendors and not skilled in mixing drinks. One of these was being sought for employment by Samuel Buffington in 1810 when he advertised for a boy "14 or 15 years of age who can read, write, and cypher, and come well recommended."[53]

The most famous of Milledgeville's saloons was the Big Indian, once operated by Gus Randolph on the north side of Greene Street opposite the Presbyterian Church. In front of this establishment was the large figure of an Indian carved from wood. He held a scalping knife in one hand while a dagger and a tomahawk hung from his belt. On one arm was a gourd five feet long and around his neck was a rattlesnake skin. Long recognized as the most popular and most elegant bar in the town, the Big Indian had a standard price of ten cents a drink, "plain or fancy," while others sold plain drinks for five cents. To the dismay of many legislators but with the applause of wives and mothers, the Big Indian was destroyed in October 1853 when a catastrophic fire swept away a large portion of the business district north of the Statehouse.[54]

The advertising of alcoholic beverages usually was confined to wholesale merchants who ran commission warehouses, such as R. J. Nichols, William Bowen, and Thomas Wiley, all of whom publicized a long list of exotic wines and other beverages.[55] Their listings of groceries were greatest during the winter months and always included Irish potatoes and salt, neither of which was produced in commercial quantity within the state at that time.

Pickled pork and beef were rare, but salt for meat-curing was in great demand, as were salt mackeral, herring, and salmon, green coffee, cheese, sugar, and split peas. Many hogs were supplied by drovers from Tennessee.[56]

Advertising in local papers increased perceptibly just before the legislature's annual sessions in November and December. Thomas Wilkinson announced during the 1810 session that he would be at Olmstead's tavern, where he would "take profiles of such Ladies and Gentlemen as may please to honor him with their commands." In the same year Mason Locke Weems appeared during the session of the superior court to take orders for his books, among which was his famous *Life of Washington*. Weems remained in Milledgeville through part of the legislative session. His lecture at the Statehouse on the importance of education was well attended, and he later received a testimonial from Governor Mitchell.[57]

The paucity of good reading material was a characteristic of frontier communities. To fill this deficit, several local citizens subscribed to a circulating library organized and run from Lucas' tavern.[58] By 1820 Arthur Ginn had established a bookstore on Wayne Street. He announced a list of books on home medicine, theology, history, philosophy, and religion. On his shelves were books of such classical distinction as Adam Smith's *Wealth of Nations*, Plutarch's *Lives*, Hutton's *Mathematics*, Montesquieu's *Spirit of the Laws*, Vattell's *Law of Nations*, John Locke's *Essays*, Ferguson's *Lectures*, and works by Shakespeare, Cervantes, Goldsmith, Byron, Scott, Swift, and Coleridge. In addition, he sold maps, surveyor's compasses and platting instruments, and offered bookbinding service. However, it was not until 1827 that a complete bookbinding shop appeared in Milledgeville.[59]

Dry goods merchants were few in number, and their line of merchandise was a simple one. Their shelves took on a more sophisticated appearance during the fall months, again reflecting discriminating patronage during legislative sessions. William Butler announced a fall and winter supply from Philadelphia in which were to be found "superfine blue, brown, green, and black broadcloth; blue, black and mixed casimeres; red, white, and yellow flannels, Irish linens, silk striped vestings, black and pink cambric, silk flag handkerchiefs, and hose made of cotton and of wool." Aaron Hanscomb sold "Baltimore made hats and boots ... of the newest fashions." John Haas, living at Jarrett's boarding house, offered to sell at the lowest prices neatly finished upper leather as well as "strong Negro leather." More indicative of the attire of the common people was the inclusion of such items as osnaburgs, homespun, Negro plains, sheetings, shirtings, plaids, and stripes.[60]

Ready-made clothing, except for hats, was almost nonexistent. Most shoes were made locally, and no attempt was made to shape rights and lefts. Shoemakers, good seamstresses, and good tailors generally were in short supply and, like all good craftsmen of this period, they took pride in their work and in the social standing of their patrons. Eighteenth-century fashions of knee breeches, silk stockings, and three-cornered cocked hats were fast disappearing as Milledgeville completed its first decade of existence. However, a few examples of these styles could still be found on its streets as late as 1820. At this time a broadcloth coat could be tailored for five dollars, while a pair of pantaloons would cost $1.25.[61]

The black, high-topped hat was a common piece of wearing apparel for gentlemen in the early part of the nineteenth century. The well-dressed gentleman might also be found in a claw-hammer tailcoat with a black velvet collar, a pea-green waistcoat, and fawn-colored long trousers. The top hat was soon to come out in improved style. Made of polished silk or beaver, it was unusually tall after 1820. It enjoyed the longest popularity of any part of a man's wardrobe, probably because its upper story was found useful in carrying papers, letters, and even money. Long after the Civil War Peterson Thweatt, Dr. Thomas F. Green, and Seth N. Boughton were still wearing these hats. Governor Troup in 1825 was described as wearing a plain white hat, a coarse osnaburg round jacket, silk socks, and nankeen crepe pantaloons. In the same year, when James Moran married, his wedding attire was of white cotton homespun—no doubt woven on primitive equipment, using thread spun from lint which was picked from the seed by hand. His coat was a roundabout jacket. Tomlinson Fort's wedding apparel was more fashionable. Married in October 1824, he wore a blue swallowtail coat with brass buttons, a white vest, blue trousers, low-quartered shoes, and silk stockings.[62]

The federal tariff controversy of the late 1820s revived the use of homespun clothing. Such clothing usually was carelessly tailored, and the texture and quality of the cloth were uneven. Some of the trousers "stood off . . . like a laboring woman's petticoat," while others were so thinly woven as to produce a chill to those who viewed them—much less to those who wore them. Governor Gilmer was among those who wore this grade of domestic apparel. One morning when the French consul from New Orleans knocked on Gilmer's door, he refused to believe that the poorly attired governor who appeared in the doorway was not a servant.[63]

By 1820 women's apparel also had undergone some basic changes. At that time the corset had acquired a steel busk front, and afterwards the waistline decreased steadily in girth; but the slim skirt changed to one shaped like a bell, and it barely cleared the ground. Petticoats also became a new feature of the feminine costume; they were short-waisted, with slim, long skirts. Several petticoats edged with frills showed below the outer garment. In great contrast to today's thought, the idea of women wearing pants was shocking indeed, even when they were in the form of drawers worn next to the skin underneath piles of petticoats. Women's drawers did not come to be worn until after 1830. However, even then what appeared to be a dainty pair of pantalets was often only a set of false drawers—a pair of separate tubes held in place by a string tied just below the knees.

Women's fashions, as in modern times, changed more frequently than those for men, but new fashions were slow to reach Georgia's capital. Rural people showed great conservatism in their dress. Early Milledgeville residents remembered Mrs. David B. Mitchell as still wearing a Martha Washington cap in the late 1820s, and on her bosom she always wore a white lawn handkerchief. She sniffed finely powdered tobacco (snuff), which she daintily removed from a silver box with her thumb and forefinger.[64] Tobacco sniffing was by no means confined to women, and the practice continued until long after the Civil War. Tradition says that Judge Edward R. Hines (1873–1944) was the last of the town's old-time tobacco sniffers. Although tobacco was grown for local consumption on almost all farms, the best snuff came from Virginia tobacco and was an item which frequently appeared in grocery stores.

Tobacco was one of the farm products which occurred most frequently in inventories of estates in this period. Seed cotton was another, for custom ginning had not yet come into general practice. Mechanical cotton gins were scarce until after 1820, when Augustus J. Brown opened a gin-making shop near Jarrett's spring.[65] Plows were also relatively scarce, for much cultivation was still performed with a hoe. Pit saws for the hand sawing of lumber were common, as were crosscut saws, hoes, axes, and rakes. There were also Dutch ovens, pot hooks, spinning wheels, churns, split-bottom chairs, pine tables, stone jars, kettles, glassware, and occasionally a loom. The well-to-do, however, were not without luxuries. Daniel Sturges, the surveyor general, possessed feather beds, elegant china, queen's ware, decanters, a dozen windsor chairs, an excellent library, and a dozen knives and forks.[66]

Not until after 1835 did forks come into general use in the dining rooms of Milledgeville's elite. At that time Dr. Tomlinson Fort was presented with a tea service containing some spoons and forks by the family of John Clark, whose son Dr. Fort had nursed during a smallpox epidemic. The Fort family did not use the spoons and forks for many years. "We did not care to incur the odium of putting on airs," explained Mrs. Fort.[67] Indeed, the absence of tableware of any description was not unusual among common people of this era. Duke Bernhard, on visiting the state penitentiary in 1825, noted that the prisoners ate their food directly from the surface of a wooden table without the assistance of knife, fork, or spoon.[68]

In a frontier community bread was more often in short supply than meat, and Bernhard saw none of the former on the day of his visit to the prison, although the institution's ration called for one and a fourth pounds of "Indian meal" each day. The convict's ration also included a daily issue of three-fourths pound of pork, in lieu of which he received one pound of beef or a half pound of bacon. There were limited allowances of salt and vinegar as well as a weekly allowance of three gills of molasses during six months of the year. The ration given slaves generally approximated that assigned to prisoners, and it was usually served in the same manner—without plates, knives, or forks. The ration for slaves and prison inmates was considered to be adequate for that day—it was almost identical to that of the Fort Hawkins federal garrison in 1808, except that the soldier also received each day a gill of rum, whisky, or brandy.[69] Throughout the antebellum period the price of pork per pound was half that of cotton, and the cost for boarding a slave remained at approximately $100 a year. The cost for feeding mules exceeded this figure by 25 percent.

By 1830 Milledgeville was slowly emerging from its frontier character. Troup-Clark political factionalism, which once divided the town, had now subsided. Except for a final confrontation with the Cherokees, Indian removal was an accomplished fact, and Georgians were turning their attention to agricultural expansion. The beginning of upcountry banking and plantation-scale cotton-growing in the recently ceded areas were beginning to be reflected in a more settled economic life which reached some degree of maturity only a short time before the Civil War. Along with these developments were significant changes in the town's social and cultural life.

Early Social Life

Throughout the antebellum period legislative sessions were held in the late fall and early winter after most farmers had completed harvesting. At this season Milledgeville was filled not only with important visitors attending legislative matters but also with farmers from outlying areas. On these occasions normal legal restraints which the town imposed on its citizens were not always enforced. Gamblers and sportsmen held high carnival on the streets. Games of chance were openly conducted, and prostitution flourished. One observer called the town "one of the gayest capitals in the South."[1]

Since alcohol was thought by many to possess a certain medicinal value, there were no restraints on its sale and consumption. Yet overindulgence produced some tragic figures among the town's leading citizens. One of these was Captain Ambrose Day, once editor of the *Louisville Gazette*, who transferred his notable journalistic talents to Milledgeville in 1811. Here his unrequited love for a local girl is said to have driven him to excessive drinking. In time he was reduced to living in a single-room shanty on Wayne Street with only a pile of newspapers for a bed. Frequently he was found sleeping on the sidewalk with his cane and tattered plug hat lying by his side. Because of his scarecrow appearance he was ridiculed and tormented by the town's youth.[2]

While drinking to such excess was thought to be no more than a harmless expression of one's own fancy, any kind of indulgence in gambling usually was regarded as highly reprehensible. Gambling was the town's earliest vice and the first to come under local regulation. A legislative resolution in 1811 requested the town commissioners to pursue a more vigorous policy against gambling and to arrest all operators of faro banks and to "put the vagrant law into full force." Professional gamblers, referred to as "the Black-legged Fraternity," were the subject of numerous grand jury presentments.[3]

No regulations succeeded in bringing gambling under control. A Darien bank note circulating in Milledgeville in the late 1820s bore evidence of a tragedy which had befallen a youth victimized by local gamblers. Across the face of the note appeared this message: "This is the last dollar which I can call my own out of an estate of $10,000—and what have I lost? Not only my fortune but my character . . . [and] my health. I am this day . . . far from any friend or relative and without a place to lay my head."[4]

Gambling was also a leading cause of homicides. A notorious adventurer named Bennett once entered the dining room of the Lafayette Hotel with blood on his shirt cuffs, causing some ladies to scurry from the room. Later it was discovered that the barkeeper had been stabbed to death in a gambling dispute.[5]

Bennett was among a large number of undesirable transients who had drifted into Milledgeville during the legislative session of 1830. So great was the influx of people on these occasions that legislators and others having legitimate business in the community often found it difficult to obtain accommodations for themselves or their families. One lady complained that she had searched for lodging until midnight before succeeding. Nelson Tift, a legislator from Albany, arrived at the end of October 1841. Although the legislature had not yet assembled, he found every house in town already crowded to overflowing. Among the transients were a large number of job-seekers whom Tift claimed outnumbered legislators. "Some [are] importunate and tiresome or disgusting, [while] others are exceedingly affable, courteous and attentive to all the rules of pleasing . . . a few despise the cloak of the hypocrit and appear as they are," he stated.[6]

Tift's diary suggests that he spent his time between legislative meetings more constructively than many of his associates. On a Sunday in November he heard a Universalist sermon at the Statehouse during the morning, and in the evening he listened to a lecture on religious liberty. On the following day he attended the funeral of Senator Bradford of Crawford County, and on the evening of the next day he was a guest at the house of Dr. Tomlinson Fort, where he played four games of drafts with Fort's oldest daughter, Julia. On Saturday night he was again at the Fort residence where he played chess with Joseph Fannin, Fort's brother-in-law, while Mrs. Fort and her daughter played the piano and sang for their guests. On the Sunday following he remained in his room to read and to do some writing, but in the evening he was again at Dr. Fort's; here he was introduced for the first time to Governor McDonald, with whom he had a long conversation on a free system of banking and other subjects. When he returned to his lodging he "took a cup of coffee and a piece of biscuit, wrote, argued politics and religion," and then retired.[7]

Two days later, on November 23, Tift was among a large number of male guests invited to supper at the Executive Mansion. "There was an abundance of liquor, wines & apple toddy in an anteroom connected with the saloon [sic]," he wrote. "At a little before 7 o'clock we were called to the dining room where two tables running the whole length of the house groaned under the necessaries & luxuries of life. All ate at the same time standing." Tift amused himself watching the varying expressions of those who arrived at the well-loaded table. It was evident that they had come solely for the purpose of eating, for they dined with enthusiasm and left as soon as they were finished.[8]

A few of the wealthier members of the legislature brought their families to Milledgeville, some of whom arranged to live in private homes. Many brought servants and sometimes horses and a carriage. Most of them however, arrived by stage or by horseback. Since it was expensive to have a horse stabled and fed over a period of several weeks, some who disdained to ride in a stagecoach had their servants deliver them, after which horses and carriages were returned to the plantation until the end of the session. Among these was James A. Bryan of Houston County, who arrived in a barouche driven by his servant, Joe. He requested his wife to have Joe return for him at the end of the session when all the stages again would be "rammed and crammed by departing lawmakers and a great many stranded." He ordered that his servant be made to "scour and cleanse himself well, and to put on his best clothes and . . . fetch one or two extra shirts."[9]

A far more practical lawmaker was Etheldred Swain, who represented Emanuel County in both the House and the Senate intermittently from 1827 through 1843. Swain may well not have possessed a horse; but if he did, he saved the cost of stabling and maintenance, for he walked the distance of some sixty miles from his home to the capital. To reduce expenses for his own food and lodging he brought along a bedroll, frying pan, rifle, and a tent which he pitched on the banks of Fishing Creek. A clever fisherman and an excellent marksman, he seldom lacked for food. His periodic thirst for strong drink apparently was adequately relieved. Once, deep in his cups, he took a pot shot at the eagle which had been painted on the south front of the Statehouse by a drifting artist named John Malcom. When friends restrained him, he paid a high compliment to Malcom's artistry by claiming that he had believed the eagle to be real.[10]

Compensation for legislative work in the antebellum period was barely sufficient to cover expenses even at the most modest rates for board and lodging. In 1807 members received a per diem of three dollars and an additional three dollars for every twenty miles of travel to and from the capital. Four years later the legislators reduced the governor's salary from $2,500 to $2,000 but left their own compensation unchanged. In 1819 their per diem and travel allowances were each increased to five dollars, but later these were reduced to four dollars. These allowances were not changed again until the beginning of the Civil War.[11]

Until 1857 legislators were not required to base their travel allowances on the shortest route between their homes and the capital. In the meantime the coming of railroads to Milledgeville made it acceptable to use rail mileage in determining these distances. This method, however, still was not generally practiced in 1852 when the electoral college met in Milledgeville to cast Georgia's vote for president. The two elder statesmen on the board, William Schley and Wilson Lumpkin, each about eighty years old, refused to use rail mileage whenever it exceeded that of the shortest route. Because of a wash-out on the Central Railroad near Millen, Schley had to travel from Augusta to Atlanta and then to Macon and Gordon to reach Milledgeville. By the time he returned home he had traveled a total of 622 miles—more than 400 miles in excess of the shortest distance by stagecoach. Even so, he requested compensation only for the shorter distance.[12]

Milledgeville remained relatively inaccessible even after the building of the state's basic rail system, and the inadequacy of transportation to the capital generated much criticism during the 1850s when there was heated discussion in the legislature over moving the capital to another location. However, there was little criticism of the town's capacity for entertainment once a visitor had arrived and become comfortably lodged. Typical of the itinerant shows which came to the town was the Washington Circus, which in 1827 made the first of many appearances in the capital. Six trained horses were featured at the performance, where crowds were entertained by tunes of "Hail Columbia," "Away Melancholy," and "Paddy Carey," played on instruments known as King David's Cymbals, the Triangles, Pandean Pipes, and the brass drum. The show was climaxed by a performance of horsemanship by "the Drunken Hussar."[13] In 1841 the first Negro minstrel appeared, making its debut in November, during a session of the legislature. The large frame building located on Elbert Street near the east entrance to Statehouse Square was filled to its capacity. There were no printed programs, and no one knew exactly what to expect. During the course of the evening's entertainment the performers sang "Old Dan Tucker." This was the first time that the song had ever been heard in Milledgeville, and at the end of the first chorus the entire audience was on its feet, cheering, shouting, and throwing hats into the air. They beat the floor with their feet until the performance was temporarily halted to prevent the collapse of the building. The players were dumbfounded at such a response. They discovered later that a local planter and owner of many slaves was Daniel R. Tucker, who was known throughout the county as Old Dan. The audience had assumed that the song was written exclusively for him.[14]

Entertainment of a more sophisticated nature had already begun in 1820 with the organization of the Milledgeville Thespian Society. Its first performance was a comedy, *The Poor Gentleman*, written by "Coleman the Younger." More than a decade later the Milledgeville Lyceum announced its first meeting, to be held at the academy "at early candle light," where a lecture was given by Charles Wallace Howard, local Presbyterian minister.[15] At this time some attention was directed toward the fine arts. Abner Locke operated a museum on the corner of Wayne and Hancock streets where for twenty-five cents admission one could view "antiquities, curiosities [both] natural and artificial, . . . portraits, paintings, etc." while listening to Jacob Skinner's music on the organ or the violin. In attendance also was "a portrait and miniature painter from New York."[16] Monsieur Bange was soon to open a fencing class at Huson's Hotel. At Beecher and Brown's Hotel R. N. Mount was already conducting a dancing school where the latest Austrian waltzes could be mastered. Appearing soon were announcements of balls held in the long rooms of local hotels and taverns. Tickets for these events were seldom available for less than five dollars, and this excessive price eliminated most devotees of the country dance.[17]

Military balls, arranged by local volunteer or militia units, soon became fashionable. These usually were held during the evening following a dress parade or a military review. Military parades were among the most popular events and they were staged at the slightest provocation. The Lafayette Company of Equestrians held an exhibition in 1828 for the benefit of a blind widow of the town. A large crowd assembled and voluntary collections were made.[18] Far more exciting, and drawing the largest number of viewers, was the annual review of the Third Division of the Georgia Militia, for which all military units from the six surrounding counties assembled at the capital late in August during the slack season in farm activities. Milledgeville was headquarters of this division, and its commander, General John W.A. Sanford, and its inspector, William S. Rockwell, resided there.

The Fourth of July was celebrated with all the splendor the frontier community could muster. The 1809 celebration was attended by a Yankee resident of the town who described the orator of the day—one Olmstead, the son of the local tavern-keeper—as "much of a fool." His speech was the product of his own efforts and those of a French refugee living in the town. It was replete with such phrases as "Glorious day," "Immortal heroes," and "God-like Jefferson," and the observer noted that "it was without head, body, or tail . . . the gaping Crackers swallowed the expressions whole, and nothing has been heard of them since." He noted, however, that the speech possessed one virtue: it lasted only twelve minutes. When it was over, the citizens and the soldiers dined apart. The observer went on to report that the dinner, which cost three dollars, was very poor. Sherry was served in place of Madeira, and New York ale was substituted for the Port wine which had been advertised.[19]

With the passage of time a few changes were wrought in the general pattern of these Fourth of July celebrations. The one held in 1810 featured a parade by five volunteer companies, representing infantry, cavalry, and artillery.[20] By 1820 the orations were held in the Statehouse, and the diners could either partake of a meal on the capitol grounds or gather in smaller groups at local taverns, where the toasts inevitably took on the coloring of Troup-Clark political factionalism. In 1821, for example, one referred to the liberal land lottery system as "the indisputable offspring of misguided policy," while Dr. Tomlinson Fort rejoined with the statement that "Georgia, true to its policy, peoples its territory without impoverishing its treasury."[21] Always present at these early occasions and occupying the head table were the Revolutionary War veterans. Among these was veteran Oaty Prosser, who may have been the first of the town's professional flag-wavers. He was often seen walking back and forth, and weeping as he reminisced about the war.[22]

The make-up of this annual event kept pace with the town's changing character. In 1828 the day began with the firing of a cannon at sunrise. A procession formed at eleven o'clock at the Eagle Tavern, consisting not only of various military units but also of citizens. They marched to the new Methodist church, where a prayer was offered, followed by the reading of the Declaration. Dinner was served at McCombs' Tavern. That evening "a very neat oration" was made by John R. Wiggins at the church before the Cliosophic Society and a large group of citizens.[23]

The 1840 celebration was the largest of its kind which had ever been seen in Milledgeville. An estimated 2,000 persons were in attendance and the orator spoke for two hours from the steps of the Statehouse while a large audience stood in respectful attention. Among the listeners were delegates to the Georgia Democratic Convention which met at the capital that day. The large crowd feasted on barbecue served from eighteen long tables under a brush arbor erected on the Statehouse Square.[24]

Throughout the 1850s, as the Civil War approached, there was even greater interest in these annual patriotic events. On July 4, 1857, an estimated five thousand persons were present. Volunteer companies from various counties were represented by more than a thousand soldiers. Governor Herschel V. Johnson addressed the crowd gathered on the capitol grounds and later reviewed the volunteer companies in a meadow on the east bank of the Oconee River. Dinner, which was served under a temporary structure, was delayed until the middle of the afternoon. The delay was not unwelcome, because champagne flowed freely throughout the long period of waiting.[25]

Gala holidays other than the Fourth of July were also celebrated. Among the earliest of these was that scheduled in 1825 for the visit to the capital by General Lafayette, who arrived on Sunday, March 27. A procession headed by Governor Troup met the general's entourage on the east bank of the Oconee, and the two dignitaries rode into town in a barouche drawn by four bay horses. Citizens who lined the road all the way from the river to Government House proclaimed his welcome amid the firing of cannon and the peal of church bells. Twenty-six veterans of the Revolution lined the walkway leading from Greene Street to the front door of Government House. One of these, the ubiquitous Oaty Prosser, was recognized by the general, who took him by the shoulders and gave him a Latin embrace.[26] For a brief moment Prosser was the most distinguished citizen of Georgia.

On the day of his arrival the visiting Frenchman attended service at the Methodist church, then a fragile wooden structure located in Cemetery Square. Later he was a guest at a Masonic meeting held in the lodge rooms at the Darien Bank. A reception was held for him at the Statehouse, followed by a barbecue, accompanied by the lively tunes of "a band of musicians." His visit was climaxed by a formal dinner at the Statehouse given by local women. Then came the grand ball where "epaulettes, swords, sashes, and other trappings [were mingled with] a matchless array of ladies skimming in the dance like fairies." The dance continued until three in the morning, five hours after the guest of honor had retired to his room at Government House.

The people of the town never forgot General Lafayette, nor did they ever cease to revel in the honor which he paid them on this visit. His death in 1834 inspired a local memorial service almost equal in magnitude to the occasion of his visit nine years earlier. All business in the town was suspended, and a large funeral procession marched from the courthouse to the new Methodist church, where Charles Wallace Howard gave an appropriate funeral sermon. Bells tolled and funeral music filled the air.[27]

There was also an annual celebration of Washington's birthday, observed each year throughout the first half of the nineteenth century. These occasions were all characterized by military parades, processions, oratory, a public dinner, and the firing of cannon.[28]

The occasion which most nearly matched that of Lafayette's visit was the appearance in Milledgeville of the Whig party leader, Henry Clay, who came to the Georgia capital in 1844 at the invitation of members of the local Whig club and others throughout the state. The Kentuckian arrived on a clear and beautiful March morning in an elegantly accoutered barouche. He was escorted by such prominent local Whigs as Seaton Grantland, Augustus H. Kenan, John S. Thomas, Iverson Harris, and Mayor James R. Washington. He spoke to a crowd estimated to number 5,000. The speaking platform was erected on Wayne Street in front of the McComb Hotel, which had just been re-christened the Henry Clay House and where the guest was furnished a suite of rooms and a reception parlor. Clay's chair on the speaker's platform was on the north end, where the noonday sun was beating down upon him. A fellow guest on the platform came over and gallantly offered to exchange positions with him, suggesting that he might be more comfortable on the opposite side of the platform. Clay accepted his offer, stating that he was happy to be on all sides.

After his introduction by Governor George W. Crawford, Clay spoke for almost two hours, during which discourse he praised General Lafayette and the Georgian, William H. Crawford, who had been one of his opponents for the presidency in 1824. He traced the tedious history of the Missouri question, the nullification movement, and the compromise of 1833. He explained his position on the tariff and on the Cherokee treaty of 1835, both of which positions most Georgians had opposed. Yet he affirmed his sympathy for the state in the Indian controversy. His sense of humor was apparent in his narration of a personal experience involving a farmer who listened to his speech from a sitting posture on a nearby lumber pile. When the candidate came by and the farmer reached to shake his hand he lost his balance and almost fell before Clay caught him and prevented the accident. "Hooray! " shouted the farmer. "He saved the Union twice and me once! "

During the evening Clay appeared in the ballroom of the hotel, and on the following morning he was introduced to citizens who had assembled at the recently renamed State Rights Hotel. Then there was a similar exchange of hand-shaking at the Henry Clay House. The remainder of the day was spent with Governor Crawford at the Executive Mansion.[29]

It is not surprising that the Whig party's leading figure should have chosen to visit Milledgeville in his quest for the presidency. Already five of the town's citizens had served in Congress, and a large number of presidential electors had resided in the town. Since so many public offices were appointive and subject to legislative approval, the capital was a mecca for those seeking political preferment. Many of these became permanent residents, for politics was the town's principal enterprise. Despite its raw character, the Georgia capital had taken on some characteristics of the Greek city state.

Common job-seekers increased over the years. Their approach to securing an appointment was seldom artful and suggests that the spoils system was much in vogue. C. G. Witherspoon of Lumpkin County, wishing to be chaplain and gatekeeper of the penitentiary, applied to the governor's benevolence as a Masonic brother. He suggested that in lieu of employment at the penitentiary he might be placed elsewhere. "Say to me whether I may go to Milledgeville . . . with any hope of getting an appointment or not," he urged. Carlisle P. B. Martin, a local Presbyterian minister, applied for the principal office at the penitentiary and offered only one qualification: he believed that he could "manage the Institution better than [he had] ever seen it managed." One of Governor Howell Cobb's supporters in Savannah sent him a box of cigars with the request that he find an opening for his friend R. F. Aiken, who was "without a dollar in the world [and yet] able to write an excellent hand."[30]

Local residents enjoyed greater political preference than others, and many became permanently identified with the lower echelons of government service. In some cases this identity was inherited by their sons. In recommending Peter Fair to be one of Governor Cobb's executive secretaries, William

Mitchell noted that Fair was the son of a long-time statehouse functionary by the same name and that the applicant had experience as a bank teller and bookkeeper. "He writes a good hand and is a man of much integrity [though] not a man of talents," wrote Mitchell, who also hinted that Fair had an unusual talent for fatherhood: "He is poor and with many children and a bed ridden wife for 15 years and is good for a child every 15 months."[31]

Milledgeville also possessed an unusual attraction for lawyers, whose profession was represented throughout the first two decades of its history by more than a dozen local attorneys. Among the earliest of these was Thomas Fitch, who arrived in the town in 1808 from New Jersey and soon acquired a lucrative practice and a reputation as the leading barrister in the capital. By 1810 his annual legal fees of $2000 equaled the salary paid the governor and far exceeded that of any other statehouse or judicial official. Fitch acquired a wife, a servant, a horse, and a town house, and invested in land. In 1811 he moved to Florida, where he became a federal judge at St. Augustine; he died in 1822.[32]

Not so successful was Daniel Mulford, Fitch's old acquaintance in New Jersey who was now studying law. Mulford's poor health doubtless contributed to his discouragement and to his poor impression of Georgia's new capital. He estimated the town's population in 1809 as "about 2000 souls," but he was extremely doubtful if they all had souls. "Prospects for business . . . for a person without connections are miserable," he wrote. He described those with whom he had to deal as "keen, hawk-eyed fellows" whom it was difficult to cheat but by whom it was easy to be cheated. Mulford described the manners of the young people of the town as "corrupt beyond any idea you or I could form." Soon he moved to Sparta and later to Savannah in search of better health. He finally returned to New Jersey, where he died of tuberculosis.[33]

Litigation over land titles, foreclosures, and bankruptcies provided a great part of the civil docket in this period. In 1815 alone there were thirteen foreclosures instituted by the town commissioners for delinquent payments on public land sold within the corporate limits.[34] The docket for criminal court was relatively heavy, and it was in this court that lawyers won their reputation for excellence or mediocrity. The town came to life on court days, when great crowds attended the proceedings.

The number of lawyers in the town greatly exceeded the office space available for them. Samuel Rockwell was among those who operated from his dwelling house. The firm of Archibald Martin and Edward B. Jenkins rented part of the surveyor general's room in the Statehouse. Hansell Hall and Thaddeus Holt constructed a small office on the north side of the Statehouse Square. Hines Holt, who was collector of federal taxes for the district, had his office at his plantation near the confluence of the Oconee and Little rivers.[35]

While the number of attorneys was double that of medical practitioners, the latter formed the second largest professional group in the community. Because they all were general practitioners, and because toothache was a general complaint, these doctors pulled teeth on occasion and did what dental practice they could. Also a number of itinerant specialists known as tooth-pullers wandered in and out of town. Actual dentists were exceedingly rare. In 1828 only one member of this profession, J. B. Badger, was living in the town. He seems also to have been a drifter, having rented an office in the Darien Bank only for the duration of the legislative session.[36] As late as the Civil War there was no resident dentist in Milledgeville.

Physicians of that day generally were poorly trained. Long experience combined with a genuine scientific curiosity were the principal guarantees of a successful career. Fitting this category were Tomlinson Fort and Benjamin Aspenwall White, who were among the more outstanding physicians in the state. Fort attended the University of Pennsylvania Medical College for one year. There he was schooled in Dr. Benjamin Rush's methods, though he did not receive a degree. He returned to Milledgeville in 1810, set up a practice at a time when not even a license was required, and practiced for thirty-six years without a professional degree. He finally was granted an honorary doctor's degree by the medical college at Augusta which he had helped to establish.[37]

In 1825 Fort was instrumental in the passage of the first medical legislation in Georgia. This law provided that no person could practice medicine or surgery in the state without a license. In 1828 Fort became a member of the newly organized licensing board, called the Board of Physicians, which met in Milledgeville in 1828. Nine men were licensed to practice solely on the basis of diplomas presented, while nineteen more were licensed after presenting theses and passing the board's examination.[38] At this time, and for many years following, the great majority of practicing physicians had never attended a full course at any medical school, even though only two six-month courses were required by most schools for the granting of a medical degree.

For the full half century that Fort resided in Milledgeville he was among the town's most noted citizens. In 1812 he took time from his budding medical practice to organize and lead a local company in the War of 1812, in which he received a leg wound that left him crippled for the remainder of his life. He represented Baldwin County for eight years in the state legislature and later served a term in the United States House of Representatives. A Unionist and later a Democrat, he served on numerous boards and was a leading figure in liberal and progressive movements of his day. For thirty years he was the physician for the state penitentiary. It would be difficult to match either his reputation as a physician or as a statesman.[39]

Some indication of the extent of Fort's medical practice is seen in his average annual income, which was approximately $10,000—ten times greater than the average earnings of physicians in that period. This figure is even more remarkable when it is remembered that Fort's patients included not only governors, plantation masters, and statehouse officials but also slaves, convicts, lunatics, and small landowners. When Governor George R. Gilmer became ill in 1839, Fort visited him three times each day for several weeks and then called at his house daily for many weeks during the period of his recuperation.[40]

Fort was largely instrumental in the passage of a bill in 1837 for the establishment of the Georgia Lunatic Asylum near Milledgeville. With two other local physicians, David Cooper and Benjamin A. White, he donated his professional services to this institution in its formative years. The Asylum was slow to become organized, and it was not until the end of 1842 that the first patient was admitted. Although the Asylum was designed for the care and treatment of mental and epileptic patients, for many years only custodial care could be provided, except in cases of routine illnesses which might respond to the normal skills of the physician. In 1845 Dr. Thomas A. Green succeeded Dr. Cooper as superintendent, at which time there were only eight employees for the sixty-seven patients.[41] Dr. Green, the son of an eccentric local schoolteacher, remained for the next twenty-nine years at the institution, where he was successful in bringing the Asylum through the most trying period of its long history.

The inferior standards of general medical care in Milledgeville during the antebellum period are dramatically reflected in the prevailing attitude toward such diseases as smallpox. While vaccination against this disease had long been known, few people in rural Georgia had been immunized, because they considered vaccination equally as dangerous as the disease. Fort once related the story of a waggoner who had come down with the disease while on the road. No one would go near him or render him aid. One courageous farmer opened a passage in his fence and permitted the victim to drive his team into a barn, where he lay starving and neglected for several days until he died. The treatment given his corpse was equally as savage as the lack of attention shown him: the barn was simply put to the torch, and the body was cremated.[42]

A smallpox epidemic appeared in the town in the spring of 1835, at which time Fort and others advised general vaccination. Although the state provided free vaccine, few were willing to be immunized. Victims were placed in a pest-house on the outskirts of the town, and few people ventured into the streets, thus giving the town a deathlike stillness. When Fort urged those who had gained immunity by reason of having recovered from the disease to serve as nurses for the afflicted, a furious argument appeared in the local press.[43]

One of the victims of this epidemic was John W. R. Clark, the youngest son of a former governor. Only nineteen years old, he had begun to study medicine under Fort and had just returned from a visit to Florida. Since no one else would go near the patient, Fort attended him in person and cared for all his needs. People of the town called a mass meeting and declared that Fort was endangering the lives of all his patients and should cease attending Clark for fear of spreading the disease. When this failed to produce results, the door to Clark's room was padlocked, to which Fort responded by using a ladder to gain entrance to the bedroom through a window. He placed a gun by his door and dared any man to deter him from his duty.[44] The doctor finally succeeded in employing two nurses for Clark before he died. Later a group of twenty-six citizens signed a statement expressing their appreciation for the physician's high ethical standards and his fearlessness.

Again, in 1842, an outbreak of smallpox began when a slave girl at the Carnes house on Jefferson Street became ill with the disease. The mayor appointed all doctors in the town as a committee of health. A tenement was converted to a hospital, and guards were posted at various points in the town. Waggoners and others traveling through the town were required to encamp on the west commons near the Eatonton road. The night police patrol was strengthened and vaccination again was encouraged. Nurses were now more easily employed than previously. By 1863, when still another outbreak occurred, vaccination was generally accepted, and the cost in many cases was borne by the municipal government.[45]

Late in life Fort wrote a book entitled *A Dissertation on the Practice of Medicine*, which he hoped might be of use to do-it-yourself family practitioners as well as to trained physicians. Some medical journals refused to review the book because they opposed the idea of every man becoming his own doctor. Despite this, the book was eagerly sought, and it greatly increased Fort's popularity. In this publication Fort paid ample tribute to his old professor in Philadelphia, Benjamin Rush. Fort's occasional disagreement with Rush's views was indicative of the former's open mind and his original thinking. On the use of blood-letting, for example, Fort was far more guarded and conservative than his mentor, despite the fact that his view arose from a false premise: Fort thought that blood, once taken from the patient, could never be restored.[46]

Fort's book is of historical significance not only because it reflects the primitive state of medical practice at that time but also because it identifies those diseases most prevalent in the area during the period of the town's development. Malaria was given the most attention, although Fort, like his contemporaries, did not understand its cause. Also called bilious fever, malaria not only caused the most illness but also was the most feared disease. It never failed to appear during the summer and fall. Fort stated that it caused the death of five percent of the community's population each year from 1808 to 1813. He attributed its cause simply to dampness arising from stagnant pools of water around the town, where the process of clearing and drainage was difficult with a small number of settlers living under frontier conditions. In 1822 half of the town's deaths were still caused by this disease. It was not until after the advanced settlement of the surrounding farms that the process of drainage eliminated breeding places of mosquitoes and suffering from this disease was somewhat alleviated.[47]

Other diseases menacing early settlers were scarlet fever, typhus, dysentery, childhood fever, and typhoid fever, the last being second to malaria in importance. The great number of open wells which began to appear throughout the town, together with the contamination of springs with surface water after heavy rains, added greatly to outbreaks of typhoid fever. While Fort noted the frequent recurrence of the disease among prisoners and guards housed near the southeast corner of the penitentiary compound where water was obtained from a particular well, he never connected the disease with a contaminated water supply. Rather he attributed its cause to poor ventilation of the prison cells and their proximity to the foul odors of the nearby tanyard.[48]

Tuberculosis was considered to be entirely hereditary and noncontagious, and Fort saw little purpose in attempting serious treatment. Because everyone recognized the disease as terminal, he generally withheld his diagnosis from the patient. One of the many diseases which often appeared in epidemic form was typhoid pneumonia, an outbreak of which occurred in 1817 and in each of several years thereafter. In the first year of the town's settlement there occurred an influenza epidemic (then called grippe), which caused an unusual number of deaths and brought great consternation to those who had only recently moved to the locality. Hookworm was frequently encountered, as was infestation by round worms, although the tape worm was unusually rare.

The more common fatal diseases of the mid-twentieth century—cancer and heart disease—were relatively rare in Fort's day and often were not recognized. Since in this period only 56 percent of all the people born in America survived to the age of fifteen, and only 4 percent lived to the age of sixty, it is not surprising that people rarely succumbed to degenerative diseases.[49]

The first three decades of the town's history not only were a period of epidemic diseases but also were unique in other ways. The absence of scientific understanding increased the people's apprehension, and they sought what solace they could from religious exercise. Organized religious life centered around the Methodists, Baptists, Presbyterians, and Episcopalians, somewhat in that order of numerical importance. All four groups had well-established congregations long before the Civil War.

The Methodists constituted the most numerous religious group of the early decades. Using the technique of the camp meeting revival and a dedicated and devout clergy practicing ascetic habits, this group had an evangelical character which had a special appeal to frontier people. In the summer of 1806, before any church was established on the west side of the Oconee, a famous camp meeting was held near Sparta. At this meeting were twenty-seven preachers and an estimated total of 4500 people, many of whom were recent settlers in the trans-Oconee area. When Reverend Jesse Lee, who was in charge of the Sparta circuit, came to Milledgeville later that year, he visited several Methodist families and conducted two funerals, including that of Judge Stith, who had been a Deist. At this time Georgia was part of the South Carolina conference, with only two districts, these being separated by the Ogeechee River.[50] The Milledgeville church was organized in 1808 during the period when the great influenza epidemic and malaria took an unusually large number of lives. This church was given the status of a Methodist station in 1811 when Samuel M. Meek became the pastor. In this year Meek organized the first Methodist Sunday School of which any record has been found.[51] At this time also a large group of Creek Indian chiefs who had gathered for a conference with Governor Mitchell attended services at the church, which was located a short distance from their campsite on Fishing Creek. This occasion was a prelude to the later establishment of a Methodist mission school for the Creeks near Coweta Falls in Alabama, where William Capers was in charge. Among the students at this school was Croesy, the youngest daughter of Chief William McIntosh. However, because of difficulties growing out of Governor Troup's militant attitude toward Indian cessions and removal, this mission was abandoned in 1830.[52]

Only two other Methodist stations existed in Georgia at the time of the founding of the Milledgeville church; these were at Savannah and Augusta. Of the three, the Milledgeville church was once the most prosperous. However, it lost its status after three years when it reverted to an appointment in the Cedar Creek circuit. It again became a station in 1823 when William Capers was placed in charge, while yet keeping a watchful eye over his Creek mission on the Chattahoochee.[53]

Capers was a particularly energetic minister. Each Sunday at sunrise he preached to the prisoners at the penitentiary and was at his church by eleven o'clock, again at three in the afternoon, and yet again at night. While it was fashionable for ministers to be outright enemies of Governor Clark, Capers remained that governor's friend. Governor Clark's wife was a Methodist, and she prevailed upon her husband to offer Capers and his family the use of Government House during the summer of 1823 when the executive family was absent. This act led to the acquisition of a parsonage in the following year, which relieved Capers' generally anti-Clark congregation from the embarrassment of having its minister occupy Clark's house The Milledgeville parsonage was the third ever provided a Methodist minister in Georgia.[54]

The early Methodists generally bore the brunt of much ridicule by more fashionable and sophisticated groups, most of whom came from older communities. Among them was Lieutenant John R. Vinton, an Episcopalian from New England who, while spending several days in Milledgeville during the winter of 1827 attended funeral services conducted by Samuel K. Hodges in the house of the deceased. Vinton described this Methodist

minister as a dedicated man of great talent, although "the ranting & boister-
ous style of his discourse & [its] general irrelevancy were poorly calculated
to soothe the bereaved hearts of the relatives." His patience finally was
exhausted by Hodges' long dissertation on abstract points of theology and
he concluded that the "simplicities of Methodism is [sic] perhaps well
adapted to a people of no higher degree of refinement than these, but the
officious tediousness of such preaching cannot be well calculated for the
extension of religious faith or practice generally."[55]

Like so many other observers, Vinton displayed ignorance of the psychol-
ogy of frontier people, to whom certain visible signs of religious manifesta-
tion had an unusual appeal. The Methodist clergymen were a well selected
lot; in both dress and demeanor they presented the example of a life devoted
to hard work and ascetic traditions. In these two respects they had been
influenced by Daniel Asbury, who was the model for all early Methodist
preachers. A simple, straight-breasted coat was their most visible mark of
nonconformity with the world of sin. Their hair was cut short, and they
wore neither wig nor beard. Simple French pantaloons, worn without sus-
penders, were part of their dress. They accepted no money for their preach-

The Methodist Church on Statehouse Square, built in the late 1820s

ing. Often rising as early as four in the morning, summer and winter, they
spent the first two hours of the day in prayer and study. A New England
visitor who attended a quarterly meeting in Milledgeville in July 1809
heard a sermon by the young presiding elder, Lovic Pierce. While he had no
plaudits for Pierce's sermon, he was greatly impressed by the preacher's
countenance, which he described as "resembling what he fancied that of an
angel to be."[56] He also stated that he had never witnessed a stronger man-
ifestation of a well-grounded hope in future happiness than was shown by
those attending this meeting.

These Methodist ministers took great pride in their ability to induce in
their hearers "the holy exercise" of physical paroxysms, but the opposite
reaction was sometimes achieved. Lovic Pierce once stated that he had
known "scores to fall senseless" while listening to sermons preached by his
older brother Reddick.[57] On one occasion Pierce tried his sermon at a
Baptist meeting, having responded to a general invitation to the congregation "to say a few words," and experienced equally effective results.

The camp meeting was perhaps the most sensational and hence the most
effective evangelical device which the Methodists were accustomed to use.
One such meeting, held in the Ogeechee circuit in 1808, was described by
an Englishman who had been drawn to the scene by the loud voice of the
exhorter and the screams of his audience. "He uttered such terrible impreca-
tions upon sinners," wrote he, "[that] . . . one half of his congregation were
groaning and weeping in the worst pitiable manner; he seemed to take
delight in viewing their distress, but I rather think it was owing more to the
terrifying loudness of his voice, his furious looks, and the vehement gesticu-
lations than to a real sense of their own wickedness." He characterized the
clergy as "artful designing men, who continue to delude the simple and
unwary into the most shameful and blasphemous excesses."[58]

Camp meetings were held in open fields, as well as under brush arbors,
usually at some distance from any habitation. The "religious exercise" invariably took on an hysterical character and often continued for days until
the participants were physically exhausted. Those who came brought along
their own food and slept in the open or in tents—"the old and the young,
men and women, the vigorous male near the unblushing female, black and
white, all together."[59]

Such a meeting took place at Milledgeville in 1827, conducted by James
O. Andrew, John Howard, Lovic Pierce, and Stephen Olin. Held under a
brush arbor on Fishing Creek, it lasted four days and resulted in more than a

hundred conversions. Again in the fall of 1828, at a meeting held on the Tucker plantation with Seaborn Jones as one of the exhorters, about fifty persons joined the Methodist Society.[60] Arthur Fort, father of Dr. Tomlinson Fort, described an incident in his own religious conversion wherein he felt himself raised several inches above the ground and, on attempting to walk, he found himself gliding forward through the air instead. He claimed that he was able to see clearly the smallest object at a much greater distance than the eye could normally reach. Beholding pleasant apparitions in the sky, he claimed that his own fingers appeared transparent and had the smoothness of ivory. "I then attempted to eat but was too full of heavenly manna to care for earthly dainties," he declared. Then they "all began to sing and praise God with one impulse . . . until we retired to rest. Next morning . . . we continued until the servis [sic] was over and Camp meeting was dismissed . . . from that day I have never had a doubt."[61]

Arthur Fort was well advanced in years when he had this experience, but the young appear to have been even more susceptible to such sensations than the elderly. One observer described seeing a girl about eighteen years old rushing from her tent at sunrise, led by two men. All three were shouting and crying in great agony as if begging for their lives. They explained that a lake of fire and brimstone was flowing before them and that the devil was trying to push them into it. Finally their behavior became infectious, and the scene became one of general and horrible confusion. "Children paled with fear [and] young girls fainted."[62]

It is obvious that hysterics such as these meetings provoked had varying effects on different individuals who sought an outlet for their tensions, which were not always relieved by shouting and gyrating. What some young people did for relief when they wandered beyond the reach of torchlight is a matter of speculation. Many sly references to "camp meeting babies" found in the literature of this period suggest that their behavior was not always pleasing to their elders.

The effect of the camp meeting on the religious life of the slave is difficult to assess. Slaveowners in general encouraged them to embrace the Christian faith and to follow its teachings. The church's emphasis upon such virtues as meekness and humility was an asset in keeping the black man in the condition of thralldom. Blacks were included in the membership of all churches, and they attended services with their masters, usually occupying segregated pews located in the balcony. Because of the curfew they were forbidden from attending night services unless by special permission. As church members they were accepted into full Christian fellowship and in church minutes they frequently were referred to as "our colored brothers." An occasional black, such as Wilkes Flagg, became a minister, usually in the Baptist faith, and led an exemplary life.

Membership in the Baptist church at Milledgeville never reached 100 at any time during the first three decades of the nineteenth century, and the majority were slaves. By 1845 the total membership had reached 190, 87 percent of which were blacks. In 1865 two-thirds of a total membership of 416 were blacks. Because of this ratio the Baptist church always remained in a weak financial condition.[63]

The paucity of Baptists in the white community was not a result of an inferior clergy, for among Baptist ministers in the town were such men as Edmund Shackelford, Adiel Sherwood, Iverson L. Brooks, and Shaler G. Hillyer, who also served as rector of the Scottsboro Male Academy. Jesse Mercer was a frequent visiting minister. A staunch friend of Governor Troup, Mercer often betrayed his own political bias in his sermons. Of all the town's early ministers, Sherwood was easily the most scholarly. Educated in New England, he married the widow of ex-Governor Peter Early after coming to Georgia. He was minister of the Milledgeville church from 1827 to 1833, during which time he began the writing of his popular Georgia gazetteers. An ardent supporter of Sunday schools and foreign missions, Sherwood became one of the leaders of the movement to break away from the conservative traditions of the church. He was also personally acquainted with most of the leading political figures of the day, and knew both Thomas Jefferson and Andrew Jackson.[64]

Edmund Shackelford moved to Milledgeville in 1816, where he supplemented his small ministerial salary by farming and teaching. He was a brother-in-law of Governor William Rabun, who was himself an ardent Baptist and who was accused of changing the governor's residence into a house of prayer. Rabun did not move his family to Milledgeville when he became governor, but rather commuted to his plantation in Hancock County on week-ends, where he continued to serve as clerk of the Powelton Baptist Church.[65] Governor Lumpkin also was prominent in Baptist circles during his term as governor from 1831 to 1835, serving both as clerk and deacon in the local church. Perhaps the most prominent Baptist of all the Milledgeville governors was Joseph E. Brown; yet there is no record of his membership in the local church.[66]

The great Baptist revival which swept Georgia during the spring and

summer of 1827 hardly touched Milledgeville, although it had great results
in surrounding rural areas. At Crooked Creek Church in Putnam County
seventeen converts were baptized. At the high shoals of Murder Creek there
were forty-two, and similar results were recorded at Powelton and Island
Creek in Hancock County. At a single baptismal exercise nine men and
their wives were immersed, in addition to a widow and all members of her
household.[67]

Being congregational in its organization and possessing a less disciplined
clergy than the Methodists, Baptists were often plagued with doctrinal
disputes leading to voluntary withdrawals and even to a few instances of
excommunication. In the Milledgeville church James Barrow, who was the
principal founder of the church as well as its leading financial supporter,
became the center of conservative dissent which came to a head in the late
1820s. His opponent was Iverson L. Brooks, a highly educated North
Carolinian who arrived in town in 1823 as the church's third pastor. Brooks
possessed some independent means which, together with his wide acquaintance—including such men as James K. Polk and Thomas Hart Benton—
placed him at once in the upper ranks of the town's society.[68] He and
Barrow soon became engaged in a controversy over foot-washing to which
Brooks was opposed.

This dispute generated considerable ridicule from the Methodists.
Whether the Baptists were exposing to public view their dirty linen or their
soiled feet, the Methodists were gleefully observing their predicament from
their own neutral position. Brooks faced a real dilemma, which he revealed
in a letter to Basil Manly, a friend in North Carolina. Manly, who was a
leading Baptist of that day, advised him to beat a hasty retreat and surrender
to the foot-washers. "And if the Methodists say a word," he suggested,
"sprinkle them well with the dirty water and stop their mouths with the
towel."[69]

The conservative group led by Barrow not only favored the washing of
feet as a church ritual, but also opposed such innovations as Sunday schools,
foreign missions, and all benevolent societies. Moreover, they had no particular respect for an educated clergy, which Brooks represented, since they
believed that God called men to preach irrespective of their learning and
that the Holy Spirit instructed the preacher at the time he delivered the
sermon.

The sincere piety of the Baptists was unquestioned. Their belief in and
practice of closed communion and baptism by immersion were useful doc-

trines in their evangelical endeavors. During their early years in Milledgeville, fasting and prayer were practiced on certain days set aside for such purposes.[70]

By 1840 the schism which had appeared in the late 1820s had resulted in two distinct groups of the Baptist sect. There were the Primitive or "Hardshell" Baptists and the Missionary Baptists, the latter prevailing in the towns and among the more sophisticated groups. As a result of these disputes, the Milledgeville church withdrew from the Ocmulgee Association around 1834 and entered the Central Association. It was at this time that the church dropped the name of Mt. Zion and became simply the Milledgeville Baptist Church.[71] During the same period the Methodist camp meeting lost much of its earlier appeal within the town. Both groups were showing signs of maturity and decorum consistent with the receding frontier.

Indicative of these developments was the organization in June 1826 of the Milledgeville Presbyterian Church, which was followed fourteen years later by the founding of St. Stephen's Episcopal Church. St. Stephen's was incorporated in 1841 with John R. Cotting and Charles J. Paine as wardens and John S. Thomas, Michael Kenan, and William S. Rockwell as vestrymen. Local families early identified with this church included those of Holmes, Herty, Tinsley, Scott, and de Graffenreid. State Geologist John R. Cotting served as vestryman for more than twenty years. Henry C. Wayne, Adjutant General of Georgia, often served as vestryman, and Charles J. Jenkins served as senior warden during his term as governor of Georgia. By far the least evangelical of all local religious groups, its total number of parishioners remained small throughout the remainder of the century, although it did receive some additions from the younger members of Methodist and Presbyterian families.[72]

The Presbyterian group did not remain small for long, and it soon exceeded the Baptists in membership. It easily surpassed all other denominations in its zeal both for a trained clergy and an educated laity. Among those who gave the Presbyterians early leadership were Dr. John Brown and Dr. Moses Waddell, both of whom had been president of the University of Georgia, and Joseph C. Stiles, a Yale alumnus who was among the earliest ministers of this faith to preach in Milledgeville. On the early rolls of the church were such statehouse officials as Governor Herschel V. Johnson, Peterson Thweatt, David C. Campbell, and Charles C. Mills. Prominently identified with its early history in the town were the families of Peter J.

Williams, Benjamin A. White, Elijah H. Burritt, Seaton Grantland, William Y. Hansell, Iverson L. Harris, William McKinley, Miller Grieve, R.J. Nichols, William Flinn, Samuel Rockwell, Carlisle Pollock Beman, Charles W. Howard, Samuel K. Talmadge, and James Woodrow. The last four were residents of Midway community where they taught at Oglethorpe University, a Presbyterian college which operated largely under the aegis of the Milledgeville church. A great majority of Presbyterians were newcomers to the state, and many were of New England background. There is little doubt that they represented the capital's elite in wealth and learning. James Woodrow, who was the maternal uncle of Woodrow Wilson, is said to have been the first professor in a Georgia college to hold the Doctor of Philosophy degree.[73]

The great majority of the people both in the town and in the county remained unchurched throughout the antebellum period and pursued a life style which must have amply convinced the Methodist circuit rider that the world was indeed one of great sin and ungodliness. While records on divorces for that day are revealed only in legislative statutes and appear to have been relatively infrequent, the statistics are misleading. Other documents show that happy marriages were far from universal. Typical is a public notice signed by John Stucky stating that his wife Rebecca had "left his bed and board without any just provocation" and warning all persons against trading with her on his account. William Parker had more serious problems with his spouse Patsy, about whom he wrote: "[She] left me and her home [in August, 1815] in as much peace and harmony as ever existed between man and wife to go and see her mother in Emanuel County; but the base insinuations of John Wolf . . . have destroyed all my earthly peace by kidnapping or deluding my wife from me." The deserted husband located Patsy in Wolf's house, but the latter refused to let her depart with him. The abductor later placed her in the safe-keeping of Ned Cowart in an adjoining county, and again she was taken off and concealed. Cowart could be easily identified, wrote the distraught Parker, "as having had the end of his nose bit off in a fight." He warned all persons against boarding Patsy or trading with her, being determined not to pay any of her contracts while she was misbehaving in such a manner.[74]

While not all the private immorality which occurred ever reached the ears of those who chastised the devil from the pulpit, there was ample evidence of its existence. Church people in general disapproved of such activities as cock-fighting and horse-racing, both of which were well under way in 1812 and continued throughout the antebellum era. During the late 1830s entrance fees for local horse races ran as high as $1,000.[75] The McKinley plantation was the scene of many of these frequently held events, and betting was a universal practice. These races helped to draw professional gamblers to the town, and there were occasional reports of small fortunes being won and lost through dishonest manipulation. A man named Bennett, who later was knifed in a barroom by one of his victims, once purchased a fine race horse and had him secreted on a farm near town. His accomplice rubbed off the animal's hair where a collar and plow traces would have chafed him, and in other ways imparted to the horse an unkempt and grubby appearance. Then, dressed as an old farmer, his accomplice drove the animal into town hitched to an apple cart and stopped in front of the hotel where Bennett was lodged. In the presence of several witnesses Bennett pretended to buy the horse for a trifling sum, affirming his belief that the animal had hidden virtues. He then proceeded to make bets on the animal for the next race. There were many takers at favorable odds who lost large sums of money in the final results.[76]

Perhaps the greatest blot on the town's early reputation was its propensity for harboring bordellos. A census made in 1828 by the town marshal listed fifteen white prostitutes out of a total of 346 white females of all ages; this was ten percent of all women in the town between the ages of fifteen and forty. It is little wonder that respectable young women seldom ventured on the streets without an escort. Police regulation of slaves was too rigid to allow them to be openly professional, but a number of free black women and mulattos are known to have followed this ancient trade also. The town's bordello district lay on the western end of Franklin Street, some two blocks south of the governor's residence, in a swampy and mosquito-ridden location. Because civil action against such establishments had to originate from complaining neighbors, operators in this area were reasonably safe from molestation by the law.[77]

One of the more notable of Milledgeville's early prostitutes was Phoebe Brown. In 1813 she, together with Mary Baily, paid the annual license fee of $10 each to permit them to retail liquor at their house. To obtain this license it was necessary to give security of $300 to guarantee "an orderly house." Farish Carter provided the deposit, and the two women were placed in business at somewhat an advantage over most of their dry competitors.

Phoebe's house was far from orderly, however. She was still in business at Milledgeville in the 1830s, although her functions apparently had become largely administrative. At this time she had the misfortune to become the central figure in a quarrel followed by a gun fight at her house in which one of her paramours was killed. The murdered man was Lem Smith, an itinerant actor who was a brother of the world-famous comedian Sol Smith. His antagonist was one Flournoy, a member of one of Putnam County's prominent families. Defended by Augustus H. Kenan, young Flournoy was acquitted in a trial which produced great sensation and considerable controversy.[78] The house at which this event occurred stood until 1960 just east of the old site of Cox's pond.

At the time of the Flournoy trial the Baldwin County grand jury called upon the legislature to enact a law forbidding occupants of every building "known by common fame as a lewd house" to obtain a license for retailing spiritous liquors. Noting the attempt of the Presbyterians to establish a college in the Midway community not far from Milledgeville, they called attention to the existence, "without restraint, of certain sinks of depravity and crime" in the populous part of Milledgeville. They warned that parents would not send their children to such a contaminated atmosphere nor would teachers "hazard the loss of their labors and reputation to circumstances so forbidding."[79] Indeed, during discussions of where to locate the college, one of Oglethorpe's founders strongly objected to placing it in Milledgeville, "which was so distinguished for its immorality." He stated his belief that the town would always be more or less impure so long as the government was located there. "The town's moral pollutions," he continued, "arise not from its permanent inhabitants but from that floating population which the Government and the Legislature call here."[80]

The Hopewell Presbytery, whose early jurisdiction included all of Georgia, finally did accept Midway as the location of the college. Although it was situated more than a mile south of the capital, the trustees immediately enacted regulations which, for all practical purposes, isolated the students from Milledgeville. To avoid the necessity of students going into town for their mail, a post office was established near the college.

The founding of Oglethorpe was the climax of a prolonged period of interest in education by the people of Milledgeville. The town was barely organized before a number of families joined together to employ a teacher for their children. Occasionally they advertised for one who could teach Latin and Greek as well as the elementary subjects. Generally held in residences, such schools did not enroll more than fifteen or twenty pupils. Tuition varied from ten to twenty dollars a year. The higher rate was charged for the upper branches, which included the classical languages. Board in the town for rural children could be obtained for $50 a year. The teacher's compensation was derived solely from tuition and it was extremely low, especially since tuition often was difficult to collect.[81]

In 1816 there appeared in Milledgeville a highly educated but eccentric scholar named William Montgomery Green, who recently had been discharged from his professorial position at the University of Georgia. Born in Ireland in 1767 of a family prominent in political circles, Green took as his first wife Anna Maria Wilkes, a niece of John Wilkes, the lord mayor of London who was famous for his sympathy with the American cause during the Revolution. As a result of his participation in the Irish rebellion of 1798, Green came to America, finally settling in the South, where he found a climate more congenial to his wife's failing health. At Milledgeville he and his wife opened two private academies, one of which was for young women.[82] His male academy had an advanced and comprehensive curriculum organized into four departments: the preparatory department, the classical and scientific department, the department of moral philosophy, and the department of belles lettres. Greek, Latin, French, and ancient history were taught in the early years, together with logarithms, algebra, trigonometry, moral philosophy, logic, and rhetoric. The final course included elocution, composition, and modern history and geography.[83]

Notwithstanding the availability of such a comprehensive curriculum, there was not a suitable building in the town available for instruction, and many parents could not afford Green's high tuition. The Baldwin grand jury requested that the state apply some of the money it collected from the sale of lots in the town to the construction of an academy building. Since no land in the town had been reserved for public education, the legislature complied with this request, and six one-acre lots were set aside for an academy. Later a square of four lots in the northwest part of the town, at Montgomery and Jackson streets, was donated for the academy building. In December 1821 the commissioners of the Baldwin County Academy announced that Dr. William Green "would again be rector of the academy" and that "an able Classical Assistant and a competent instructoress would be employed to aid him." They also announced that a library had been added and some scientific apparatus acquired.[84]

At this time no public school existed anywhere in Georgia. However, a beginning was made in 1817 when the legislature set aside a school fund, the income from which later was used partly to finance the operation of academies and partly for the tuition of children whose parents were unable to enroll them in private schools. The annual income available for these purposes was never large, only $20,000 being available for statewide distribution annually throughout the 1820s. Early in that decade Tomlinson Fort and Joseph Singleton joined Wilson Lumpkin in urging Governor Clark to recommend a program for a common school system to provide adequate statewide support. Fort, with David C. Campbell, also sponsored a public seat of learning for females which he hoped might be established near Milledgeville. Both programs were defeated.[85]

Fort was successful in obtaining special legislation setting up a common school system for Baldwin County which would be supported by local taxation. Passed in 1823, this law was remarkably similar to the statewide law enacted just before the Civil War. It provided for the election of five county school commissioners who were to lay out school districts, appoint trustees for each, levy a county school tax, and to examine and license teachers. Trustees of local districts were charged with providing suitable school housing, and for this purpose they were empowered to levy a small district tax. Milledgeville was defined as a single school district, and the original trustees of its academy were retained to serve under the new law.[86] Tomlinson Fort was one of the more active of these trustees, and he was later appointed to the University of Georgia's *Senatus Academicus*, whose annual meetings were held in Milledgeville after 1811. Fort served on this board for twenty-six years.[87]

The experiment in a locally financed public school system was short-lived, for the law had a built-in provision which insured its early demise. A county referendum could suspend its operation at any time, and this apparently is what occurred after four years. By 1828 the Baldwin Academy was operating like any other academy in Georgia. Its income was derived largely through tuition, but it also received some voluntary contritubions and a small additional sum provided by the state. The county's public fund was shared by Corinth Academy in the western part of the county and by Lonicera Academy for boys at Midway, both chartered in 1826.[88] The state fund was woefully inadequate, even for children of poor families who shared it. In 1827, although there were an estimated 200 county children eligible for this aid, the total county allotment was only $316.50 for ten tutors. The payments ranged from $75 for Michael Smith to $18 for John Hannon. In 1833 Milledgeville's Baldwin Academy, with twenty-five students enrolled, had in hand a total of $557.15, a two-year carryover of public funds which was increased in the following year by only $184. The trustees were reserving this money for the employment of "competent teachers." At that time the academy was operating under two instructors who had possession of the academy building as tenants at will and who received only the tuition for their services. In the following year the trustees employed David Kiddoc, a graduate of Jefferson College in Pennsylvania, as rector, but because of sparse enrollment no assistant was provided.[89]

Since it was judged improper to have males and females in the same school building or even in the same part of town outside of the family context the education of young women was left entirely to private enterprise. No school building was provided for them until 1835, at which time two new academy buildings were constructed on the vacant south side of Penitentiary Square. Funds for this construction came from proceeds from the sale of lots on the town commons.[90]

If interest in education was lagging within the town, it was going forward at great speed in the Midway and Scottsboro communities, which already had become the center of education in the county. It was in the latter community that the first complete academy for girls in the vicinity of the capital was established in the summer of 1828. Known as the Scottsboro Female Institute, it began operation in the house of Farish Carter, one of its sponsors, who seems to have engaged in the widest variety of activities for young women. Board was provided in the home of the rector Robert C. Brown or with other Scottsboro families at $80 a year. For a tuition payment of $60 pupils might study "all the solid branches of English Education, the French language, Drawing, Painting, Music, etc." Brown's school was a complete prototype of the young lady's seminary of the antebellum period in which the curriculum was designed to create a more socially oriented woman, to make her more attractive to men and, through her artistic skills, to become an embellishment to the home.[91]

The institution at Scottsboro was soon flooded with applications from parents seeking to enroll their daughters there. The school moved into enlarged quarters, and the rector employed five people to assist him. On his staff were Lucien Lataste of Columbia, South Carolina, and a Mr. Kellog, a former principal of a seminary in New York. Brown's high regard for professional standards is revealed by his leadership in the creation at Milledgeville in 1831 of the first teacher's organization in Georgia (called The Teacher's Society and Board of Education). Its purpose was to promote improved training of teachers and the upgrading of professional standards.[92]

In 1836 the Scottsboro Female Institute was acquired by Lucien Lataste and his brother Victor, now a music teacher at the institute. They promised to employ able assistants and to supply complete scientific equipment. They changed the name of the institution to Georgia Female College and later built on the campus a girl's gymnasium, said to be the first such facility anywhere in the South.[93] Those who graduated were required to pass a rigid examination.

So successful was the school that a rival institution, called the Hermitage Female Seminary, was opened at Scottsboro, and still another in the capital, called the Milledgeville Female Academy. The Scottsboro Male Academy was also opened in 1832 with Washington Baird as rector. In contrast to the curriculum at the girls' school, Baird taught the classical languages, literature, and history, the sciences and mathematics, as well as surveying, rhetoric, logic, moral philosophy, and political economy.[94]

Baird (1807–1868) was not an ordinary teacher. He came to Scottsboro from Pennsylvania, where he had graduated from Jefferson College. A Presbyterian minister, he later became editor of the *Southern Presbyterian*. After moving on to pastorates in Arkansas and South Carolina, he returned to Milledgeville and, during the Civil War, he employed his talents in writing Confederate school books and in tutoring the grandchildren of his old friend, Seaton Grantland.[95]

The Presbyterians, always in the vanguard of educational developments in the community, opened the Midway Seminary in January 1835. Originally designed as a manual labor school, this institution was sponsored by the Georgia Presbyterian Education Society, on whose executive committee were such local Presbyterians as Charles W. Howard, Samuel Rockwell, Baradel Stubbs, and John A. Cuthbert. Selected to head the new school was Carlisle Pollock Beman (1797–1875), who had come to Hancock County from New York in 1813. He was a student of his brother Nathan at Mount Zion and later an instructor there. After returning to New England and graduating from Middlebury College he again came to the Mount Zion Academy and later was licensed to preach in the Hopewell Presbytery, under whose jurisdiction the Midway school which he headed was soon placed.[96]

Beman was a hard taskmaster, and his discipline was as rigid as his teaching was thorough. His personality made an indelible imprint upon his students, who for the remainder of their lives referred to the institution at Midway only as "old Beman's school." Their rector was described as having "a short stalwart form," somewhat overweight, with his hair kept in crew-cut fashion to give him the appearance of a Prussian drillmaster. His voice was cold and metallic, and his steel gray eyes peered out above a pair of undersized spectacles. Apparently incapable of a smile, his face was as grave as that of a pallbearer. His standard threat to erring students was "I'll whip the very filling out of your shirt."[97]

The school soon abandoned the manual labor feature and inaugurated two academic sessions a day, beginning early in the morning and continuing until sundown. There was a three-hour study period after supper, and all of Sunday afternoon was devoted to study, after which a short walk might be permitted. On Sunday morning all were lined up and marched to the Presbyterian church in Milledgeville. There was no room for boyishness at the seminary. Beman allowed no nick-names to be used, and all straight-bladed knives and other weapons were confiscated. On each Friday (called "Black Friday" by his students) a half day was devoted to a review examination of the week's work. Anyone who failed this examination was soundly caned. Friday afternoon was devoted to public speaking from original compositions. Again, a poor performance might result in the command, "Come down!" This was preliminary to a caning by the master.[98]

The perils of composition and public speaking were navigated with difficulty by some of Beman's students. Most of the boys wrote themes on such topics as "The Animal Most Useful to Mankind." Becoming bored with so much discussion of farm animals, one young scholar, John R. Bonner, chose the topic "War." He captured a few paragraphs from Weems' *Life of Francis Marion* and purloined some ideas from other sources, but he ended with a fiery eulogy of his own on the American eagle and the national flag. Beman listened through to the end, but he had no compliments for the student's efforts. Instead he cautioned him in future to stick to subjects he knew something about—whereupon Bonner returned to livestock.

On another occasion a boy recited the line "Sink or swim, live or die, survive or perish" without either a gesture or intonation. Beman's observation was, "You ought to put on a brimstone shirt and set it on fire." Apparently taking his cue from this remark, another student, Robert Howard, decided to recite a stirring poem by Fitz-Greene Halleck. Howard sawed the air with gestures, charged from one end of the rostrum to the other, and single-handedly fought off an entire battalion of Turks. When he closed, Beman said simply, "Some boys have too much." Alec Martin was noted for his scarecrow appearance. Because of his awkwardness he had a great dislike for gestures and animations and had no relish for public speaking, which exposed his ungainly features to public view. He began his oration by stating, "You'd hardly expect one of my age to speak in public from a stage," to which Beman quickly rejoined, "Come down, Martin. Come down! You're a pretty infant!" Robert Jamison once had failed to memorize his lines and asked to be excused. When this request was refused, he got up and began to recite the multiplication tables, embellished with gestures and inflections. After he finished the first table, Beman intervened, "You think that is right smart, Jamison. Come down!"[99]

Beman's school originally was located on the lot later occupied by the Midway Elementary School, for which Farish Carter had donated land. The headmaster's house, later occupied by Baradel Stubbs, was still standing in 1976. Approximately one hundred boys were in attendance, many from other parts of the state. Board was available in private homes for $100 a year.[100] In 1836 the original location was abandoned and the school was moved farther into Midway, where a new academy and a dormitory were built to accommodate a growing enrollment. The new location was in proximity to the Bingham house on what later became Allen Memorial Drive.

During the same year that this move was made typhoid fever broke out in Steward's Hall where approximately sixty boys boarded and where they lived four to a room. These rooms were only ten feet square, each having only a single window for ventilation, and they were infested with rats and vermin. During the epidemic the students were sequestered and assigned to families living one to three miles away. In the following year they were again required to live in Steward's Hall but shortly after school opened the building burned down. The students were again placed in private homes, some going to Scottsboro. Some fifteen went into the Bozeman home, and a few boarded with an elderly widow, Mrs. Underwood, whose humble abode was amply compensated for by her motherly care and kindness.

Beman always greeted his students each morning on the steps of the academy building after their long two-mile walk. "You come towards school with heavy looks," he would say to them. Despite the long distance involved, Beman took to horseback and continued to make his nightly rounds to inspect his charges. Only rarely did he leave this duty to his assistants after one of them had been attacked from ambush.[101]

In the meantime, the Hopewell Presbytery had begun plans to convert the school into a college. The charter, under the title of Oglethorpe University, was granted in December 1835, and the trustees set about raising a building fund. This accomplished, Central Hall was constructed, and the university opened its doors in January 1838 with 125 students. Beman was retained as president of the college but he resigned in 1840, being dissatisfied with the trustees' rule that no boy above the sophomore class could be flogged. Also, Beman favored the New School theology, which already was beginning to divide the Presbyterian Church throughout the country. He went to LaGrange, where he founded a new academy to his liking. Six years later, however, he returned to Mount Zion, where he again founded a private boarding school for a select number of young men. Beman's successor at Oglethorpe was Samuel K. Talmadge, who guided the institution's development for the next twenty-four years.[102]

Beman was one of the better-known schoolmasters in the state during the antebellum period. While his discipline was severe, his results were unquestioned: he represented the ideal and successful type of academy teacher during the age in which he lived. His former students developed a filial respect and a genuine appreciation for him as they grew to manhood and assumed the responsibilities of adult life. To be known in Milledgeville as "one of Beman's boys" was a peculiar distinction which persisted well into the twentieth century.

Social life in the average Southern town was far more limited and much less commonplace than it was in the state capital. Elsewhere such events as militia musters, court sessions, camp meetings, and quarterly church conferences provided the principal relief from boredom. Yet Milledgeville could offer in addition all the excitement which normally flowed from the seat of the state's government. A problem which all towns shared in common, however, was the organization and administration of municipal government. In this activity, no doubt, the capital on the Oconee must have been essentially similar to Augusta, Louisville, Macon, and Columbus.

Municipal Regulation: Slaves and Citizens

During the first two decades of the town's history its annual budget averaged approximately $2,000. It was a taxpayer's paradise. Receipts came largely from the rent and sale of land in the commons and from the leasing of fishing rights in the two streams bordering the community. In 1815 revenue from regulatory license fees on such items as spiritous liquors and faro banks amounted to only $185. While barrooms were not yet discouraged by special tax levies, hard cider could not be sold on the streets in quantities of less than five gallons.[1] All shows were taxed, but these revenues were negligible. One showman paid a fee to exhibit a female baboon, another to display some wax figures, while a third was granted permission to operate a show called "artificial comedians," probably a puppet show. Fines amounted to $51.50, the greater part of which came from respectable citizens who chose this alternative to performing the required work on the streets. There were no poll taxes and no levies on businesses, trades, or on property of any description within the corporate limits.

The largest single expenditure for 1814 was for street improvement, which amounted to $198.50, and the next largest sum was $128.31 for keeping the springs in a sanitary condition. Following in descending order were the annual salaries paid to the marshal, the board secretary, and the treasurer; these were $90, $55, and $30, respectively. Miscellaneous items included printing, room rent for town meetings, stationery, repairs to the market house, overseers for roads, and court fees.[2]

Consistent with the town's growth and the passage of time, both the cost of local government and the methods of raising revenue were expanded. By 1828 both real and personal property taxes were levied, as well as taxes on all trades and professions. In addition, the revenue ordinance now provided for a tax on all free persons of color in the community. This tax varied from six to sixteen dollars according to age and sex. It appears to have been largely regulatory and designed to discourage growth of the free Negro population. To further achieve this goal, a special tax of fifty dollars was levied on free Negroes who entered the town for the purpose of making it their permanent residence. Slaves who were compelled to live apart from their owners were assessed a tax of sixteen dollars for this unusual privilege. Taxes on slaves as personal property were begun at an early date. On the eve of the Civil War the levy amounted to forty cents on every $100 of returned valuation, which was identical with that on other forms of personal property and on real estate.[3]

An ordinance of 1816 placed a prohibitive tax of $200 a week on "all Pharo [sic] banks, Rowlett [sic], Equality, ABC, E or O or any other table of like construction for . . . gaming." This heavy fee later was reduced and all billiard and bagatelle tables were taxed each at thirty dollars annually. For "keeping a Spanish Needle" the tax was forty dollars. To discourage the proliferation of barrooms a special license costing $21 was required in 1828 for those who sold liquor by the drink.[4]

In the meantime, by 1827 the marshal's salary had climbed to $350, and the secretary was now drawing $150 annually. The town was paying a stipend to those doing patrol duty, which added $270 to security costs. Street work was lagging, apparently because of the failure of citizens to perform assigned road duty. The offer of free whisky by the town did not improve the citizens' enthusiasm for this work, and finally an annual street tax of two dollars was levied. All street work now came to be performed by slaves hired from their masters, which, with the cost of their subsistence, amounted to almost $500 annually. The largest single outlay was for sinking two public wells on Hancock Street at a cost of $582.[5] In 1832, a tax of fifty cents per wheel was levied on carriages, wagons, and carts. Also all males of military age were required to pay a tax of one dollar for commutation of patrol duty. Later all of these taxes were increased, including one on pleasure vehicles. However, the tax was lowered on wagons and carts used for transporting freight.[6]

The marshal's salary had increased to $500 by 1850, at which time he had the assistance of a deputy who served only on special occasions at one dollar a day. The salary of the city clerk, who had in fact become the principal executive officer of the board of aldermen, now reached the princely sum of $2,000.[7]

Taxes and expenditures continued to rise throughout the last decade of the prewar period. The depression of 1839–41 temporarily halted these trends when a money stringency seriously curtailed income. At the beginning of this depression the board of aldermen issued $14,400 in money bills in denominations ranging from twenty-five cents to five dollars, some of which were still in circulation during the 1850s. The money panic was all but forgotten in 1848, when town authorities issued $30,000 in 7 percent bonds for the completion of a railroad from Gordon to Milledgeville. This undertaking necessitated raising the tax levy on all freeholds, and it was the community's first experience with a bonded debt.[8]

By 1860 the annual cash receipts amounted to $8,700, of which the largest single item was the $5,800 derived from taxes. More than $1,000 came from ferry toll. A total income figure of $13,700 included approximately $5,000 which was due but as yet uncollected. This was roughly equivalent to the municipality's total obligations, not all of which had been paid.[9] At no time during the antebellum period did any official of the town issue a balance sheet or make an orthodox financial statement. Fiscal affairs continued to be conducted in an unbusinesslike fashion throughout the remainder of the nineteenth century.

The management of the town commons and related activities occupied the greater part of the commissioners' attention during the early period. Until 1837, when an elected mayor and council replaced the intendant and commissioners, citizens were allowed to take wood from the commons, but such wood could not be used for burning bricks, nor could trees be skinned for tanbark. Trees which were cut had to be chopped up and removed and used only for firewood.[10] Land in the commons generally was leased to the highest bidder for a term of two years, although in 1856 a tract of eight acres on the north commons was leased at twenty-five dollars an acre for a term of one thousand years. There were five prime fishing leases on the Oconee just east of the town and one on Fishing Creek, the annual rental of which varied from fifteen dollars to $100 each.[11] Nearly all of the town's early financial transactions involved considerable credit, and authorities were plagued with problems of collections and foreclosures. Occasionally the state intervened in the resale of lots under foreclosure proceedings and sent its own representatives to make bids in behalf of the state. In the older section of the town sales of lots had been made outright under conditions set forth by the legislature and the proceeds had gone into the state treasury to be used for the construction and repair of the Statehouse and other facilities.[12]

Beginning in the 1820s streets underwent considerable improvement. Fences were removed from certain impassable thoroughfares, and drainage ditches were cut across streets at low points and covered with planks. At a few places, such as the intersection of Wilkinson and Franklin streets, a causeway was constructed. Ditches were dug on both sides of the streets and a gentle grade from the center took the water to the side. Such improvements were extremely costly and frequently placed a strain on the town's resources. To alleviate this problem a street lottery was authorized in 1831. Despite such efforts, however, the uneven terrain of the town continued to make street improvement difficult. Throughout the nineteenth century the town was maligned for the deep gullies which bisected its thoroughfares.[13]

Tree-planting for reclamation of the natural beauty of the area began in 1830 when the town marshal was directed to "plant a line of trees in front of the fence north of the Statehouse . . . about 12 feet from the fence." This activity continued throughout the remainder of the century. At the same time a system of garbage collection was begun when the editor of the *Recorder* launched a clean-up campaign. He stated that no town in the country had so many nuisances or was in a more filthy condition. "A blind man," he affirmed, "so long as his sense of smell remained, could . . . swear to their existence." A town scavenger was appointed, and public carts were provided twice each week for the removal of "all offensive matter and filth from the streets and alleys." A stiff fine was provided for those who failed to cooperate.[14]

In 1836 a law for the first time took notice of the encroachment of buildings on the public right-of-way and limited such encroachments to no more than eight feet on the sidewalk or street. When John W. A. Sanford added to two sides of his house a colonnade, which extended ten feet onto the sidewalks of Greene and Clarke streets, some of his neighbors became annoyed and asked the council to enforce the encroachment law.[15]

Milledgeville's streets were unlighted at this time. Three years later thirty oil lamps were acquired, most of which were placed on Wayne Street. At the same time a public hearse and "a gentle horse" were bought by the authorities, and a sexton was employed who conducted burials, secured the cemetery, and kept a book of registry. He received a fee of six dollars for opening a grave and making the interment, although slaves were buried for a smaller fee. The town treasurer was frequently called upon to finance the burial of paupers. There appeared to be no regulations or policies concerning segregated burials, and none appeared until after the Civil War. However, certain distinctions were manifested during the 1850s when a second hearse was acquired and used solely for the burial of blacks; it was somewhat aged in appearance and in need of paint. About the same time the city began to sell cemetery lots nineteen feet square at the price of ten dollars. The cemetery block underwent gradual enlargement by the acquisition of adjacent land. It was the final resting place not only of the town's elite and members of the legislature from other areas, but also slaves, convicts, and, after 1840, an occasional patient from the lunatic asylum.[16]

Aside from two or three minor regulations, no building code existed at any time before the Civil War. No ordinance attempted to regulate the location of privies in relation to residences and the various sources of drinking water, nor was terrain considered to be a deciding factor in determining the location of such facilities. However, authorities made an attempt to keep the springs cleaned and in good order. Bids were let for the keeping of each spring, the price ranging from six to twenty-four dollars annually. To prevent dogs and livestock from fouling the water, each spring was enclosed with a fence. Efforts to prevent the overflow of surface water into the springs were often ineffective.[17]

The sinking of wells to augment the water supply was begun as early as 1815. Ten years later, as a result of numerous petitions, a well was added at the intersection of Wayne and Greene streets near the market house, and in two more years another appeared at the junction of Wayne and Hancock. Both wells were seven feet in diameter and walled with stone. By the early 1840s hand pumps had been added to these wells. When the Executive Mansion was built in 1838, a well was added at the junction of Clarke and Greene streets; this served the Newell and the John W. A. Sanford houses as well as the Executive Mansion, which already had two wells on its property. Soon public wells appeared at all street intersections in the more populous areas of the town. Numerous cisterns were also constructed, though these were confined largely to the business section. All were equipped with pumps, and the stored water was used for fire-fighting.[18]

The elimination of fire hazards and the control of fire were constant problems throughout the antebellum period. No fire-fighting equipment existed during the first two decades. "Our houses are all wood," wrote a citizen in 1816, "and would burn like tender [sic]. Where are our water buckets, our Engine and our fire hooks? We have nothing of the kind [that are] found in all well regulated towns." Seven years later citizens still were deploring the total absence "of new wells, patented pumps . . . ladders and buckets."[19]

Instead of purchasing fire-fighting equipment, however, the commissioners in 1820 required each home owner to keep on his premises a ladder sufficient to extend to the roof. They also ordered a fine on those who should "suffer . . . chimneys to be fired at any other time than when it is raining." It was later declared unlawful to have a chimney or fireplace made of wood daubed with clay, and all stems or flues had to extend no less than thirty inches above the roof.[20]

During the winter of 1824 a fire destroyed five houses on South Wayne Street, including the house of Peter Jaillett south of the Statehouse Square. The incident aroused new interest in the organization of a fire company and in construction of cisterns. An attempt to finance a fire company through public contributions failed, and not until 1828, when the legislature authorized the town commissioners to do so, did they organize one. Coming into existence in the following year, this organization had eighty members who met for training sessions once a month under a chief engineer. The company was divided into five sections—the engine, fire hooks, ladder, bucket, and safety departments.[21]

Soon after the organization of the company, a disastrous fire started by the convicts destroyed the state penitentiary, despite the efforts of all local fire-fighting equipment and techniques. Two years later, during a session of the legislature, the Statehouse caught fire from a chimney spark, and its complete destruction was only narrowly avoided. Legislators and townspeople rushed to the scene, bringing water, wet carpets, and blankets. At one point the high winds spread the flames over the entire wood-shingled roof, well beyond the reach of the fire pump's jet, which barely reached the eaves of the building. Wells were some distance away, and the water supply was inadequate. Furniture, official records, and money from the Central Bank and the state treasury were taken to safety. After persevering for almost an hour, however, the crowd subdued the flames.

Emerging as the hero of this episode was a slave named Sam Marlow. Despite the steep pitch of the roof, he ascended to the cone where the fire had begun and remained on the roof during the entire time. When the flames burst forth near the eaves, he made his way down the treacherous, wet incline without a rope or other security, removed the burning shingles, and then returned to the top. "Everyone looked on with agonizing solicitude," wrote an observer, "fearing any moment that they would see him slip and fall from that tremendous height." Sam was rewarded by the legislature for this outstanding service when they appropriated $1,600 for the purchase of his freedom from his owner, John Marlow.[22]

Milledgeville was never again without an organization and equipment for meeting such emergencies, although these proved inadequate for many fires which struck the town's business section in the years which followed.

Conflagrations set off by incendiaries continued to plague penitentiary officials. Twice in 1837 fires were set to flammable materials in the various shops, which now were constructed of masonry. In November 1843, a short time after dark on the day that Governor George W. Crawford was inaugurated, flames simultaneously engulfed all shops in the compound. The setting of this fire was the prisoners' protest against the regime of General Charles Nelson as principal keeper. Nelson, who had commanded a regiment of state troops in the Seminole War, was a stern and merciless official. As the fire raged, he refused to allow the cells to be unlocked, despite pleas from inmates and bystanders. "Burn, damn you, burn!" he yelled to the convicts, reminding them that it was they who had started the blaze. One observer stated that "such howlings and moanings . . . we have never heard before." Finally Governor Crawford himself ordered the cells unlocked and the prisoners were made to lie down outside the walls while being guarded by a local military company. Although the prison had its own fire-fighting equipment and an elevated water tank, the destruction was excessive, particularly in view of the fact that all new construction in the past twelve years had been of stone and masonry. The estimated damage to the buildings was $30,000.[23]

Masonry construction had never been ordained for the town, whose new buildings continued to be constructed largely of wood and inadequately spaced. The most destructive of all the fires experienced by Milledgeville during the antebellum period occurred on a windy and dry October day in 1853. The blaze started in a barber shop on Hancock Street, where the new market house and, later, the city hall would stand. It swept down that street to the corner and then up South Wayne Street to Greene, where it turned east to consume almost an entire square. The progress of the fire was slowed by dynamiting the house of Nathan C. Barnett opposite the Presbyterian Church. With greatest effort the blaze was prevented from crossing Wayne Street and destroying the entire business section. On viewing the devastation, Governor Howell Cobb pronounced it the worst that he had ever seen.[24] The loss was immense, for only a few owners had their property insured under the excessive rates which prevailed at that time.

Almost as stubborn as the problem of fire safety was that of getting livestock, particularly hogs, off the streets and out of the alleys. Since the fences enclosing the commons were inadequate for confining hogs, whenever the animals were found on the streets they were captured and impounded in a twenty-foot square pen of notched logs which stood near the Statehouse. Owners of these animals might reclaim them by paying a fine of one dollar. In 1851, however, hogs finally were permitted the freedom of the streets (where they picked up loose garbage), but only if they wore nose rings to prevent their rooting under fences. The impounding fee, now reduced to fifty cents, went to the marshal whose duty it was to enforce the law. Later still the town provided nose rings but charged the cost to owners.[25]

If the revised regulations seemed to relent somewhat on the hogs' confinement, this liberality had been compensated for somewhat by a renewed effort to enforce the fencing of private premises. In 1839 unenclosed privies "so exposed that hogs [might] have access to them" were outlawed. Also, the council frequently found it necessary to issue special orders to property owners who failed to fence their land in the business section. The enforcement of local fence laws remained a problem as long as livestock enjoyed free range outside the town—and it was not until 1891 that state laws and a local referendum forced farmers to enclose their livestock. After this fences began to disappear not only from around arable land but also from around dwellings, cemeteries, and the limits of towns. This single development did more to change the appearance of Milledgeville than has been generally recognized.[26]

Closely related to the problem of livestock running loose on the streets was that of cattle mysteriously disappearing from the surrounding countryside and particularly from the town commons. From the beginning branded horses and cattle were permitted not only the freedom of the commons but also free range elsewhere in the countryside. Some were known to disappear in the swamps and revert to wildness; others were slaughtered surreptitiously and consumed by those who possessed an unusual hunger for fresh beef. Some rustling of these animals was reported throughout the antebellum period. Therefore, all who sold animals for food were required to transact their business only at the Market House, where a nominal fee was charged, but where a heavy fine was levied for failure "to furnish the clerk with ears, marks, brands and color" of all animals slaughtered.[27]

Another of Milledgeville's ubiquitous problems was prostitution. Throughout the first half of the century the penalties for this practice were mild, and they fell largely on the individual practitioner. But in 1858 a new ordinance placed on the owner as well as upon the renter or occupant of brothels a fine of up to $100, and imprisonment of not less than ten days for each offense. The offender also faced the possibility of banishment from the town.[28]

The case of one white prostitute possessed an unusual dimension. Having five children and a husband who was incapable of supporting them, Martha Butts was represented to the board as "a great nuisance to the citizens and a common nuisance to the community." The marshal was directed to remove her children to the house of relatives in Hancock County and to take the woman and her husband to a point outside the limits of the town with orders that they were never to return.[29] In the control of prostitution, blacks came under the same regulations as whites, although there is evidence that the enforcement of the law was highly discriminatory. Because of the complaints about the conduct of one Rachel, "a free woman of color," the commissioners in 1828 simply ordered her to leave the house she was occupying. Her guardian was then notified to give bond to guarantee her future good conduct. Again, Ann Norman, a free black woman, Rose Butts, a slave, and Penny Sanford, a white prostitute, all were reported as creating a nuisance. Rose was ordered to leave town, but Ann was allowed to remain, although she had to leave the house she was occupying and secure a guardian who could protect her and see that she "conduct herself orderly." No disposition seems to have been made of the white woman's case.[30]

As a rule, black women were not often the subject of special ordinances. Slave women who sold cakes, pies, and confectionaries had to be granted a special license to do so, but the restrictions placed on free Negroes—such as giving bond for good behavior and producing a certificate of good character—were not applied to a certain number of washerwomen.[31]

Generally, however, ordinances against Negroes either free or slave, trading any article whatsoever were extremely severe. The restrictions began very early, when a city ordinance of 1819 prohibited blacks from keeping or selling spiritous liquors, or keeping for their own use any cow, horse, or hog. Later the ordinance was extended to embrace "any article of provision or other valuable property" which, if found in their possession, would be seized and sold. Finally, in 1861, slaves were prohibited from buying within the town "for speculation" chickens, eggs, and butter under the penalty of thirty-nine lashes for each offense. In a law aimed primarily at preventing the theft of cotton, white men who traded with Negroes were subject to grand jury indictment and heavy penalties.[32]

Apparently the regulation against a slave dealing in articles of food did not apply to game and fish, nor was his right to own a dog ever challenged. Since the slave could not own or fire a gun, the dog's usefulness to him was restricted to hunting animals such as opossums, which could be captured alive. In 1860, however, a canine tax of two dollars practically eliminated the possibility of a black man owning even a dog.[33]

Residential regulations were equally severe. Blacks in Milledgeville were subject not only to the municipal code but also to the state and county codes. A legislative statute of 1807, applying to Milledgeville as well as to Washington, Louisville, Augusta, and Savannah, was the first of these laws ever exercised in the town for the purpose of regulating free Negroes, who were looked upon with fear and suspicion. It stated that all free Negroes, mulattoes, and mestizos would be subject to the same police regulations as slaves, and it fixed a penalty for any white person who rented a house or tenement to such persons. An ordinance of the town commissioners in 1810 made it unlawful for a free Negro to remain either in the town or on the commons. In the event of his having to transact business in town, he was limited to a visit of only three hours. The penalty for violation of this ordinance was fifty lashes, the maximum such penalty ever fixed by local regulations. No white person in the town was permitted to employ or harbor free Negroes in any way.[34]

In spite of such harsh penalties free Negroes tended to gravitate to the town, where nonagricultural employment was available and where the commissioners soon softened their prohibitions against them. After 1822 free Negroes were permitted to reside in the capital only by paying a special tax, showing a certificate of good character, and giving a bond for good behavior.

Slaves, of course, were much more strictly regulated. An ordinance passed in 1813 required that slaves live on the same premises as their master, and in 1822 it was added that no assembly of Negroes or any kind of disorderly conduct on these premises would be tolerated. Furthermore, to discourage a slave from purchasing his freedom, he was forbidden to hire his time from his master or to make work contracts. Three years later, however, slaves were permitted to hire their own time and to live apart from their masters on payment of a license fee. Such slaves were required to wear a tin badge showing that they had been so licensed.[35]

By 1830 the town's population included twenty free Negroes, a figure which doubled in the next ten years. In addition there were twenty-nine free

Negroes who lived in the county outside the limits of the town. At this time the town's slave population of 1,048 exactly equaled that of the white inhabitants, and in the county and town combined, slaves comprised 56 percent of the total population of 7,250.[36]

Throughout the remainder of the antebellum period the town continued to discourage the increase of free Negroes in the community. When Governor Brown requested that he be allowed to bring a number of these people to Milledgeville in 1858, the request was reluctantly granted, with the provision that he pay a tax on them.[37] The status of free Negroes in the community was in some respects less satisfactory than that of slaves, particularly those slaves who were fortunate enough to have benevolent masters. This explains why Wilkes Flagg, who had early acquired his freedom from Tomlinson Fort, chose to remain ostensibly his slave throughout the antebellum period. It is said that few people in the town ever knew the exact relationship which existed between Fort and Flagg.

Flagg was easily the most remarkable black man in Milledgeville during his lifetime. In 1831 Fort acquired him and his mother, "a Bright Colored Negro Woman [named] Sabina," from the Lamar plantation on Little River.[38] Flagg was set to work in a shop where he became a skilled blacksmith. The Fort children taught him to read and write and to keep accounts. His master permitted him the use of the shop after the normal day's work, and with the money he was able to earn from his extra work he bought his freedom and that of his wife Lavinia and their son; eventually he bought the shop and also a house. It is said that by the time of the Civil War Flagg owned property and securities which exceeded $25,000 in value. He had made many loans in Fort's name and that of Fort's son, George.

Flagg has been described as "copper colored, six feet tall, with the manners of a Chesterfield." Although known largely as a highly skilled artisan, his early life as a waiter provided him with an additional accomplishment. He was said to be the most competent head waiter in Georgia. None of the Milledgeville governors, from Wilson Lumpkin to Joseph E. Brown, ever gave a state dinner at the Mansion without obtaining Flagg's services. His language was precise and courteous, his dress was in good taste, and his manners were always gracious and refined. In his informal conversation Flagg espoused the cause of abolition. Yet he never expressed these sentiments in public meetings nor from the Baptist pulpit from which he spoke. Because of his recognized honesty and his sincerity, he had the complete confidence of the white community.[39] It is doubtful that the fear and distrust of free Negroes would have extended to Flagg even if people had known that he was not a slave.

The distrust of free Negroes stemmed largely from the fact that they were in a position to incite slaves to insurrection or to encourage runaways. The Georgia capital was an early focal point for the capture and incarceration of slaves who had taken refuge in the Oconee swamps or had fled to the Creek Nation, which until 1826, was just a day's journey to the west. Daniel McDuff became so experienced in recovering slaves from the Creeks— through his acquaintance and influence with their chiefs—that he advertised his services at $150 for each capture. This was considered a bargain price for such a recovery.[40]

Early advertisements for runaways, and other documents giving names and descriptions of slaves, provide a fascinating insight into the character of slavery on the Georgia frontier during the first third of the nineteenth century. Often the name reflected not only the sex but also the physical appearance of the slave, as well as the classical or biblical interests of his or her master. Among Zachariah Lamar's slaves, for example, were Big Flora, Hercules, and Samson; African Peter, Esau, Gabriel, Moses, Abraham, and Joshua; and Scipio, Augustus, Caesar, Selah, and Edinborough.[41]

Advertisers for runaways often made a distinction between "African Negroes" and "Country Born Negroes." One of the former was described in 1810 as having "his country marks on his cheeks, filed teeth, [and a] pleasant countenance when spoken to." William Robinson in 1818 asked for the capture and return of John, a slave of "yellowish complexion, straight and spare," who had "holes in his ears and commonly [wore] ear-rings." Though apparently of African birth, he was described as having such "a remarkable [sic] good address, simple and artful" that he would probably attempt to pass as a free man under the name of John Edwards. "He was a sailor by profession," continued Robinson, "and still has that appearance."[42]

Seaborn Jones offered a reward for the return of French Ned, who, said he, spoke only broken English. Accompanying French Ned was a runaway named July, "about 24 years old, brought from Africa when a small boy," who had been working as a boat hand. Samuel Rockwell sought the return of Sam, about twenty-two years old, of black complexion, five feet ten inches in height, "well made, has rings in his ears [and wore away with him] a Gingham Coatee, white pantaloons, [and] a half worn Beaver hat." Another runaway was described as dressed in simple white homespun of mixed cotton and wool, while still another, who must have pillaged his master's wardrobe before departing, was dressed in "Northern homespun trousers, with blue stripes, Bombazine coat, Morocco boots, linen shirts [and] a Beaver hat."[43]

These fugitives from slavery often demonstrated unusual artfulness and great sagacity. One took away with him a bridle and pretended to have been sent to look for his master's horse. John Clark described his runaway waiting man, Grig, as very intelligent and well acquainted with the country. He thought his slave might head for one of the coastal cities or perhaps Florida or the Creek Nation. "He may attempt to pass down the [Oconee] river as a boat hand and it is not unlikely that he may have forged a pass or instrument to show his freedom." Thomas B. Stubbs offered a reward for a mulatto truant named Elijah, whom he thought would change his name and pass as a white man. He had blue eyes and straight hair and very little appearance of mixed blood. However, to insure that Elijah would not be mistaken for white, Stubbs had branded him on one cheek with the letter S, which, the master warned, he might endeavor to obliterate. "He has been accustomed to boating on the Oconee and Altamaha rivers, and I think he may attempt to join the Patriots in East Florida."[44]

These records all possess a note of high tragedy, but none can match the drama produced by those incidents in which free Negroes were captured, smuggled away to a distant community, and then sold into slavery. Such an incident involved a fourteen-year-old youth who appeared in Milledgeville in 1819. He was arrested by Fred Sanford, the jailer, who suspected him of being a mulatto or of having Indian blood because of the dark hue of his skin. The youth claimed that he had been born of a free mother and was the son of Philip Southerland of Virginia. He related how he had been stolen from Louisa County by speculators, hired out by them, and later taken into the Creek country. He was now making his way back to his home in Virginia.[45]

The descriptions of many fugitives who were jailed at Milledgeville betrays evidence of whipping and physical abuse prior to their running away. One Burrill was described as "having a downward look" and showing the marks of a whip on his back and arms. His owner, Stephen Pearson, denounced him as a murderer and proclaimed that he would pay all expenses for his recovery, even if he were taken dead. Pearson had been attacked by the Negro and almost killed while escorting him home from Savannah, to which he had originally escaped.[46]

The Milledgeville slave code might more properly be called the black code, since it made little distinction between free Negroes and slaves. This code, like that which applied to free Negroes, consisted of a number of ordinances passed from 1808 to 1865, during which period some were repealed and others amended or modified. Basically these regulations fixed the slave's place of abode, limited his freedom of assembly, his right to own property, and required him to observe the curfew. In addition, his general behavior was regulated, often in great detail. In 1813, for example, Conrad Peterson, the town's spring-keeper, was authorized to inflict "reasonable corporal punishment" on any Negro found washing in or abusing any spring, and they were forbidden to use the springs after nightfall. For unlawfully cutting trees on the commons or around the springs, thirty-nine lashes might be imposed in addition to a fine to be paid by their owners. (A fine ranging from $5 to $20 levied against a master was equated with thirty-nine lashes inflicted on his slave.) A regulation of 1843 made it unlawful for any Negro to smoke cigars in the streets or on the sidewalks. At the same time blacks were denied the privilege of building their own church on city lands, although they were permitted to hold their own services in the Methodist and Baptist churches on Friday and Saturday nights. These services had to be under the supervision of the white pastor or some acceptable white person. The council also permitted them to extend their period of evening worship thirty minutes beyond the sounding of the curfew. Likewise, Negro musicians were permitted to practice after the curfew, but no later than 10:00 P.M. and only when some suitable white person accompanied them.[47]

Social dancing among Negroes was discouraged; yet they were permitted to have balls during the Christmas holidays—though only in the daytime. Permits were granted only after the application by owners and guardians, who had to give assurance that white persons would be present to preserve order. In 1853 the aldermen placed a complete prohibition against Negroes engaging in public or private dances within the town, but after a few weeks the ruling was repealed. Later, however, when Buck Kenan, "a person of color," petitioned for permission to give a Christmas ball he was flatly refused.[48]

It was the marshal's responsibility to enforce all of these ordinances. He or his deputy not only administered corporal punishment to violators but at the same time often filled the role of judge, jury, and prosecutor. The black man's hatred and distrust of the local police must have been considerable.

Apparently, until 1865 no Negro was ever tried for a misdemeanor in the Mayor's Court, where he might have acquired more respect for the rule of law.[49]

When the marshal rang the curfew at nine o'clock at night his daily duties were over. At this time the patrolmen assembled at the Market House to begin their duties, which usually ended at three in the morning. Originally comprised of a captain and twelve men "liable to do military duty," the patrol operated only three nights each week on a schedule unknown to the general public. Occasionally they began their duties at 10:00 P.M. and ended them at four in the morning. Membership changed each month. The neglect of duty by either the captain or a patrolman was heavily penalized, as was failure to heed a summons to serve. Despite this, few citizens of prominence rendered this service, preferring to pay the fine instead. Among those who were fined for neglect of patrol duty were Joel Crawford, former congressman, Augustus H. Kenan, intendant, and Judge L.Q.C. Lamar.[50]

The difficulty in securing willing and capable patrolmen led to a change in the system in 1823. The marshal was now required to divide the citizen list into thirty squads, and each squad was required to serve one night each month. One could buy exemption for $6 a year. After two years the system was again changed. Now called the Town Guard, the patrol's ranks were filled by volunteers who received a small stipend for their services. Finally, in 1831, the patrol was reduced to five persons who were required to patrol every night. Three sergeants, each drawing a salary of $100 a year, commanded the patrol in succession.

The principal function of the patrol was to enforce the curfew and to prevent unlawful assemblies and riotous conduct. The fear of arson, rape, and murder and the possibility of insurrection always lurked in the minds of citizens. Slaves found outside their cabins without a pass were placed in the guardhouse and released after the marshal had administered twenty-five lashes and had received the payment of a fine of one dollar by their masters. Only under exceptional conditions were members of the patrol permitted to enter the yard, kitchen, or other buildings on the premises of citizens.[51]

The Nat Turner insurrection in 1831 increased the sense of danger in all slaveholding communities throughout the South, and Milledgeville was no exception. The local patrolmen were cautioned to exercise greater vigilance. They now were charged to take care to check every assembly of Negroes and to treat religious gatherings in the same manner as other meetings. During the fall of that year the commissioners examined nine blacks for suspected leanings toward insurrection but dismissed all except one, who was kept in jail for not having "a lawful ticket." He remained there until his master provided one. Apparently to discourage provocative acts by irresponsible whites, the board also ordered that all guns be taken away from intoxicated persons, particularly "from boys parading the streets," and that the law be vigorously enforced against firing weapons within the town limits.[52]

A few cases involving the enforcement of the slave code became part of the town records. These give an insight into some of the problems involved in the exercise of local police power over the slave. Once Marshal Ezekiel Ralston complained to the board that young Billy Flagg, a blacksmith and the slave of John Lewis, had evaded his questions and had refused to give an account of himself, "and moreover [he had] made his brag that no marshal should whip him." The marshal was forthwith ordered to take Billy to the Market House and "there on the bare back inflict the number of twenty lashes with a common cowskin." On another occasion the marshal and Richard Mayhorn, a member of the patrol, brought a charge against Nathan, a slave of Edward Cary, claiming assault and battery by Nathan against Patrolman Mayhorn. Cary, Nathan's owner, appeared before the board without the slave and claimed that Mayhorn had violated the town ordinance and transcended his authority. He then introduced certain evidence to substantiate this charge, whereupon Mayhorn was discharged from the service of the town and the case against the black man was dropped.[53] This incident illustrates the effectiveness of the master's intervention in protecting the rights of his slave.

Again, the patrol charged a free Negro named Hubbard with cursing, assaulting, and bruising Billy Woodriff, a slave of Seaborn Jones. The fracas occurred in front of Billy's shop in the presence of white witnesses. Two white men testified that Hubbard's attack was brought on by Billy's having had an affair with Hubbard's wife. Despite this mitigating circumstance, Hubbard was remanded to the custody of the marshal, who was ordered to give him a mere ten lashes "moderately laid on." For disorderly conduct, Maria, slave of Dr. C. I. Paine, together with Hannah Edmundson, slave of A. W. Callaway, were kept in the guardhouse for three days and on each successive day they were given ten licks each with a paddle. Their owners, who had acquiesced to the mild punishment, were directed to pay the cost of the flogging.[54]

Slaves who lived outside the town and worked on the plantations often had to observe a plantation code. These regulations involved working conditions as well as personal behavior and were administered by the overseer much as the marshal administered the town code. A state law of 1811 provided that certain crimes and misdemeanors charged to rural slaves could be tried in the local justice court. However, all capital crimes committed by Negroes were to be tried by a jury impaneled in the Inferior Court of the county. Any resulting penalties were executed by the sheriff. Therefore town Negroes, as well as those living on the plantations, fell under the jurisdiction of this court.

A few records of the trials of slaves for capital crimes have been preserved in the minutes of the Inferior Court of Baldwin County, but they extend only from 1812 through 1826. These records afford a rare view of the range of court action in such cases as well as the variety of penalties inflicted upon the victims. Typical of these was the trial and conviction of John, slave of William McGehee, for stealing a hundred-dollar bank note. He was taken immediately to the Market House to receive "39 lashes on the bare back . . . on three successive days and then within 30 days to be taken outside the state to which [he was] not to return on pain of Death." A slave of John Neeves was adjudged guilty of committing rape on Suzanna Cobb and ordered to be hanged. A slave of John A. Jones was found guilty of burning down a ginhouse containing a quantity of cotton belonging to his master. He was hanged eight days after being sentenced. A slave belonging to Andrew Elliot was tried for assault and attempt to murder and to commit rape on Lillie Lankford. He was found guilty and hanged seven days later. Dave, the property of William Johns, was convicted of assault and attempt to murder a white man with a long-bladed knife. He was hanged. Also hanged was a slave of Israel Jordan who attacked a white man with a hickory stick while traveling on the Clinton road. George, property of John Ponder, was hanged for the burglary of clothing and money valued at $150. On the other hand, Tom, a slave of Joseph Andrews, was adjudged guilty of beating to death another Negro named Czar. The murderer was branded on both cheeks with the letter M, given thirty-nine lashes on each of three successive days, and then discharged. John, a slave of William Robinson, was found guilty of breaking open and entering a barroom and was sentenced to thirty-nine lashes on each of three successive days and then branded with a T (thief) on his right cheek. A slave named Alick, who pleaded guilty to striking a white man, could have received the death penalty under the slave code, but instead he was sentenced to fifty lashes on each of three successive days.[55]

These records offer unmistakable evidence that slaves fared poorly in cases involving offenses against the white establishment, while, on the other hand, offenses against other blacks were seldom prosecuted, and when convictions were made, the sentences were mild. For example, a Negro woman Fannie, property of William Micklejohn, was charged in 1811 with the murder of an infant belonging to Polly Sanford, another slave. Prosecution of the case was dropped. A similar charge was dismissed against a Negro boy accused of murdering a slave belonging to Devereaux Jarrett. Finally, when Peter, a slave of Eden Taylor, was found guilty of killing a slave at the house of John Sharp, he was declared guilty only of manslaughter and given thirty-nine lashes on each of three successive days.[56]

The preceding records suggest that discrimination against those who possessed black skins existed in every phase of life during the slavery regime. It was literally a cradle-to-grave aspect of the Negro's existence. On the other hand, segregation was a rare and unimportant part of his experience. It is impossible to measure the degree of opposition in the white community toward an institution so violently undemocratic and so morally indifferent to the human rights of the other half of its inhabitants.

After 1831, when Southerners everywhere became conscious of the dangers of insurrection, it became increasingly impossible to discuss the subject of slavery openly and critically. Before that date, however, public comment indicates that there was a surprising degree of dissent concerning both the economic merits of slavery and the ethics of slaveholding. One of these dissenters, writing in the *Southern Recorder* in 1820, admitted the claims of some that slaves were better off economically than many free inhabitants of the North but did not believe that such an argument should be used to defend slavery. "Freedom is the same to the Negro as to the white man," he wrote. "Let us see whether *we* should not prefer freedom with poverty to the best condition of the slave."[57]

Despite the sinister absence of such opinions after 1831, there is some evidence that slavery became more humane and tolerable with the passing of the frontier conditions of the early third of the nineteenth century. During the waning years of its existence there were numerous manumissions and a growing spirit of *noblesse oblige*. "I wish my man, Grigg, to be held as the nominal property of such master as he may choose but enjoy all the fruits of his labor or at his option to be manumitted and sent out of the State," directed Joel Crawford, who died in 1858. He allowed other slaves to select their future masters, and in no instance did he permit families to become separated. The aged and infirm received a comfortable support from his estate.[58] With the waning years of the slavery regime there was a growing tendency to deal with the slave as an individual and to respect his personal dignity wherever this could be done in a manner consistent with thralldom.

By 1860 Baldwin County had nearly 100 free Negroes, the greater part of whom resided in Milledgeville. Fifty-five percent of the county's 9,078 people were black. The town's population was 2,229, of whom approximately half were Negroes. The value of slave property in both the town and the county exceeded the combined value of all real estate. The community remained essentially an agricultural town except for a brief period each year when legislative sessions dramatically changed its character. However, 72 percent of the county's 147,000 acres of farm land was as yet unimproved.[59]

Free Negroes in the town tended to dominate such trades as barbering, blacksmithing, brick laying, carpentry, and tailoring, while town slaves performed the more menial jobs of cooking, cleaning, grooming, gardening, and personal service. The names of eight free Negroes appeared on the town's tax digest in 1860, along with those of 327 white taxpayers. While there is no record of free blacks in Milledgeville owning slaves, such a circumstance did exist in the neighboring community of Sparta, in Hancock County.[60] However, the ownership of all other types of property by blacks was well under way before the Civil War.

As the state's limits of settlement expanded to the line of the Chattahoochee River, the town matured in growth and became attuned to the semi-urban character of its permanent citizens. By 1840 most of the roughness of its early frontier ethos was perceptibly diminishing. This was manifested in various forms, the most ostensible of which was the building of elegant and more spacious houses. Some were of masonry construction and bespoke a sense of stability and permanence. There was also a growing public interest in improving the state's facilities in the town, but a parallel movement to relocate the capital greatly interrupted this development.

6

Toward a Maturing Society

Throughout the late antebellum period Milledgeville was barely able to hold its own against the attractions of the rural countryside. Not only were investments in land and slaves proving profitable, but planting was deemed a more honorable pursuit than any other calling, with the possible exception of politics. Many townsmen-turned-planters continued to be absentee planters and remained in the town, but those who resided in the country often owned houses and other property in town as well. There were at least twenty-five such families in 1860.[1]

The most significant single characteristic of these gentlemen planters in the Milledgeville area was their adherence to diversified farming. In 1860 very few of them fitted the traditional image of large cotton planters. While some, such as Stith P. Myrick, produced more than a hundred bales each year, there were others who grew none at all. Individual slaveholdings in general were modest, although sixteen Baldwin County planters owned more than fifty slaves in 1860.[2] The group produced no outstanding agricultural leaders such as were found in the adjoining Hancock county, yet they were identified with the innovative production of fruit, grapes, and pecans. Perhaps the first pecans ever grown in Georgia were those planted in Tomlinson Fort's garden in 1849. Five years later a local editor described in detail their size, color, and foliation, and announced that although the pecan was considered an ornamental tree, it might also prove valuable for its fruit. By 1883 these trees had grown to a height of forty-five feet and were twenty inches in diameter. Their fruit production was well established, and Milledgeville became an early center for the distribution of pecan trees throughout the southern half of the state.[3]

If planters who resided in the capital and its rural environs lacked a strong dedication to growing cotton, they were not unfamiliar with the way of life usually associated with that pursuit. Both in town and in the countryside, they created some of Georgia's more graceful residential structures. The ideal site for a home, whether in town or on the plantation, was thought to be in the midst of a grove of hardwood trees, at an appropriate distance from

the thoroughfare and on the crest of a hill. The finest of the county's plantation houses were all located within an hour's ride of the capital. Many of
these houses were still standing in 1976, and their lasting elegance suggests
that their owners, though representing a small minority of the people, could
lay claim to most of the romantic traditions of the full life under the plantation regime.

Lockerley Hall—Daniel R. Tucker's home, built sometime after 1840
near Midway—is considered by many to be a perfect example of the plantation house. Standing in a grove of trees, the masonry house had two stories
above a ground floor and displayed six Doric columns across the front. Its
stairway was graced by a mahogany balustrade, and the doors were made of
solid walnut.[4] In 1965 the house and its ample grounds became the center
of an arboretum operated by an educational foundation.

Also in Midway was the house of General Stith P. Myrick. Built in 1838
by the New England attorney, William S. Rockwell, it had been the home of
Herschel V. Johnson before its purchase by Myrick. Situated on a high
ridge overlooking Milledgeville, where it still stood in 1976, the house
boasted a spacious banquet hall, kitchen, larders, store rooms, and laundry
on its ground floor. Unlike most plantation houses, this one did not stand in
the center of, or even near, its owner's vast domains—Myrick's 3,200 acres
lay in other parts of the county.[5]

Six miles east of Milledgeville was Mount Nebo, the seat of David B.
Mitchell's thousand-acre plantation. It commanded the most breath taking
view in Middle Georgia. Built in 1809, the house had nine rooms, a two-
tiered front portico, and a rear piazza which looked out over the slave
quarters and other buildings arranged in a quadrangle behind it. This
messuage included two frame buildings, each of which measured 36 by 18
feet, stood one and a half stories high and had four fireplaces built into a
central chimney. One of these houses was used for a kitchen and laundry,
while the other was used for weaving and for servants' quarters. Also in the
quadrangle were a brick dairy house, a smoke house, an overseer's house,
barns with a grain-storage unit, blacksmith and carpenter's shops, a thresh-
ing floor, a cotton gin, and cabins to accommodate thirty slaves. It is said
that this complex and its site were so admired by the trustees of the University of Georgia that they came close to choosing it as the location of the state
university. In 1834, having run into financial difficulties, the Mitchell heirs
sold Mount Nebo to Robert McComb, so the house also came to be known
as McComb's Mount. By 1860 the plantation had ceased to produce cotton,

Mount Nebo (later McComb's Mount), originally the plantation home of Governor David B. Mitchell. Built near Milledgeville in 1809.

but the house and its complex remained unchanged until their destruction by fire more than a century later.[6]

Less than five miles from the capital, in the Scottsboro community, the plantation house known as Woodville was built by Governor John Clark in 1819. Fifteen years later, when it was offered for sale by Seaton Grantland, who had bought it from Clark, this seven-room, double-story house was the center of a 2,100-acre plantation. "I have no skill in planting," wrote Grantland, "yet I have made on this place the past year with 13 hands about fifty heavy bags of cotton and 350 barrels of corn, besided a quantity of small grain." This plantation later passed to the DuBignon family through the marriage in 1844 of Anne Grantland to Charles DuBignon of Jekyll Island.[7] The house was still standing in 1976.

Charles W. Howard in the 1830s owned a 700-acre plantation near Midway known as Beckham's Mount (later Pomona), where vineyards, fruit trees, and meadows flanked a handsome two-story house. Here Howard combined the roles of Presbyterian minister and Oglethorpe professor with the pursuit of farming until 1840, when he moved to North Georgia to become editor of *The South Countryman*, an agricultural journal devoted to the promotion of grass-and-livestock farming.[8]

Some two miles east of Beckham's Mount, at Scottsboro, there stood until the 1960s the oldest house in Baldwin County. It was the residence of Farish Carter, who owned an immense acreage which he held largely for speculative purposes. His large holdings in North Georgia, ideally suited for grain, inspired a famous colloquialism, the principal element of which referred to the abundance of Carter's oats. Among Carter's neighbors at Scottsboro were Singleton and Lorenzo Buckner, who together possessed an orchard of 7,000 apple trees, mostly of the Shockley variety. When Lorenzo sold his crop at inflated Confederate prices in 1863, it brought $70,000.[9]

About the same distance from the capital as Carter's house, but in the opposite direction, stood Westover, the plantation mansion of Benjamin S. Jordan. Located at the center of a 950-acre tract, Westover possessed a complete assortment of plantation structures, most of which were still standing in the 1960s when the mansion was destroyed by lightning. The principal features of this establishment were its orchards, flower garden, and its formally landscaped grounds. In 1860, like many of the farms in the Milledgeville area, this plantation produced large quantities of milk, grain, vegetables, and livestock, but no cotton. When Benjamin Jordan died in

1855, R. E. Launitz of New York, creator of the Pulaski monument in Savannah, was commissioned to execute his monument. In 1976 the Jordan monument remained the largest and most impressive memorial stone in the Milledgeville cemetery.[10]

The most singular plantation in the vicinity of Milledgeville, and perhaps the most noted grain and livestock establishment in Middle Georgia, was the 1,200-acre Barrow-McKinley livestock farm on the east bank of the Oconee. Its owners encouraged horse-racing as an incentive to the breeding of these animals, but they never permitted cotton to be planted on the land, nor did they allow trees to be cut except by special contract. Eventually the plantation came under the sole ownership of William McKinley, the attorney, who was an avid reader of agricultural journals and followed the precepts of the New York agricultural writers. In 1858 he completed a large brick plantation house with materials obtained on the plantation, but the plan of his house was Gothic rather than Greek Revival and came directly from the form book of Andrew J. Downing, a New York architect.[11]

Unlike the many striking residences in and around Milledgeville, the structures which appeared in the business section of the town generally were mediocre and nondescript in style. One exception, however, was the Masonic Hall on the corner of Wayne and Hancock streets, by far the most elegant building ever placed in the commercial area. Dedicated on June 24, 1834, this three-story Georgian building with its spiral stairway was still in use in 1976.[12]

Construction of the Masonic Hall was funded through a lottery authorized by the legislature. Its architects were John Marlow (also its builder), James Doyle, and Samuel Tucker. In 1832 the cornerstone was laid, with Samuel Rockwell serving as Grand Master. After these ceremonies the large crowd moved in a procession to the Methodist Church and heard Rockwell's address. The fraternity then repaired to the Benevolent Lodge in the Darien Bank building where, "in exercise of brotherly love, they partook of a social and temperate collation, and [then] dispersed at an early hour."[13] There were two masonic lodges in Milledgeville up to 1838, at which time the Benevolent Lodge No. 6 and Fraternal Lodge No. 20 merged to become Benevolent Lodge No. 3.

The new building soon became a major attraction for the town's loafers. Its Georgian-style front faced the south, and on its broad sidewalk, shaded with trees, were chairs, tables, and benches where men gathered to discuss politics and agriculture and where they read and also played checkers.[14]

The Masonic Hall was of masonry construction, being one of only four such structures in the business area in 1834. The others were the Lafayette Hotel, the Darien Bank, and the Waitzfelder building, the last being a mercantile establishment. Built before 1820 on the west side of Wayne Street near Eagle Tavern, the Waitzfelder building had a slate roof, iron shutters, and dormer windows above its second floor. It was the only structure in that block which withstood numerous conflagrations of the nineteenth century.

The portion of West Hancock Street between Penitentiary Square and the Masonic Hall remained partly a residential area until after the Civil War. During the 1860s two residences still stood on the north side of the block, one being that of Secretary of State Nathan C. Barnett. On the opposite side of the street fully half of the frontage was undeveloped, although two dilapidated houses and a barroom stood there. Just east of the Masonic Hall was the residence of Dr. C. C. Mitchell. On the northwest corner of Hancock and Wayne was the double-story frame structure owned by George T. Leikens; it had a barroom entrance on Wayne and a millinery shop facing Hancock. Long after the war this building was moved north some thirty yards to occupy part of the old site of Wilkes Flagg's blacksmith shop. It remained in 1976 as the oldest commercial structure in the town.[15]

The shifting center of the town's business establishments may be traced in the changing post office sites. In 1850 this office was in the Masonic Hall. Later it was moved to a location east of the Statehouse, where it remained throughout the Civil War, when Ezekiel Candler was postmaster. After the war James C. Shea replaced Candler, and the office was moved to rooms in the Milledgeville Hotel. Later still, after Jeremiah Fowler became postmaster, it was operated from the basement of his house on North Wayne Street.[16]

Although, as has been noted, several masonry structures had been erected in the business section, no residence of masonry, either in the town or in the county, is known to have existed prior to the completion of the Executive Mansion in 1838. The construction of the Mansion had its origin in a senate resolution passed in 1835. Responsibility for making building arrangements fell upon Governor William Schley, who immediately communicated with H. A. Norris, a West Point graduate and New York architect and engineer; Norris had participated in the planning of the U.S. Customs House in New York. Early in May he sent to Governor Schley a plan for the house which the governor had outlined to him. Norris's description of this plan strongly suggests that Schley's concept of the house was the basic one on which the Mansion finally was constructed. Norris commented as follows:

In arranging the plans of your house, I have in mind your directions as to the size on the ground (40 feet wide and 60 feet front) the width of the entry (14 feet) and having but two floors. But I found that it would be very inconvenient to make a portico of four columns reaching from the ground to the roof. Columns of that length would require a large space between them and that would spread out the portico over the front so as to interfere with the adjacent windows. . . . After trying it several times I gave up the idea, satisfied that such a portico would be too heavy for the building and that the space on each side of it would appear too insignificant. In my design the portico has two ranges of columns over each other, the lower ones square, the others round. The columns being *smaller* the space between them is *smaller*; and the spread of the portico suits the width of the entry. . . . I have made no arrangements for the servants rooms, kitchen, etc. for I presume you wish these in a separate building. The side portico is on the end of the house nearest the Statehouse and it is intended as a more private entrance. [Here he described the first floor to be used as a breakfast room, family sitting room, parlors, and a large salon. The upstairs was designed for sleeping, storage, and family uses.]

Should the design suit you, it can be constructed of any material you choose; but when finished it should be one color as near as may be. Many persons think they gain a point by painting their walls red, their cornice raw white, etc. but anyone that has seen a beautiful edifice of marble can easily see the difference between a piece of patch-work architecture and one of the right stamp. If the masses are well arranged the single effect of light and shade is infinitely more grand and beautiful than all the house painter can accomplish.[17]

In January of the following year the governor's office announced a prize of $100 for an "Approved Plan of a House for the Residence of the Governor," which should be three stories high and approximately 60 by 70 feet. It was further stipulated that the basement or ground floor be constructed as a kitchen "and other offices" and that this floor and one immediately above it each contain a salon running the entire length of the building. The building was to be constructed of brick and covered with a copper roof.[18]

Subsequently, on March 10, John Pell was paid from the governor's contingent fund the prize of $100 for the best plan "as approved by the committee." One month later C. B. Clusky received the same amount by legislative appropriation "for the best plan . . . for the Residence of the Governor."[19] It appears, therefore, that three architects—Pell, Clusky, and Norris—all had a part in the planning of the structure, not to mention Governor Schley and his building committee comprised of Augustus H. Kenan, Iverson Harris, and Charles D. Hammond. It is certain that both the style and the size of the structure, as well as its projected cost, expanded considerably in the two years following 1835. Ultimately the cost reached $50,000—from an original projected figure of $15,000.

Ultimately, the person most responsible for the final appearance of the Executive Mansion was its builder, Timothy Porter (1802–1876) of Farmington, Connecticut. Porter's connection with the enterprise probably originated through his brother-in-law, John C. Phelps, who was a resident of Milledgeville and whose brother Jonathan lived at Macon, where the latter died in 1836.[20] In August 1837 Governor Schley sent Porter a payment for certain materials to be purchased in New Haven or New York, and his letter urged him to be on hand as early as October. The governor was eager to get the work started before the meeting of the legislature. "The brick and lumber are now being delivered," he wrote, "and if you think the lime now being made in Washington County . . . will do for laying brick it can be furnished here at about $4 per barrel. . . . It is certainly not as good as the northern lime."[21]

Porter arrived early in October, bringing with him twenty-eight large boxes containing Redford Crown Glass, hardware, tools, mouldings, and other materials. Accompanying him were members of his family and twelve carpenters and bricklayers, all of whose transportation was paid by the governor.[22] It is not known how many local artisans, if any, were employed in the construction of the Mansion, but the number must have been insignificant. An inescapable conclusion is that the building was the product of Yankee workmanship and ingenuity. A careful observation of its structural details, particularly those above the rotunda, reveals a rare fidelity to accuracy and perfection and suggests the work of highly skilled shipwrights.

The house was ready for occupancy by the fall of 1838. Because the cost had exceeded the total appropriation by some $3,000, the fence and outbuildings were not constructed until 1840, at which time much of this work was done by convicts from the penitentiary. These accessories included stables, a carriage house, and bathing rooms, "all corresponding in style to the principal building." All of these out-buildings were destroyed by fire in November 1855 and rebuilt two years later.[23] In the meantime, in March 1851, a tornado swept across the town uprooting trees on the Mansion grounds and destroying the fence. It also tore off part of the copper roof and caused considerable water damage to the interior of the house.

The Mansion appears to have been inadequately furnished for a number of years following its occupation by governors' families. Governor Schley was able to purchase only a few pieces of simple mahogany furniture from

New York to supplement the simple furnishings transferred from Government House.[24] Many subsequent occupants of the Mansion brought much of their personal furniture with them. It was probably because of inadequate furnishings that the house saw only limited use for social functions in its early years. Ailing Governor Gilmer had barely become settled with proper furnishings in the new house before his second gubernatorial term expired in 1839. His successor, Governor Charles J. McDonald, held his inauguration ball at Huson's Hotel. The new mistress of the Mansion, who had recently become the governor's second wife, was the daughter of Judge Spencer Roane of Virginia. A woman of great charm and intellect, Mrs. McDonald used her persuasive powers in the interest of obtaining more appropriate furnishings for the house. As a result, all rooms on the middle floor were refurnished in elegant taste, including an Axminster carpet. Unfortunately, the white ground of this carpet was soiled and greatly damaged on the first night after it was installed when several hundred men attending the governor's levee walked in from a heavy rain with mud on their shoes.[25]

When Governor Cobb was making plans to move into the Mansion in 1851, he made enquiries about the furnishings and the general condition of the house. "[There] is a sufficiency of furniture to begin with," wrote back W.N. Mitchette, who listed "a good tea and dining set, two castors, 4 feather Beds and seven mattresses." He also noted some bureaus and bedsteads, knives, and forks. "I presume you had better bring with you your silver plate . . . the bed clothing is old. . . . the house wants refurnish[ing] very much."[26]

By the time Elizabeth Grisham Brown, the wife of Governor Joseph E. Brown, became mistress of the Mansion in 1857, she found the governor's house more than adequate for the life style to which she was accustomed. In a letter to her mother she described her abode in Milledgeville as "a very large house and well furnished with most things," although she lamented the absence of adequate silver and china, which every Mansion hostess seemed to find lacking. She listed the contents of the living quarters as consisting of seven feather beds, fourteen underbeds, nine large bedsteads, two small beds, a cradle crib and seven bureaus. Although neglecting to list the contents of the downstairs reception rooms, she described the size and arrangement of these compartments in great detail.

If the style of Mansion living to which the Browns had fallen heir proved unexpectedly genteel, this was not yet the condition of the Statehouse and its occupants. One visitor to the town in 1857 was disappointed in its general appearance, although he found the people he met there warm and hospitable. On observing the legislative session, he was astounded by the absence of parliamentary decorum in both the House and the Senate. During official sessions members were walking the floors, some were seated with their hats on, "and feet propped up, talking, laughing, joking, smoking, etc." It was said that a dozen legislators, mostly from the mountain counties, could neither read nor write.[27]

While the Statehouse itself had only recently undergone extensive repairs, its interior still lacked the appearance of distinction which its Gothic exterior suggested. The nine full-length portraits of early state and national leaders which adorned the walls of the Senate Chamber and Representative Hall were described by Sidney Andrews as "job work style." The two hallways which crossed in the center of the second floor were lined with peanut vendors and other plebeian appurtenances, all within earshot of the governor's office and those of other officials. The arsenal which stood just west of the Statehouse was described as "an inferior brick building . . . going to decay." This structure, as well as the magazine on the opposite side of the capitol, was totally lacking in any architectural style whatever. In refusing to vote a $200 annual salary for a keeper of the arsenal, one lawmaker stated that it was not worth twenty-five cents, and suggested that twenty dollars be appropriated for powder to blow it up. "It looks like the house down there," he said, pointing to one of the privies on the hillside east of the Statehouse.[28]

The repairs which the Mansion and the Statehouse had recently undergone were indirectly the result of a plebiscite held in 1855 in which the electorate reaffirmed the legislative decision made fifty years earlier to make the site on the Oconee the permanent seat of government. This reaffirmation came after years of controversy. The first expressions of dissatisfaction with the Milledgeville location had appeared as early as 1828, when it was suggested that the capital be moved to Macon, on the Ocmulgee River. A north Georgia legislator is said to have put the issue to rest at this time by declaring his conviction that all the oxen in Georgia could not drag it a single mile. However, as the state continued to grow and to shift its population center northward and westward, the issue was revived with increasing seriousness and vigor. By 1848 citizens of Macon appeared willing to construct new state facilities there without cost to the taxpayers. Soon bids came from other cities, including Griffin and Atlanta.[29] Dissatisfaction with Milledgeville centered on its inaccessibility and on its lack of adequate accommodations for visitors.

Criticisms of the town as the permanent seat of government made some impact upon the public mind after the first phase of railroad building had failed to relieve the isolation of the capital. Then in 1841 the Georgia Railroad from Augusta through Warrenton and Athens was completed, reaching northward toward DeKalb County. In 1843 the Central Railroad finished its line from Savannah to Macon, and two years later it was completed to Atlanta, where it joined the Western and Atlantic, a state-owned railroad running to Chattanooga. Other railroads later were to join at Atlanta, making it an important and growing transportation hub.

Milledgeville citizens were by no means oblivious to the significance of these developments to the future of their town. In 1838 the Baldwin grand jury stated that unless some countervailing movement was made, the metropolis of the state would be reduced to the condition of a deserted village. It suggested the building of a branch line to one of the principal railroads, either the Central road at Macon or the Georgia road at Warrenton. A meeting of citizens held in 1841 began a local railroad movement, but the Milledgeville and Gordon Railroad Company was not formed until five years later. Its stockholders were largely Milledgeville people. In the meantime, improved hack and stage lines were set up to run daily to Macon and to Warrenton. There was also a stage line to Gordon which passed over corduroy roads in swamp areas and through deep sand elsewhere, sometimes slowing travel to a half mile per hour.[30]

The Milledgeville–Gordon railroad, seventeen miles in length, was opened in 1851 after the Central Railroad Company, with whose line it joined, agreed to take stock equal to the cost of the iron for the tracks. This arrangement greatly relieved the financial burden of the community. The line had broad-gauged tracks, laid on stringers of pitch pine attached to cross ties of the same material. The tracks were "flange rails" rather than the T-rails then being installed on new roads. The passenger cars were fitted with cross-benches which had cushions but no backrest. A center isle permitted the passage of the conductor who collected fares. This official, addressed as "Captain," could stop the train at any time to eject non-paying riders, drunks, and rowdies.[31]

When the Milledgeville and Gordon Railroad Company began construction, the people of Putnam County, after making financial arrangements with the Central Railroad similar to those made by the Milledgeville group, started a venture to extend the railroad to Eatonton. This road was completed in 1853.[32] At the same time convict labor at the penitentiary constructed a spur track from the railroad at Milledgeville a few hundred yards into the prison yard. Part of the penitentiary now became the railroad shop for the state, which operated the Western & Atlantic Railroad.

In addition to these developments Milledgeville's leaders were making plans to connect their town to the Georgia Railroad at Warrenton and perhaps also to have this line extended from Milledgeville directly to Macon. Despite the uncooperative mood of Macon, whose interest lay in promoting roads to the south and west, the idea of a Warrenton railroad persisted throughout the remainder of the antebellum period. In 1860 a county referendum resulted in an overwhelming vote for a tax levy to support the Warrenton road. However, the advent of the Civil War brought these plans to a temporary halt.[33]

The railroad from Gordon to Milledgeville brought to the capital two immediate innovations: the first carload of natural ice arrived in town during the summer of 1860, having been brought from Savannah to which port it had been shipped from northern ice ponds—and Herty and Gesner's drug store was fitted with a soda fountain, the first ever installed in the town. Also, in the preceding year, a telegraph line from the capital to Macon was completed after long and frustrating negotiations during which a collection agent absconded with local subscription funds. As a result of this development in communication, the *Southern Recorder* announced that it would issue its paper daily during sessions of the legislature.[34] The increase in rail travel also made it possible after 1854 for the legislature to adjourn for the Christmas holidays and return to Milledgeville in January.

Despite the use of railroads for commerce and travel, steamboat traffic on the Oconee River did not abruptly end. A few enterprising boat-builders attempted to compete with railroads until long after the Civil War. In 1859 a 12-by-26–foot boat loaded with five hundred bales of cotton and capable of navigating in only three feet of water was reported plying the Oconee from Milledgeville to Dublin.[35]

Neither did the construction of the railroad end the agitation for the removal of the capital. The controversy reached a new peak in 1847 when a bill favoring the relocation of the capital was introduced in the legislature. Representative Nesbit of Bibb County was the most vocal opponent of Milledgeville's interests and during the debate which followed he engaged his oratorical talents in denigrating everything in and about the capital. Even the stately Executive Mansion did not escape his condemnation. He called it an "immense, half-finished and already dilapidated monument of folly," which did not deserve the few repairs to its outbuildings then being planned. He described the Statehouse as a "patched up" edifice which had a fair exterior but whose interior was in ruins. "Year after year appropriations have been made to . . . cover over its rents, fissures, and patchwork," said he, "and yet it looks like a riddle." He stated that the public records, books, and archives were unprotected "from blight, mildew and ruin." He was equally critical of the arsenal but saw no reason why the penitentiary should not remain in Milledgeville.[36] Other lawmakers charged that Milledgeville landlords took advantage of limited accommodations and overcharged for board and lodging.

Baldwin County Representative Iverson Harris met all these arguments with quiet logic. He promised the legislature that the railroad to Gordon would be completed in two years, and suggested that the legislature itself held the solution to the high cost of food and lodging: it should simply raise the *per diem* from four to five dollars. Harris also reminded the legislature that the state had a moral obligation to the people of Milledgeville, who had paid unusually high prices for residential lots because the town had been legally designated as the permanent capital. Probably the most effective argument, however, was his admonition that "the penitentiary follows the capital." Whoever obtained the capital would have to take the penitentiary along with it. Harris pointed out that the local merchants and artisans suffered from the competition of penitentiary labor. He also mentioned the large number of entire families of prison inmates who settled in the neighborhood of the prison in order to be near their convicted kin, and added that often these people resorted to crime for a livelihood or threw themselves upon local charity. Moreover, many convicts remained in the town after their release, some erecting shacks on the commons.[37] Milledgeville's spokesman went on to mention still other liabilities in being the seat of government, obviously it was not an unmixed blessing.

The debate continued. Those who favored the removal of the capital acquired new arguments in 1853 when the great fire destroyed a large part of the town's business section. The cost of board was higher than usual during the 1853–54 session of the legislature, and accommodations were inferior—one legislator claimed that he was given a camp bed to sleep on and a diet of bread and water. Landowners were reluctant to rebuild the burnt area because of the uncertainty of the capital's final location. Governor Cobb raised this issue in his address to the legislature in 1851. Because the controversy was unfair to the town and impeded its normal growth, the governor urged that the question be settled once and for all.[38]

A few businessmen, however, decided not to wait on the vicissitudes of politics to determine their future, and now began to rebuild. The most significant new structure, and one which best symbolized their faith in the future, was the Milledgeville Hotel, completed at a cost of $80,000. Constructed of brick and standing three stories high, it had a frontage of 210 feet on Wayne Street, and a wing of 180 feet which faced Greene Street and the Statehouse. Capable of lodging 300 guests, the building was described in 1855 as having "an iron balcony in front and a splendid piazza in the rear, and corridors running the whole length of the building." The barroom, barber shop, and billiard room were in the basement "and protected from an undesirable publicity." There were both public and private sitting rooms and parlors. On the premises were ample servants' rooms, a large kitchen, a smoke house, and store rooms. An Atlanta editor called it "the finest [hotel] that we have yet seen in the State" and stated that it had a more pleasing effect than the Statehouse. The hotel company was headed by Pleasant M. Compton, who soon announced the employment of "one of the best bands of music in the State" and his intention of giving two cotillion parties each week during the session of the legislature.[39] Although it suffered considerable damage by fire in 1872, the building survived, with numerous modifications, until 1970.

Of course, the new hotel was not the only accommodation in town. Other lodging houses available at this time included the Lafayette Hotel, McComb Hotel, Washington Hall (a frame building on the north side of West Hancock Street), the D. M. Edwards house, and the boarding houses of Peter J. Williams, Mary C. McComb, F. S. Harrison, Ezekiel S. Candler, James Haygood, Isaac Newell, and others.[40]

While boarding accommodations were increasing in number, however, they were also increasing in cost, and the legislature which assembled in the fall of 1854 was faced with a growing demand for removal. In response to Governor Cobb's suggestion that the matter finally be settled, a bill was introduced calling for the removal of the seat of government to Macon. It passed the House by a single vote. When it was considered by the Senate, Milledgeville's interests were eloquently defended by a group of senators from various sections of the state. As they completed their remarks, bouquets of flowers were showered on these senators by local women sitting in the balcony. But the opposition also had its say. Senator Moseley of Spalding County was Macon's principal non-resident sponsor. Upon receiving from the gallery a few audible manifestations of disapproval, the senator stated that he needed "no Dogwood blossoms and cedar from these ladies" to prompt him in his duty. He then launched forth on Macon's greater accessibility and its nearness to the population center of the state, and denounced the dilapidated condition of the Milledgeville Statehouse. The debate lasted until a late hour. As finally passed the bill provided that the question be placed on the ballot in the next general election and that those favoring removal be required to indicate on the ballot the city of their preference.[41] The latter clause had been added through the insistence of those who wished to have the capital moved to Atlanta.

The referendum, held in October 1855, was a complete victory for Milledgeville. Of the 84,326 who voted, more than 56 per cent favored no removal. Of those who favored removal, 34 per cent chose Atlanta, while Macon was the choice of only four per cent. In announcing these results, Governor Herschel V. Johnson recommended to the legislature that improvements on the Statehouse and Mansion be funded immediately so that this work could begin without delay. "Now that the [removal] question is put to rest, we may hope for the continued and certain advancement of our community in all the elements of permanent prosperity and happiness," wrote a local editor.[42]

Governor Johnson was one of only three governors who had resided in the Milledgeville community as a private citizen. Manifesting a keen interest in the improvement of the state's facilities in the town, he recommended not only that the Statehouse be repaired but also that it be enlarged, and that serious considerations be given to the construction of a new building. He also recommended that the twenty-acre square be graded, planted with shade trees, and enclosed by a substantial iron fence to replace the old wooden enclosure. The arsenal, the magazine, and the four church buildings on the square were all eyesores, he declared, and should be removed. He urged the construction of large cisterns on each side of the Statehouse and the purchase of a fire engine. The suggested expenditure for all these improvements was $125,000 to $150,000.[43]

Since architects estimated that it would cost almost $100,000 merely to remodel the Statehouse, and that a new structure would cost $1,000,000, the legislature refused to follow through on Johnson's major recommendations. It appropriated only $12,500 for repairs to the Statehouse and the Mansion and, in the following session, voted $2,200 for furniture for the latter building. A small appropriation for a keeper of the grounds was rejected.[44]

By utilizing convict labor and by drawing on his contingent fund to a total of $15,000, as well as by giving his personal supervision to the work, Governor Johnson was able to make the improvements which he most desired. Both the Statehouse and the Mansion were given an outside coating of soft red—almost pink—stucco, thus changing them for the first time from their original gray color. This choice of color for all state buildings may have been Governor Johnson's response to Henry Rootes Jackson's "The Red Old Hills of Georgia," which had been published in the preceding year. The color which he selected is not uncommon in the Milledgeville area, where white kaolin and red clay have blended. These buildings had the appearance of having grown out of the red soil, and their new color possessed a peculiar aesthetic quality which harmonized with their surroundings.

The interior of the Statehouse was replastered and repainted; the roof was given a covering of composition and rendered fireproof by a topping of pebble stones. The Mansion received the same treatment, except for the roof. Both the capitol square and the Mansion lot were graded and planted with elm trees and then enclosed with new wooden fences. Brick paving was laid on the streets bordering the north and west sides of the Statehouse Square, on Greene and Wayne streets. However, the governor was unable to remove from the square the wooden structures he found so unsightly.[45]

Thus it was not until the eve of the Civil War that public sentiment reluctantly registered a need to upgrade the state's facilities at Milledgeville and to give them an elegance and style befitting Georgia's new title as Empire State. With the exception of the Georgia Penitentiary, very little industrial activity had invaded the quiet seclusion of the community before 1860. The town's total manufacturing enterprises, exclusive of those carried on in the penitentiary, represented an invested capital of only $146,000, and these employed a total of only 123 men and seventy-nine women. Wages averaged but $200 annually. Manufacturing consisted of leather and leather goods, brick, furniture, wine, patent medicines, flour, meal, woolen and cotton cloth, and iron castings. The penitentiary produced a small number of more sophisticated products, such as steam engines and railroad cars.[46]

The principal manufacturing establishment in 1860 was the textile factory below Jarrett's Spring on North Wayne Street. It employed 130 operatives in a five-story brick building constructed in 1845. The water-powered Oconee Mill, built by Peter J. Williams in 1823, had been greatly enlarged and was now operated by Hugh Treanor with nine employees. Duffey, Perrons, and Company operated a small iron and brass foundry near the Central Depot, where they made such articles as syrup kettles, machinery for cotton gins and grist mills, and an assortment of ironware. Near Scottsboro, at Stevens Pottery, was the beginning of a brick and ceramic enterpise which, for a time after the Civil War, was the county's largest industry. It was also the harbinger of a multi-million-dollar clay industry which developed in the area after 1900.[47]

Contrary to what is generally believed, Southern industrial development did not originate with the Civil War or with the new departure movement of the postwar period. In this and other aspects of life the war and its aftermath simply speeded up processes which already were well under way.

The refinements in both economic and social life, then, were beginning to emerge in Milledgeville by the 1850s, when new rail connections with other parts of the state and a vote of confidence from the electorate seemed to assure the permanence of the capital.

Late Antebellum Life in the
Executive Mansion

During the years immediately preceding the Civil War the Executive Mansion was the center of the town's social life as well as the seat of the state's political power. The character of this life varied with the temperament of the executive family, for the governor's wife was largely responsible for its grace and style.

The sophistication of the wives of antebellum governors usually was adequate for the social demands required in the small community of Milledgeville. Occasionally they faced such problems as how to avoid offending those who could not be invited to an important function at the Mansion. Such a situation occurred in May 1843 when the daughter of Governor Charles J. McDonald was planning her wedding to Colonel Alexander Atkinson, an aide on her father's staff. Facing the problem of a guest list, Mrs. McDonald chose to invite only young people who were particular friends of the wedding couple. However, she was artful enough to send to a few close neighbors by oral messenger an invitation to a tea following the wedding. "[It is] very little form, I think, for the head of the state," complained one who had been overlooked.[1]

Such attention to informal civilties and etiquette as was paid by Mrs. McDonald and her predecessors at the Mansion came to a temporary halt later in the year when her husband left office and was succeeded for two terms by George W. Crawford, the only Whig in Georgia ever to hold the office of governor. Crawford found Milledgeville's people amiable, for many of them, like himself, possessed strong Whig convictions. (Having already served in Congress, the governor was a personal friend of such national Whig leaders as Henry Clay and Zachary Taylor, and became the latter's secretary of war in 1849.) During their stay in the Executive Mansion, the Crawfords were able to maintain a remarkable balance between fashionable decorum and rural simplicity. Mrs. Crawford was a person easily accepted as a neighbor by residents of the town in all ranks of life. For example, once when the first lady stopped in a local tavern to call upon the wife of world-famous geologist Sir Charles Lyell, the landlady easily made herself one of the party and entered into the conversation as if both distinguished ladies were her own guests. The woman even succeeded in turning the conversation into one embracing commonplace topics, including a detailed description of her method of soap-making from ashes and pork grease.[2]

In less than a decade the Executive Mansion would see a radically different life-style. No family who occupied the Mansion ever matched the ostentatious glitter of the Howell Cobbs, whose tenure of two years ended in November 1853. Part of that family's great wealth in land and slaves was at Hurricane plantation, a few miles north of Milledgeville. Here in 1852 were 150 slaves under the direction of an overseer. Cobb's brother-in-law, John Basil Lamar, served as steward over this and numerous other properties throughout the state which represented Zachariah Lamar's legacy to his remaining two children. Hurricane was primarily a cotton plantation, but it possessed 400 head of hogs and 100 head of cattle in addition to many sheep, mules, and horses.[3] From the proceeds of this establishment alone the Cobbs could live in unusual comfort.

In contrast to Governor Crawford's experience, Cobb found Milledgeville

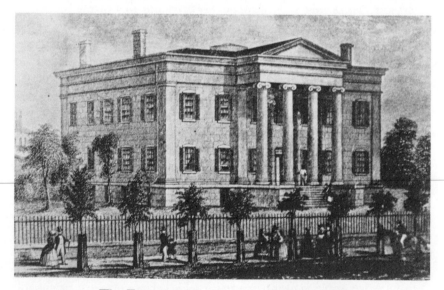

The Executive Mansion, completed in 1838

to be uncongenial, if not at times downright hostile to him. Although he had been elected by an overwhelming majority of the people and the legislature was controlled by his own Constitutional Union party, the town's leading paper, the *Federal Union*, strongly opposed him, as did nearly all statehouse officials, who had favored his opponent, ex-Governor McDonald.[4] A few local citizens even avoided him on the streets. Owing in part to these circumstances, Cobb disliked both the town and his job as governor and spent as little time in Milledgeville as possible.

For long periods Cobb remained at his home in Athens or made extended visits elsewhere, during which times Mrs. Cobb would often visit her relatives. Throughout most of the summer and fall of 1852 the Mansion was vacant, Mrs. Cobb being in Athens and the governor in New York and Washington. "The town is exceedingly dull," Cobb wrote to his wife on returning briefly to Milledgeville, "and I shall not trouble them with my company a moment longer than I am obliged to."[5]

Of course, extended absenteeism was not an unusual practice among statehouse officials in the antebellum period. The salary of the secretary of state and the surveyor general each was only $1600 a year—a sum which holders of these offices considered insufficient to require their full attention. In 1860 the surveyor general paid his office so little attention that it took in some $500 less in fees than his provided salary. During the preceding two years the secretary of state, E. P. Watkins, resided in Milledgeville only six months, spending the remainder of his time at his law practice in Atlanta. During his absence he kept no regular clerk on duty, the business of his office being discharged by other statehouse officials.[6]

Much of Cobb's absence from Georgia's capital, however, was not so much the result of a disregard for office as it was the product of his restless spirit and his driving urge to keep abreast of national political developments. He was perhaps the most consummate politician of all Georgia's antebellum governors, having begun his career at an early age. Immediately after graduating from the University of Georgia he had gone to Milledgeville to begin his political training. Here, in the winter of 1834–35, he observed legislative procedures and began the cultivation of older people who held political power. While in the capital he boarded with John Basil Lamar, a college acquaintance and fell in love with John's sister, Mary Ann, who was a student at the Scottsboro Academy. They were married in May 1835. Mary Ann's wealth at this time is estimated to have been at least $100,000.[7]

Although he had been admitted to the bar, Cobb never applied himself intensely to the practice of law, his overriding interest being politics. Becoming solicitor-general of his circuit at age 22, he was seldom out of public office again and almost never out of the public eye. He entered Congress in 1843, where he served four consecutive terms and became Speaker of the House. He opposed the Southern fire-eaters and supported the Compromise of 1850. It was largely on these issues that he was elected governor in 1851. As Georgia's chief executive he pursued and instituted certain reforms which clearly were a product of his deep and abiding Jacksonian heritage. After leaving the governorship he again was elected to Congress in 1855, still opposing the Southern extremists. In 1857 President Buchanan appointed him Secretary of the Treasury.

It is one of the great ironies of Cobb's career that he should have been made keeper of the nation's purse strings when the record of his own personal finances was one of an improvident if not irresponsible spendthrift. The president once found it necessary to rebuke Cobb when he learned that the secretary had rented a house in Washington at $1800 a year while he had not yet discharged his own personal obligations to creditors. Buchanan suggested that if Cobb was unable to pay off these obligations, perhaps his wealthy wife might be willing to do so. When Cobb left the treasury department at the end of 1860, the federal government was operating on a deficit and barely surviving on borrowed funds.[8]

Somewhat typical of the plantation-owner class with which he was identified, Cobb habitually lived beyond his means, always expecting the next crop of cotton to be larger than the preceding one and hence sufficient to cover a back-log of debts. Falling upon the hard times of the early 1840s Cobb found his financial problems gradually mounting. These were alleviated only after John Lamar gave him blank endorsements to draw upon the Lamar account—a privilege which Cobb often abused and which Lamar doubtless lived to regret: after 1840 most of the Cobb family expenditures appear to have come from the Lamar estate.[9]

The standard of Cobb's lavish style of living was demonstrated by the reception which he gave at the Executive Mansion in December 1851 following his inauguration. It was described as "the most showey [sic] and elegant [levee] . . . which had ever distinguished the Executive Mansion." In attendance was a large crowd of all ages, conditions, and shades of political sentiment. "The display of beauty and fashion was rich and attractive [and] would have graced the most stylish metropolitan entertainment."

There were "pyramids of snowy cakes, of spun candies, candied fruits, jellies, ice creams and blancmanges . . . turkeys, oysters, hams, salads, etc." However, for reasons difficult to explain, there was neither liquor nor wine—a condition which, wrote one observer, "was a departure from a reprehensible custom." [10]

In spite of this one exercise in moderation, Cobb's household records show ample outlays for such items as cognac, brandy, sherry, and ginger. At one time he ordered 1,000 cigars from Savannah. His personal account with Milledgeville merchants Beecher and Horne in one instance had mounted to nearly $900, and the purchase list included such items as alcoholic beverages, nuts, fruits, plug tobacco, cigars, sperm candles, and lamp oil, in addition to an assortment of groceries. [11]

Oysters and ice for the levee were sent by train from Savannah on the day of the reception. Food preparation and final arrangements were placed in the hands of a Macon confectioner who attended to these tasks after the food was placed in the Mansion kitchen. A fifty-pound cake stood in the center of the long table in the dining room, accompanied by two smaller cakes at either end of the table. There was an abundance of grapes and oranges, although the host had been able to locate neither apples nor bananas "that were fit to put on a gentleman's table." There were nearly 200 pounds of cakes of all varieties, all known assortments of candies, and twelve gallons of ice cream. The occasion was further enhanced by a group of musicians playing two violins, a bass viol, a clarinet, and a tambourine. [12]

Complementing Cobb's lavish style of entertainment were his social graces. His gregarious nature combined with his epicurean tastes to make him an exceptional host, and his wit made him a popular guest at all social events. Although he lacked intellectual depth and had no special talents, he was at least well rounded. Particularly fond of children, he delighted in taking his sons fishing with their friends or romping with them on a family outing. [13] It seems ironic that so genial a man found so little warmth in the state capital.

More ironic, however, was the life of Cobb's wife, Mary Ann, one of the most tragic women who ever filled the role of mistress at the Mansion. A gracious person who was popular with her neighbors, she had life-long friends in Milledgeville and never let her husband forget that it was her native community. She was a devout member of the local Baptist church, while Cobb was a borderline agnostic. She was in marked contrast to her husband in other ways as well, possessing a temperament generally inadequate for public social occasions. Typical of her demeanor was her failure to appear in the receiving line at the governor's inaugural reception in 1851.[14]

Only four of Mary Ann's seven children had survived to the end of her husband's gubernatorial term. Zacharias died in 1840; two other sons, Basil and Henry, died in Washington during the cold winter of 1848. Finally, in October 1852, she lost her younger daughter, Laura, who succumbed to "bowel complaint and teething" a few hours after her father reached her bedside. This loss complicated the mother's long-standing nervous condition and caused the governor to place her in the charge of a New York specialist.[15]

Always in delicate health and possessing irritating nervous sensibilities, Mrs. Cobb faced mounting problems with each succeeding year. Sorrows over family deaths, long periods of separation from her husband (whose marital fidelity she strongly questioned), and her heartbreak over his religious agnosticism must have contributed much to her condition. She also suffered great humiliation over the forced sale of some of Cobb's properties and the transfer of others to Lamar family members to protect them from foreclosures. Finally she lost her hold on reality and was given to screams of hysteria and despondence. She once wrote that she "needed to cry from morning to night."[16]

After her return from New York late in 1852, Mary Ann engaged her energies in the cultivation of a garden on the Mansion grounds, where she produced a great variety of spring and summer vegetables. During this period she was frequently seen trimming hedges and roses near the Mansion while keeping a watchful eye on one of her sons who was riding his pony bareback around the Mansion grounds. In July she returned to New York, where she stayed with her children at Saratoga Springs in the hope of recovering from her recurring physical and mental ills. Attending her were Lavinia Flagg and a governess for her children.[17]

This adventure was an unusual one for the Cobb children who previously had suffered the trauma of their mother's illness and the long absences from home of their father. During these periods their schooling often presented serious problems. From 1851 to the end of 1853 the Cobbs were patrons of private schools in Milledgeville, Athens, Macon, and Roswell. Beginning in June 1852 the two older boys, John and Lamar, were sent to Nathanael Pratt's School at Roswell, where Lamar developed an illness that required the presence of his parents for several days in August. As a result of his infirmity the youth developed an eye infection which necessitated his withdrawal from school. During that fall Howell and his sister, Mary Ann, were placed in school at Athens. Howell, the youngest son, had already developed some juvenile problems. "I don't think he will go to [Mr. Scudder's] school long before he will get the lash, if he has not got it already," John wrote to his mother from Roswell. In the same letter he admonished her to take good care of his game rooster.[18]

The schoolboy correspondence of brothers John, Lamar, and Howell must reflect the childhood experiences of many Milledgeville youth during this period. From home, Lamar wrote to his brother John that "Sister's rooster died not long ago [and] Howell's hen has got seven chickens. I have got your poney [sic] in town to ride. . . . Howell went out to the plantation with Uncle Bob in the wagon to carry some pigs." Later Howell reported a trip which Lamar made on his pony to the Scottsboro Female Academy, where he "gallented [sic] . . . Miss Ada Mitchell and Miss Fanny Williams."[19]

Such news surely was not calculated to temper the feeling of homesickness which John must have been experiencing at Roswell under the stern discipline of the headmaster there. "Tell Lamar that he had better mind how he is staying away from school, that he cannot catch up with me," wrote the young scholar to his father. "I am in the third book of Virgil and . . . I have started Greek."[20]

In the meantime Cobb had made preparations to leave Milledgeville and the governor's office. He found himself once again in debt and begging his brother-in-law to rescue him from financial embarrassment. "Our purse is entirely dry," he wrote. Mrs. Cobb's condition had not greatly improved. However, after leaving Milledgeville she bore four more children, one of whom died during the war soon after Mrs. Cobb's brother, Colonel John Basil Lamar, succumbed to a wound received during the fighting at South Mountain, Maryland, in 1862. By this time her three older sons had grown into men whom the war rapidly matured. These sons and their father all survived careers in the Confederate army.[21]

Cobb's successor in office was Herschel V. Johnson, who had moved to Milledgeville from Jefferson County. Both of these communities were Whig strongholds, and it was said that Johnson, a staunch Democrat, could not have been elected a justice-of-the-peace in either county. In order to pay for the education of his step-son and his wife's half-brother, he opened a law office in the capital, a move which apparently improved his political status.

Despite his party affiliation, local people accepted him with good grace and with all the pride normally shown a successful native son.[22]

Mrs. Johnson, a niece of former President James K. Polk, was an effective and popular first lady. To a vivid imagination and a lively intellect she added a fine command of brilliant language. It was said of her that "all gentlemen preferred her company to the most fascinating of belles." The younger female contingent of the town were quick to sense this situation and their reaction was often unkind to Mrs. Johnson. After one of her receptions, Sue Fort was moved to call the hostess "a great show . . . with her opera coat that she has had for 5 or 6 years" and which the young lady suggested was inappropriate for the occasion.[23]

In contrast to his sparkling and gracious wife, Governor Johnson was a stern and unsociable person. Yet he possessed a native beneficence and a tenderness of heart which those who knew him intimately never forgot. It was said of him that he had no superior in the eloquence of his public speaking. A scholarly man, he wrote with elegance and polish and with a flawless penmanship. His correspondence is replete with allusions to classical and modern philosophers. A newspaper editor said of him that he was the best proofreader he had ever known.

Nothing was so commonplace to Johnson that he could not invest it with charmed interest. He could lay brick as well as any skilled mason. Often he would leave the executive desk, go into the penitentiary, and instruct convicts in masonry construction. In the woodshop he would explain to them how to detect flaws in any part of a wagon, and likewise at the blacksmith's he would display a certain horseshoe and explain why it would not properly fit the animal's foot.[24]

In his operation of the executive office Johnson was equally astute and capable. To reduce the cost of printing he once asked the state printers to omit five or six lines of an enabling act clause which formed the preamble to each of several hundred acts to be printed, directing them instead to substitute "Be it enacted, etc." for each of these long preambles. When the printers remonstrated, he ordered them from his office.[25]

Johnson's levee at the Mansion in 1853 was described by a guest as being so unusually well attended that there was "neither eye room nor elbow room." The usual array of beauty and fashion graced this occasion, although some ladies were observed to be dressed in gowns which "once had colors but which had yielded to the touch of time and water." There were gay widows and sprightly widowers "buzzing, bumping in one incomparable but picturesque cmnibus." This observer noted "a piney woods plebeian" who, having eaten his fill from a well-laden table, repaired to an empty room and took a position before an elegant mirror. He then took from his pocket a jack-knife and applied it vigorously to his teeth while gazing at his image in the mirror with apparent satisfaction.

While the governor himself never partook of alcoholic beverages, he permitted them to be served at state social functions, and his levee was no exception. One member of the General Assembly pitched into the syllabub with the greatest of gusto, announcing to all bystanders that it was very good soup. "These levees, however much may be done to make them agreeable, are incorrigible bores," wrote the observer. He concluded that "the public convenience no less than the comfort of the Governor, requires that they be abolished."[26]

Rather than suffering extinction, however, the governor's levee appears to have grown into an intrenched tradition during the waning years of the pre-war period. Coming early in December, it was a fitting prelude to the Christmas season and provided to an otherwise dull community an excellent excuse for a full complement of social activities that brought to the town a long season of rare gaiety. One local belle spoke of Johnson's second levee as "one of the most pleasant," though by no means the most elegant, of the parties that she attended during the winter season of 1855. Conspicuous at this gathering were a number of families representing the laboring and artisan classes of the town. This may have been a reflection of Johnson's experiences as a self-made man, which gave him a great respect for the dignity of labor. Sue Fort noted "a great many factory people" there, and their unfashionable and sometimes gaudy attire drew some unkind comments. "You would have laughed if you had seen old blind Garrison's wife," she wrote to her sister. "Uncle Joe [Fannin] declares that she was painted. She was the gayest sight I ever saw."[27]

By no means did all the town's humbler citizens gain entrance into the Mansion for this occasion, though some of them did find a way to dine there without troubling themselves with the intricacies of social etiquette. These people, called "malcontents" for reasons which are not entirely clear, could be found standing in the darkness just outside the open windows of the basement dining room. One showed enterprise by fashioning a hook on the end of a long pole with which he removed whole hams and roasted turkeys from the table.

The round of minor social activities which preceded and followed the governor's inaugural festivities sorely taxed the wardrobes of many young women of the community. "Cousin Matt and Sally wore their handsome rose colored silks," wrote Sue Fort, "and [they had] braids across their head." Margaret Armstrong was described as nicely dressed, but "her face looked as it always does, you know her face is made by herself and there is no change day or night. . . . I was dressed in a black velvet basque and white tarleton skirt with bows on my head and [wore] white kid gloves." She reported that all the ladies received their share of attention at the governor's party—"at least enough to keep them in good humor."[28]

Among the minor social activities was a dance given by Mrs. Carnes on Jefferson Street in honor of her visiting nieces from Macon and Athens. Mrs. Daniel Tucker opened Lockerley Hall for "a splendid party with plenty of beaux and Champagne," wrote one.[29] There was always a military parade to be witnessed among these occasions, and at this time the governor reviewed the volunteers of Baldwin, Putnam, and Bibb counties. The review was held on Greene Street on the north side of the Statehouse. "A bevy of beautiful ladies crowded the windows and balconies of the Milledgeville Hotel near by." A dance followed in the evening. Participating in both of Governor Johnson's inaugurations was the battalion of cadets from the Georgia Military Institute at Marietta. About 100 in number, these cadets encamped near the Central Depot and attracted great interest. The military ball of December 1859 included a large number of visiting military units and was said to have been the gayest and most delightful group of young people ever assembled in Milledgeville. In that period each military company chose its own uniform, which was distinctive in color and style. One observer noted "25 or 30" different uniforms on the spacious dance floor of the Milledgeville Hotel.[30]

Such occasions were not without their share of social catastrophes. One visiting belle found herself socially ostracized by her companions for committing certain indiscretions. The offending girl's hostess suggested that she return to her home in Eatonton, which she did. "I hope she will not come [again] for she has made a name here that she will never get over," wrote one of her critics.[31]

Governor Johnson's successor in 1857 was Joseph Emerson Brown, who at age thirty-six had been elected governor as a dark horse from the hills of north Georgia. He was the only Milledgeville governor of the prewar era not identified with the cotton belt. While Brown became one of the most effective chief executives in the state's history and remained in office for nearly eight years, his arrival in Milledgeville was met by a degree of haughtiness on the part of many of the town's residents. Local tradition and folklore have dwelt more upon the parsimony of the governor and the commonplace artlessness of Mrs. Brown than upon their high moral rectitude and their worthy qualities of simple frugality and common sense. The unaffected grammar imputed to Mrs. Brown in most of these stories is hardly substantiated by the correspondence in her own handwriting which has survived—although the same cannot be said of some of Mrs. Brown's in-laws.

Elizabeth Grisham Brown shared her husband's penchant for thrift and frugality. She made a few significant references to the expenses of Mansion life. "Mr. Brown has hired a meat or every day cook at 75 cents a day and a boy to wait on the table and answer the bell at 25 dollars a month," she wrote, "and if Emma [who was ill with typhoid fever] does not get well soon we will have to hire a woman to wash and iron." She quoted the price of a pound of butter at forty cents, while cured ham and lard were twenty-five cents per pound. Beef and pork were selling at eight and ten cents, respectively, yet she considered these prices excessive. "I can hardly see how we can afford to live here," she wrote, yet she hoped there might be some recompense from the vegetable garden on the Mansion grounds. She also noted the existence of very comfortable outbuildings of all kinds. "[Yet] with all these things around me, I am lonesome," she confided, and she longed to be back at her old home in Canton.[32]

Mrs. Brown's simple life and frugal administration of the executive household, suggest that in her managerial talents she was a facsimile of the governor. Both were also Baptists and deeply religious. They allowed no alcoholic beverages to be brought into the Mansion at any time. This policy was adopted by Governor Jenkins who succeeded Brown in 1866.[33]

Governor Brown's first levee was well attended, but here ended the similarity between it and its immediate predecessors. There was no music other than an occasional song by small groups around the piano. As was customary, tables were loaded with an abundance of food, but most of this was prepared by Mrs. Brown with the assistance of her neighbors. "We had plenty of meat and bread left over for another [such occasion]," wrote Mrs. Brown to her mother. "This large house was crowded, I have never seen the like. . . . We found the material and got the baker to make $15 worth of cake for us, he baked for ten cents a pound, without iceing [sic] or trimming and I had more than as much more baked at home besides. Sweet cakes in abundance. . . . We sent to Savannah for fruits, candy, nuts, beef tongues, oysters, etc. . . . We set one table of meats and one of cakes, etc. . . . it was a splendid affair. We got to bed about two that night." She then thanked her mother for sending a box of preserves, the freight on which was less than she had expected. She deplored the high price of eggs, which she reported cost twenty-five cents in Tennessee plus express charges to Milledgeville.[34]

When they came to the capital in 1857 the Browns brought with them five children, four of whom were boys. Later two sons and another daughter were born. Shortly after the war the three younger boys died, two of whom had barely reached adulthood. After the death of the governor's mother during the latter part of the war, the governor's father, Mackey Brown (b. 1797) and his two spinster daughters came to Milledgeville and resided in the Mansion.[35] This extended family of twelve members was described in some detail by John Cobb's young wife, Lucy Barrow, who saw them in the summer of 1864.

You can't turn 'round without having some little deformed face peering at you from behind a corner. I never saw such an afflicted family. There is bleary-eyed Joe [Joseph Mackey Brown, who was elected governor in 1909 and again in 1912] . . . the most uncouth specimen I have ever met with; then comes Franklin Pierce (Mrs. Brown told me she had some big names among her children, Franklin Pierce and Charles McDonald) the poor little cripple with the crooked spine and the knot on his chest. *very* smart & *very* disgusting. Elijah comes next in the catalogue of afflictions, who is as his grandfather expressed it a little hard o' hearing—Sallie the baby [b. 1862] has a breaking out on her head which I believe to be scrofula & last and vilest of all is the negro nurse with a consumptive cough, & the most obsene [*sic*] looking scrofolous face I ever beheld. I avoid him as I would the plague. And the old man Brown! My conscience, how I dread him! But his old withered hanging jaws with their curious prying look. . . . Miss Nancy Jane, how can I describe her! Picture to yourself a face with jaws hanging . . . & lovely ringlets becoming a maid of 35, tall, gaunt figure of gurlish [*sic*] ways in perfect accordance with the ringlets. . . . The younger sister is Joseph's self in petticoats.[36]

These impressions doubtless were greatly influenced by deep prejudices which the aristocratic Cobb family bore toward Governor Brown as well as the fact that Cobb and Brown were at the time the bitterest of political enemies. Shortly after these lines were written, the Browns were in anguish at the death of the governor's brother, Colonel John M. Brown, age twenty-five, who was wounded near Atlanta on August 22, 1864, and brought to Milledgeville, where he died three days later. Prior to this his youngest brother, George, had died in Virginia, where three of Brown's brothers were serving the Confederacy. It was while standing by the bed of his dying brother that the governor was called upon to provide a defense of the capital against an enemy cavalry raid.[37] The Browns all were grief-stricken by these events, and the town was quick to offer them sympathy and consolation. Lucy Barrow Cobb may have regretted some of the harsh appraisals of the Browns which she had made earlier.

In almost every aspect of his personal and political affections, Brown stood in towering contrast to Howell Cobb. Some of Brown's best friends in Milledgeville had been Cobb's worst enemies. The *Southern Recorder* opposed Governor Brown's wartime measures, while the *Confederate Union* approved them. Moreover, unlike Cobb, Brown had only a modest slaveholding. According to his tax returns of 1860, the governor had five slaves in Milledgeville and eight in Cherokee County, and his total taxable property was only $3,600. By the end of the war he had acquired plantations in Dooly and Lee counties, as well as additional landholdings in the Canton area of North Georgia, but at the time of their emancipation his slaves numbered only twenty—the largest number he had ever possessed.[38]

Like her husband, Mrs. Brown disliked the idea of relying heavily upon the services of numerous slaves. She believed that having slaves around the house discouraged her children from learning to perform manual labor and also tended to corrupt their morals. Slaves which the Browns brought to Milledgeville were somewhat advanced in years; they performed light domestic work and cultivated a vegetable garden. On occasions when the Browns spent long periods of time in North Georgia, the Mansion was left in charge of a trusted black retainer named Jim. In July 1861 James A. Green wrote to the governor in Canton to inform him of Jim's death. "We done all we could for the old man," wrote Green. "I hired Mr. Gentry to Stay at the Mansion with him, and after he was took away we collected all the keys we could find. . . . The outside door under the steps leading into the basement is not locked. We could not find any key to lock it."[39]

Much of Brown's absence from Milledgeville was a result of his intense interest in the efficient operation of the state-owned W. & A. Railroad—an interest which, in the mind of the governor, placed him in the role of a railroad president. He was extremely conscientious in fulfilling this trust. In fact, he was so successful in the management of the road's operations that by 1860 it was earning the state a profit of a half million dollars annually. Brown and his superintendent, John W. Lewis, were accused of walking the tracks to pick up loose coal which had dropped from the cars. This facetious charge was an only slightly over-stated illustration of Brown's frugal habits and his business acumen as he gave his attention to the smallest of business and financial details.

Brown demanded, and usually received, every cent of value which others were obligated to render—a rule that applied to his personal as well as to his public relationships. Once he refused to pay $300 to a contractor for repairs made on his house until the job was done "in a workmanlike manner," as the contract stated. "The whole job is exceedingly rough," he complained. "Some of the closet doors are not worth hanging. . . . Some are so tight they will not shut while others are so loose they do not fit. . . . The columns are not set upon any basement but upon the floor. The brick pillars under the house will have to be built over. . . . In several other particulars too tedious to mention the contract has not been complied with."[40]

Soon after the war Brown had an exchange of correspondence with Mrs. Richard M. Orme, the wife of a local editor who had opposed his war-time measures. In question was the payment of an account for the tutoring of the governor's son. Joseph Mackey Brown had attended her school for four months during the spring and summer of 1865 under an agreement by which she was to be paid $100 in Confederate Treasury notes. Before the end of the term, at which time payment was due, the war had ended and Confederate money had become worthless. Mrs. Orme insisted that she be paid $35 in gold or $45 in greenbacks. "You are entitled to what you agreed to take and I agreed to give—no more—no less," replied Brown. "The fact that Mr. Orme has to support a large family or that provisions [now] can only be purchased with gold or greenbacks is no reason why I should pay, or you should charge, what I did not agree to give . . . nor can that fact make $100 in Confederate notes worth $35 in gold." The governor finally agreed to pay in gold or greenbacks, including interest, what the Confederate money would have brought in the market at any time from the day his son entered her school to the day the term ended.[41] Thus the amount which Mrs. Orme received was exceedingly meagre in comparison to the services which she must have rendered.

Possessing such extraordinary talents for the careful conservation of resources, if also for some degree of parsimony, the Browns made ideal tenants of the Mansion during the years of austerity during the Civil War. Social functions were limited in number, simple in style, and without needless display of effort.

Despite General Sherman's brief occupancy of it, the Mansion survived the war unscathed although it never recaptured during Reconstruction the distinction which it had earned during the 1850s. After the last of the Milledgeville governors had closed its doors and its furnishings were gone, the building fell upon evil days. At one time it was used briefly as a flophouse where a traveler might spend the night for twenty-five cents. Later it became a college dormitory. It was destined, however, to become once again the center of the town's social life. This phase of its destiny began more than a quarter of a century after the war, when it became the official residence of college presidents.

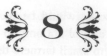

8

Secession and Wartime Activities

If we follow traditional guidelines and consider a holding of twenty slaves as the dividing line between farmers and planters, there were sixty-five of the latter in Baldwin County in 1860. Of a total of 4,867 slaves on the county's census for that year, 2,600 were owned by these planters who had an average of approximately forty slaves each. Four individuals—Nathan Hawkins, John Basil Lamar, William Sanford, and Thomas Humphries—each held over one hundred. Twelve others each owned over fifty. In addition there were 437 farmers who each held fewer than twenty slaves; the total holdings of this group amounted to 2,267, or slightly over five slaves for each one. Thus the average slaveowner might be said to have held two families totaling approximately ten slaves. Of course, the number of white families who owned no slaves at all far outnumbered those who did.[1]

Contrary to what is generally believed, the ownership of slaves played an insignificant role in determing individual attitudes toward secession. This issue and the controversy leading to it centered in the growing opposition in the North to the expansion of slavery into the territories, a policy which would have discriminated against the South. Southerners would have developed much of the same attitude they held toward certain Northern politicians had they been deprived of the right of taking any other kind of property into the territories. There was one important difference, however. The prohibition of slavery in the territories would eventually have resulted in the abolition of slavery everywhere. What might result if the black man were set free in a white man's country was difficult for the white Southerner to contemplate dispassionately.

As the controversy moved toward a climax in the movement for secession, Governor Joseph E. Brown added a fresh note to the South's pro-slavery argument. If the Negroes should be set free and remain in the South, he reasoned, they would be in direct competition with thousands of slaveless white men and would demand (and eventually obtain) economic and political equality with them. Many small white freeholders would be reduced to the status of tenant farmers. The inevitable consequence, at least on the lower levels of the social scale, would be the amalgamation of the races. This logic carried a special appeal not only to the people of Brown's native northern Georgia, but also to small farmers throughout the South.

When the Republican party wrote its platform for the 1860 presidential campaign, many Southerners were bewildered. The platform declared not only that slavery was illegal in the territories but also that neither Congress nor any other power could make it legal there. The platform contained nothing which indicated that Lincoln hoped to attract the vote of a single Southerner. Had Lincoln's opponents remained a solid block, it is possible that he might have been defeated, but his opposition was split into three separate splinters. The largest of these factions nominated Stephen A. Douglas of Illinois as president, and Herschel V. Johnson of Georgia as vice-president. Had Southerners been blessed with reasonable foresight, they would have given full support to the Douglas-Johnson ticket, for had this ticket won, Johnson would have succeeded to the presidency when Douglas died in 1861. In addition to sparing the country a devastating and bloody conflict, they would have placed the federal government in the hands of a Southerner who was vitally interested in preserving the Union.

Lincoln's election was followed in December by the secession of South Carolina. This action increased tensions elsewhere. In Milledgeville the two local volunteer companies—the Baldwin Blues and the Governor's Horse Guards—tendered their services to the mayor. Subsequently they were authorized to act as a special patrol and cautioned to be particularly careful to see that all blacks observed the curfew. Two assistant marshals were appointed, and a number of Colt's repeaters were acquired. The governor increased the size of the Statehouse Guard.[2]

Such precautions proved expedient, for throughout the following three months several unsolved acts of vandalism and arson broke out in the town. Ropes fixed to buckets at the public wells were cut and had to be replaced with chains. The academy building was damaged, and on the night of February 26, a fire destroyed the courthouse and many of its records. While the exact cause of this fire was never positively determined, all evidence pointed to arson.[3] It was in an atmosphere of increasing tension that the Secession Convention met in Milledgeville on January 16, 1861.

Milledgeville had never before hosted such a large number of people at a political gathering, nor had it ever witnessed such excitement. In addition to 300 state delegates with voting rights, observers from other states were given seats, among whom were Robert Barnwell Rhett of South Carolina,

Edmund Ruffin of Virginia, and Judge W. L. Harris of Mississippi. "Crowds and crowds of people have gone to Milledgeville," wrote Mary Nisbet of Macon. "Ten cars went off from here Tuesday, [and] as many Wednesday." Admitting that she had "never been able to endure Milledgeville for a longer period than a few hours," she planned to go there on Saturday to witness the final act of the state's separation from the Union.[4]

Two hours in advance of the second day's meeting the galleries and lobbies of the Statehouse were crowded, and many delegates found their seats taken by spectators. On Friday the convention adopted the closed door rule, barring not only spectators but newspaper reporters as well. One reason given for this action was the need to eliminate the loud applause of spectators to speeches and remarks made by pro-secession delegates. Unable to occupy seats in the galleries, visitors thronged the streets, and street corners were monopolized by impromptu speakers.[5]

By Friday afternoon the outcome of the voting was easily predictable, and the celebration of the state's independence began that evening. It continued through Saturday, when formal voting by the delegates was completed. The jubilation now took such forms as the firing of cannon, ringing of church bells, serenades, a torchlight parade, and the illumination of private residences.

There were many people, however, who did not rejoice. Herschel V. Johnson remained in his room and paced the floor in anguish. He stated that it was the saddest day of his life. Mrs. Tomlinson Fort, now two years a widow and with a mother's perception, saw visions of a martial struggle into which her three sons would inexorably be drawn. While her twenty-one-year-old Tom was out leading a torchlight parade, Mrs. Fort sat brooding in a darkened room. Other families, as well as the local press, were divided. The *Southern Recorder* opposed secession while the *Federal Union* favored it.[6]

Baldwin County's three delegates to the convention were Lucilius Briscoe, a thirty-one-year-old lawyer and owner of two slaves; Augustus H. Kenan, also a lawyer and owner of three slaves; and Dr. Samuel G. White, age thirty-six. White, a Milledgeville physician, was owner of a large plantation in the Salem community on which sixty-five slaves were working. Briscoe—like ex-governor Johnson, for whom he once had served as executive secretary—was an outright Unionist. As a former member of both branches of the legislature, his sentiments were well known. Kenan, who later was elected to the Confederate Congress, was a moderate secessionist, believing that the Southern states should secede only by cooperative action and as one body. White was known as an independent secessionist, and of the three he was the only one who might be called a fire-eater. It can be assumed that these three men represented fairly accurately the community's varying sentiments on the basic issue of secession.[7] Once separation from the Union was accomplished and there was no turning back, local people appeared to forget their differences. All worked for unity and final victory.

The contribution of Milledgeville women to war efforts was tremendous. Despite her misgivings about secession, Mrs. Tomlinson Fort became a prominent organizer of local preparations. With the help of Wilkes Flagg and the labor of only eight slaves, she ran the Fort plantation, now the family's principal source of income. She maintained a steady and cheerful correspondence with her three sons in Confederate service, but she fretted because her youngest did not have a commission. "Captain Beck's company left yesterday," she wrote to one of her older sons. "John is second corporal, a low place but better than private. I feel badly . . . and cannot write you a long letter. . . . I have worked hard to get the company off. . . . Today is the first day the town is deserted." In the pursuit of a commission for John, she had enlisted the aid not only of members of her family but also of some of Dr. Fort's old political friends as well.[8]

Lieutenant Tom Fort was discouraged by the slowness of his own military promotion. He was seriously considering resigning from the army to become a sutler when his mother intervened. "If it is considered dishonorable in any way don't let him touch it," she wrote to her son George, who was a surgeon in northern Virginia. Making money was all very well, she continued, but many other things were far more important.[9]

The Fort boys eventually received the promotions they sought, and their mother hoped that this might lessen the danger to which army life subjected them. "I hope you will get into some house and not stay in a tent," she wrote to George, and she suggested that they should get a transfer to the Georgia or South Carolina coast where they might escape the hazards of both the climate and the fighting in Virginia. Yet, while constantly reminding them to guard their health, she also cautioned them never to shirk a responsibility. "Learn all you can in your business, if others neglect their duty don't you follow their example," she wrote. On hearing of Tom's penchant for profanity, she rebuked him with unmitigated severity. "I have never heard you swear," she wrote, "but Kate tells me now that a lady wrote her that you are the most profane man in your regiment. . . . It is the vice of a low vagabond and not a gentleman. . . . It is a habit you have acquired in the army. . . . [I] beg you to cease the low sinful habit unbecoming your name and family."[10]

Mrs. Fort supplied her sons constantly with extra food. Her custom was to send a box of food by soldiers returning from furlough. Heavier articles such as blankets, shoes, clothing, and even an occasional mattress were sent by express. Once John remonstrated and asked his mother not to send the two blankets which she mentioned. "In the first place, I do not need them and in the second place I could not transport them," he wrote, "for if we made a hasty retreat at any time I may be obliged to leave behind or burn up some of my baggage."[11] John's correspondence suggests unusual literary gifts, but he often disquieted his mother by needlessly dwelling upon the dangers and privations of army life in which he was happy to be a participant. After writing about awakening one morning to find frost in his hair, John received from his mother a knitted woolen nightcap.

In early July a Soldiers Relief Society was organized by Mrs. Fort at her home on Greene Street, where one of the few sewing machines of the town was available. Within a month this organization had made 1,500 garments for Baldwin volunteers. At the end of six months some $6,000 had been raised and expended. Carpets from Phi Delta Hall at Oglethorpe University were donated for conversion into blankets.[12] Now known as the Ladies Aid Society, these women for a time made upwards of 3,000 "buck and ball" cartridges each day. Made for muzzle-loading rifles, these cartridges consisted of one round ball and three buckshot enclosed in small paper envelopes. The powder, measured for each load and wrapped in waterproof paper, was provided elsewhere.[13]

Outfitting the army became a townwide operation. Complete uniforms were made in Milledgeville on the primitive "putting out" system. The Milledgeville Manufacturing Company wove the cloth, which was cut to pattern at the penitentiary, and then sewed and finished by women in their homes. Beginning in the summer of 1862, the penitentiary operated an armory under the direction of Peter Jones, former armorer at Harper's Ferry; this shop soon was turning out several hundred rifles and other arms each month. Tents were also made at the penitentiary. The firm of R. C. Cyphers and S. J. Kidd manufactured oilcloth overcoats with large detachable capes, and also made canvas leggings, havelocks, and oilcloth blankets lined with wool or cotton. The firm of Waitzfelder and Company which had a government contract for army clothing, paid out annually $25,000 for sewing alone.[14]

When the government took over the responsibility of supplying uniforms and accessories after the first year, the women's war-time work was modified. The management of convalescent homes, nursing, and similar activities became predominant. Since Milledgeville was not on a main rail line, no Wayside Home was established in the capital until 1865, after the town and the countryside had been impoverished by Sherman's march.[15]

The most effective and tireless of the town's women in promoting nursing and related activities was a former schoolteacher, Mrs. C. C. Mitchell. After the Battle of Manassas she went to Richmond and offered her services as a nurse, in which occupation she became highly skilled. She returned to Milledgeville only after her son, Herbert P. Mitchell, who had been a medical student in Baltimore, was killed at Chancellorsville. After the fighting at Chattanooga, Mrs. Mitchell collected from her neighbors both money and supplies for a Confederate hospital in Atlanta. She went there with several servants to aid in that enterprise, taking with her such articles as paper fans made by local school children and fresh vegetables from the school garden of Carrie Fair.[16]

Mrs. Mitchell arranged numerous concerts and other benefit attractions, usually held at Newell's Hall. These were organized for a wide range of worthy causes. Once on a cold and gloomy evening she raised $110 for the benefit of "the Atlanta exiles" who had come to the capital in advance of Sherman's invasion. On another occasion she raised money for the relief of the town's poor. She found time to have enclosed with a fence the grave of Philip Gurlinger, a foreigner who died in the service of the Baldwin Blues. She also enlisted the help of the wife of a former governor of Maryland, then a refugee in Milledgeville, "for the benefit of barefoot soldiers."[17]

As Sherman moved southward from Chattanooga and deep into northern Georgia, the women of Milledgeville were called upon to organize a hospital to accommodate 100 wounded soldiers. Subsequently, on September 26, 1863, eighty-five convalescent soldiers arrived by train. The Ladies Aid Society secured the use of the two academy buildings near the penitentiary. Later they acquired the armory belonging to the Baldwin Blues and some empty store rooms, all on South Wayne Street. Merchants contributed cloth, mattresses, and other materials, while food supplies were provided by the municipal government.[18]

In July of 1864, just before the fall of Atlanta to Sherman, Governor Brown ordered the hospital for the state militia removed from Atlanta to Milledgeville, where it became an adjunct to the original hospital. Now enlarged and called the Brown Hospital, it was staffed by eleven surgeons and a number of volunteer nurses. Tents erected on the south side of Penitentiary Square took care of an overflow of patients. Newell's Hall on South Wayne Street was also acquired. As the military situation around Atlanta deteriorated during the summer of 1864, the Brown Hospital was suspended. On September 12 all patients who were able to bear arms were ordered to the front while the others were sent home.[19] The Confederate Hospital on Penitentiary Square, often referred to as the Stout Hospital, continued to function under Confederate authority.

Before its requisition for hospital use, Newell's Hall had been a center for the town's social life where musical performances, charades, tableaus, concerts, and social dances were held. Wartime gloom appeared to have no effect on the number of such events in the town. In 1863 the annual May festival, held as usual on the Statehouse Square, was well attended and pronounced a great success—although one observer noted that the rude and noisy crowd, "combined with the gobbling of a few silly geese," made it impossible either to see or to hear much that transpired. After the main event the young people secured a band and retired to Representative Hall, where they danced until nightfall.[20]

While the tide of war advanced and Sherman's legions brought the realities of the conflict nearer to the state's capital, young women of the town enacted their feminine role with remarkable fidelity to the standards of that age. Anna Maria Green recorded in her diary the major events of the period and often confided her intimate reflections during those days of turmoil. Yet throughout her entire journal it is apparent that the only real interest of her schoolgirl heart was the young men in Confederate uniform who moved in and out of Milledgeville and who touched her own personal life in various ways. She developed a serious romantic interest in four of these men in as many years, but a larger number stood very near the periphery of her amorous circle. One of the latter was Dr. William Gesner, an official of the Confederate Ordinance Department. Gesner, whose proposal of marriage she rejected, was a widower with two small children.

Apparently Anna Maria's interests were directed chiefly toward officers—at least, if she ever became infatuated with a private, she never bothered to mention him. During the great excitement preceding Sherman's entrance into Milledgeville, she confided to her journal that her visit into town from her home in Midway had not been so satisfactory as she had hoped. "I do not think I left a very pleasant impression upon either . . . Captain Darling or Lieut. Ketner," she wrote.[21]

Rank-and-file solders, far more frequently than officers, were ill prepared to accept any kind of social opportunity. Because of their ragged and vermin-infested clothing and the unsanitary style of camp life, they were inclined to shun the presence of women. Yet, despite their sensitivity to these matters, privates often were surprised to find that many young women were eager to overlook their tattered clothing and lack of personal grooming, for they were inclined to equate raggedness, hunger, and dirt with bravery and personal sacrifice. In fact, knowledge of a soldier's slowness to volunteer, or his identification in any way with a needless military defeat, could be far more disastrous to his social acceptability than his personal appearance. Once a Milledgeville girl invited a soldier to attend a dance, whereupon he declined with the excuse that he had nothing suitable to wear. She then offered to provide him with some woolen jeans. Later, when he told her that the valise containing his clothing had been lost at Missionary Ridge, she withdrew her invitation. "No one who ran from Missionary Ridge can wear Sue Woodall's jeans," she explained.[22]

Casting a smile in the direction of soldiers, even though sometimes contrived, was an acceptable practice among single young ladies. However such flirting was considered highly improper by young matrons whose marital status denied them such indulgences. "Miss Mary Adams flirts with every soldier that comes and is getting to be quite adept in the art," wrote Lucy Barrow Cobb, who was staying at the McKinley plantation. Lucy's own talents for entertaining young men in gray uniforms were extremely ladylike and refined. Raised in Athens and educated in the best traditions of the young lady's seminary, Lucy was an accomplished performer at the piano. It was Lucy's custom to balance a few Confederate ballads with a number of jigs, polkas, and marches. Indeed, wherever young couples gathered, piano music and singing prevailed. The more popular war ballads included "Who Will Care for Mother Now," "Home Sweet Home," "Nellie Gray," "Just Before the Battle, Mother," and "The Girl I Left Behind Me."[23] However, because these songs reminded one of the closeness of death and awakened nostalgic memories of home, often bringing tears to the cheeks of homesick youth, young women of perception soon learned to emphasize the playing of martial music instead.

Milledgeville was noted for the hospitality it dispensed to soldiers at home on leave and to hundreds of others who passed through the town. Not even the scarcity of food seemed to slacken the pace of social life in which the town's youth indulged. One girl stated that "if one of our boys comes home . . . we would run the gauntlet and boil syrup and have a candy pulling." Once a group of escaped Federal prisoners, dressed in gray uniforms and claiming to be Confederate soldiers on furlough, were treated with unusual hospitality by the citizens, who even shared with them their meagre rations.[24]

The town experienced almost as much hunger and privation during the war as it did in the period which followed. As soon as the war began, wheat bread almost immediately became difficult to obtain. In the fall of 1861 a local bakery was advertising "a new corn bread at 10 cents a loaf." During the legislative session then in progress a large number of beggars—mostly boys too young for military service—were found on the streets. They were a particular annoyance in the Statehouse and on the streets leading to it. The marshal finally was instructed to arrest them and place them in the guardhouse.

The inadequacy of firewood was a particular problem in some families, the most needy of which were supplied by municipal assistance. Many more families felt the effects of the shortage of food supplies. Early in 1863 sixty families were on the town's needy list. F. L. Brantley, a miller, agreed to grind donated wheat into flour for distribution to these families. In December of that year the Ladies Aid Society attempted their last Christmas buffet supper. Although it succeeded in raising funds for soldiers' relief, the repast itself was a catastrophe. The food was placed on one long table, and "after the floodgate was lifted, . . . in two minutes not a crumb remained." Many who had paid their fee went away unfed.[25] Thereafter, instead of serving food in buffet style, they learned to measure it out and serve it on individual plates.

Some basis for estimating the actual extent of hunger in this period may be found in an incident which occurred on April 10, 1863. While much of the town was attending Good Friday services at St. Stephen's Church, a hungry mob of citizens broke into stores and warehouses, pillaging them for food and other articles which were in short supply. The mayor, councilmen, and local police looked on in utter helplessness and later were either unwilling or unable to make arrests and bring the rioters to trial. As a result, a detachment of state militia was dispatched to the scene to make arrests.[26]

The cause of this food riot—as similar outbreaks in Macon and Atlanta were called—was a combination of several factors. While food and other commodities were scarce, merchants had taken advantage of inflation by overvaluing their inventories and charging exorbitant retail prices. Also the General Assembly was in session, and local hotels and taverns had bought up all surplus food supplies in the neighborhood. The act which triggered the riot was a charge made by Judge Iverson Harris to the grand jury in which he made an emotional reference to "speculators and extortioners" who were robbing the destitute wives and children of Confederate soldiers. Harris later repented this rashness and appeared on the streets to make another speech in which he condemned the riot as an "outrageous violation of the law" and urged the end of such behavior.[27]

By the end of 1863, as problems mounted on the home front, the military aspects of the war were growing more acute. When the conflict had begun, Georgia's militia system had been largely a paper organization consisting of eight divisions, each having two brigades. In the early 1850s the system had been in such chaos that Governor George W. Towns had advocated its total abolition and the substitution of volunteer companies upon which the state might rely for meeting any crisis. Ten years later, on the eve of the state's greatest crisis, no basic improvements had been made. In 1860 Major General John W. A. Sanford, who commanded the Third Division, complained to Governor Brown of its deplorable condition as to organization and equipment. Explaining that the division was largely without officers, he renewed the plea made a decade earlier that volunteer companies be substituted and that the state provide their equipment. Already volunteer companies were enjoying wide acceptance. Forty-five new companies, including the Governor's Horse Guards at Milledgeville, were incorporated by the legislature in 1859.[28]

Although the legislature agreed to appropriate money for arming and equipping volunteer companies and making them subject to the governor's call, the old militia laws remained on the books.[29] For all practical purposes the militia system was paralyzed by the Confederate Conscription Act of 1862, yet Governor Brown was determined to have one. Independent of Confederate control, the militia provided Brown with the only instrument by which he could justify his title as commander-in-chief of the state's military forces. Known by hardened veterans as "Joe Brown's Pets," the Georgia militia was made up of a rag-tag group of youth and old men who were just outside of the ever-expanding perimeter of the Confederate draft.

Further inroads upon the residual manpower of the state were made by the Confederacy late in 1863 when the Georgia State Guard was created. Commanded by Howell Cobb, its authorized strength was 8,000 men, who were to be enrolled expressly for local defense. This organization lasted only a few months and was succeeded by the Georgia Reserve Force, which had its headquarters at Macon. The latter, comprised of all able-bodied men between the ages of seventeen and eighteen and between forty-five and fifty, was to fight only within the limits of the state. Once again it was Howell Cobb, Brown's long-time political and personal enemy and now a major general, who was ordered by Richmond authorities to raise this new force. Brown placed numerous obstacles in the way of Cobb's enrollment of officers, such as unusually liberal exemption laws under which one could easily disquality himself.

It was the local volunteer company which bore the burden of the early months of the war and provided the training and experience later imparted to new cadres. Three such units existed in Baldwin County at the time the state seceded. The oldest of these was the Baldwin Blues, organized in 1848 by William Steele, Clerk of the Superior Court, and by William A. Harris, who had just returned from the Mexican War. This company was formally incorporated in 1858. The other companies were the Governor's Horse Guards, under Captain Charles DuBignon, and the Black Springs Rifles, under Captain Thomas W. White. Formed in that year were two additional groups called the Troup Artillery, under Captain Benjamin Beck, and the University Guards, comprised of students and alumni of Oglethorpe University.[30] Also formed at Milledgeville in March 1861 were companies H and I of a single regiment of state troops known as the First Georgia Regulars.

The University Guards was the first local company whose organization stemmed directly from the excitement of secession. When that event occurred students began immediately to withdraw from the university and to volunteer for Confederate service. On February 24 about fifty students met and formed the company. Governor Brown promised to arm them from state arsenals, but he refused to disrupt their studies by ordering them into service away from Milledgeville.[31] Despite the governor's orders to exempt Oglethorpe students from military duty, the exodus from the campus continued. Many students such as Sidney Lanier, returned home and entered volunteer units which carried no prohibitions against service outside the state. Because of this situation the trustees decided to end the term two months ahead of schedule.

Many of the faculty displayed as much zeal for war as the students. Professor Nathanael A. Pratt proceeded to organize another company, called the Jordan Grays, and became its captain. Dr. James Woodrow enlisted as a private. However, both men were soon detached for work in ordinance and supply, where their superior scientific skills could be utilized. The university struggled through the 1862–63 academic year with both volunteering and military conscription eroding its student rolls; then it closed for the duration of the war. It operated only briefly after the conflict was over.[32]

A number of additional volunteer companies were formed before the end of 1861. These included the Milledgeville Grays, the Oconee Volunteers, the Myrick Volunteers, the Independent Volunteers, and the Baldwin Volunteers. After 1862 the Baldwin Cavalry and the Georgia Guards came into existence, their ranks being filled largely by conscripts. Formed in 1863 were the Capital Guards, the Milledgeville Guards, and the Armory Guards. The latter three were organized exclusively for local defense, and their ranks were filled by men excluded from the draft.[33]

Some local companies enrolled men from adjoining counties and even a few from other states, while a number of Baldwin men enlisted in other than home units. For example, the Oconee Grays was made up of Baldwin and Wilkinson County youth with the latter predominating. The company was commanded by John Shinholster. Richard L. Harris, son of Judge Iverson Harris, was elected captain of a Louisiana company. John W. A. Sanford became colonel of an Alabama regiment. In 1862 Tomlinson Fort, Jr., was captain of a company which was made up entirely of men from Atlanta and Fulton County.

While the surplus officer material flowed over into other units, men resigned with reluctance the privilege of serving with their own relatives and friends. There was a tendency for local men to form a group when offering their services to other units. The First Georgia Regulars, for example, had among its officers Miller Grieve, Jr., Marshall deGraffenreid, Tomlinson and John P. Fort, Pierce Horne, William A. (Rough) Williams, and Lewis H. Kenan. Significantly, these officers all received their commissions by appointment from the governor, but there is no evidence that they needed to exercise political influence. Kenan, for example, had been educated at West Point.[34]

As these early volunteer companies departed for war, great pageantry and excitement prevailed. There was usually a ceremony in which a banner was presented to the company. Such an event took place at the Daniel B. Stetson (Sanford) house in December 1861 when Elizabeth Stetson made the presentation of the flag to Captain Pratt of the Jordan Grays. A large crowd filled the double portico of the mansion and overflowed onto Wilkinson Street. Lucilius H. Briscoe gave an address, at the close of which the Grays "marched in deployed column, with music, before the dwelling . . . and waved a handsome salute." Fannie Williams presented the Baldwin Blues with their first banner in a similar ceremony from the stone steps of the Peter J. Williams mansion. The University Guards received their flag at the Midway Female Academy.[35]

Military volunteer units organized in 1861 were largely equipped with uniforms and accoutrements provided by local people. A few wealthy planters such as Leonidas Jordan and Stith P. Myrick equipped entire companies. These men also subscribed large sums for Confederate bonds.[36]

The first companies to depart for the battle area were attired in their own distinctive uniforms, and there were great variations in color and design. Later recruits were dressed in Confederate gray, the shade of which varied from brown to light blue. The shoes, shirts, and in some instances trousers, were not considered part of the uniform of volunteer units, and the men's varied attire often imparted to them a nondescript appearance. Adjutant General Henry Wayne suggested that white and red flannel shirts be avoided since they made targets for enemy riflemen. He also suggested that forage (kepi) caps be worn and that high-heeled boots be avoided; brogans and ankle bootees were recommended instead. "Each man [should take] with him a flannel band . . . 8 to 10 inches wide, provided with strings to be worn over the abdomen [next to the skin] for the prevention of camp diarrhea or dysentery," he cautioned. If a laxative were needed, he recommended a mixture of corn meal and water.

In addition to his rifle, a blanket roll, and a canteen, the soldier most likely carried with him both a knapsack and a valise. In the latter might be found a change of clothing, extra shirts, socks, and drawers, a black tie, and handkerchiefs. In his knapsack he carried articles of food, a comb, pocket knife, tin cup, and an iron spoon, knife, and fork. On long marches the soldier's ammunition and heavy accoutrements were transported by wagon.[37]

The Blues, being already fully equipped and trained, were the first to depart from Milledgeville and the first to arrive in Virginia. Headed by Captain George Pierce Doles, the company left in April with seventy-one men; this number was soon augmented by additional recruits. Of sixteen

German-born men of military age in Milledgeville, six were already members of the Blues, and one or two of these had already had experience in the Austrian army. One such veteran, sizing up the company's rank and file, wrote: "They are mostly poor men but their heart is in the right place." It was believed that their inurement to hard outdoor labor would make them successful soldiers.[38]

Although the Blues were to leave on an early morning train, they were accompanied to the Central Depot by the Horse Guards and a crowd of over a thousand citizens. There were flowers, speeches, short addresses, and a prayer, all punctuated by the firing of cannon. "All wept, old and young alike," wrote an observer.[39] When the Blues boarded the cars, they were met by the Brown Rifles from Eatonton.

By far the most notable military company ever identified with the capital, the Blues became Company H of the 4th Regiment of Georgia Volunteers and participated with distinction in all the important battles fought by Lee's army in northern Virginia. Despite its high casualty lists, the company's ranks were relatively easy to fill with recruits early in the war. At one time it was announcing its casualties in the same communication which called for replacements, asking that these be men who were not up for the draft. However, as available manpower dwindled throughout the latter part of the war, this policy was modified. By the end of 1863 the Blues were offering a fifty-dollar bounty to all who would enlist, including those subject to conscription.[40]

The company enrolled a total of 152 members during the course of the war. Of its original component of sixty men, only seven were present at Appomattox. Its muster roll at that time was thirty-five, among whom fourteen were prisoners of war and eleven were either on leave or were sick. Two of its members had deserted. Of its war-time total of ten officers, only two escaped wounds, capture, or death. Wallace Butts, who rose from the ranks to become a captain in two years of service, suffered the loss of both a hand and a leg.[41]

Two more companies left Milledgeville shortly after the Blues, and they too were sent on their way in grand style. The Baldwin Volunteers left on June 11, and the Horse Guards departed on July 5. The latter unit became part of Phillips' Legion, which assembled for further training at Camp McDonald near Marietta. Traveling by horseback directly to Marietta, the cavalrymen were treated with great hospitality along the route, which took them through Hillsboro and Monticello. "In truth, it was a perfect ovation at every farm house," wrote one of the soldiers, "the farmers giving us their provender free of charge." The men were particularly high in their praise of Colonel W. S. Moughon, at whose plantation near Hillsboro they were received as picnic guests.[42]

The Myrick Volunteers did not leave Milledgeville until March 1862, at which time they went into training at Camp Stephens near Griffin. It was the seventh company formed in Milledgeville entirely of volunteers. At that time the county had provided approximately 500 volunteers for Confederate service—just 200 less than the number of registered voters in the county.[43]

The first units to leave were naturally the greatest sufferers in total casualties. Sad tidings of death reached the town almost as soon as soldiers reached their stations in Virginia. James A. Darnell of the Baldwin Volunteers died of typhoid fever near Manassas early in August, followed soon by Littleton Pugh of the Horse Guards and Jesse Moran of the Blues. Andrew J. Micklejohn, who fell at Pensacola early in the war, was Milledgeville's first battle casualty. The cold weather of November offered the opportunity to return his body to the town, where he was accorded a military funeral attended by city officials.[44]

Such deference to the war dead was soon to prove burdensome to the community, for throughout 1862 and 1863 casualties mounted alarmingly. In a single engagement near Richmond in the summer of 1862, three Baldwin companies were engaged and thirty-four casualties were reported. Among the wounded was Dr. Henry S. Orme, son of the editor of the *Recorder*. Earlier in the year Editor Orme had complained of the long obituaries and resolutions on deceased soldiers and declined further to publish them if they exceeded ten lines. Later he set a printing fee on obituaries which exceeded five lines in length. As a result, obituaries diminished in both length and number, as well as in eloquence; those of officers now predominated.[45]

A surprisingly large number of the town's dead were returned to Milledgeville and reinterred in the local cemetery or in family burying lots. At first the transportation of disinterred bodies was undertaken only in cold weather, but later a method was found which made it possible to do so at any season. The body was placed in a coffin without charcoal or disinfectant but with sufficient packing to prevent jostling. A cotton osnaburg which had been dipped in boiling tar was wrapped around the coffin, which then was placed in a box with more packing.[46]

Frequently there were difficulties in locating and identifying bodies of men who had fallen in battle. For example, Alonzo West was wounded, taken to the rear, and never seen again by his comrades. His captain, Charles Conn, placed notices in the Richmond papers enquiring of his location, not knowing whether he had survived. Later it was learned that Sergeant James Holmes of Darien had seen him in a fodder shack with several other wounded men. Unable to speak because of a serious jaw wound, West indicated his need for food and water. Holmes made some pap from hard biscuits and water, but when the wounded man tried to eat, the food passed out through a hole in his jaw. During the night West and two others died, and their bodies were laid out in front of the shack.[47] Apparently his identity was lost in a mass burial.

The remains of Memmenger Campbell and Captain Jesse Beall were among those which were not returned until a year after the close of the war. Memminger's mother enlisted the aid of the MacGill family at Sharpsburg, Maryland, in locating the remains of her son. The problem of distinguishing her son's body from numerous other rotting corpses must have been an anguishing experience for his widowed mother, but it gave her the satisfaction of knowing that he would finally rest in the family lot alongside his father and other kin.[48]

As the fighting wore on through 1864 and the first half of 1865, Milledgeville's casualty lists began to show a relatively large proportion of officers. Men at home on furlough frequently wore citizen's clothing to help give them a more complete respite from army life. Yet they often noted among the townspeople a sense of defeat not generally shared by those in the field.[49]

Stories of gallantry, heroism, and sacrifice drifted homeward with these furloughed men. Captain Lewis H. Kenan of the First Georgia Regulars informed his father of the terrible losses his company sustained at the Second Battle of Manassas in September 1862. Although his regiment took only 170 men and twenty-four officers into that battle, it suffered 104 casualties. A member of Myrick's Volunteers reported that not more than twenty men of that company escaped untouched from the Battle of Mechanicsville, where they were members of Stonewall Jackson's Corps. On that occasion their hunger and thirst had been less bearable than enemy bullets. "I drank water as muddy as ever came out of a hog hole," said one, "and was glad to get it." A year later, with its ranks replenished by recruits, this gallant company again suffered serious losses at Gettysburg. Lieutenant Tom Newell lost a foot there and fell into enemy hands. Years later he visited the spot where he had fallen wounded before Little Round Top. "As I saw how far our forces had driven the federals . . . over what ground they had to fight, my heart glowed with secret pride," Newell wrote.[50]

John Snead, who had joined the Blues at the age of forty, was killed in the fight in the Chickahominy Swamp; in his pocket was found an honorable discharge from the army. His kinsman, Charles W. Snead, the son of a Methodist minister, was more fortunate. A surgeon in General John Hunt Morgan's command, he participated in the Grey Ghost's famous raids into Kentucky and Indiana and survived four years of hard riding and hazardous fighting.[51] At Malvern Hill Lieutenant William A. Williams was wounded in the stomach and had an arm so badly mangled that he never recovered the use of it. When taken by wagon into Richmond, he had difficulty finding a hospital bed until he accidentally fell into the hands of a Milledgeville surgeon, Dr. James W. Herty, who placed him in the care of the Sisters of Charity. Shortly before the end of the war Williams married Bessie Grieve, whose three brothers, Miller, John, and Fleming, also came home with broken bodies and in poor health. John died in 1874 of the tuberculosis he had contracted while confined at Fort Henry. Miller, who had risen to the rank of lieutenant colonel, became a patient in the Asylum before his death in 1897.[52]

The three Grieve brothers, together with Joseph and Tom Newell, had all been students at Oglethorpe University before the war. Oglethorpe's students suffered unusually high casualties. Joseph Newell survived four years of war only to die within a year of Appomattox. With the exception of three students—Sidney and Clifford Lanier and Andrew Weems—the entire chapter of the S.A.E. Fraternity was wiped out by the conflict. "When we left for the war we expected to be back in three months," wrote Weems in 1931, "but we haven't got back yet."[53]

Among the last casualties of the fighting in Virginia, and one which brought particular grief to the Milledgeville community, was the death of Lieutenant Colonel Charles A. Conn, originally captain of the Myrick Volunteers and finally commander of the 45th Georgia Regiment. While at home recovering from a wound a few weeks before his death, Conn had married Lucia Griswold of Jones County. Upon returning to battle he was captured but soon was paroled and managed to rejoin his command. Conn was killed at Petersburg on March 25, just a few days before Lee's surrender at Appomattox. His body fell into enemy hands, but General Lee had it recovered under a flag of truce and then interred in the Presbyterian churchyard at Petersburg. The son of an Irish merchant who owned two slaves, Conn was described as "a self-made man [who rose to his rank and position] without the assistance of fortune or influential friends."[54]

Conn's old company, the Myrick Volunteers, had as Company G of the 45th Georgia Regiment participated in all the important battles fought by the Army of Northern Virginia. As with all other Confederate units, its depleted ranks could not be filled in the last months of the war, for the Confederacy had completely exhausted its military manpower. In his last defensive stand at Petersburg, Lee had pressed every staff officer and vignette into battlefield duty. Of the total of 115 men ever identified with the Myrick Volunteers, only eleven remained to surrender at Appomattox. Fourteen had been captured in the previous fighting around Petersburg; four had deserted. One of the deserters, Green M. Smith, left the picket line at Appomattox only hours before the surrender of the army. Another, Lieutenant Moses S. Pittman, had told his comrades that he was going to an island on the James River to shoot a turkey but instead went deliberately to the enemy's lines. He never returned to Milledgeville.[55]

During the course of the war many wounded Confederate soldiers were captured and imprisoned. In many ways these men were less fortunate than those who survived their wounds to face more fighting. John Myrick was so emaciated when he returned home that his mother fainted when she saw him coming up the path leading to her door. Thomas Raines had barely reached his widowed mother's house on the Monticello road when he died. Another soldier who returned from war prison had lost eighty pounds.[56]

The role of the mounted soldier in the war can well be illustrated by the Governor's Horse Guards. Since the Confederate cavalryman provided his own horse, this soldier usually came from a more affluent background than the infantry volunteer. While the government compensated the owner for a horse lost in service, it was difficult to obtain cavalry recruits because of the scarcity of mounts. This was particularly true after the summer of 1863, when the army was impressing horses for all kinds of military transportation. Largely as a result of these conditions, the Horse Guards numbered only thirty-nine men, including three officers, when they were mustered into service on July 5, 1861.[57] After spending two months in training near Marietta they were assigned to service under General John B. Floyd in northwestern Virginia. Later they were dispatched briefly for duty in the coastal defenses of South Carolina. Early in 1862 they were moved to the vicinity of Richmond and remained part of Lee's Army of Northern Virginia. Their captain was now James H. Nichols, an officer who, according to General "Jeb" Stuart, was too gallant in the line to be appointed to staff duty.[58]

The Guards were among the hand-picked horsemen who participated in General Stuart's famous raid into Maryland and Pennsylvania in September 1862. Covering as much as eighty-three miles in a single day, they rode completely around the entire Federal army and once were within two miles of 70,000 enemy soldiers. Captain James H. Nichols being ill at the time and Lieutenant George Beecher being absent, Lieutenant Mapp, third in command, was the proud leader of the company on this occasion. He wrote of capturing 1,600 horses "from a fat Dutch farmer in Pennsylvania" and of the ovation which the invaders received in Maryland. At Chambersburg they seized enough revolvers to rearm the entire company.[59]

Unlike the average infantry company, the Guards experienced relatively light battle losses. In the Battle of Antietam, for example, they sustained only six casualties. Disease and camp hardships took a high toll, however. These are graphically described in the brilliant letters which Lieutenant Thomas Kenan wrote to his father. From their station at Culpeper during Christmas of 1862 the Guards sent Oliver P. Bonner home on furlough with an urgent appeal for shoes, clothing, and equipment of all kinds, stating that these articles would be collected at Herty and Hall's drugstore by the end of the year. At that time snow covered the ground at Culpeper and water in streams was frozen to a thickness of five inches.[60]

Most of the companies raised in Milledgeville saw service in northern Virginia. One notable exception was the Independent Volunteers, who served as Company H of the 57th Georgia Regiment in the Army of Tennessee. Unlike the commander of any other local company, its commander, Captain John Richard Bonner, remained its official leader throughout the war, even though he was twice wounded, captured, and exchanged. (In his last engagement, at Bentonville, North Carolina, Bonner briefly commanded Smith's Brigade of Cleburn's Division, but the war ended before he was officially promoted.) The original lieutenants of Company H were Archibald McKinley and his cousin, Randolph Spalding, both just under twenty years old. The company suffered many casualties at the Battle of Baker's Creek near Vicksburg. Bonner was shot in the leg, and McKinley received a wound in each shoulder. Of the thirty-six members of the company who engaged in that battle, only five escaped unscathed. They were surrendered on July 4, 1863, and shortly thereafter were exchanged. On arriving in Milledgeville after the exchange, they were given a picnic feast at Carrington's grove attended by an estimated 1,000 people.[61] After some reorganization they were sent to Johnston's army in northern Georgia.

At the end of the war the company counted its losses. Two of its twelve officers had been killed and six wounded. Of fifty-six privates only eleven returned home without wounds. Twenty-seven were dead, including Thomas, Charles, and James Martin. Of the seven Russell boys—brothers and cousins—five were dead, three of them from battle wounds. The two survivors, Joseph and Samuel, were seriously wounded. The company had one deserter, David Snelling, who had defected to the Union early in the war.[62]

The army fighting in Tennessee received the services of two of Milledgeville's more significant military figures. These were Bryan Morel Thomas (1836–1905) and Dr. Andrew J. Foard (1825–1868). The latter became medical director of the Army of Tennessee, while Thomas rose to the rank of brigadier general.[63] The Thomas family of Midway was descended from Virginia forebears who brought with them to Georgia the aristocratic background of the old Tidewater. Episcopalian in faith and substantial planters and slaveowners in lifestyle, they possessed a high regard for public service. John Sherrod Thomas, the general's father, brought up his sons in the best of these traditions. One son, John G. Thomas, was educated at Yale and later married Anna Drayton of an aristocratic Charleston family. He rose to the rank of major in the Civil War. The other son, Bryan Thomas, attended Oglethorpe University and later received an appointment to West Point, from which he graduated in 1854, but he resigned from the United States Army in 1861 to accept a commission as a lieutenant in Confederate service. Bryan played a commendable role in the Battle of Shiloh as chief of ordinance and artillery under General Jones Withers and rose rapidly in rank. In August 1864, at age twenty-eight, he was promoted to brigadier general and thereafter led a mixed brigade of Alabama cavalry, infantry and artillery in the Department of the Gulf.[64]

Equally impressive, though with its roots in a much humbler background, was the career of George Pierce Doles, the only other Milledgeville native who rose to the rank of brigadier general. His father, Josiah Doles, was a tailor by trade and held no slaves. His mother was a daughter of Lovic Pierce and a sister of George Pierce, Bishop of the Methodist Church. Josiah Doles' two sons, George and Hamilton, received a small legacy from their paternal grandfather, a small farmer in Houston County, to be used for their education at the Milledgeville Academy. Upon the outbreak of the war, Hamilton was following his father's trade as a tailor. George, the future brigadier general, was struggling to support his wife, two children, and two orphan sisters on his meager salary as a bookkeeper; the value of his entire possessions did not exceed five hundred dollars.[65]

Georgia's secession offered George Doles the opportunity of a lifetime, for at that time he was captain of the Baldwin Blues. However, he did not long remain in that position. Rising rapidly in rank, he soon was elected colonel of the 4th Regiment in April 1862 without opposition; Jacob M. Carraker then took over as captain of the Blues. As the new colonel of the regiment, Doles was soon to come to the attention of General Lee, for he was a model commander. As his regiment moved into position at Seven Pines on May 31, it attracted universal attention. Those who saw the 4th Georgia Regiment file down the Williamsburg road on that morning felt a glow of pride and a swell of exultation. "Every step was cadenced," wrote an observer, "every limb was elastic, with compact and closed ranks, with precision and regularity [it] moved on [to] the field of battle."[66]

Doles' outstanding gallantry and leadership were again displayed in the Battle of Antietam, where he had replaced the wounded Brigadier General Roswell S. Ripley. At that time the 4th Georgia was part of General Daniel H. Hill's Division of Stonewall Jackson's Second Corps. Lee recommended Doles for promotion to brigadier general as the permanent commander of Ripley's brigade. Although he was only thirty-two years old, Doles' peculiar aptitude for military life was now recognized by all his superior officers. He was soon regarded as one of the best brigadiers in Lee's army—yet he had had no military training other than that received in the Baldwin Blues before the war.[67]

By May 2, 1863, when it entered the Battle of Chancellorsville, Doles' brigade had mustered 1,489 men and 133 officers. In that engagement it lost 437 in killed, wounded, and missing; thirteen of these casualties had been sustained by the Blues. In the Battle of Gettysburg, a few months later, Doles' brigade was part of the Second Army Corps under General Richard S. Ewell. As the first brigade to enter the town on July 1, it had two sharp encounters with the enemy in the streets, although after the first day's fighting it experienced only skirmishes. By the end of the battle the brigade had suffered 179 casualties, twenty-four of whom were killed. Doles' written report of this engagement is a model of clarity and precision and suggests a disciplined, well-organized military mind.[68]

Within a year, however, Doles was to meet with his first—and last—criticism. Early in May 1864 Doles' brigade found itself in position along the face of a salient located north of Spotsylvania Court House. The position which has come to be known as Mule Shoe or Bloody Angle, was dangerously vulnerable. When a charge of blue-clad soldiers emerged from the wooded cover 200 yards away, the defenders were able to manage only one volley before the Federals reached their parapet. At least 300 of Doles' men were captured (Union reports placed the figure at 1,000). This was the only real disaster which the youthful brigadier had ever experienced. His bewilderment and anguish over this incident was sharpened by irresponsible criticism of his brigade by one of the Richmond papers. It has been said that Doles' experience at Bloody Angle and the newspaper criticism which followed drove him to excessive exertion and caused him to overexpose himself to danger. That may be so, for on June 2, at Cold Harbor, this distinguished son of an obscure tailor was hit by a sharpshooter's bullet which entered his right side, passed through his heart, and shattered his left arm.[69]

Doles' loss was deeply felt. The *Richmond Whig* published a long obituary full of praise for his achievements. Ironically, it did not even mention the calamity at Bloody Angle; rather, it recalled the splendid reputation which his old regiment—the 4th Georgia—had acquired in every place it had ever been stationed in Virginia. "The excellent character of the regiment, sustained as it was by intelligent and polished Southern youths, under his administration, acquired a permanence and splendor that will not be forgotten by the people of Nansemond County," it concluded. A member of Doles' regiment said of his commander: "He was absolutely fearless . . . never flinched before danger, sickness, suffering, or death. He was prompt, resolute, and cool in the face of danger. He had a warm and affectionate heart . . . and that gentle and placable nature which so often accompanies courage. He was incapable of permanent anger . . . less capable of revenge."[70]

The flag over the Blues' armory flew at half-mast for a full week after the news of Doles' death reached Milledgeville. His body arrived on June 7 and was taken to Representative Hall in the Statehouse, where services were conducted by William Flinn, chaplain of the 5th Georgia Regiment, and by C. A. Fulwood of the Methodist Church. Upon his casket lay a simple wreath of myrtle, together with his swords, all encircled by the original banner of the Blues. At the head were the Confederate flag and the battle flag of the 4th Georgia; at the foot was a cluster of three enemy flags captured in battle. At 5:00 p.m., when the services ended and the procession was being formed, a violent storm arose. Although there was no cannon in Milledgeville to sound the general's final military salute, "the red artillery of heaven sent peal after peal along the dark canopy." The violence of the storm continued unabated until nightfall, and the casket was returned to the Statehouse, where an honor guard stood watch throughout the night. The next morning the cortege was again formed, moving through the north gate of the Statehouse Square to the center of town, up Wayne Street to Greene, thence to Liberty Street and on into the cemetery.[71]

After Doles' death his widow and infant daughter were in dire need. Warm-hearted people of the town raised funds and purchased a cottage, which was then deeded over to the widow, but bad fortune continued to stalk the family. Although Mrs. Doles eventually found employment as an attendant at the Asylum, her salary was not sufficient to meet the expenses of her daughter's illness from tuberculosis, and she was forced to sell the house to meet living expenses. When the daughter died in 1886, she and her mother were residing in the house of Henry Goodman. Old members of the Blues served as her pallbearers. Thus Milledgeville's most famous warrior left no descendants. With the death of his widow a few years later, all of Doles' earthly possessions, which largely consisted of his letters and papers, passed into oblivion.[80]

Many people who had little enthusiasm for an armed conflict were swept into the war against their better judgment. Yet when military confrontation occurred, they performed their task with remarkable fidelity to duty and patriotism. Although no complete record of Baldwin County's roster of Confederate soldiers has ever been compiled, the number doubtless exceeded that of the county's registered voters in 1860, for its percentage of volunteers was unusually high. Moreover, since a very large number of Milledgeville men qualified for commissions, the local units were well led. Indeed, one of the ironies of the community's wartime experiences was that during the invasion and occupation of the capital by the Federal army in the fall of 1864, the best of the town's military manpower was serving on distant battlefronts and was unable to come to its defence.

Sherman and the End of the War

Milledgeville's first experience with the realities of invasion occurred during the summer of 1864 when a roving band of cavalrymen under General George Stoneman struck southward from Atlanta and threatened the capital. Before his capture at Sunshine Church near Clinton on July 27, Stoneman had set in motion plans for a raid on Milledgeville. He detached 125 horsemen from the 14th Illinois Regiment and placed them under Major Francis M. Davidson, ordering him to advance first to Gordon where he was to destroy railroads, locomotives, and other property in the vicinity, and then to move on Milledgeville. Learning of these plans, Governor Brown called on Adjutant General Henry Wayne for 1,000 state troops and also asked General Howell Cobb at Macon for Confederate assistance. These reinforcements reached Milledgeville on Sunday night, July 24.[1]

It was the intention of Davidson's raiders to destroy Gordon and its railroad facilities before troops could be sent through there to Milledgeville. This done, they could then capture the capital and destroy the Oconee bridge. Had they arrived at Gordon thirty minutes sooner both objectives might have been accomplished. However, when the raiding party reached the outskirts of that rail junction, General Wayne's train carrying reinforcements was already moving out from Gordon toward Milledgeville. Hiding in a ravine, the raiders waited until the troop train passed on. Then they dashed into Gordon, fired the depot, and destroyed cars, locomotives, and a warehouse filled with food supplies. Davidson claimed the destruction of 150 passenger and express cars and nine engines. Seven of these engines were already steamed up and were demolished by being run into a smash-up.[2]

The raiders now headed for Milledgeville. They rode to within sight of the lights of the town and there detached scouting parties to probe the area. Two of these scouts, dressed in gray jeans, actually entered the bivouac of the defenders near the Central Depot, conversed with them, and learned the strength of the capital garrison. This information revealed that Wayne's Confederate reinforcements had been supplemented by a small battalion of local guards and an improvised cavalry company. The Milledgeville Guard, as this homegrown group was called, numbered no more than 200 men, all of whom were either very old or very young. (In the latter category was Willie McKinley, age thirteen, who was posted as a guard at one of the roads leading into town. Learning of his location, his mother drove her carriage into town and found the young defender on duty. To his enduring humiliation he was plucked from his post and forthwith returned to his home.)[3]

Finding the capital fortified, Davidson pushed on. Through some stragglers captured from his band the Confederates learned that the raiders had impressed a local guide and were moving north from Milledgeville on the east side of the Oconee. About twelve miles north of town they crossed to the west bank and reached Eatonton, where they joined a group of their comrades who earlier had managed to escape capture at Sunshine Church. After burning the railroad station at Eatonton, this jaded remnant of Davidson's band continued northward, riding broken-down horses and plantation mules, until they finally were captured near Athens.

The defenders of the capital were mortified that these men had escaped them. A company of cavalry under Captain Pierce Horne had been sent after the raiders, but a heavy rain had delayed their pursuit. A trainload of infantry had also been sent to Eatonton, but it too had arrived too late. The disgruntled soldiers returned to Milledgeville with only a wagonload of plunder which the enemy had left behind.[4]

While resulting in no physical damage to the capital, this raid dealt a great psychological blow to the people of Milledgeville. Throughout the entire period the town was filled with wild rumors, exaggerated stories, and deep apprehension. "What a night and what a morning!" wrote Lucy Cobb from the McKinley plantation on July 30. Her Uncle William, who had spent much time galloping between the plantation and town, reported a most pitiable state of things at the Executive Mansion. Mrs. Brown, in the absence of the governor, was in great distress, pale and terror-stricken that the house would be burned before morning, with the whole of the governor's family having no place where they could hide. A dispatch from the governor advised her to take the children to Scottsboro, leaving the Mansion to its fate and the older members of the family to shift for themselves. Forgetting his past political feuds with Brown, McKinley offered the governor's family his plantation house as a refuge, and they readily accepted. Before morning the frightened guests, along with a considerable collection of baggage, had arrived. The latter, piled high in the hallway, included such items as sugar, coffee, and syrup. The McKinleys themselves spent most of the night concealing their own food and valuable personal possessions which might be stolen by the raiders.[5]

The loss of silver, money, and other portable objects of high value was soon reported by those living along the route followed by Davidson. This inspired the *Confederate Union* to publish a long article suggesting how such losses might be minimized in the event of another raid. One of the precautions suggested was never to allow a slave to know where anything was hidden or to trust him with any article of value. It was not the possible disloyalty of slaves which was emphasized here, but rather the fact that the enemy would be resourceful enough to get the truth from them. However, because the raid had caused the loyalty of some slaves to be questioned, General Wayne later issued an order requiring men over the age of fifty-five to form mounted patrols and to devote their full time to maintaining orderly behavior and full employment of all slaves.[6]

Governor Brown lost no time in preparing Milledgeville's defenses against similar raids which might occur in the future. He ordered the impressment of 500 slaves from surrounding plantations to be employed in the fortification of the town's approaches. Some of these fortifications were still visible in 1976.[7]

With the advance of Sherman's army, the defense of Milledgeville assumed greater importance. Throughout the latter part of the summer his army had been fighting for the possession of Atlanta, a transportation hub of great strategic importance. That phase of the campaign ended with Hood's evacuation of the Gate City on September 2, at which time the flow of refugees from the Atlanta area to Milledgeville increased. Here they were joined by a number of refugees who had fled the Georgia coast earlier in the war. These displaced people not only put an extra burden on the community's resources but also served as a constant reminder of the nightmare which invasion could produce.

The most welcome of these refugees were the cadets from the Georgia Military Institute, whose campus and buildings at Marietta had been destroyed by the invaders earlier in the summer. Late in May, when Sherman was approaching Marietta, Major F. W. Capers, superintendent of the institute, obtained the use of vacant buildings at Oglethorpe Universty as a refuge for the families of his officers and for those cadets who were sick or disabled. The buildings also served as a storage place for the institute's

Wilkes Flagg

Dr. Tomlinson Fort

Captain Bernard R. Herty in full dress uniform of the Baldwin Blues

baggage and property.[8] The cadets, about 160 in number, were then sent to Troup County to do guard duty at the Chattahoochee River bridge. Later they were placed in the trenches at Atlanta, where sickness and casualties reduced their number by a third. After the fall of Atlanta they were ordered to Milledgeville, where they lived in tents on the northeast portion of Statehouse Square. Here they continued their studies but spent much of their time on military drill and similar duties. They were supplied from the state commissary.[9]

In announcing the opening of the new term on August 1, Capers listed a new academic faculty and set the fees for the term at $600. In lieu of a money payment, students might substitute food items. The cost could be met with any one of the following: 200 pounds of bacon, 100 bushels of corn, sixty bushels of wheat, two casks of rice, or two barrels of syrup.[10]

Milledgeville was well represented at the institute. Governor Brown's sixteen-year-old son, Julius, was among the new students in 1864. Francis B. Mapp left a clerkship in the comptroller general's office to join the cadets. B. C. Ward, who had been a student at the institute when the war began had enlisted in the army at age fifteen. (He was to become Baldwin County's last surviving veteran of the war.) Other Milledgeville youths who became identified with the institute were William P. Boughton, Archibald McKinley, Goodwin D. Myrick, and John L. Hammond.[11]

Hammond, at age eighteen, had resigned at the end of the 1862 session to enter Confederate service as a private. Superintendent Capers expressed regret that "so meritorious and promising [a] cadet should not complete his course," but recommended him as a "young man fit to be trusted with important duties and a true soldier and gentleman." Hammond soon received a commission, and by 1864 he had become adjutant of the 63rd Georgia Regiment. On July 7 of that year he wrote to his sister from the north bank of the Chattahoochee, saying that his regiment had marched directly through the abandoned campus of the Georgia Military Institute at Marietta and that he had marched within five feet of his old room. "I felt almost like crying," he wrote, "for though there [for] only a short time there are many pleasant associations. . . . I little thought then that an invader's army would pollute the spot or that I would ever soldier so near."[12]

The presence of the battalion of cadets in Milledgeville clothed the town with a military mien which it had not known since the first year of the war. Major Capers, whose headquarters were in a basement room of the Statehouse, was commandant of the Milledgeville post for the special defense of the capital. In addition to the cadets and local guards, he had under his command a company of mounted scouts under Captain Charles J. Talbird, an erstwhile official at the penitentiary, and Prudden's battery of artillery. Toward the end of August the governor ordered that after August 24 all businesses should close at 5:00 p.m. each day so that all citizens could assemble at the Statehouse Square for organization and instruction. There was also a military parade three times each week.[13]

However, when the vanguard of Sherman's army entered the town three months later, they found the trenches and fortifications unmanned and useless. On that day—Sunday, November 20—members of the legislature had already hastily departed for their homes. The governor and other officials were in flight and many citizens were following their examples. At sunset a group of blue-clad cavalrymen was seen lingering on the outskirts of town. They advanced cautiously through the streets with carbines cocked, cut the telegraph line, and then hurried away. These scouts discovered that the capital was wholly undefended, for on the previous day General Wayne had moved the garrison to Gordon, where it was augmented by the battalion of cadets and about 150 penitentiary prisoners who had been given their freedom in exchange for military service. Wayne's total command numbered approximately 600 men.[14]

During the next four days more than 30,000 soldiers entered Milledgeville. These were the Fourteenth and Twentieth corps, comprising the left wing of Sherman's army. The right wing, which consisted of the Fifteenth and Seventeenth corps, commanded by General Oliver O. Howard, was moving toward Clinton and Macon. Its object was to threaten Macon and then to move south of Milledgeville through Gordon and Irwinton.[15]

Only the left wing of the army, with which Sherman and his staff were riding, was headed directly for the state capital. On the afternoon of November 20 the advance column of the Fourteenth corps went into camp near Stanfordville in Putnam County, just twenty-seven miles from Milledgeville. The Twentieth Corps, accompanied by General Henry W. Slocum, the thirty-six-year-old commander of the left wing, camped near Eatonton, about six miles east of Sherman's encampment. Meanwhile, the right wing, under Howard, was encamped in the vicinity of Clinton in Jones County, accompanied by Kilpatrick's cavalry of 5,000 men.

Only the weather was able to offer much resistance to this army of 65,000 men which was rapidly enveloping the countryside around the capital of

Georgia. Throughout the night and the following day a cold rain settled on the invaders. Toward nightfall on Monday freezing temperatures developed under a biting raw wind. It was the coldest November weather in the memory of most natives.

The problem of moving so many men over two or three parallel country roads was greatly augmented by a long wagon train, artillery, thousands of horses and mules, and several thousand head of cattle. Cold, wet, and mud-caked Northern soldiers tugged at stalled vehicles, dug them out of narrow sloughs, then gathered in groups around fires made of fence rails, where they cursed the Georgia weather. Problems in crossing streams caused some units to delay encampment until midnight before making the day's required ten miles march.[16]

It was not until late in the afternoon of Tuesday, November 22, that advance columns of the Twentieth Corps entered Milledgeville from Eatonton. After a forward skirmish line found the earthworks on the northwestern part of town vacant, the division marched down Jackson Street to Greene. Here companies were formed, flags were unfurled, and the band moved to the head of the column. As they marched past the Statehouse and across the Oconee toward the place where they would make camp, the band played, among other airs, "The Battle Hymn of the Republic"; this was probably the first time that this martial song had ever been heard in Milledgeville. Although crowds of Negroes thronged the route, the long icicles which hung from the eaves of the houses must have been a more appropriate symbol of how the rest of the town felt.[17]

In the meantime the main body of the Twentieth Corps was going into camp near Meriwether Station and Butts' crossroads. Four miles to the west, on the Monticello road, the Fourteenth Corps had halted for the night on a windswept hillside just seven miles from Milledgeville. Sherman's orderly was pitching the general's tent in a clump of plum trees to give some protection from the wind when it was discovered that a substantial overseer's house and a number of slave cabins lay a short distance down the road. On reaching the overseer's house and settling himself by a roaring fire, the general learned that he had become the uninvited guest of Confederate General Howell Cobb at Hurricane plantation. The Negroes and the livestock had been moved away, but the invaders found more than a thousand bushels of peanuts and an abundance of corn, beans, and sorghum.[18] Sherman gave orders for the confiscation and destruction of everything except the slave cabins. At the same time he ordered a special guard to protect the nearby property of Andrew J. Banks, who was a North Carolinian by birth and known to be a strong Unionist.

Sherman's unusual intelligence sources on this occasion were principally provided by Lieutenant David R. Snelling, a twenty-six-year-old cavalry-man who commanded the general's escort. Some of the slaves who had drifted into camp from surrounding plantations had already recognized Snelling as the young man who had been born only a few miles from Hurricane and had spent most of his life in the community. Early in 1862 Snelling had joined Captain John Richard Bonner's company of the 57th Georgia Regiment. Never an enthusiastic rebel, he defected to the Union at Bridgeport, Alabama, in July of the same year. He was now a first lieuten-ant in the only Alabama cavalry regiment in the Union army. His knowl-edge of the people and the roads over which the army was marching made his services invaluable to Sherman. Later, in one of the last engagements of the war, Snelling would face at Bentonville his erstwhile captain, John R. Bonner, when the latter commanded a brigade of Cleburn's Division against Sherman's Fourteenth Corps.[19]

That evening Snelling obtained permission to ride a few miles ahead to visit relatives at the plantation of his uncle, David Lester, who lived in Jones County near the Baldwin County line. He returned later mounted on a fresh horse from Lester's stable—although David Lester's plantation book suggests that the horse was no gift from a loving uncle. Snelling had visited the plantation with a squad of cavalrymen, and the group had conducted a raid on the establishment, burned the ginhouse, and pillaged the premises. This unusual conduct appears to have stemmed from an old grudge which he held against his affluent kinsman, as well as from a desire to prove his loyalty to the Union.[20]

In direct contrast to Snelling's behavior was that of another soldier, who participated in an event which occurred a few miles south of Milledgeville when the right wing of the invading army was approaching Gordon. Gen-eral Wayne, with his motley group of 600 defenders from Milledgeville, was joined by a volunteer named James Rufus Kelly. Although just twenty years old, Kelly had already become a legend after much heroic fighting in Vir-ginia. Now on crutches because of an amputated leg, and with a disability discharge in his pocket, he sought one more opportunity to fight the Yan-kees.

Having no intention of pitting his rag-tag militiamen against Howard's

Lieutenant David R. Snelling, who deserted the Independent Volunteers in 1862 and returned to Milledgeville in 1864 as commander of Sherman's escort.

Lieutenant William A. Williams, who was severely wounded at Malvern Hill, where he then miraculously fell into the hands of Dr. James Herty.

Officers of Company H (Independent Volunteers) of the 57th Georgia Regiment, Army of Tennessee, 1863. l. to r.: 1st Lieut. Archibald C. McKinley, Capt. John Richard Bonner, Scott (cook), 2nd Lieut. William S. Stetson

30,000 veterans, Wayne prudently ordered them to entrain for the Oconee railroad bridge, where they might prevent its destruction by Federal scouts. With rifle and crutches slung to his saddle, Kelly rode up to the commander and berated him loudly for his decision not to stand and fight. Then he unlimbered his rifle, recruited one private Bragg to assist him, and set off to meet the entire Seventeenth Corps. Upon encountering the point of the column crossing the creek just north of Gordon, he fired upon it and forced the formation of a skirmish line, thus delaying the town's capture for almost an hour. Later, as he was being pursued, he turned his horse into the woods where the animal stumbled, unseating the valiant rider and separating him from his crutches. Subsequently he was captured and threatened with a sentence to be shot after a military trial. However, the plucky Kelly later escaped and returned home.[21] With the possible exception of the skirmish at Griswoldville, Kelly's defense of Gordon was as close to Milledgeville as the shooting phase of the war ever came.

After the war Kelly taught school in Wilkinson County for more than fifty years—a period when the public payroll provided the only approximation of an adequate pension for war-time disabilities of Confederate veterans. David Snelling also returned to his community near Cobb's plantation. Here his life was threatened, and he was forced to depart hurriedly in the night, never again to return. He went to Ozark, Arkansas, where he married and raised a family. Although he was respected by his neighbors, he was never successful in his various economic enterprises, and never talked of his past experiences. His daughter remembered him as a "tall, thin man with troubled brown eyes" who often walked alone in the fields and woods.[22]

On Wednesday, November 23, the main body of Sherman's left wing finally assembled at Milledgeville which soon resembled a vast army camp, even though the principal bivouac was on the McKinley plantation. Since the weather was unusually cold, picket fences and outhouses became the principal supply of firewood for 30,000 soldiers. Thus gardens and private enclosures were turned into open thoroughfares for horses and men. Church buildings provided greater protection from the cold than army tents—and church pews made excellent fuel—so all church buildings and their contents suffered some damage. The organ of the Episcopal Church was ruined when sorghum molasses was poured into the pipes.[23]

Army officers, from provost guards to General Sherman himself, were besieged with petitions from citizens who sought protection from seizures and vandalism, and, indeed, overt destruction of factories, residences, and warehouses was rare. Only three or four private residences in the vicinity of the town were burned; these included the house of State Treasurer John Jones and the country places of Judge Iverson Harris and Dr. William A. Jarrett. Harris had attracted Sherman's attention by urging planters along the path of the march to destroy everything upon which the invaders might subsist and thus to force them to retreat or starve. At Jarrett's plantation the overseer, Patrick Kane, had too zealously defended his employer's property. He was shot to death, and the property was burned. Kane is the only known fatality of the invasion of Milledgeville.[24]

The Central Depot and the bridge spanning the Oconee were burned by military orders. The arsenal, which stood on the east side of the Statehouse, also was burned, while, on the opposite side of the square, the fireproof magazine was blown up after six wagonloads of its contents had been dumped into the river. Although some cotton was destroyed as the result of a miscarried order, the bulk of this commodity was left untouched in the warehouses. The Oconee Mill, the textile factory, and the foundry all escaped destruction, probably because their owners were Northerners or men of foreign birth. Sherman honored almost every excuse for not applying the torch, and even accepted worthless bonds. There is no record that he ever ordered the destruction of the penitentiary, although he might justly have done so, since it functioned as an armaments factory. Rather, the fire which only partly destroyed these buildings was said to have been started by some of the twenty-odd unparoled convicts left there, most of whom managed to escape in the confusion which followed. One of these was a woman serving a life sentence for the murder of her husband. Dressed in a Federal uniform and plying an ancient trade, she found hospitality and refuge in the 33rd Indiana Regiment.[25]

While the Statehouse was not burned, it was the object of extensive vandalism. Some of the younger officers of the 3rd Wisconsin and the 107th New York regiments staged there a mock session of the legislature during which much horseplay was indulged in, including a parody on the ordinance of secession. The affair attracted a large number of soldiers who later ransacked the building, breaking windows, chairs, desks, and plaster and writing obscenities on the walls.

Many of the library books, shelved on the basement floor, were thrown out of the windows to the ground, where a soldier was seen to walk his horse back and forth over them to trample them into the mud. Other soldiers, including some officers, took the books off by the armful. Fortunately, the more valuable state archives had been secreted at the plantation of Arthur J. Butts, having been sent there by the state treasurer in wagons driven by William A. (Rough) Williams and James Shurlock. Six wagonloads of books—about a fourth of the total—and most of the court records had also been removed through the efforts of Fleming Grieve, then an assistant law clerk. Transported by train and in open wagons, these materials were sent to Dooly and Warren counties and to Columbia, South Carolina.[26] The Great Seal and the unfinished records of the recent legislature were hidden safely under the house of Nathan C. Barnett and in a nearby pigpen. After the departure of the invaders, many letters and public documents were found in the streets and public squares, which, with flour and meal emptied on them, looked as though they had been in a snow storm. The Statehouse was said to be "knee deep in papers."[27]

Farms and plantations which lay on the route followed by the army appear to have suffered greater pillage and devastation than the town itself. Swarming over the countryside, the invaders destroyed much that they were unable to consume or to carry way. "In passing through the country they left the road in large numbers passing through every field and thicket,

The State Arsenal in 1864

The Burning of the Penitentiary in 1864

consequently but little escaped them," wrote Terrell Barksdale, who lived near Meriwether Station. He enumerated his losses at two slaves, fifty head of sheep, nine hogs, and all his horses, mules, and poultry, as well as oats, carts, and a buggy. The soldiers also burned his ginhouse and cotton. The house of Mrs. Cadwallader Raines, a bed-ridden widow and mother of two sons fighting in Virginia, was near Sherman's campsite at Cobb's plantation. Her plantation was completely ravaged of all food and livestock. "They have nothing [to eat] except what the neighbors give them and . . . few have anything to spare," wrote Barksdale.[28]

Federal "bummers" who visited outlying plantations were largely unrestrained by military directives and army discipline. On the road between Stevens Pottery and Gordon, Samuel Griswold encountered a group of Ohio soldiers mounted on mules and horses taken from Baldwin County plantations and loaded with plunder tied to their saddles. Their cavalcade included a yoke of oxen, complete with a Negro driver and a cart filled with peach brandy and apples taken from the Henry Stevens plantation. They stopped at every farmhouse to warm by the fire and to ransack the premises, turning down blankets and opening drawers in search of valuable trinkets. Griswold, who was a captive of these soldiers for a few hours, noted that some of them disapproved of such looting and took no part in it.

Finney Ivey, who lived south of Milledgeville, was a guileless and oblig-ing victim of these men. Having taken advantage of the cold weather to slaughter his hogs, he had just salted the meat and placed it in his smokehouse when they came and loaded it into their wagons. His horses and mules were conveniently assembled in a barn near by—as if he had never heard of a pillaging Yankee soldier who preferred riding to walking.[29]

It is unlikely that any instance of rape would find its way into the records of this period, yet one such entry did appear in the diary of a young woman who later made an unsuccessful effort to eradicate it. This involved the wife of Captain James H. Nichols of the Horse Guards, who lived in an isolated spot in the Midway community. She was confined to her bed at the time she was visited by two Union soldiers who intimidated the Negro attendant and entered her room. The victim later died in a mental institution.[30]

Many Milledgeville people were fortunate in that their houses, being larger and more comfortable than the average, were occupied by Union officers whose presence guaranteed protection to the owners as well as to their close neighbors. However, the houses of state officials, all of whom had fled the capital, appear to have suffered most from material damage. Peter-son Thweatt, comptroller general, estimated the damage to his house on Columbia Street at $20,000. Silverware and other articles of high value were stolen, while furniture, blankets, and clothing were either destroyed or given to Negroes. William H. Scott estimated the value of goods and chat-tels taken from his plantation to have been $14,650 at pre-war prices.[31]

Governor Brown had the foresight to strip the Executive Mansion of many of its portable furnishings, including carpets and curtains. He also took away a milk cow and provisions from the larder and a servant added some cabbages from the vegetable garden. When Sherman occupied the house for his headquarters, he was forced to sleep on an improvised bed and to use a table made from boards and camp chairs.

There were several private houses at which military guards were posted. Many of these dwellings belonged to families who could claim Northern birth or who might give some evidence of Union sympathy. Mrs. Richard M. Orme, Sr., whose husband edited the *Southern Recorder*, was a native of Andover, Massachusetts—and a thoroughgoing rebel in 1864. Much to her good fortune Captain Henry Ward Beecher of a Massachusetts regiment was assigned to her house. The officer was a nephew of the famous New York divine, whose name he bore and Mrs. Orme had been childhood friends with his family. During the three days that Captain Beecher stayed at the Orme house he did not know that upstairs under the same roof was Mrs. Orme's Confederate son-in-law, Dr. James Alexander, who was there on furlough to see his bride.[32]

The house of William McKinley, being near the main campsite of the Union army, was guarded by 125 men. Among those who occupied this house with Generals Norman J. Jackson and John W. Gary was Lieutenant Stanley of New Britain, Connecticut, who was a cousin of Mrs. McKinley. However, he did not make his identity known to his reluctant hostess until after the war. Also occupying the house was another native of New Britain—Mary Andrews, a sister of Mrs. McKinley, whose visit to Milledgeville in 1861 had been indefinitely prolonged by the outbreak of war.[33]

Quartered in the elegant Jarrett house on Clarke Street*was Major James A. Connolly, who wrote in his famous diary the most favorable description of the town recorded by any of the invaders. Even at that season he caught the delicate fragrance of boxwoods growing in the gardens, and he was impressed by many evidences of culture and refinement. He observed that the streets and sidewalks were well-tended and covered with sand, and that the names of the streets were painted on neat boards attached to fences and buildings. However, when viewed from the east bank of the river, he noted, the town "presented a very shabby and rickety appearance"; this, he explained, was the quarter where many poor whites and Negroes were living.[34]

Another officer, Sergeant Stephen Fleharty, recorded his impressions of Milledgeville and its people during the occupation by Union troops. All black residents of the community appeared to be on the streets and sidewalks when the invaders entered the town, he wrote. This group was augmented by an even larger number who had been following the army. Dressed in their best attire, they were festive and happy, and, according to Fleharty, "their ecstatic demonstrations were ludicrous in the extreme." In striking contrast was the almost total absence of whites from the streets. Their houses gave the appearance of being closed and vacated—as indeed many of them were.[35]

No such assembly of blacks had ever been seen before in Milledgeville. In addition to placing a heavy drain on the town's food resources, these people put a heavy burden on the Union army, to which they looked for deliverance. The large number of women among the refugees caused some concern

* In 1910 this house was moved to a position facing Columbia Street.

over the effect which their presence might have on the soldiers. Before entering Milledgeville Sherman assembled many of these slaves at the Humphries house on the Monticello road and urged them to return to their plantations so that the army could complete its work. Such urgings appeared to have little effect. "The ruling thought in their mind," wrote Fleharty, "is thus expressed whenever . . . [they] meet, 'Is you gwine?'"[36]

A practical solution to this problem was devised by General J. C. Davis of the Fourteenth Corps. When the last of his corps had crossed Buckhead Creek, he ordered the pontoons immediately removed so that the refugees would be unable to follow. Although it proved to be highly effective, this act was denounced by one chaplain as the most heartless and cruel act of the entire campaign.[37]

One black refugee, a Milledgeville boy named Allen Brantley, was a more fortunate one. When ordered by an army sergeant to try his hand at managing some balky plantation mules hitched to a supply wagon, he performed the function so well that he was allowed to remain with the army to the end of the war. Many years later, with the help of a kindly lawyer, he was able to produce sufficient evidence of army service to entitle him to a substantial pension. Brantley used this windfall wisely to achieve lasting economic security for his family and a college education for his grandchildren. Members of his family became leaders in the social and educational life of Milledgeville's black community.[38]

The departure of the troops began on November 24—an event which gave citizens some cause to remember that it was Thanksgiving Day. However, their larders were bare and there were no festivities, although the icicles had disappeared from the eaves of their houses. The departure of the infantry regiments was punctuated by the sudden appearance of 5,000 Union cavalry. Transferred from Gordon to join the left wing at Milledgeville, the cavalry corps stopped at the capital only long enough to draw rations, then proceeded eastward. Commanding the cavalry was Hugh Judson Kilpatrick, just twenty-six years old and one of the youngest brigadiers of the army. Sherman had once called him "a hell of a damned fool," but at the same time had approved his assignment to his command. Kilpatrick's reputation for hard riding earned him the nick-name of Kill-Cavalry. More than half of his corps' original mounts were destroyed by hard riding between Atlanta and Savannah. In Kilpatrick the people got a brief glimpse of an undersized youth with dark piercing eyes who was heard to deliver a tirade to some of his officers for not effecting a more complete destruction of farm equipment, provisions, and livestock.[39]

Then the cavalry too was gone, and those who were left behind began to sort through the pieces of the life they had known. Although the Statehouse and residential mansions had survived, the town and countryside had suffered great devastation. Eliza Andrews, who passed through the area in the wake of Sherman, wrote a graphic account of conditions along the road. Fields were trampled down, and hardly a fence was left standing. Fodder stacks and hay ricks were demolished. The road was lined with carcasses of all kinds of livestock which had been needlessly slaughtered, and a horrible stench pervaded the atmosphere. She saw Confederate soldiers sitting by the roadside eating raw turnips, meat skins, and parched corn. People were wandering over the abandoned campsite of the Union army trying to recover shattered corn, half-rotted beef, and frost-bitten potatoes. At the Milledgeville Hotel she saw crowds of men in gray uniforms "pacing restlessly up and down the galleries like caged animals in a menagerie."[40] Extreme hunger was the lot of both the rich and the poor, white and black, and the next harvest was almost a year away.

The food situation was made more acute by the arrival of Ferguson's Brigade of General Joseph Wheeler's Confederate Cavalry. These troopers were described as a ragged, rollicking, and vermin-infested group of hungry and ill-accoutered men. One observer referred to them as a "plundering band of horse-stealing ruffians" whose visit to his plantation he dreaded more than that of the Yankees.[41] Whatever these men may have appropriated for their own use, however, must have been repaid when, a few days later, they delivered to Milledgeville's Mayor Boswell B. deGraffenreid fifty head of beef cattle captured from Sherman's supply trains.

Other help was forthcoming as well. Early in December the Confederate commissary at Macon, through the efforts of General Howell Cobb, sent Milledgeville 5,000 rations of corn meal and eighteen beefs. "[The mayor] acknowledged not only the corn but also the Cobb," wrote the editor of the *Telegraph*. Within the following six weeks Milledgeville also received $5,000 in relief from Alexander Collie, a London merchant who made the donation as part of a large sum which he provided for those reduced to poverty from Sherman's march.[42]

Neither Howell Cobb nor his enemy Brown could be blamed for the defenseless condition of the capital during the debacle of Sherman's

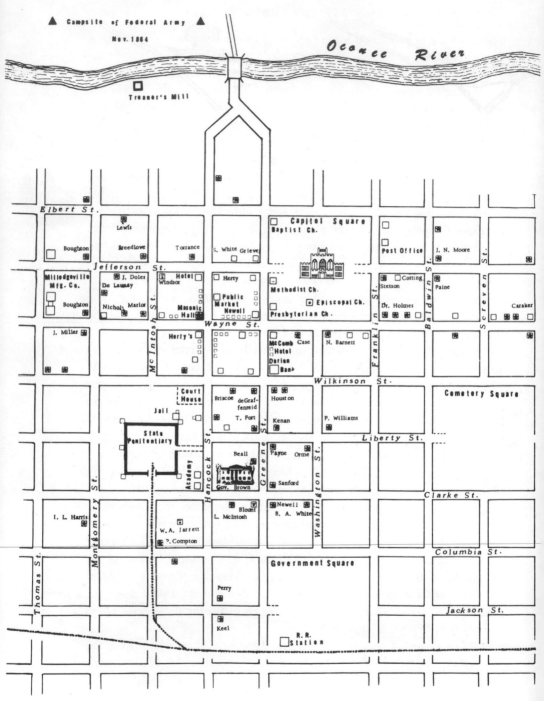

Milledgeville and

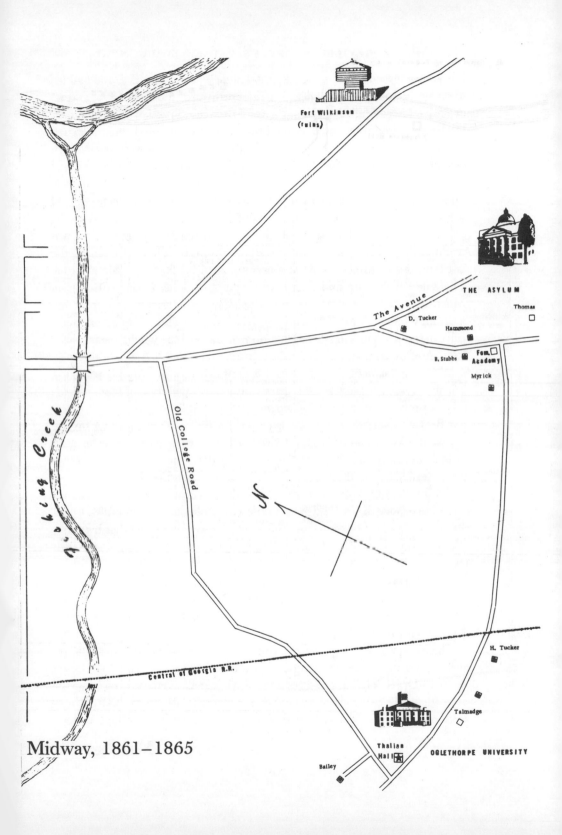

Fort Wilkinson
(ruins)

THE ASYLUM

The Avenue

Thomas

D. Tucker

Hammond

B. Stubbs

Fem.
Academy

Myrick

Old College Road

N

Fishing Creek

Central of Georgia R.R.

H. Tucker

Talmadge

Thalian
Hall

OGLETHORPE UNIVERSITY

Bailey

Midway, 1861–1865

November invasion. After the fall of Atlanta General John B. Hood had led the main body of the Confederate army northward into Tennessee, and no defensive force of fighting strength stood between Sherman and Savannah. Under the circumstances it is doubtful that anyone could have matched Brown's judgment and his decisions in this crisis. The governor's staunch defender, the editor of the *Confederate Union*, pointed out that Brown had remained in the capital an entire day after it was abandoned by the legislature and most of the Statehouse officials. He had sent his sixteen-year-old son with a gun and a blanket to the field where he fought gallantly at the Oconee railroad bridge south of Gordon. During this time Brown was working diligently to safeguard the state's property. Then he boarded the last train out of Milledgeville and accompanied his family to Montezuma. There he left them to find their own way to his Dooly County plantation, which they had never visited and which lay some thirty miles from the railroad, while he himself hastened to Macon, where he set up a temporary office in the city hall and where later, on February 15, he would assemble the legislature to complete its unfinished work.[43]

While the *Southern Recorder* was most critical of the governor for utilizing valuable space on the train for transporting his own store of food and his private property to safety, the *Confederate Union* defended him. "As Governor Brown's salary does not now even pay for the corn necessary for his use . . . we think . . . that it was the Governor's duty to take care of his meat, if he had any, his milch cows, etc.," wrote the editor, who also pointed out that the governor lost to the enemy all food that remained in the Mansion.

The most publicized event involving the governor's hasty exit was recorded in a story that he had gone to the vegetable garden and pulled up all the collards and cabbages to take with him. Brown explained that his cook, without his or Mrs. Brown's knowledge, had gathered some cabbages, but the story persisted and doubtless became exaggerated with each rendition. Its biting quality resulted from its implication that Brown was plebeian in character. The story inspired a humorous ballad from the pen of Joseph Addison Turner of Eatonton, which was reprinted in various newspapers throughout the state.[44]

The story was revived after the war when Brown became a Republican, and it dogged his career as long as he remained in politics. In 1869 Brown wrote to Dr. H. H. Tucker, President of Mercer University, protesting the ungentlemanly behavior of some Mercer students whom he had encountered on the train. Upon recognizing him the students had shouted "Josey,"

"Cabbage," "Collards," and other names which Brown did not mention but which obviously he did not relish. When the train stopped for dinner at Union Point, the students gathered on the platform and announced that they would have cabbage for dinner and would present a sideshow of Old Joe eating cabbage. Brown's reprimand availed little.[45]

When the governor returned to the Mansion after Sherman's departure, he found little evidence of the general's occupancy. Much of the heavy furniture and numerous other articles had been carted off, but this apparently was the work of local people, who also had taken property from the Statehouse and the penitentiary. Brown reported the loss of all his poultry, two barrels of syrup, forty bushels of potatoes, and numerous other food items. More than half of the blankets had disappeared, nearly all the tinware, water pails, buckets, bowls, mirrors, and even the andirons. Later, when the governor threatened legal search and forcible seizure to recover these articles, an unsigned paper defying the governor's power to recover the plunder appeared on a barber's pole.[46] The dearth of materials, tools and workmen prevented the Browns from replacing what had been destroyed at the Mansion.

Like many other families that spring, the Browns spent much of their time seeing to their own basic needs. They planted a garden, and the three cows brought from Dooly County provided their dairy needs. Mrs. Brown took charge of restocking her poultry yard but for lack of a rooster she made slow progress. Betraying ignorance of the most elementary principles of poultry breeding, she wrote her mother that she was at a loss to know why the eggs did not hatch.[47]

The older members of the governor's family remained for several months in Dooly County, where they found food but experienced hardships and difficulties. Nancy, the governor's sister, wrote in broken English of her quandary. "I don't know what to do about going home. I wish I was their today but I have nothing to pay my expences not no one to go with me. . . . If I have had known I would have stayed hear this long I would have taken up a school and tryed to have maid sumpthing."[48]

Brown, who had always fretted about Milledgeville's poor location, now found the capital more isolated than he had ever known it. Railroads, telegraph lines, and bridges had been destroyed. The only connection with the outside was a hack service to the railhead at Mayfield, to which a line had been constructed from the Georgia Railroad during the war. While the Central Railroad to Gordon was put back into limited service in February

1865, the Oconee at Milledgeville could be crossed only on pontoon bridges which had to be taken up in rainy seasons. Conveyances and animals for transportation were practically nonexistent, and prices for these were unusually inflated. The municipal government, which was without funds, obtained street hands by offering them a bare subsistence of four pecks of meal, twelve pounds of bacon, and a half gallon of syrup each month.[49]

Service at the Milledgeville Hotel was tenuous. Four months after Sherman's invasion a young woman who was an overnight guest complained of being kept awake all night by "cockroaches, bed bugs and noise in the streets where men were cursing and singing rowdy songs." She survived on a cold biscuit. Her room was without a water pitcher or towels, and the fireplace was described as a dump heap. The water supply came from a large tub at the head of the stairway, where every one stopped for a drink. "Those who did not have cups . . . stooped down and drank it directly or lapped it up with their hands," she noted. Despite its shabby state, the hotel received some prominent guests during this time, including Generals P. G. T. Beauregard and Daniel H. Hill; Mrs. William B. Howell and Mrs. Wardlaw, the mother and sister respectively of Mrs. Jefferson Davis; and George R. C. Todd, who, although a brother of Mrs. Abraham Lincoln, had served as a Confederate surgeon throughout the war.[50]

For the first time conditions on the home front might have appeared to be even more chaotic than those in the field. Soldiers' furloughs, which had always been granted with liberality, now abruptly diminished in number, and news of home conditions disquieted soldiers and broke the morale of many. Some no longer considered desertion dishonorable. John Hammond wrote from Mississippi early in 1865 describing the Army of Tennessee: "a thoroughly disorganized, demoralized mass, incapable of the slightest resistance. . . . With its best leader slain, more than one half of its artillery taken, a third of its number killed, wounded and captured, it now presents a gloomy aspect," he stated.[51]

The situation in Virginia and the Carolinas grew increasingly hopeless as the spring of 1865 approached. Lee surrendered on April 9, followed by the capitulation of Joseph E. Johnston's army at Durham Station nearly three weeks later. These events were a welcome end to a bitter struggle in which overwhelming manpower and industrial might had been the most decisive factors. The news of the war's end brought mixed emotions to the people of the town, as it always does to the vanquished. The Georgia Military Institute cadets, now increased to 200 in number, displayed the greatest evidence of unhappiness. "They were the saddest looking troops I ever saw," wrote a chaplain who was with them at the time.

One final act of lawlessness punctuated the tragic news from Appomattox and Durham. A mob of citizens and some soldiers broke into the quartermaster and commissary stores and the express office, where they ransacked and robbed for two days before the disturbance could be quelled. Those who had participated rationalized that the goods would have been confiscated by the victors. Returning soldiers, for whom the supplies had been intended, now had to go hungry or seek supplies from other stores.[52]

This incident created a new emergency. Hundreds of paroled men from Lee's army were drifting through Milledgeville on their way home. Since the train to Macon was not running at the time, the town became filled with a backlog of these men. The townspeople did what little they could for them, but the problem could no longer be managed by the Wayside Home and the Ladies' Aid Society. General Wayne, under a flag of truce, sent a large number of these men to John H. Wilson, the Union general at Macon, where he hoped they might be supplied from the Federal commissary there.[53]

Ironically, life at the Executive Mansion in the meantime went on almost as if the war had never occurred. Mrs. Brown wrote on April 27 of attending a wedding at the house of Major Williams, of the illness of Mr. Flinn, of the death of Mr. Stetson, and of hosting a dinner at the Mansion for the Baptist minister and his wife. The governor and Julius were away from home. As usual, Brown was diligently involved in the troublesome affairs of state. He had just arranged to send Leopold Waitzfelder to London to recover money for cotton shipped there by the state early in the war.[54]

Governor Brown had already surrendered all state troops to General Wilson and had received a parole from him. However, despite this parole, Brown's arrest and confinement by Federal authorities was already being planned. On the night of May 9 a squad of cavalrymen, sent from General Wilson's headquarters at Macon, reached Milledgeville. They entered the Mansion and called for Governor Brown, who was occupying an upstairs bedroom. Coming to the rail over the rotunda, he was informed of the orders to arrest him. After doing some minimal packing he accompanied them to Macon, whence he was sent under guard to Washington. "I was truly glad brother Joseph could go off so cam [sic] and composed," wrote Nancy Brown.[55]

The governor was kept nine days in Carroll Prison before being released

on city parole; after a week he was allowed to return to Milledgeville. On
June 29 James Johnson, a Columbus lawyer and a well-known Unionist
before the war, was appointed Provisional Governor of Georgia by President Andrew Johnson. Brown resigned the governorship on the following
day.[56]

Despite its escape from destruction, Milledgeville experienced greater
suffering from Sherman's invasion than any other community between Atlanta and Savannah. Moreover, it never experienced the tranquility which
the end of hostilities was expected to bring, for new political and economic
forces generated by Reconstruction were to lead finally to the removal of the
capital, and the town's energies and resources were to become almost completely exhausted in efforts to reclaim it.

10

Reconstruction: Removal of
the Capital

Provisional Governor James Johnson arrived unexpectedly on July 12 and stopped at the Milledgeville Hotel. Since he contemplated only a short tenure in office, he did not move his family to the capital, nor did he occupy the Mansion except as a boarder with the Browns, who continued to live there until November. During his term as provisional governor Johnson remained in Milledgeville only three or four days at a time, and occasionally he was absent for an entire week. During these absences his private secretary, Lucilius H. Briscoe, performed the necessary day-to-day functions of his office.[1]

Johnson's concept of his responsibility was to safeguard the state's property until an elected governor could be installed under a new state constitution, which it was also his duty to inaugurate. Accordingly he issued a proclamation for the election of delegates to a constitutional convention to meet at the Statehouse late in October.[2] The main purpose of this constitution was to give legal validity to what the war and military defeat had in fact already accomplished. Voting requirements for delegates to this convention had not changed since 1860, except that a few high-ranking Confederate leaders had not yet received a pardon and could not vote. The Negroes, who now were called freedmen, were not yet citizens and hence took no part in these political activities.

Many of the 285 delegates chosen for the new convention had been members of the convention which had passed the Ordinance of Secession in 1861, but every aspect of this new gathering was in stark contrast to the earlier one. The conservatives who had opposed secession were now in the ascendancy, and Herschel V. Johnson, an old Unionist, was the presiding officer. Some of the delegates, however, were of the old Confederate leadership; a great many of these were war veterans and showed up at the convention in their gray uniforms.

Charles J. Jenkins was elected governor under the new constitution. An aristocrat in manner and bearing and a member of Phi Beta Kappa, he possessed a scholarly approach to law and government. His writings reflect a mastery of historical detail. His inauguration on December 14 was without the usual display "of gallantry, chivalry and beauty."[3] The cold, rainy day proved an appropriate harbinger of the future, for this was the last guber-natorial inauguration that would ever be held in Milledgeville.

Jenkins had had no opposition in the election. While Brown had received a full presidential pardon early in September, he was wise enough to retire temporarily from active politics. However, he was quick to place himself squarely behind President Johnson's policy of reconstruction and was happy to offer the president advice about who in Milledgeville should or should not receive a pardon. Brown urged the president to deny the application of his old enemy, Augustus H. Kenan, whom he described "as the late con-gressman and tool of Mr. Davis." A few citizens of the town, such as Pleasant M. Compton and Boswell B. deGraffenreid, like Brown himself, soon became conspicuous for their eagerness to cooperate with the victors. Compton was rewarded with the Milledgeville postmastership, while deGraffenreid obtained other preferments.[4]

When members of the legislature assembled for the November session, they found the town in great physical and economic disorder. The peniten-tiary was in ruins and without food for its inmates. Patients at the Asylum fared only a little better than the prisoners. All public buildings were leak-ing and in need of general repair. The public squares were filled with rubbish and filth. Inside the Statehouse the furniture was either destroyed or defaced. Most of the wooden fence around the square had disappeared as firewood. Bridges throughout the county had also disappeared, and most of the roads leading into town were impassable in wet weather.[5]

Although the town now had a larger number of stores than before the war, they were shabby-looking and poorly stocked. Competition was so great that no merchant could earn a reasonable profit. A fitting symbol of the general state of affairs was the new post office sign with its letter S painted backwards, a slip-shod detail which irritated the editors of both newspapers.[6] The post office might well have omitted the sign altogether, since for a time it was impossible to obtain postage stamps. The lack of mail service caused the *Federal Union* to suspend publication for two months during the summer of 1865.

The municipal government was in great financial disarray. With money almost nonexistent, such commodities as eggs, corn and vegetables were used in a barter economy to meet necessary expenses. State bank notes and Confederate currency were worthless, and the municipal council authorized the lithographing of $4,000 in change bills; however, it failed to announce the terms of payment. Financial needs were so great that authorities threatened holders of cemetery lots with disinterment of family members already buried there if purchase contracts were not immediately complied with.[7]

The problem of getting the freedmen back to the plantations or into some form of productive employment was one of universal concern. For the first time Negroes were now able to come to town at will, to own firearms, and to ride a horse. Relishing their new-found freedom, they were likely to take off on a long journey while cotton rotted in the fields. Women of the town had difficulty obtaining servants, and it was even more difficult to keep them in constant employment.[8]

Municipal authorities finally ordered that all disorderly freedmen found on the streets should be placed in the guardhouse to await trial in the Mayor's Court, and stipulated such penalities as "ball and chain, bread and water, work on the streets, and confinement in jail or stocks . . . according to the offense." This problem was so widespread that it led to the enactment of a vagrancy law by the legislature in December. This law, which was careful to apply equally to whites and blacks alike, might impose a fine or imprisonment on anyone who was not visibly employed. Convicted vagrants could contract their labor to employers in exchange for the immediate payment of their fines.

While it took several years for the physical character of the plantation messuage to change perceptibly as a result of the black man's emancipation, the town underwent immediate changes. Whereas formerly Milledgeville's black population had been somewhat evenly distributed throughout the town, living for the most part in small houses at the rear of or alongside their master's or guardians's residence, now, augmented by a large number of freedmen who had drifted in from the plantations, the blacks formed special communities of jerry-built shacks on the outskirts of the town. Here disease took a dreadful toll, and municipal authorities often were hard pressed to provide minimal burial expenses. Blacks were interred in the cemetery plots nearest Fishing Creek, and segregated burials now became general.[9]

Only partly sustained by free rations from the Freedmen's Bureau or such agencies as the Southeastern Relief Commission, hungry blacks made nocturnal forays on chicken houses or pig pens. They would also frequently take stolen cotton to some deadfall establishment, where it was surreptitiously exchanged for whiskey or tobacco. Citizens of the town complained of freedmen appropriating fence railings, pickets, and timber from public bridges for use as firewood. The dozens of small foot-bridges at street intersections were particularly vulnerable to theft and soon had to be replaced with culverts.[10]

Problems such as these grew in intensity as the Reconstruction era unfolded. During these years Federal troops were in control everywhere in the state, although most of the elected officials in office at the time of Appomattox were allowed to remain. During 1865 the Federal garrison in Milledgeville was a small one. In July it consisted of a commander, Lieutenant George Buchanan, and twelve enlisted men. They were courteous to the inhabitants, all of whom praised their conduct. "They are very polite and gentlemanly," wrote a local veteran, "and unlike Yankees generally, always take the white man's part."[11]

The most obvious reason for their popularity was their orthodox attitude on the local vagrancy problem. The garrison commander went so far as to issue a directive to former masters of slaves requesting them to punish those who failed to work and to require that they conform to the old curfew law.

The Masonic Hall, built in 1832, and the fire tower, 1890

He tried to prohibit freedmen from selling articles without authority and also announced that he would punish anyone who harbored a runaway freedman. For this generous application of military authority in favor of the white establishment—a policy in direct conflict with that being established by the Freedman's Bureau—Buchanan was relieved of his command and his directive was canceled.[12]

The local office of the Bureau was conveniently located in the Masonic Hall, which also housed the garrison's headquarters. Officially entitled the Bureau of Refugees, Freedmen, and Abandoned Lands, this agency was created more than a month before the end of the war and was extended by subsequent acts of Congress until 1870. During its operation under the War Department it supplied food to both blacks and whites who were displaced by the war. However, with the surrender of Confederate forces the Bureau's work took on a more varied character. It now assisted freedmen in finding work, fixed the wages and terms of their employment, and protected them from discrimination. Sometimes serving as a probate court in untangling marital problems, the Bureau also assisted in establishing Negro schools and filled other functions generally associated with public welfare activities. Headed by General Oliver O. Howard, it had a strong organization in the Southern states. In April 1867 the Assistant Commissioner for Georgia, Colonel C. C. Sibley, was ordered to move his headquarters from Macon to Milledgeville; later, however, his office was returned to Macon.[13]

The local Bureau office in Milledgeville served Baldwin, Putnam, and Jasper counties. Its first agent was Thomas W. White, who was succeeded by J. D. Rogers; Matthew R. Bell replaced Rogers in December 1867. Contrary to what is generally believed, these men were not carpetbaggers, nor could they properly be called scalawags. White, for example, was a lawyer, and his father was one of the county's largest slaveowners in 1860. Bell and Rogers had come to Milledgeville during the war. Bell, who was a native of Forsyth County, had served as an enrolling officer with the rank of captain in Confederate service. His work as Bureau agent is said to have come "as close to giving satisfaction to both races as it was possible [to do]." Because the office gave him great influence over blacks, he later was elected to political office with ease; yet he appears always to have exerted his political influence wisely.[14]

The records of the Bureau agent's office at Milledgeville reflect nearly all of the varied problems with which that office was faced during Reconstruction. These records reveal that Bureau officials did not exhibit that partiality toward freedmen which is commonly attributed to such officials; nor did they ignore local tradition and try to remake Southerners into the Yankee mould, as it was sometimes claimed. Often they forced freedmen to adhere to work contracts made with white employers which the former desired to dissolve, and they settled differences between black parties as frequently as between blacks and whites. Since their problems were profuse and there were no precedents to follow, these officials often were at a loss to know how to proceed. The following note sent by Bell to the district office at Macon suggests the kind of frustration to which they were subjected: "How shall I compel parties to appear at this office? What shall I do with col'd children whose parents are dead? How can I get an old colored man into a hospital? How can John M. Tucker be forced to pay the wages he promised to pay 6 negroes when he has already sold the cotton and his land and stock already mortgaged?"[15]

Many of the freedman's problems grew out of matrimonial tangles left over from the days of slavery. These involved child support, rights of inheritance, and an occasional polygamous marriage. A former slave named Paul Freeman deserted a bad-tempered common-law wife and their two children, then remarried. While he was not forced to take back his original wife, he was orderd to pay four dollars monthly for the support of the two children. During the beginning of the cotton picking season freedman John Spivey ran his wife off with the apparent intent of harvesting for himself all the cotton which the two had cultivated. He was forced to permit her to return to his roof and then to harvest and sell her half share.[16]

Agent Bell was faced with a most unusual problem when a freedman, Ben Braxton, sought his assistance in recovering a sum of money which an imposter with a perverted sense of humor took from him in the nation's capital. Bell related the details in a letter to General Howard, chief of the Bureau in Washington. Braxton, who had been discharged from the army, had started home with $350 in his possession. The imposter, who gave his name simply as General Lee, and represented himself as an official of the Freedmen's Bureau, convinced the guileless Braxton that it would be unsafe to travel on the train with so much money and that he should entrust it to Lee so that it could be expressed to Milledgeville in care of the Bureau office there. "The man . . . wishes to know what has become of the money," wrote Bell. "He does not remember General Lee's [full] name." Howard simply informed him that "no Gen. Lee is known at this office."[17]

Most of the agent's attention was given to the making and supervision of work contracts. A list of seventy-three such contracts made in January 1867 included leases of small acreages to be worked in shares as well as a number of contracts stipulating direct payment for labor performed. The latter group, which largely represented contracts by town freedmen, were by far the most frequent. A typical example is the agreement made between John W. Moran and freedman Kane Helms, his wife Hester Hays, and their two children. Each of the adults was to receive $100 annually in addition to food and clothing for all four members of the family. Before emancipation this was the usual rate for the hiring out of slaves, and only a skilled artisan could expect to command a greater sum.[18]

The apprenticing of minors required only a simple contract with the parent or guardian. For example, for one dollar Nancy McIntosh apprenticed her daughter Mary to William H. Scott who agreed to keep her until she reached the age of eighteen and to provide her only with food and clothing. This was not the bargain for the master which it might seem, for food and clothing were in extremely short supply. Freedmen were in such need of these necessities that they often had to be supplied by local charity. Charles W. Lane of Midway once made a single contribution to freedmen of 100 pairs of shoes valued at $150.[19]

A surprising number of freedmen were able to make rental contracts for the use of their own livestock for cultivation, thus increasing their share of the crops produced. This appears to have been made possible by the large number of abandoned horses and mules picked up by blacks along the line of Sherman's march. "Unless the white people clearly establish a previous ownership [to these animals]," wrote a high Bureau official, "the freed people will be allowed to retain them." The Bureau also declared that the date from which freedmen should be entitled to compensation for their labor would be January 1, 1865 rather than the date of Lee's surrender in April.[20]

A few white men made contracts on which they later attempted to default. However, the Bureau considered the worker as having a lien on the crop which he produced, and the landowner could be arrested and the crop seized. The Bureau was authorized to use the local military garrison in the exercise of this authority, but such services appear to have been used sparingly and with restraint. Usually cases were settled with a hearing. For example, freedman Tom Burkett complained that John Roberts not only had broken his contract with him but also had beaten him up. Roberts countered that he had struck Burkett because he was fighting another freedman in his yard and using profanity in the presence of his mother.

Roberts was exonerated of all charges, and Burkett was ordered to resume work for him. On the other hand, Skelton Napier was ordered not to remove nine bales of cotton from Dennis Station until certain freedmen were paid for their labor in producing it. When freedman Peter Murray and his wife complained that J. W. Myrick had left the state owing them $200 for labor, some of Myrick's property was seized and sold to discharge the debt.[21]

Since freedmen showed little inhibition and less judgment in taking all manner of petty complaints to the Bureau agent, it is not surprising that many whites believed that the agent took the black man's side against them. These circumstances are aptly illustrated in the following letter written to the agent by Asenah Wells, a white schoolteacher:

I write . . . to know if you told that negro that has been running to you all the week about what my husband owes her . . . if you told her you would give him until Saturday to pay her and if he did not . . . you would put him in jail and . . . send him to the Penitentiary . . . what more would you have us to do for her we have had $4 worth of provisions here for her every [sic] since the first day of the month. I have to take everything my pupils parents are willing to pay me and my husband had to take provisions for his work. . . . I expect . . . she has told you a great many things that are not true and I expect that you would believe her before you will your own color.[22]

While no Ku Klux Klan or similar activity was reported in the county, conflicts between whites and blacks over Bureau policy sometimes flared into violence, although such outbreaks were infrequent. However, threats and intimidation generally prevailed. "My life is severely threatin By Mr. Reid as fair [far] as twice without a cause," freedman Christopher Bradley informed the local agent. "I have not parted my lips to him no way but he is sworn to kill me he put me to a great dele of truble. I do not see any peace I am afraide to go out at night even to go to church."[23]

One of the more famous cases of violence occurred in August 1865 when the younger Daniel H. Tucker was charged with shooting a freedman named Randall Smith. Tucker, in the company of a Federal soldier from the local garrison, entered Smith's house seeking his brother Daniel Smith, who had made a verbal labor contract with Tucker but had not appeared for work. At the time of the visit Randall Smith was in bed and in no mood to answer questions concerning his brother's whereabouts. The soldier struck Randall, whereupon he arose from the bed in anger and Tucker shot him with a pistol, crippling his leg. The wounded Smith asked for damages of $1,000. Tucker was arrested, taken to Macon, and placed under bond.

Later he deposited $350 in the local Bureau office, and the Smiths signed a statement saying that they had received ample indemnification and were withdrawing the charges. The local agent recommended that the case be closed. However, Bureau officials at the Macon office refused to allow this settlement because the offense was a criminal one which had to be prosecuted on its merits in the regular courts. By the time the case could be tried in the state courts, however, the lapse of time had deprived the prosecution of any chance for success, and Tucker escaped possible conviction for assault with intent to murder.[24]

Another type of Bureau activity involved efforts to assist black parents in establishing schools for their children, an enterprise in which a surprising number of local white citizens also gladly participated. Since no public schools existed in Georgia during the Reconstruction period, the children of poor parents of both races were without educational facilities other than what could be provided through local charity and assistance from outside agencies. In Milledgeville during 1866 nearly 100 children of poor whites received instruction in the factory settlement on North Wayne Street, where teachers donated their services and where citizens made contributions of textbooks and paper. As the year 1867 opened it was stated that "good schools [would be available] in almost every part of the city"—despite the fact that no common school fund was available and no local tax levies had been made. Prominently mentioned were the private schools of Lafayette Carrington, Castedana Cotting, and Miss Davidson. The Masonic Lodge took over the Male Academy and opened a school there. However, rural children outside the town were largely without schools. It was estimated that not more than 22 percent of them were in school in 1870.[25]

The American Missionary Society opened the Eddy School, in which 272 black children enrolled. Five white teachers were provided by the Bureau. On May 1 these children staged a procession to the west commons, where they crowned a queen of May, enjoyed a picnic dinner, and heard an address by Wilkes Flagg. In the following year the town donated a lot on which a substantial school building could be erected. This structure, which stood near the cemetery and close to Fishing Creek, was dedicated on March 19, 1869. Both races had contributed to its construction. More than 350 black children were now enrolled, and the Peabody Fund contributed twenty-five cents a month for each pupil.[26]

Black parents demonstrated in many ways an intense interest in their children's education. This is illustrated dramatically in a letter written by a freedman, Asbury Catchings, who lived in an adjoining community. Dated April 1, 1868, and addressed to the local Bureau, it reads as follows:

Mr. Bell Cier   We have Auganze [organized] a Chool and we are redy for your to seen them teechers we can get a 100 Childron . . . if they can get and opotunyty we could pay 35 dollars at leese we have a long Congragaton of our people together Sunday and they seem verry Anxsious. . . . Answer as quick as you can.[27]

The most active and effective black leader in Milledgeville during this period was Wilkes Flagg. When the war closed he suffered as others did, but his blacksmith shop prospered. He believed that the blacks should have been educated and provided with citizenship experience before being emancipated and that it was his duty to lead and instruct them in their new status. He acquired a plantation on which he established a colony, and on Franklin Street he built a Baptist church known as Flagg's Chapel. Here he assembled members of his race for instruction which was social and economic as well as religious in character. When the freedmen became voters, some leaders encouraged them to participate in politics, but Flagg frowned upon such advice. It was perhaps as a result of this that a schism developed in his flock which led to the formation of a rival church known locally as "the Hamp Brown Church." Flagg continued to work diligently, but old age found him financially insolvent. When he died in 1878 he left only a house for his widow, Lavinia, who for half a century had lived in relative luxury as his wife. After her death her body and that of Flagg himself were enshrined in the Baptist chapel which he had built.[28]

Flagg's Chapel and the Hamp Brown Church were the first of Milledgeville's segregated churches. Then, as the Negro community grew and developed its own identity, more blacks gradually withdrew from integrated churches. By 1873 black Methodists had formed the Trinity Colored Methodist Church. The black Presbyterians also began to follow this pattern, but their transition to segregated religious life in the town was so gradual as to be almost imperceptible.[29]

Social life in the white community was not so drastically changed by the war as it was among the black residents. However, the Reconstruction era was characterized by a number of innovations. Although the colorful military parades had disappeared, pageantry of a paramilitary nature was much in evidence. One of the more popular substitutes for prewar excitement was the tournament, organized by young men of the town to "keep alive the spirit of chivalry." Great crowds of all ages and of both races gathered to enjoy this event.

Typical of these touranments was one held as part of the Christmas festivities in December 1868. The Knights, dressed in their distinctive costumes, met at 10:00 A.M. on Jefferson Street and proceeded in a parade through the center of town and thence to the Orme Mansion on Liberty Street, where a track of 100 yards had been laid off. In order to qualify for entrance into the games, the knight had to cover this distance on horseback in eight seconds. Eleven young men qualified as participants. To earn points in the contest the rider was required "to cut off the head" at the end of fifty yards, and to "tierce the ring" at the end of the run. If all this was done in eight seconds a maximum of three points was scored. That evening at a ball held in Newell's Hall, the champion knight selected his Queen of Love and Beauty, while the next three highest scorers each chose a Maid of Honor. Richard Stubbs, Knight of the Golden Cross, won first prize and chose Mary White as his queen.[30]

Another tournament was scheduled for New Year's Day, but because of bad weather it was rescheduled for January 8, on the anniversary of the Battle of New Orleans. Seaton DuBignon won this contest and received a cavalry saddle. Miller Grieve presented the awards after delivering a patriotic address in which he noted that although "our cruel taskmasters have taken from us the privilege of forming military companies, . . . the Tournament will serve to keep alive the spirit of chivalry." He also expressed his delight that so many beautiful young women were present.

In a tournament held the following year, Ed Bain, Knight of the Golden Horseshoe, was adjudged the winner and received a steel engraving of General Robert E. Lee. West's "brass and string band" provided the music for the dance that evening, where Frances Goddard reigned as Bain's queen.[31]

The term *chivalry*, together with references to all of its honorable implications, now appeared more frequently than it had before the war. This emphasis upon the gentlemen's code appears to have served as a refuge from some of the hard realities of the lost cause. Unfortunately, this code at times took its own toll. Lewis Kenan, for example, had survived four years of hazardous fighting in the war only to fall to John Strother's bullet in the streets of Milledgeville five years later. The two had indulged in an extended feud involving Kenan's honor and pride. "Honor was his idol," read his obituary, "and he worshipped at its shrine with all the devotion of knighthood." Dicey Kenan, a former slave of the family, traveled nearly 300 miles from Thomasville to view the fresh grave of a member of the family in whose escutcheon she had learned to take great pride.[32]

The afflictions of defeat encouraged interest in various new types of social organizations. The local lodge of the Independent Order of Good Templars which met regularly at the Statehouse, boasted the second largest membership in the state. The Baldwin Farmer's Club was revived, reaffirming the community's acceptance of the agrarian order of life. Not outlawed by military authorities in spite of its overtones, was the Merchants and Mechanics Fire Company under Captain James H. Nichols, which drilled, marched, and held its annual parades and its balls. This group soon was as much a social embellishment to the town as it was a protector against conflagration. Its grand ball, held in November, opened the festivities of the legislative session of 1866—a session which otherwise was wholly without spirit and at which the few visitors were characterized as "despondent and indifferent." Meanwhile the revived Milledgeville Lyceum was relieving some of the humdrum life of lawyers and other professional people, few of whom had many clients. Among its weekly debates was one on the subject, "Should women be given equal rights with men?"[33]

The women of the town were not seeking equal rights at that time, but they were suffering equal despair with men—they were doing more than their share in dispensing what relief and charity they could afford. In March 1868 they organized a highly successful subscription supper for the benefit of maimed veterans (for whom the state in 1866 had agreed to provide free tuition and board at Oglethorpe University but as yet had failed to make an appropriation). Earlier they had formed an association to raise funds for Mrs. Jefferson Davis. In 1868 they also erected a monument "To Our Unknown Dead" to stand where soldiers who had died in the Confederate hospital lay in unmarked graves. This is said to have been the first Confederate monument ever erected in Georgia. On April 26, 1871, the ladies brought Confederate Memorial Day in Georgia to full bloom in exercises involving the entire community. Business was suspended, and citizens gathered for a sermon at the Methodist church, followed by a procession, the decoration of graves, and finally a chauvinistic address on the virtues of the Confederate soldier.[34]

In addition to organized social activities, various other forms of amusement became popular during the Reconstruction era. While the once-prevalent horse-racing and cock-fighting were not revived after the war, the traveling shows which had taken their place sometimes offered gamblers a rare opportunity to place an exciting bet. One of these was a highly advertised fight between a bear and three dogs, preceded by a dog fight, all held in a vacant warehouse. "The bear came off victorious, although McComb's dog stayed in the fight longest and came out greatly injured," wrote one spectator, remarking that it was the first show he had ever seen that offered more than it advertised.[35]

Yet another novelty, Robinson's Circus, arrived in town in the spring of 1868 after having been isolated by rain for several days on the east side of the Oconee without provender for its animals or food for its crew. Its principal feature was a performance by the famous clown, Charles Covelli; the rest of the show, however, was more of a zoo than a circus.

The activities of young people appear to have been little affected by the poverty which for many was the aftermath of the war. Innovations at this time included a skating rink at Newell's Hall and the new game of baseball, introduced by veterans who had discovered the game during the war. The first contest was played in the spring of 1871 in a meadow near Treanor's Mill. Soon a local club was competing against teams representing Sparta, Macon, and Eatonton. These games all ended in exceedingly high scores, inspiring a novel form of sportswriting in which no single play or combination of plays was mentioned. Instead there was an emphasis on each team's standing in runs at the end of each inning. Stars were picked on the basis of the low number of put-outs made against them and the total number of runs which they scored. Second-baseman Whiddon achieved stardom when he suffered no put-outs and scored nine runs.[36]

The first Christmas which followed the war was marked by the absence of the traditional fireworks and by cold, damp, and dreary weather. Only a few people appeared on the streets, and these had little money. Nevertheless, remarked one celebrant, "Egg-nog, Tom and Jerry, Bust-head and Tanglefoot took a general spree." Serenading, which had become a popular Christmas pastime, was also in evidence.

While social pastimes still could be freely pursued for pleasant associations, political life did not offer such agreeable results. During the final months of Governor Jenkins' administration the course of state political developments began to affect drastically the life of those who resided in the capital. Throughout most of 1866 and part of the following year, attention was given to the physical repair of the state's facilities in the town. In his

The old Statehouse as it appeared in 1830

only message to the General Assembly late in 1865 Provisional Governor Johnson recommended that these renovations be made as soon as possible, and he sought the beautification of the Statehouse Square and the removal of four church buildings from these grounds. "It is proper and expedient that the capital itself here be declared permanently located," he concluded. His successor, Governor Jenkins, reaffirmed these sentiments suggesting also that a separate supreme court building be constructed. Following a legislative appropriation for renovation, Colonel B. W. Frobell, who had been chief engineer in Hood's army, was made superintendent of public works and placed in charge of the project.[38]

With the help of convict labor, Frobell was able to renovate all buildings, making them tenable by the end of 1866 and to start construction on the covered bridge across the Oconee which opened in the fall of 1867. Since the state was not allowed a military establishment, the arsenal and magazine were not rebuilt. A number of modern innovations resulted from Frobell's efforts and enterprise. Gas lights and running water were added to the Statehouse and Mansion. To eliminate moisture in the ground floor of these two buildings, a dry moat was constructed around the base of each structure. A chronic leakage problem around the skylight over the rotunda of the Mansion was solved by constructing what Frobeil called "an observatory" which completely enclosed the old cupola; unfortunately its Gothic style was an intrusion on the original classic design of the building. For eight months during which the Mansion was undergoing these additions the governor lived in the Peter J. Williams mansion, which the state rented for his use.[39]

The Statehouse Square was laid off with curved walks and flower beds and was enhanced by a water fountain. The dilapidated wooden fence around the square was replaced by a low brick wall topped by three white rails. Three Gothic entrance gates also were constructed. The smallest of these, which has since disappeared, was a pedestrian entrance facing South Washington Street near the Episcopal church. Citizens of the town planted trees along parkways on the streets leading to the square.[40]

At the Asylum a new building was under construction for the accommodation of insane freedmen. However, most of the Asylum buildings were in poor repair, the mastic having fallen from the exterior walls. The penitentiary was rebuilt in improved style and several new structures were added, including a hospital, chapel, and an office building. The Penitentiary Square of twenty acres was enclosed with a neat plank fence, and the compound within this enclosure now had a capacity for 500 convicts. However, the vicissitudes of Reconstruction politics were soon to bring about the complete abandonment of this institution.[41]

With the opening in the fall of 1867 of the new railroad linking Milledgeville directly with Augusta and Macon, the physical recovery of the capital was nearly complete. It now seemed that the town had at last laid to rest all of the criticisms leveled at it during the abortive attempt in 1854–55 to remove the capital to a new location.[42] It is extremely doubtful that anyone in Georgia suspected that the legislature, which adjourned in Milledgeville on December 29, 1866, would be the last one ever to assemble in the town and that the refurbished legislative halls would never be used for the purpose for which they had been so carefully redesigned.

A new train of events destined to change drastically the course of the town's history had begun in March when Congress inaugurated its plan of military reconstruction. This new plan ignored the almost completed work which President Andrew Johnson had done in reconstructing the Southern state governments. Johnson's plan was now set aside, and the process began all over. Georgia became part of the Third Military District, with its headquarters at Montgomery (later Atlanta), and on April 1 General John Pope arrived in Atlanta to take command. He divided the state into eight military posts; Baldwin and twenty-one other counties comprised the Macon post.[43] Military occupation and control now became a new burden which the people had to bear.

Under the direction of congressional leaders, Pope further divided the state into forty-four political districts, each having three counties (although the three largest cities each comprised a single district). It was through these forty-four political divisions that Pope and the army undertook to shape the political future of the state. He proceeded to register those whom the military authorities would permit to vote. These included all black males of voting age and most of the white males who had not been conspicuous rebels; approximately 10,000 whites who had formed the state's political leadership during the war were refused registration. Since the registrars received twenty-six cents for each person enrolled, it was not unusual for them to permit multiple registrations and to register all who had drifted in from other states. The new registration list was identical to that which the Fourteenth Amendment stipulated, although that amendment had not yet been ratified.

The registration board sat for five days in Milledgeville during July and registered 916 blacks and only 450 whites. The apathy shown by those white men who could qualify disturbed the editor of the *Federal Union*, who urged everyone to register. The board returned in August and gave them another chance to enroll, but only an additional 210 whites did so, while an additional 184 blacks also were enrolled. It was only after the books closed that Pope gave the registration list a new importance by ordering all state courts to select their juries from the new registration lists.[44] The apathy of local white men slowly changed to bewilderment. They had believed that Reconstruction was over and had settled down to picking up the loose ends of their lives. Now, more than two years after Appomattox, it was as if the war had just ended.

General Pope's next move was to order voting on a convention to draw up a new constitution to replace the one of 1865. The voting was to continue for five days beginning on October 29, and 166 delegates would be chosen. These delegates were apportioned to the forty-four districts somewhat arbitrarily. The twentieth district, comprised of Baldwin, Hancock, and Washington counties, was allotted six delegates; some districts were given one and others as many as eight. The apportionment seemed to favor the urban centers toward which many freedmen had migrated; and it also favored the non-plantation areas of North Georgia where there was much residual

Unionist sentiment. Jere N. Moore, editor of the *Federal Union*, charged that the apportionment was rigged so as to make the white vote "63 per cent less valuable than the negro vote." For such unflinching criticism of the military authorities the *Federal Union*, by Pope's orders, lost its public advertising. Other conservative papers suffered the same penalty. This prohibition continued until the following year, when the order was repealed by Pope's successor.[45]

Under the voting system inaugurated by Pope it is extremely doubtful that anything devised by the white electorate could have prevented a favorable vote for holding a new constitutional convention. In some counties there was the hope that a wholesale absence of white voters from the polls might render a convention impossible. As a result of this possibility only seven white men voted in Baldwin County. However, more than a thousand blacks voted for the first time in their lives. In the state as a whole there was a total of 106,410 voters from a registration list of 188,671, and the vote for the convention easily carried with 102,283 votes. From the Twentieth District four blacks and two whites were chosen as delegates. No rigid residence requirements were enforced either for voters or for the delegates chosen by them. Some of the latter had only recently come to the state. One of the black delegates, C. C. Richardson, who represented the Twentieth District, gave Baldwin County as his residence, although no one of either race in that county seemed to recall having voted for him.[46]

The political complexion of the convention was Republican. While thirty-seven delegates were blacks, the leadership of the body was composed largely of white men, most of whom were not native Georgians. The old political leadership was conspicuous by its absence. Seth Boughton, now editor of the *Federal Union*, referred to it as a "conglomeration of scullions, boot-blacks, and black legs with a smart sprinkling of wandering Yankees in search of adventure," and he vowed that most of them "[did] not know the difference between [the words] constitution and constipation." The *Southern Recorder* was only a little less vitriolic in its characterization of the group. These long-standing rivals had at last found an important issue on which both could agree.[47]

Up to the end of November it was assumed that the convention would assemble at Milledgeville in the newly refurbished Statehouse. Then, without warning, General Pope issued a call for the delegates to meet at the Atlanta City Hall on December 9. This was the initial step in Milledgeville's undoing as the capital of the state.

Pope never fully explained his reasons for shifting the convention site to Atlanta. A number of reasons appeared obvious, but there were others of a subtle nature and perhaps more significant. Among the former was the fact that Pope's own headquarters stood within ear-shot of the Atlanta City Hall. Also hostility of the Milledgeville newspapers was in contrast to the situation in Atlanta, where there had developed a friendly radical press, one of which was the *New Era*.

While Milledgeville's problem of accessibility by rail to all parts of the state was now solved, the town still was criticized for its lack of hotel accommodations for a large number of visitors. It was argued that most of the elected delegates were poor men who would seek lodging in private homes, and the black delegates would find it unusually difficult to find any kind of accommodations in Milledgeville. Furthermore, it was not certain whether, or if ever, the delegates would receive compensation for their services.

Far more significant than the question of housing, however, was the formation earlier in the year of a group of business men and others in Atlanta who were working quietly with the radicals to obtain primarily for themselves and incidentally for their community anything which was possible for the military regime to grant. Chief among these men were Henry P. Farrow, soon to become a Republican leader in Georgia and an office-holder in the radical administration of Governor Bullock; E. L. Hurlbert, Samuel Bard, James L. Dunning, O. L. Pease, and Asa L. Harris, all of whom later received political appointments under Bullock; Richard Peters, a real estate developer and a member of the Atlanta City Council; and John H. James. The last had been born near Atlanta but had refugeed to Canada to wait out the Civil War; now a rising banker, he was soon to become mayor of the city to which he had returned.[48]

Farrow was the original sponsor of this group, which became known as "the Atlanta Ring," a term which appears to have been coined at this time by the Milledgeville editors. Dusting off old arguments used in the abortive efforts to obtain the capital in 1854, the group now added a single new tactic—one which proved highly effective in dealing with the military authorities. It was quietly rumored that Milledgeville had placed a special tax on all occupants of hotels and taverns and that the proprietors of these establishments had entered into a conspiracy not to entertain Negro and Republican delegates.[49] While it is quite likely that idle talk of such a maneuver may have occurred on the streets of the town, there is no record of a public meeting at which such tactics were discussed. Such a conspiracy was flatly denied by responsible local spokesmen.

Not yet realizing the full implications of Pope's order to assemble the convention in Atlanta, the editor of the *Recorder* registered only mild disapproval of the convention site and stated his dislike "of such a grasping spirit" as that shown by the Atlanta leaders who tendered Pope the use of the city hall. He rationalized that after all it might be well that the people of Georgia be spared the sight of seeing "the Yankee emissaries and negroes" fill the seats once occupied by such men as Troup, Crawford, Toombs, Cobb, and Stephens.[50]

Indeed, the convention which assembled at Atlanta in December was quite unlike any group of political functionaries which Georgians had ever seen before or were likely ever to witness again. A reporter from the New York *Herald* characterized the opening session as "decidedly rich," a tongue-in-cheek reference to parliamentary procedure and to the physical appearance of the delegates. The latter were described as "unshaven, uncombed, unwashed, and in most cases very dirtily dressed." Their conversation "was interrupted by the continuous squirting of tobacco juice into small tin spittoons, of which there are over two hundred scattered over the room." The city hall room in which they gathered was a small, dingy apartment without adequate space for visitors. It was equipped with pine desks and reed-bottomed chairs. Faded green calico of varying shades covered only the windows behind the president's chair; the rest were left bare to the sun.[51]

The Milledgeville editors did not fail to note the contrast between this room and the refurbished legislative chambers at the state capital. However, they also pointed out many stark contrasts between the Atlanta assembly of delegates and those of previous conventions held at Milledgeville. Commenting on the character of the members of the current convention, Seth Boughton of the *Federal Union* quipped—with a lamentable lack of prudence—that Atlanta washerwomen were chasing the members in every direction to collect their pay, although "from a personal inspection . . . [the delegates] had not had any washing done since they left home, so they could not have owed the women anything *for washing*." He insisted that some of the members could not obtain credit at home for a pint of peanuts and that many were never known to have worn a white shirt.[52]

The terms *scalawag* and *carpetbagger* were not in Editor Boughton's vocabulary at this time, but he did castigate the convention's membership with the epithet, "skohegan skunks." He also rebuked the editor of the

Atlanta *New Era* for pursuing the hypocritical and expedient role of praising the radicals while advocating Atlanta as a new seat of government. Quoting General Pope's well-known statement that his saddle was his headquarters, Boughton equated the Atlanta editor with the hind part of a horse's anatomy, declaring that the *New Era*, being the organ of Pope's government, was "as near the seat of General Pope's government as was agreeable." He further suggested that if the commanding general would move to Milledgeville as soon as the convention adjourned, he could rid himself of "the swarm of hungry office-seekers and toadies that torment him day and night and ... [who] come to his bed chamber and even [to] his kneading trough."[53]

The hammer blow to Milledgeville's pride and her dignity as the state capital came suddenly, on the last day of February 1868 when a simple clause providing for the removal of the capital to Atlanta was inserted into the new constitution. S. P. Richards, an Atlanta diarist, had earlier called the convention "a menagerie ... [and] a great burlesque on law and order" which had done nothing but spend money at the rate of $2,000 a day. Now, however, he lauded the convention for its act in incorporating the removal clause. "The fifth Saturday in February!" he wrote, "When shall we see another? Atlanta has been promoted to the dignity and importance of being the capital of Georgia ... by our great Convention ... so this is a capital place."[54] The insertion of the removal clause had won for the radicals new friends from unexpected places.

The constitution of 1868 had yet to be ratified by the voters, but since the voting list for the referendum was the same as that which had authorized the constitution and named the delegates, the outcome of this plebiscite was easily predictable. It was stated that the document would be approved even if it fixed the capital in the middle of the Atlantic Ocean.

Meanwhile another event from the same general quarter greatly agitated the people of the state as much as it did those living in Milledgeville. Early in 1868 General Pope had called upon Governor Jenkins and certain other elected officials for $40,000 from the state treasury to pay the costs of the convention. Jenkins had refused to issue warrants for this money on grounds that no constitutional authority existed for such a purpose. Before the question was resolved, Pope was succeeded by General George H. Meade. Not sharing Jenkins' concern for the rule of law, Meade appointed General Thomas H. Ruger, commander of the post at Atlanta, to duty as provisional governor of Georgia. At the same time Captain Charles F.

Rockwell of the Army Ordinance Corps replaced John Jones as state treasurer. Captain Charles F. Wheaton was appointed to the office of comptroller general, replacing John T. Burns, and also to the office of secretary of state in place of Nathan C. Barnett.[55]

When General Ruger presented himself in Milledgeville on January 13, he found Governor Jenkins confined to the Mansion and on crutches as a result of an accidental fall. Jenkins asked Ruger if he had been instructed to use force if necessary. The latter replied in the affirmative and produced his orders to that effect. "Well, sir," responded the governor, "you have the army of the United States at your back, and I can summon not even a respectable police force. I therefore elect to bow out to you rather than to a file of soldiers with muskets and bayonets." Jenkins then denounced the proceeding as an

General Thomas H. Ruger,
the last of the Milledgeville governors

outrage on the rights of the people of the state, adding, "Had I adequate force I would resist you to the last extremity."

Ruger's behavior was courteous. He went so far as to offer the ousted governor the privilege of remaining in the Mansion. However, Jenkins soon left for his home at Augusta. On the night of his departure citizens of the town expressed their appreciation for him in a torchlight parade.[56]

Before he left, Jenkins was careful to remove from the Statehouse both the Executive Seal and the Great Seal. These were committed to the custody of Richard M. Orme, Sr., who placed under his bed the small trunk in which they were concealed. In May of the following year Jenkins requested that the trunk be expressed to him, together with the sealed key. Meanwhile he had gone to Washington in an unsuccessful attempt to obtain from the Supreme Court an injunction against those in authority at Milledgeville. He also had deposited $400,000 of state funds in a New York bank, safe from seizure by the military government. He then went to Europe for an extended visit and did not return until 1870—an absence which may have prevented his arrest by military authorities.[57]

The other evicted officials did not fare as well as Jenkins. After being arrested by Ruger, John Jones was placed under city parole. Comptroller General John T. Burns, who was in Rome on the day his office was seized, was imprisoned by miliary authorities for his sharp criticism of Meade's action. Only Barnett escaped without great difficulties. The behavior of these officials was denounced by Meade as "acts of contempt and disrespect to the authority of the United States."[58]

Ruger was the last of the Milledgeville governors. During his five and a half months in office his acts were largely those of an efficient and responsible caretaker. His background was ideal for the role in which he now found himself. He was a graduate of West Point, where he had stood third in the class of 1854; later he had resigned from the army and had practiced law in Wisconsin before the war. The son of an Episcopal rector, the provisional governor attended services at St. Stephen's church, where Jenkins had served as Senior Warden. Wholly without arrogance and always friendly and considerate toward his neighbors on Clarke Street, Ruger came to be highly regarded by the people of the town and he surely won their approval when he ordered the entire military garrison into action to help control a fire on Wayne Street. On another occasion he ordered the regimental band of the Thirty-third Infantry to his headquarters at Milledgeville to give the town a free concert.[59]

Only one official act of Ruger's administration has left a note of reprehension to be sounded by those who, with all the superior advantages of hindsight, write history. Because the emancipation of slaves had removed all penal functions from the plantation, freedmen who had suffered conviction by civil courts soon taxed the limited capacity of the penitentiary. Accordingly the legislature of 1866 had given the governor discretionary power to lease convicts and relieve the state of prison expenses.[60] However, Governor Jenkins, who supported the penitentiary system over all other devices, was careful to make no leasing contracts. General Ruger was not so discerning. He inaugurated the infamous convict lease system on May 11, 1868, when he leased 100 prisoners to William A. Fort of Rome for work on railroad construction. The state received approximately seven cents per day for each prisoner. Two days before Ruger left office he executed a second lease under which the state received only three and a half cents per day for each convict. His successors expanded this policy in the years which followed.

The final stages in the rebuilding of the penitentiary were in progress even while the initial steps were being taken to lease its prisoners and to empty its cells. The total abandonment of these structures was a tremendous waste at a time when the state could least afford it. After 1868 the penitentiary buildings began to decay from disuse, and soon they passed into oblivion. This travesty received little notice in Milledgeville, however, because the people were willing to accept almost any workable substitute for the prison which had stood since 1816 like a festering sore in the center of the town. Indeed, many believed that the provisional governor had rendered the community a great service in helping to bring about an end to this institution.[61]

When he was relieved of his duties on July 4, 1868, General Ruger received a demonstration of appreciation by local citizens in a set of resolutions which cited his kindness, courtesy, and general deportment. The tempestuous *Federal Union*, which had raged so furiously about recent acts of tyranny, admitted that the town had been exceedingly fortunate in having such an officer sent there.[62]

Three months before Ruger left Milledgeville the new constitution with its removal clause was ratified by voters in a referendum. Friends of Milledgeville had been unable to find any effective manner of resisting the inclusion of the removal clause in the new constitution. They could only argue that removal of the capital had not been an issue in the contest for seats in the convention and that voters should now be given a separate opportunity to register their decision on the matter. This Meade would not permit.[63] The *Federal Union* later observed that there seemed to be an unholy liaison between a certain group of Atlanta businessmen and the state's new political rulers, and it ridiculed several social events at which Meade and his staff were guests of honor.[64]

Voting statistics showed, however, that Atlantans were by no means in agreement on the removal issue. Fulton County voters gave an overwhelming majority to the Democratic gubernatorial candidate, John B. Gordon, and also gave only a 210-vote majority for the new constitution. In contrast the statewide tally gave Republican Rufus Bullock the governorship and ratified the new constitution by a majority of over 17,000 votes.[65]

It is difficult to judge to what extent fraud and irregular voting procedures may have determined the final outcome. Absence of voting lists and un-numbered ballots made it impossible to check plural voting. The *Federal Union* quoted the Macon *Journal and Messenger*'s claim that had the removal clause been considered separately, the Milledgeville location would have been sustained by a majority of 100,000 votes.[66] While this was an exaggeration, there is little doubt that voters, given a separate referendum, would have sustained Milledgeville as the capital.

Not long after the consitution was ratified by the State, the town's mayor and aldermen directed a memorial to the Fortieth Congress requesting that body to strike the removal clause from the constitution when it was submitted for approval. The memorial reviewed all the reasons for maintaining the capital in its traditional location, citing its climate, geography, and the recent expenditure of $100,000 to repair the public buildings. As in the struggle of 1854–55, emphasis was placed on the state's moral obligation to Milledgeville's citizens, who had funded the original cost of public buildings through the excessive prices they had paid for lots in a town officially designated as "the permanent capital."[67]

One hundred fifty citizens—Republicans and Democrats—signed the document. A number of blacks were among the signers, including Peter O'Neal, the local political leader, and Wilkes Flagg. Boswell de Graffenreid, the town's leading Republican and a former mayor, was chosen to deliver the document personally to General Grant, for which occasion the municipal council purchased a new suit of clothing for him.[68]

The local committee's confidence in de Graffenreid may have been misplaced, however, for traveling to Washington on the same train with him was Henry Patillo Farrow of Atlanta, who later styled himself the custodian of the state's new constitution. When de Graffenreid presented the memorial to Congress, Farrow was ready with a long and detailed rebuttal, during which discourse he was careful to exonerate de Graffenreid of any attempt to subvert the plans of the Reconstructionists. Shortly thereafter, and to no one's surprise, Farrow became Bullock's attorney general—and Milledgeville's former mayor received an appointment as the governor's executive secretary.[69]

Farrow's rebuttal had characterized the memorialists as hypocritical "wolves in sheep's clothing." They were, said he, "chiefly the aristocratic property-holders of Milledgeville." He coined the adjective "fossiliferous" to describe both the people of the town and their habitations. "Old fogyism must give way to young America," proclaimed this thirty-four-year-old rising Republican leader. Citing Atlanta's population at a figure which proved to be in excess of 9,000 to that given in its official census two years later—while understating Milledgeville's size to the same relative degree—he left no doubt of his belief that size was a major factor in a city's qualifications as well as its right to be the capital of the state. In words which almost captured Henry W. Grady's image of "The New South," Farrow described Atlanta as a city of growth, progress, and industry, with its face turned toward the future.[70]

Thus Milledgeville's plea fell to Reconstructionist rhetoric, and the townspeople had only the barbed humor of the *Federal Union*'s editorials for consolation. Apparently Farrow had served with the Confederate Nitre and Mining Bureau during the war and at one time had occupied a shack on the banks of the Oconee River while engaged in the recovery of nitre from beneath not only old buildings and smoke houses in Milledgeville but also privies, both public and private. When apprised of this aspect of his wartime activities, the *Federal Union* was quick to remark upon certain similarities which it saw between Farrow's services as a Confederate and his growing politicial career as a Reconstructionist.[71]

In the meantime arrangements were being made in Atlanta for the legislature to occupy a rented floor in an unfinished opera house owned by Kimball and Company. This transaction was destined to have many interesting ramifications. It produced one of the first scandals in Bullock's administration and came close to wrecking Atlanta's plans to secure its hold on the state capital.

The Atlanta City Council offered in a resolution to supply suitable space for the government for ten years and to donate land on which it could eventually construct permanent buildings. Some time before the 1868 legislature met there the Atlanta Opera House and Building Association began the construction of a building containing a large auditorium on the southwest corner of Forsyth and Marietta streets. By the time the outside walls were up, construction funds were exhausted and the company went into receivership. Later the unfinished building was acquired by Hannibal I. Kimball and his brother for $31,750. Kimball now promised to have it finished for the occupancy of the legislature by the beginning of 1869. He proposed that the Atlanta City Council rent part of it for a state capitol at $6,000 a year. At the end of five years the state could exercise an option to buy it or erect a new building on another site. These arrangements were accepted by the city and by Governor Bullock, who had made Kimball his financial advisor with unprecedented influence over his administration.

In these transactions nothing was said about who should furnish water, lights, heat, and furniture for the building. To secure these Bullock advanced Kimball $54,500 in state funds without reporting the transaction to the state treasurer, Nedom L. Angier. This was done despite the fact that most of the state's furniture and office equipment had already been removed from Milledgeville.[72]

When it was completed, the capitol had four full stories above a basement, and a fifth story with dormer windows under a mansard roof, all topped by a clock tower facing the main entrance on Forsyth Street. The structure abutted the sidewalk on two sides, leaving no space for grass, shrubbery, or trees. It never earned a more dignified title than Opera House; in fact, some of its less ardent admirers gave it such nicknames as "Pigeon Rookery," "Owl's Nest," and "Buzzard's Roost."[73]

On the occasion of its grand opening in January 1869 it was brilliantly illuminated with gas lights, and a band from the military post held forth in the Representatives Hall. However, only a small part of the building was equipped for governmental uses. To the astonishment of many, the top floor had been transformed into a lodging area with signs labeled "Sleeping Rooms For Rent." Also under the same roof with the legislature were gambling, eating, and drinking saloons. Only a few pieces of the Milledgeville furniture were visible in the state rooms. After some effort, Milledgeville editor Seth Boughton was able to locate in a saloon some of the furniture brought from Milledgeville. He wondered if this would not also be the final destination of the old portraits of state and national leaders which once had adorned the walls of the old Statehouse.[74]

The Opera House had been occupied for barely six months when it began to settle and the plaster began to crumble from its walls. Engineers discovered in its foundation a defect which was difficult if not impossible to repair. The upper floors became uneven and openings began to spread, causing windows to jam and doors to drag. The doors of the Supreme Court Room refused to close, and the area was later abandoned because the outside walls swayed so perceptibly that it was declared unsafe. On several occasions the legislature refused to assemble until a committee had inspected the basement to determine if the building were safe.[75]

No sooner had the building's defective construction been discovered than Kimball began to complete plans to unload it on the state. He obtained the support of Governor Bullock, who recommended its purchase by the legislature. This was followed by some unusual political maneuvering. Originally the House had voted to table the motion by an eleven-vote margin. Within the next few days, however, the original opponents of the measure grew strangely quiet and tractable. Attempts to refer the matter to popular vote were defeated. The Speaker once refused to allow opponents of the measure to be heard on points of order. Four days after its original vote the House registered a change of opinion by forty-one members. It was rumored that food, whisky, and political threats all had been used to obtain a favorable vote. The House approved a purchase price of $380,000; a Senate resolution raised the figure to $390,000. Eventually the building was exchanged for state bonds.[76]

This transaction and its sordid implications won new friends for Milledgeville. During the debates on the measure the Opera House had been called "a rickety fire trap" which was so noisy that nothing spoken within its walls could be heard. It was bordered on two sides by structures that cut off air and light, and its steam plant stood on a rented lot that was not included in the sale. But what stunned the people most was the revelation, made after the sale, that the building was encumbered with a mortgage of $60,000. This information was the climax of the most serious threat to Atlanta's continued hold on the capital—a threat sufficiently alarming to cause the Atlanta City Council to pay off the mortgage and to clear the title.[77]

In the legislature the thirty-odd black members easily held the balance of power between the radical and the conservative factions, and Bullock worked diligently to curry their favor. The problem now facing the Atlanta regime was how to find some practical modern use of the facilities at Milledgeville which would remove the persistent argument that these empty buildings represented a waste which the state could ill afford. A motion was defeated which would have transferred the Statehouse and Mansion to the trustees of the Asylum, who sought funds for expansion of that institution, now struggling with the longest waiting list in its history.[78] Failing here, Bullock recommended to the legislature that the Milledgeville facilities be used as a "Negro State University," and a bill to this effect was introduced by Henry McNeal of Bibb County, perhaps the most outstanding black member of the legislature. This move was challenged by those who argued that not a single Negro in the state was known to be prepared for entrance to such an institution. However, the measure was finally defeated by poor management within its own ranks and by extravagant demands of Negro legislators who sought an independent black council to act with finality on the matter.[79]

The *Columbus Sun* stated that "Bullock intends to have the Statehouse in Milledgeville fired if necessary to carry out his rascally schemes."[80] There is some evidence that the governor's proposals were designed largely to intimidate the people of Milledgeville with the threat of destroying the town's pleasing environment and to punish them for their hostility towards the new regime in Atlanta. Milledgeville's Seth Boughton had usually been the first to expose and ridicule the policies of the radicals. If he could be subdued in some fashion, their remaining plans might face less opposition.

These plans included the acquisition of a governor's residence. Atlanta's promise of a mansion for the chief executive had never been fulfilled, although the city provided him commutation of rent at a hotel. One of the final acts of the 1870 General Assembly was the approval of the purchase of the John H. James house at Peachtree and Cain streets. James claimed that the construction of the house had cost $53,000. The sale price of $100,000 included rugs, furniture, and equipment and also the use of a private waterworks system. Democrats who abstained from voting on this issue claimed that they succeeded in preventing a quorum, but the Speaker put the question and later announced the bill's passage.[81]

Oddly enough, this procedure, which was reprehensible to many, did not draw the same degree of editorial fire that had followed the Opera House swindle. Nevertheless new rents soon developed in Atlanta's armor. Mass meetings were held in many parts of the state where the return of the capital to Milledgeville was favored, and newspaper support increased. These efforts were directed toward having the issue submitted to the people, in which case it was believed a popular vote would result in returning the capital "to the halls of our fathers." On one occasion such a resolution received a two-thirds vote for approval. However, parliamentary obstacles mounted until a three-fourths vote was needed to overcome them, and the resolution was lost. The *Macon Telegraph* stated that Georgia's rural virtue had been seduced by city fashions.[82]

Indeed, Atlanta was enjoying a bustling growth and prosperity which few Georgians had ever imagined. Her people believed in their city's future and became its incurable boosters. Milledgeville, on the other hand, remained unchanged, and her friends felt that they were custodians of the Old South and its finest traditions. They saw in Atlanta's rhetoric only boastful arrogance and vulgar ostentation. Commenting on Atlanta's boast that it was a wide-awake city and easily accessible by railroad while Milledgeville was an isolated and sleepy rural town, Seth Boughton reminded them that Satan's domain was also a very bustling place and, like Atlanta, it was quite accessible.[83]

As early as 1868 Atlanta businessmen were already thinking of the possibility of their city becoming an international center through the building of a river port on the Chattahoochee. "We would not be surprised," observed Boughton, "if [the Atlanta City Council] should pass an ordinance to have the Savannah River [change its course] . . . and make Atlanta a great naval base." Indeed, continued Milledgeville's wry commentator, if the Atlantans would simply learn to suck as hard as they blow, the ocean would be at their doorstep.[84]

Boughton saw a close similarity between Atlanta's success in luring Oglethorpe University away from Milledgeville in 1870 and what he called the stealing of the capital. Both procedures reeked with shameful fraud, he said, and both institutions had taken years of toil and thousands of dollars to build. The university had begun at a Presbyterian prayer meeting in Milledgeville in 1835. Now, in Atlanta, it had forsaken its old liberal arts traditions and wedded itself to the ideals of the New South. Perhaps in reflection of this turmoil, the institution was forced to close in 1872, although it did reopen in 1913.[85]

By the time Oglethorpe closed its doors, the Bullock regime had run its course in Georgia. Elections of December 1870 secured for Democrats the control of both houses of the legislature. Soon certain members of Bullock's ring were officially charged with crimes punishable by penitentiary confinement. In October 1871 Bullock himself resigned and secretly fled the state. Kimball followed his example. With characteristic ridicule,

Boughton referred to the flight of Bullock and Kimball as "another New Departure" and called Bullock "our runaway ex-excellency."[86]

Soon some of the key underlings of the Bullock ring were reported under arrest, and Boughton's pen moved with renewed zest. Henry "Potash" Farrow was reported incarcerated along with Foster Blodgett and charged with plundering the state railroad and taking money under false pretenses. Also arrested was Asa Lyman Harris, who was charged with fraud. Harris was an Ohio-born ex-army mail official who remained in Georgia after Sherman departed and became one of the ring's most versatile members. His weight was well over 300 pounds, and Boughton always referred to him as "Fatty," although in Atlanta he bore the dignified title of Colonel.[87]

In an editorial Boughton pretended to give some advice to the jailors of Farrow and Harris. "Potash Farrow," he wrote, "has a great affinity for moisture and he should by all means be put away in a dry place, less he become all lye. Let Fatty Harris be kept in the same room—then as they melt and run together they will form a large mass of soap, which is probably the only thing that either of them is good for." He suggested that while the "Atlantese" might have very little interest in old fashioned soap, it was something for which they had a great need. In a more serious vein the editor predicted that the trials to be held in March would result only in the conviction of some petty thieves, while those who had stolen thousands and millions would go unpunished. His predictions were accurate. After several years' absence both Bullock and Kimball returned to Atlanta and stood trial, and they were cleared of the charges against them. Both resumed a life of respectability in Atlanta.[88]

With the Bullock regime out of power and its leaders in temporary disgrace, the state was redeemed from the radicals. Georgia's Reconstruction era came to an end early in 1872. The controversy over the capital now centered on the attempt by sponsors of Milledgeville to call a constitutional convention which would repudiate the worst features of the 1868 constitution, including the removal clause.[89]

The first move to obtain legislative sanction for a new convention was made in 1874. On the evening before the legislature was to vote on the bill, however, the entire Senate was entertained by O. L. Pease at a dinner at the Kimball House. New arguments against changing the constitution at this time were put forth. These included the cost of a new convention, estimated at $30,000, and the danger of retaliation by the Federal government if the Reconstruction consitution were tampered with. It was argued that federal officials might restore military authority along with black political domination. Ironically, these arguments were the opposite of those used in 1868 to obtain the removal of the capital from Milledgeville. The convention measure was defeated in the House by a vote of 100 to 65, and the Senate bill, would simply delete the removal clause from the existing constitution, lost by a vote of 19 to 16.[90]

The issue was bound to reappear and a new constitution was inevitable, but time was working in Atlanta's favor. Memories of that city's association with the excesses of Reconstruction were rapidly fading, and Atlanta was successful in making life exciting for lawmakers. This was achieved, according to Boughton, at the expense of no-quorum legislative assemblies on days following a night on the town.[91]

A state constitutional convention finally was assembled in the summer of 1877, after the prospect of federal intervention had ended and the Southern states everywhere were turning to home rule. The Georgia convention framed a conservative document which actually was more in conformity with the ideals of rural Milledgeville than with those of urban Atlanta. No one held the least doubt about voter approval in December. However, Milledgeville was to be victimized by a reversal of the tactic that had robbed her of the capital in 1868. This time the question of the capital's location was to be voted on separately from the constitution itself!

Atlanta's citizens now waged an all-out campaign to keep the capital. They formed a committee, collected donations, mailed out pamphlets, and sent out speakers to all parts of the state. Speakers representing Milledgeville were met with organized rebuttal on every platform. Proponents of Atlanta not only introduced new arguments, some of which were absurd and naïve, but also secured the endorsement of such men as Alexander H. Stephens, Joseph E. Brown, and Huke Smith. Robert Toombs remained uncommitted: : "I do not care whether the capital is Atlanta or Lickskillet," he announced, "so long as we have a good constitution."[92]

Milledgeville's battle plans were well known by the opposition, but even more disadvantageous to her in this final phase of the struggle was the exhaustion of her financial resources. Only recently a tornado had swept across the town, killing nine people, injuring sixty others, and destroying ninety-four dwellings and the Oconee bridge. Prior to this two disastrous fires had destroyed fully half of the town's business section, including the new Milledgeville hotel and Newell's Hall, the latter alone valued at $75,000.[93] The community still owed a large debt for railroad bonds which it had authorized earlier so that the town might no longer be criticized for its inaccessibility to visitors. Finally, her limited manpower was severely diminished early in 1877 by the death of Seth Boughton.[94] No one remained who could match the biting editorials and the humor and logic which this editor had been capable of producing.

As the voting date approached there was a perceptible shift of public sentiment toward Atlanta. An observer from McDuffie County stated that one month earlier pro-Atlanta voters could be counted on one's fingers, but on election day they were swarming everywhere. Atlanta won the capital by 43,934 majority votes. Forty-two counties, most of which lay south of Atlanta, returned a majority for Milledgeville. Three coastal counties with large black populations voted overwhelmingly for Atlanta.[95]

The new editor of the one remaining local paper took the defeat philosophically and in good grace, calling the outcome simply "an illustration of the potency of pluck, industry, and cash." He could now turn his attention to other problems.

Georgia was the only Southern state which had its seat of government permanently relocated as a result of the confusion of Reconstruction politics. In 1870 Milledgeville's population was 2,313, of which 51 percent were blacks. Of the remaining capitals of states in the old Confederacy only Tallahassee had fewer people, yet only four capitals were cities of more than 10,000 population. Atlanta, with 21,289 inhabitants, did not surpass Savannah as Georgia's largest city until 1880.[97]

Sherman's invasion, the physical destruction, and economic disorder wrought by the war and by natural catastrophes were transitory. They were of little significance to the people in comparison with the spiritually debilitating policies of Reconstruction. Milledgeville's loss of the capital was an added humiliation to a courageous community already burdened with more than its normal share of adversities.

Epilogue: A Community in Transition

Following the removal of the capital the people of Milledgeville passed through a period of great spiritual affliction. Many established residents moved to other communities; a number of these were political functionaries who followed the government to Atlanta. Partly because of this loss and partly because of other difficulties the town's postwar growth was slow. Only 3,332 inhabitants were recorded in 1890.[1]

Typical of the pattern by which many old family names disappeared from the community are the records of the Orme and Fort families. Some of the members of the Orme family moved to Macon, while others went to Savannah, Atlanta, New Orleans, and even to California.[2] One of the Orme daughters, Mrs. Charles P. Crawford, remained in the family mansion in Milledgeville, which was still occupied by her descendants in 1976. The Fort family also moved to Macon, whence members of that distinguished clan later dispersed to other communities. Tomlinson Fort, Jr., was elected mayor of Chattanooga in 1876.[3]

Like Fort, most of these emigrants found improved opportunities for their talents in the communities to which they removed, and many enjoyed remarkable success. John Hammond became president of a bank in Savannah. Here, too, Fleming DuBignon developed into an outstanding lawyer and legislator, serving as president of the Georgia Senate in 1888. John Sanford became attorney general of Alabama, and Jordan C. Compton presided over that state's senate at Montgomery. Among a group of future writers and journalists who departed for New York were Frances Way Williams, who became society editor of the *New York Herald*, and Alfred Newell, who worked on the *Brooklyn Eagle*.[4]

Only a small number of those who refugeed to Milledgeville during the war remained there after that conflict ended. Among these was William Gibbs McAdoo (d. 1894), who arrived from Tennessee in 1864 with his wife and infant son who bore his full name. Here McAdoo practiced law in an office in the old Statehouse and for a time served as county school commissioner while Mrs. McAdoo taught school. In 1878 he returned with his family to Tennessee, where he was appointed to a professorship in the University of Tennessee at Knoxville. While the family was living in Milledgeville, the younger McAdoo attended school at Midway and, to help support his father's large family, he worked in the printing office of the *Union-Recorder* and sold newspapers in the streets. Years later this young man would wed Woodrow Wilson's daughter and eventually become the secretary of the treasury in Wilson's cabinet.[5]

On a sentimental visit to Milledgeville in 1923, traveling in a private railroad car, William Gibbs McAdoo renewed his acquaintance with numerous childhood companions in the town. His recall of the names of black friends that he had known was phenomenal. He was surprised to learn that so many of them had moved away, just as many of his white friends had done.[6]

The emigration pattern of blacks was only a little different from that followed by whites, but there is little data on which to judge their success or failure in their new environment. While a few moved to Northern states, most relocated in the more prosperous urban centers in Georgia. None are known to have settled west of the Mississippi, where they might have secured free homesteads on which to begin a new life. A few went to Liberia. Among these was Allen Yancey, who left early in 1873. Others included the families of Nathan Barnes, Sandy Gannoway, the Tuckers, and the Wallaces. Writing from New Philadelphia in April, Yancey told of losing three children to whooping cough and worms, and of the death of his mother. Despite these tragedies he was determined to remain in Liberia, where he believed his opportunities were excellent. Not sharing his optimism were Nathan Barnes, who was sick with fever, and Sandy Gannoway, an elderly immigrant afflicted with incurable homesickness. The latter returned to Milledgeville in 1874, somewhat embittered, if wiser than when he had departed. His family had been stranded in New York without means for further travel, and an appeal was made to local charity to aid in their return to Milledgeville.[7]

With the end of Reconstruction, new and stable work relationships between white employers and black laborers quickly evolved. In agriculture this relationships was based on the system of sharecropping. Those who had lived in town before the war continued to work in much the same manner as they had under slavery. Now, however, they faced competition from those who had left the plantations in order to avoid the rigors of agricultural labor. While a few of the black townspeople operated their own businesses, most were employed in personal services and menial labor on a wage scale that provided only bare subsistence.

Of the 311 mulattos who lived in the county before the war, more than a third now resided in Milledgeville, most of them operating their own shops. Since it had been the custom for white masters to grant freedom to their children born of slave mothers, a large number of mulattos had long been freedmen—at least by implication. Many of these continued to enjoy a paternalistic deference in their economic pursuits under the new regime. As a group they fared unusually well during the post-Reconstruction period,[8] dominating the barber's trade until well into the following century.

Certain standards of demeanor for black citizens were informally established and then rigorously enforced. Industrious habits, fidelity to one's employer, and a Christian humility and forbearance were important imperatives in their conduct. Punishment was extremely harsh for petty larceny and theft, and vagrancy was not tolerated. Since vagrancy laws had been frowned upon by federal authorities, the most effective controls over this offense were informal. During the Spanish-American War, for example, the black man was encouraged to believe that the army draft was his only alternative to steady employment. A few strangers were engaged to carry yardsticks around on the streets pretending to measure vagrants for army uniforms.[9]

Any attempt by whites or blacks to disturb existing employer-employee relationships met with intense reaction. The only incident of post-war violence in the town arose when such relationships were challenged. Peter O'Neal, the county's leading black political organizer, remained undisturbed as long as he confined his activities to black political functions. In 1887, however, after he had met with a white political organizer, he was warned to leave the community. This he did, but not before his house in the Seatonville district was burned.[10]

The black man's freedom was far from complete. After Reconstruction many blacks found themselves in a quasi-slavery system which was sanctioned both by state law and custom. Because blacks often received harsher punishment for their crimes than did whites, they comprised a large percentage of the penitentiary's population. Beginning in 1868 most of the state's convicts were leased to railroad contractors and other corporations; however, a number were contracted to small operators and to cotton planters. Henry Stevens, for example, obtained fifty convicts in 1874 for work at his pottery plant south of Milledgeville. His contract called for him to pay the state only twenty dollars per year for each convict, and the lease ran for two years. In addition, Stevens had an agreement with county authorities who sent to him for employment all persons convicted of petty crimes and misdemeanors who were unable to pay the fines assessed upon them. He then compensated the county by paying the fines and court costs.[11] This was a convict lease system at the lowest level of local government.

Stevens' convicts were engaged in brick-making and in manufacturing various ceramic products. They operated the steam plant, saw, and grist mills, and cut firewood. Supervised in squads, they were under guard at all times. After learning of an insurrection by convicts in Washington County, Stevens acquired a cannon, loaded it with nails and scrap metal, and mounted it near the gate of the stockade as a warning to the men who worked under his lease. Despite such unusual procedures Stevens' management of convicts does not appear to have been harsh in comparison to standards followed by the larger corporate leaseholders. He reported no serious injuries and no deaths in 1875, and the food he supplied was adequate in both quantity and quality. At a Christmas dinner that year the prisoners were served "roast pork, turnips, greens, and wheat bread"; after dinner they sang Christmas hymns for Stevens' guests.[12]

It should be noted here that a great majority of Milledgeville's black citizens were never charged with any crime or misdemeanor. They managed to meet their obligations and to enjoy a degree of respect. Some were even recognized for their unusual worth to the community—a fact attested to by numerous obituaries penned by white editors. Invariably, the quality most highly praised in these vignettes is the close adherence of the deceased to those informal standards of conduct which had been set for their race. The death of Bob Spencer (formerly McComb) in 1879, for example, called forth the comment that he had worked at the Milledgeville factory for twenty consecutive years. "During all this long time, as a slave and as a freedman," wrote the editor, "Spencer has been faithful to every duty assigned to him, and diligent in and out of season, bearing an irreproachable name with both races. [He was] temperate, polite and industrious. . . . Such men are respected in every community where industry, honesty, and temperance are pronounced virtues."[13]

Frank Foarde was cited for "his good sense, his intelligence, and his blameless Christian life." July De Sauseaure, who died a Methodist minister in 1886, had been a slave of David C. Campbell. He was described as "much above the average in intelligence and good judgment, and never used these endowments for other than good purposes." It was also noted that he had "retained and manifested his affection for the children of his former master ... which was reciprocated by them."[14]

Bill Marlow (Marlor) was a brick mason who died in 1873 at the age of fifty-six. He was said to have worked on every brick building in the town and to have constructed most of the cemetery vaults. He was praised as having been "intelligent, affectionate, amiable, tender-hearted, industrious and liberal to a fault." His services were held in the old Methodist church building in the cemetery, where both white and black ministers officiated. His former master, Dr. Samel G. White, paid all his funeral expenses.[15]

Asa Wilson, a shoe-mender, was a rather eccentric black man of unusual accomplishment. Having once been a janitor at the University of Georgia, where he had learned many Latin words and phrases, he commanded an unusual and impressive vocabulary. He also collected rock specimens. Dick Betton was a barber who during the war went to Virginia with a local company but later returned to Milledgeville. "Here, amid many vicissitudes he continued to live with undiminished affection for his native town until his death." The obituary of Nancy Holmes, who died at Midway in 1873, cited her good character and emphasized the fact that she had "remained an acceptable member of the Baptist Church for the past 15 years."[16]

There appears to have been no insistence upon segregation in either the black- or the white-dominated religious groups which existed during the post-Reconstruction period. When P. G. Reynolds and Minnie Hitchcock were married in Flagg's Chapel, a large number of their friends of both races were present. Before the wedding the groom hosted some of his white friends at a dinner prepared by his mother. It was pronounced "a delightful feast." Performing the wedding ceremony was C. H. Brightharp, who had succeeded Wilkes Flagg as the leader of the most distinguished black congregation in Milledgeville.[17]

Toward the end of the century, however, the only institution in the town which remained racially unsegregated was the city jail. Still called the guard-house, it had one compartment for men and another for women. Once when a white man charged with drunkeness and disorderly conduct fought a black cellmate for the possession of the cell's single mattress on the floor, the former was released from custody without further ado.[18]

Segregation in its first legal form appeared in the common school law of 1870, which clearly provided that black children should be taught in separate schools but should have the same facilities as whites. Significantly, the original law did not forbid white teachers from instructing black children, and this procedure was pursued in some parts of the county. However, this practice became increasingly unpopular and soon disappeared. By the end of the century segregation had become a well-established tradition.[19]

Reconstruction politics did little to help public schools. The emancipation of slaves had doubled the number of children to be educated in the community while reducing by half the base upon which school taxes could be levied. Furthermore, mismanagement of the state school fund by Governor Bullock in 1871 delayed the beginning of the public school system. Not until 1873 were there schools in all local districts of the county and in Milledgeville. In the fall of that year "a free school," bearing the impressive name of Capitol School, opened under J. H. Allen in the basement of the old Statehouse. At the end of three months, when the common school allotment was exhausted, the institution converted itself into a private school with tuition charges. During 1874 there were three small private schools in the town in addition to the Capitol School, each of which operated both as a public and a private school. At Midway the Talmadge School opened as a high school under B. T. Hunter, but lack of patronage forced it to close after two years.[20] The community was left without a high school or an academy until 1880, when a military college opened on Statehouse Square.

The Eddy School, said to have the largest schoolhouse ever constructed in Georgia by the Freedman's Bureau, was opened in Milledgeville soon after the war, and by 1886 it had an attendance of 300 pupils. At the end of the century it was the only high school serving blacks in a large area of Middle Georgia. While it received aid from philanthropic sources not available to white schools, its classrooms were overcrowded and its teachers underpaid. A total of 250 pupils were taught in only three rooms designed to seat fewer than 200. Two teachers occupied a single classroom packed with almost 200 pupils.[21]

Problems of educating white children of the county were complicated by their wide geographic distribution. School districts in 1879 followed the same boundaries as military districts. Within one of these—the 318th—lay the once-famous plantations of the Scott, Furman, Sanford, Myrick, and Howell Cobb families. This district contained nearly 500 black children but fewer than forty white pupils. The latter were scattered over an area of 100 square miles, yet only two schools were provided for them, and they had to travel great distances to reach their schools.[22] The schools provided for black children were more numerous and closer to their homes but were severly overcrowded.

As late as 1900 the teacher's salary for the county prescribed only $35 per month for white teachers holding a first grade license. For holders of second and third grade licenses the figure was $25 and $20, respectively. Black teachers holding these licenses received only $24, $20, and $18, respectively.[23] Even for a six-month term, which only recently had been provided, the maximum annual salary was only $210. These salaries were based on a scale of low-paid farm labor wages and gauged by the scale of bare literacy—the ability to read, write, and "cypher" was the only qualification required of teachers.

Because many tutoring classes were held in private homes throughout the town, the quality of education in Milledgeville was superior to that in the countryside, where schools were held in abandoned houses, barns, and hastily constructed shacks, all with inadequate heat and light. There was no provision for a local tax levy for schools before 1879. At that date there appeared the first fruition of a series of events destined to change completely the character of Milledgeville, transforming it from its postwar role as a purely agricultural town to one having a high degree of institutional eminence.

This development originated in a minor skirmish which unfolded between Milledgeville and Athens over the location of a proposed state college of agriculture. This issue arose when Georgia's quota of federal land grant funds under the Morrill Act, amounting to $243,000, became available in the latter part of 1871. Public colleges to which the state might direct this fund were required to teach agriculture and military science. The trustees, alumni, and friends of the University of Georgia urged that the federal grant be given to the university at Athens.[24]

At this point a group of Milledgeville leaders headed by William McKinley and Seth Boughton urged support of a plan to have their town become the seat of the proposed agricultural college. Not yet willing to surrender his dream that the capital might eventually be returned to Milledgeville, Boughton urged the use of the old Oglethorpe campus, which, he claimed, had a value of some $200,000. Within view of the town the state already owned 3,200 acres of agricultural and forest land acquired for supplying firewood for the Asylum. Together these investments exceeded in value more than a million dollars.[25]

McKinley rested his case for the town on a single argument. He stated that the existence of a truly agricultural college and a college of liberal arts on the same campus at Athens would be fatal to both. He characterized the university as "the old Scotch-Irish preachers' college of Latin, Greek, etc." and called attention to its conservative traditions. He believed that disruptive social stratification would result when agricultural students wearing work smocks were placed on the same campus with students preparing to enter the professions.[26]

In the summer of 1872 the Georgia Senate voted to withhold all land grant money from the university. The House of Representatives passed the same bill but amended it with the positive stipulation that the agricultural college be located in Milledgeville. It was assumed, although not positively specified, that the proposed college would occupy the vacant public buildings in Milledgeville. By the time the bill was returned to the upper house, the legislative session was in its final hours and the bill was never reconsidered.[27] Since the question of the permanent location of the capital was still open to debate, the use of the vacant Statehouse and Mansion for college purposes would have removed Milledgeville from contention as the seat of government. As a result of this situation the college bill had enjoyed support from unusual sources. In the end the land grant fund was awarded to the University of Georgia but a part later was distributed to five branch colleges. Governor James M. Smith was the final arbiter of the controversy. He maintained that the fund could not be designated for an institution not already chartered and operating.[28]

Not accepting the finality of this arrangement, another group of community leaders, headed by Mayor Samuel Walker, met some time later with state agricultural leaders and the trustees of the university. They secured the endorsement of a college in Milledgeville which would qualify for a share of the land grant fund by offering instruction in agriculture and military science. Subsequently, in October 1878, the plan was approved by the legislature. The institution, called the Middle Georgia Military and Agricultural College, opened in January 1880 as a branch of the University of Georgia. In the first year it employed nine instructors and enrolled 385 students.[29]

At the time of the endorsement of the Milledgeville college, the state transferred to the university trustees, in the form of a lease-loan, all of its Milledgeville property on which the Statehouse, Executive Mansion, and the old penitentiary stood. Penitentiary Square had already been cleared of most of its unused prison facilities and was considered valuable only as

rentable commercial property.[30] The identification of the local college with
the remaining two historic facilities gave it a great advantage over other
branch colleges at Hamilton, Dahlonega, Thomasville, and Cuthbert.

Adequate financial support for the institution was the foremost concern of
the city council for many years. In the original agreement of 1879 the
university trustees allocated only $2,000 annually for the support of the
branch college at Milledgeville. Five years later they reduced the amount to
$1,500 and declared their right to withdraw the assistance entirely, which
eventually they did. The municipal government now had to make a substantial increase in its own contribution. This annual allocation, which originally
was $2,000, at first came from the sale of land in the commons but later was
provided through new tax levies. Although the college was forbidden by its
charter to charge tuition, it collected the maximum matriculation fee of ten
dollars from each student.[31] While college officials claimed a larger registration than that at the University of Georgia, their figures included all persons
enrolled, a majority of whom were primary and high school students.[32] This
comparison with the university, blatantly proclaimed throughout the state,
did not win friends for the college among supporters of the university.

The Cadet Barracks of the Military College, 1900

By 1888 the total annual income of the college had reached $8,100. In addition to the land grant allocation and the donation from the city, it received $1,000 from the common school fund and an equal amount in rents for the Executive Mansion and the Penitentiary Square. Two thousand dollars came from matriculation fees, while an additional $600 came from the Gilmer Fund used in the training of teachers. Graduates of the college received a license to teach in the common schools and were permitted to enter the junior class at the university.[33]

In 1889 the legislature made an appropriation of $2,000 to each of the five branch colleges but failed to renew it two years later. Near the end of the century the town levied a school tax of five mills, nearly all of which went to the military college. At this time the annual municipal appropriation had reached $4,800, which did not include the cost of funding bond issues.[34] This figure increased over the years which followed.

Boarding cadets were a small percentage of the total registration, but they comprised approximately half of the cadet corps of some eighty students recorded in the early 1890s. Beginning in 1880 the Executive Mansion was used as a barracks. Five years later, when that building was released for other purposes, the Darien Bank Building was used briefly as a dormitory. During the depression of 1892, as an economy measure, boarding cadets were removed to quarters in the old Statehouse, where they occupied the north wing of the building. With all college functions thus confined to that single building, however, it became too crowded. It was under these conditions that the Statehouse caught fire and was largely destroyed on January 1, 1894, along with furniture and a library of 3,000 volumes, the nucleus of which had come from Oglethorpe University.[35]

At a called meeting of citizens on the following day a firm resolution was made to rebuild the structure around the old walls, and a decision was also reached to construct a separate barracks for which bonds later were voted. In the meantime the Peter J. Williams (Ferguson) mansion was rented for classroom space. Boarding students were placed in tents and in private homes. College classes were resumed on the third day following the fire and there was no further disruption of routine activities.[36] The new barracks opened in 1897.

The military aspect of the college flourished from the beginning. It qualified for federal assistance in 1894 when Lieutenant Albert B. Scott was detailed by the War Department to provide military instruction. Arms, accoutrements, and ammunition were also provided. The first annual inspection by the War Department occurred in the following spring, accompanied by a gala round of social activities in which all public officials as well as a large number of citizens participated.[37]

Since the institution had never offered courses in agriculture other than certain peripheral courses such as natural science, there was little justification for its continued designation as an agricultural college and its receipt of land grant funds. By the end of the century, when these funds were withdrawn, the name of the institution was officially changed to Georgia Military College. Throughout the first quarter of the new century it maintained high academic standards, although its rank became that of a preparatory school. It officially became a junior college in 1930, but it never ceased to operate also as a high school.[38]

From its opening to the end of the nineteenth century the military college had six presidents, some of whom were outstanding leaders. The most distinguished and colorful of its early presidents was General Daniel H. Hill, who had been one of General Lee's major generals in the Army of Northern Virginia. Hill came to the college in the summer of 1885 from the presidency of the state university in Arkansas. He had resigned his former post because of difficulties over student discipline in which he lost faculty support. Yet he found his work in Milledgeville equally taxing. "The students here do not interest me as much as they did in Arkansas," he wrote, "and they are much less law-abiding. That unprincipled set [in Arkansas] were five years in working up trouble [but here] they could have done it in five weeks." On the other hand, the general's wife, who was the sister of Stonewall Jackson's widow, found the people of Milledgeville to be "more congenial companions" than any she had ever encountered.[39] The Hills were provided with an apartment in the south wing of the Statehouse.

Despite advanced age and a prolonged illness, Hill never missed a day at his post except on occasions when he was away giving lectures on his favorite subject, "The Old South." He was also present at all military drills. He kept notes on cadets who were absent either from drill or from other duties, and held numerous conferences with them. Students loved the twinkle in his eye and they appreciated the laconic style of his written communications, which often were peppered with sarcastic humor.[40]

Although trained in mathematics and a former professor of that subject at Davidson College, General Hill often stated his teaching preference to be history. Indeed, he would have accepted such a position at Milledgeville in preference to an administrative post had it been available. (Hill's son, who had been with the college from its first year, held the post of instructor in history.) The mathematical problems that the general had submitted to his students at Davidson had often betrayed his strong pro-Southern sentiment. Once referred to as "Southern Mathematics," these problems often involved calculations to determine how much money a Yankee gained by his fraudulent selling of wooden nutmegs, or the rate of travel made by a cowardly Northern militiaman retreating in great haste from a battle line in the Mexican War. Noted everywhere for his rampant Southernism, he always emphasized his devotion to the Confederacy and sought to impress upon his students "the honest and honorable traditions of the old South." Unlike General Lee, who never used a harsher term for his adversaries than "those people," Hill referred to them as "those infernal Yankees."[41] In nonacademic conversation he was known to use an even harsher expletive.

Because of his increasing illness Hill was given an indefinite leave from the college in the summer of 1889, and in August he submitted his resignation. He died of cancer a few days later, at age sixty-eight.[42]

Hill's successor as president was J. Colton Lynes who had studied in Paris and Berlin and held the Doctor of Philosophy degree. As might be expected, Lynes attempted an ambitious upgrading of academic standards. Apparently this is what brought about dissention within the faculty and led to Lynes' resignation after three years.[43]

During the first year of Lynes' tenure other developments were coming to a focus which were to have importance in the development of higher education in Georgia. In 1886 the town attempted without success to obtain the Georgia School of Technology, which had been authorized by the legislature in the previous year. While Milledgeville's offer of land was ample, it was able to promise only $10,000 in cash. Other communities offered more, and the institution finally was located in Atlanta, which had doubled Milledgeville's cash offer. Five years later Milledgeville offered the old Oglethorpe campus for the Negro Industrial College, which later was established in Savannah.[44]

What eventually would prove to be the town's most successful educational enterprise was the girls' industrial college, which, like its all-male counterpart, the school of technology in Atlanta, was a product of the New South philosophy. These two institutions were designed chiefly to prepare young men and women for industrial occupations and represented quite a departure in outlook from the young lady's seminary of prewar days and from liberal arts colleges and military schools preparing young men for the professions.

The location at Milledgeville of the Georgia Normal and Industrial College was accomplished almost entirely without fanfare or the pressures of local public sentiment. All preliminary work was done quietly in Atlanta cloakrooms by a small group of astute politicians. These included the senators Robert Whitfield and S. R. Harris, the president of the Senate, Fleming G. DuBignon, and House representatives Leonidas N. Callaway of Baldwin County and Robert H. Lewis and Ivey W. Duggan of Hancock County.[45]

The industrial college bill was strongly backed by William Y. Atkinson, a representative from Coweta County who later became governor. It called for an initial appropriation of $75,000 for construction of facilities, but no location was specified. Gainesville, in North Georgia, was a leading contender for the college, and other cities were ready with attractive offers of land and cash donations. In an effort to reduce the potency of Milledgeville's bid, a bill was offered in the legislature to require the state to sell the property

Main Building of the Georgia Normal and Industrial College, 1890

which it held in the town as well as that which it held at Indian Springs near Griffin. This bill was defeated with the help of Ivey W. Duggan and others. This accomplished, the industrial school bill was amended so that the initial appropriation of $75,000 was reduced by half. To make up the difference of $35,000 the Executive Mansion and Penitentiary Square were to be relinquished by the military college and offered for use by the new school. Thus the final bill stipulated that the college be located in Milledgeville. Die-hard opponents offered a resolution requiring a local cash donation of at least $10,000, but this was voted down. The law was approved on November 8, 1889.[46]

While providing it with a board of directors, the original law also made the college "a part of the University of Georgia" and therefore under the control of its chancellor and board of trustees. Its appropriation was to come from rentals of the W. & A. Railroad and was to be used solely for construction. "Suppose the Railroad [is] not rented, or sold . . . then the school is a myth," wrote a local editor. He stated that the military college was "worth 50 times as much to the community as the Girls Industrial School,"—and there were many who agreed with him.[47]

Such expressions of skepticism concerning the future of the college did not weaken the town's willingness to invest in it. Bonds in the amount of $22,000 were voted to aid the building program. Of this amount, $5,000 was spent on repairing the Mansion, which was now partitioned into thirty-five dormitory rooms. Paneled ceilings replaced the broken plaster overhead, and interior blinds were substituted for the rickety shutters.[48] This was the first of many bequests made by the community for the development of the college.

The opening of the college in September 1891 took place without public participation of any kind. President J. Harris Chappell spoke briefly to the eighty-eight students assembled in the little auditorium, confining his remarks largely to registration procedure. The registration of new students continued throughout the fall and reached 171 at the end of the year. This figure grew steadily over the next few years, reaching 400 by the end of the decade. The annual cost to the student during these years never exceeded a hundred dollars. Students were received on the county allotment plan, and local applicants were permitted to fill places not taken by students assigned from other counties.[49]

The school's charter provided that all students be instructed in at least one of the industrial arts, including typing, bookkeeping, telegraphy, cooking, and dress-making. Normal courses (teacher education) were particularly stressed, but there was some emphasis on "the collegiate branches" (liberal arts) as well. Faculty salaries averaged $1,190 annually. Instructors were required to teach courses in more than one department.[50]

One of the early instructors was Julia Flisch, who appears to have been above the average among her associates in intellectual outlook. She taught stenography in addition to classical history and English. Among the very few who held a master's degree, she was a popular teacher and made significant contributions to the community and even to the outside world of scholarship. In a paper published by the American Historical Association entitled "The Common People of the Old South,"[51] she was among the earliest historians to focus attention on the need to give more study to this segment of antebellum Southern society in order to fully understand the region's past. Letters which she wrote to newspaper editors and other comments she made on public affairs reveal her liberal educational philosophy and depth of intellectual interests.[52] She ably defended the industrial aspects of the Milledgeville college against its critics and was impatient with those who were reluctant to embrace the spirit of the New South. She disparaged the section's adherence to military traditions. During the Spanish-American War she was distressed that the South in its poverty and need should be so anxious to send its young men off to war again. "[We are] too far behind in manufacturing . . . to go to war," she wrote, "and we have already lost too much."[53]

Among Julia Flisch's friends in Milledgeville was a young history student at the University of Georgia, Ulrich Bonnell Phillips, who was destined to become a distinguished historian at her alma mater, the University of Wisconsin. His earliest published research was based upon the exploration of the town's archives. Phillips' mother joined the faculty of the college in 1897 as head of the Department of Dress-making. His father, Alonzo Rabun Phillips, served as the college's first superintendent of buildings and grounds and also taught a class in floraculture. In the former capacity he laid off walks and flower beds and planted pecan trees on the front campus.[54] Results of his work were still visible in 1976.

The acquisition of two flourishing colleges was an exceptional achievement for a community of fewer than 1,700 white inhabitants. Indeed, there were some who believed that this achievement had regained for the town much of the glory it had lost when the state capital was relocated.

Some of the old gaiety of the town's social life returned with the inauguration of the military college. At its first commencement, held in 1880, Governor Alfred H. Colquitt came to the campus to review the cadets and a number of military companies that paraded with them. The dance held that evening at the Mansion provoked nostalgic comments from older citizens. Within a few years the "commencement hop" had become so popular that it had to be staged in the large dining room of the Oconee House. There the quadrille, lancers, waltz, and polka were on happy display to what was yet the largest social gathering of young people in the town since pre-war days.[55]

Life was considerably less gala at the industrial college, whose girls were denied participation in such affairs. In fact, during the early days of the institution it was only on rare occasions that the girls were allowed to venture into town, just one block from their dormitory. On such trips they always walked in groups and were carefully chaperoned. Social life was restricted to whatever the campus could provide, and this seldom included male companionship. Once President Chappell bent the rules enough to allow some students to conduct through the Main Building a group of excursionists from Macon, among whom there were a number of Mercer University boys. When the procedure took longer than usual to perform, Chappell was constrained to probe the students' dilatory record. "But by a singular coincidence," wrote one, "nearly every girl had a first cousin among the Mercer boys."[56]

At the girls' college only a brief holiday was granted for Christmas, and neary all students remained on the campus for this season. However, restrictions appear to have been slightly relaxed on these occasions. Students were entertained by numerous serenades, and on Christmas morning they might even be served the traditional eggnog. In the evening there was a great display of fireworks, after which a group of carefully selected guests spent the hours until midnight in dancing and playing games in the great dining room of the Mansion.[57] As might have been anticipated, these Christmas parties soon got out of hand and it became necessary to warn uninvited elements from the town to keep away.

Rowdyism among certain local youth presented the college administration with some of its most frustrating experiences. This behavior was a natural response of young men to the college's stern regulations and its unrelenting efforts to enforce them. In its conversion to a college campus the old Penitentiary Square had failed to lose completely its old image. Outsiders were not permitted to walk or to ride a bicycle across the campus, and a permanent guard was employed to keep them away. This was in complete contrast to the policy at the military college on the Statehouse Square, which was open to the public at all times. Black children used its athletic field; cows and chickens grazed undisturbed on the campus; and farmers drove their conveyances across it in every direction, cutting new paths which ignored well planned driveways.[58]

Town authorities obligingly cooperated with the administration of the girls' college in enforcing regulations against intrusions. Hoping to escape the wrath of the campus policeman, boys would gather at the Central Depot to meet all trains bringing girls to the campus after holidays or the summer recess. To render their presence there less annoying to authorities, they often were accompanied by the Apollo Brass Band. The musicians not only welcomed the students but also led their march of three blocks to the campus, where they were inclined to linger after exhausting their repertoire of incidental music.[59] Then, along with the other boys, they were forced to retreat to the streets bordering the campus, to which college regulations did not extend.

A religious revival in the fall of 1897 was credited with giving the town a respite from the rowdyism in which many young men indulged, but it did not last long. On a Sunday afternoon a year later a number of boys gathered on a hill behind Atkinson Hall and with spyglasses gave the back of the dormitory a thorough inspection. The young women who were attracted to the windows by their shouts were greeted with rude signs and gestures. President Chappell applied to these disturbers of Victorian propriety such epithets as "sneaking scoundrels" and "ill-bred hoodlums."[60]

The grounds in front of Atkinson Hall were usually the scene of great activity as students engaged in calesthenics and athletic contests. Here, in April 1895, occurred what might well have been the first official game of basketball ever played in Georgia. The local editor called it "a new and rollicking out-door game" and announced the arrival at the college of "a full outfit of implements and apparatus" from Boston, where the game had only recently been invented. Only intramural games were played, and no scores were announced. "The screams and shrieks and yells of ecstatic players may sometimes be heard a half mile away," wrote one observer. "It is full of snap and vigor, and is a splendid thing for girls who have been cooped up all day poring over books," he concluded.[61]

Leaving basketball solely in the care of young women, the cadets began playing football as early as 1892, although no intercollegiate matches were played for the next fifteen years. The development of this sport was delayed by the death of a University of Georgia athlete, Richard V. Gammon, in a game played in 1897. The university team was disbanded and other colleges proscribed the game, as did the Atlanta City Council, which forbade it in that city. The Milledgeville editor branded it as "brutal, cruel and dangerous," and predicted its early demise throughout the nation.[62]

With public sentiment cooled toward football, local sports interest came to be solely directed to baseball at the military college. A match with Mercer University in April 1897 was witnessed by more than a thousand fans, including 300 college girls who marched to the game in close order, all bearing the red and black colors of the local team. "Supporters waved hats, canes, umbrellas, and yelled like Comanche Indians," but the team was defeated by a small margin. Two weeks later the cadets lost to Georgia Tech by a similar score.[63]

Such local enthusiasm for baseball continued unabated long after football was restored and intercollegiate matches in that sport were organized. This enthusiasm was fed by the annual visit to the area by the Boston Braves team, which held its spring training at nearby Haddock and was managed by George Stallings of that community. In April 1913 an all-star team featuring the famous American League star Ty Cobb engaged in a game with the local cadets. More than 2,000 fans saw Cobb hit the first ball thrown to him with such force that it carried far over the fence. While ground rules allowed him only two bases, the Detroit star received a great ovation as he came to rest on second base. However, when he turned for a moment to give the college girls on the sidelines a courtly bow with a long sweep of his cap, he was caught off base and put out by a cadet infielder. Red-faced, and heckled by his teammates, Cobb returned to the bench while the upstart cadet now received the crowd's cheers. But Cobb returned to lead his team to a 9 to 5 victory.[64]

The unusual educational developments pursued by the town in the post-Reconstruction era resulted from excellent leadership and a high quality of civic enterprise. Yet these efforts involved financial burdens which the community could ill afford. Commercial life and general economic conditions were by no means flourishing. The community was still under the burden of a debt of $60,000 resulting from bonds subscribed for the completion of the Macon and Augusta railroad—an undertaking designed to quiet the earlier capital removal controversy. The complete redemption of these bonds was not accomplished until 1892.[65]

This debt, together with those incurred for the community's educational developments, hampered routine public endeavors. The county had to forego for more than twenty years the rebuilding of the courthouse, which had been destroyed in 1861. During this period part of the Masonic Hall was rented for court purposes, and later the Statehouse was used. When the latter was acquired by the military college, superior court sessions were held in Brake's Opera House. Finally, in 1884, bonds were voted for a courthouse which was opened two years later.

In the meantime a new city hall appeared, with two stories and a bell tower. The post office continued to be moved from one location to another throughout the remainder of the century. Die-hard rebels manifested some disdain for this institution, which stood as the most visible reminder of federal authority and Republican patronage left in the town. The postmaster often complained that citizens ignored his trash baskets and cuspidors. They appeared to take pleasure in scattering paper and peanut hulls over the floor "and plastering them down with tobacco juice." Finally, in 1910, the post office was permanently located in a new structure built by the federal government. Costing more than $50,000, this building was the most substantial structure erected in the town since before the war. It served the additional function of reminding the people of the power and might of the government at Washington. However, two years after its completion local citizens erected a Confederate monument at its front door, near the intersection of Hancock and Wilkinson streets.[66]

The removal of church buildings from the Statehouse Square was gradual, and the process was never completed. In 1886 the Baptist Church burned, whereupon the Baptists abandoned their old site and moved to North Wayne Street. There they built a structure having a peculiar Moorish dome reminiscent of the architecture of southern Spain.[67] The Methodists moved to a new masonry structure on West Hancock Street in 1912.

An addition to the religious community of the post-Reconstruction period came with the dedication of a Roman Catholic sanctuary erected in 1874 on the site of the old Lafayette Hotel. Approximately sixty persons were listed on the original rolls of that parish, known as the Sacred Heart of Jesus. Among these were the families of Treanor, Cline, O'Brien, Magill, Supple, and Quinn. The Milledgeville DuBignons had given up their Catholic faith but the coastal branch of the family retained it.

The Catholic community grew steadily, and it made exceptional contributions to the civic and cultural life of the town. Visiting Catholics noted the complete absence of religious intolerance in the town whose leading Catholic, Peter J. Cline, was the unanimous choice for mayor in 1889; two of his wife's sisters taught in the local school. Another prominent family was that of Catholic Joseph Miller, a local merchant, whose Lutheran wife, the former Henrietta Wideman, was one of the town's most cultured matrons. Born in Stuttgart, Germany, Henrietta Miller was fluent in three languages. She was Miller's wife from 1847 until her death thirty years later.[68]

Neither Catholic nor Protestant was the town's leading merchant, Adolph Joseph, who was born into the faith of Judah. Joseph had arrived in Milledgevile at the end of the war, at age nineteen, and had become universally popular for his kindness, his generous spirit, and his civic interests. Upon his marriage to Frances Herty in 1872, he became a welcome addition to the Episcopalian community.[69]

While civic pride did not disappear with the loss of the state capital, its true assessment is complicated by some stark contrasts. Jefferson Street, long considered the finest residential area in the town, lost none of its former elegance. Its houses were kept neatly painted and in good repair. On the other hand, the town's business houses and its thoroughfares were extremely

Joseph's Corner, *ca.* 1880

shabby in appearance.[70] Ox-drawn wagons increased in number and were particularly numerous on Saturdays. An ox might be seen feeding from the rear of a cart parked in the middle of the street while the owner stood guard to prevent loose animals from partaking of the provender. The list of offending animals running loose included geese and goats. A group of women informed the council of "a large party of goats which promanade the streets by night and often take lodging on our porches and piazzas which in the morning present . . . a filthy and disgusting appearance. . . . We cannot look upon it with Christian resignation," they declared in their plea for the removal of the nuisance.[71]

More serious than the problem of animals running loose in the streets and alleys was the grievance generated by long rows of privies behind the stores on Hancock Street and in the rear of the courthouse lot. In the summer of 1881 citizens petitioned for the elimination of these annoyances.[72] The council responded by requiring that "privies of new and modern style" be erected no farther than four feet from a water drain.

To further promote what the city council termed "the good redolence of the community," owners of dead animals were required to have them dragged to the mouth of Fishing Creek, where the carcasses were deposited in the river. A general cleanup was organized to encourage painting and whitewashing throughout the town. Weeds finally were cut from the streets and sidewalks, and the council ordered merchants to remove "unsightly sheds, platforms and protusions over sidewalks in front of their stores." Special ordinances were directed at prohibiting butcher shops from overflowing onto the streets. Those who traded in cotton were required to cease storing this commodity on platforms erected in the streets. New brick sidewalks were laid in the commercial area, although no improved sidewalks appeared in residential areas until 1915, when cement paving became popular.[73]

Soon after these improvements were completed the town experienced the last of its great fires. Occurring in the winter of 1884, it destroyed seven buildings on North Wayne Street coming perilously close to the Masonic Hall.[74] Two years later, on August 31, 1886, the Charleston earthquake sent severe shock waves throughout the area and wrought considerable damage to property in the old capital. It caused bricks to fall from chimneys and plaster from the walls of buildings. Masonry structures were rent with fissures. The walls of the Darien Bank were so out of line that extensive repairs were necessary. The old Statehouse was also damaged, as were a number of private dwellings, such as Lockerley Hall. The low rumbling sound which accompanied the quake was plainly heard, causing the McComb Hotel to become completely evacuated. At Meriwether Station a farmer was reported to have spent the entire night in prayer. A Bible salesman trudging the countryside enjoyed record sales on the following day.[75]

Floods were also added to the list of natural disasters which plagued the community during the latter part of the 1880s. Each time the Oconee bridge was swept away, the town was isolated from approximately half of its trade area, and businessmen were unusually sensitive to this condition. Four bridges were damaged or destroyed between the end of the war and 1889, when an iron bridge finally was constructed and this troublesome problem came to an end.[76]

While the untamed Oconee often brought malaise to the community, its presence at their doorstep was a constant reminder that it might still become a useful transportation artery and an asset to the business life of the community. In the summer of 1879 the federal derrick boat, the *James H. Blount*, started on its maiden voyage down the river from Milledgeville, lifting rocks and snags from the channel. Such work was intermittent, however, and was not completed until fifteen years later, when, in 1894 the river finally was declared suitable for navigation.[77] Yet at the end of the century only two commercial boats were engaged on the river, bringing to the town such items as hay, guano, and barrel staves from the railroad at Oconee Station. Far better known were the racing boat *Katie Treanor* and an excursion boat called *The Industrial Girl*. The latter on occasion brought hardwood lumber to Milledgeville from the Oconee swamps.[78]

One final development in transportation occurred in the late 1880s when a local group organized the Milledgeville and Asylum Railroad Company. Known as "the dummy line," it was designed largely as a local transit system. Always plagued with unexpected problems and expenses, it was never a successful enterprise. Yet it had a tenacious capacity for life. For fifty years, before its demise in mid-twentieth century, it was recognized as the town's greatest eyesore, causing the center of the business district to resemble a freight yard.[79]

Appearing almost at the same time as the local transit system were other innovations, such as improved streets, electric lights, the telephone, and a stable water supply. The ever-recurring problem of adequate water was of far greater general concern than anything else. As late as 1890 the town's supply of drinking water still came principally from individual wells, and its quality had long been suspect. Owing to an imperfect understanding of the relationship between impure drinking water and typhoid fever, there was an appalling death rate from that disease. During the heavy rains of 1887 many wells in the town became almost completely filled with surface water and partly as a result of this situation town authorities determined to install a water works plant.

The original plan called for securing water from O'Brien's Spring on the east side of the river, and pumping it into a reservoir near the intersection of Jefferson and Hancock streets. This plan was abandoned after residents objected to this intrusion in the vicinity of their homes. Finally an agreement was reached with the American Pipe Company of Philadelphia to provide a water plant on a rental basis. Early in 1893 the plant was completed, with five miles of pipe laid within the town and an extra mile to Fishing Creek, from which the water was obtained. There was no treatment of incoming water other than settling and filtering by the most primitive processes before it was pumped into a 15,000-gallon standpipe located on a hill seventy feet above the level of the town. The installation of seventy fire plugs within the town's limits marked the end of the town's great fires.[81]

As a result of its limited quantity and the poor processing which it received, water from Fishing Creek was never satisfactory. After 1910 some improvement was made in the purification process, but users still complained of mud sediment in the drinking water, which when boiled formed a layer of scum on the top. In 1920 the municipal government bought the plant and operated it for the next thirty years but the results still were unsatisfactory.[82] The rapid industrial growth of the community following the outbreak of World War II greatly overtaxed the capacity of the plant. In 1954 a modern plant was opened which took a plentiful supply of water from the Oconee River. For the first time in the long history of the town, citizens began to realize that the Oconee's greatest asset was the water it brought to their door. In the 1950s the Georgia Power Company completed a dam at Furman Shoals, five miles north of the town, creating the huge reservoir called Sinclair Lake. Covering more than 150,000 acres, it drastically changed the life-style of the inhabitants residing in adjacent areas.

The bountiful supply of unpolluted water from the reservoir and from the river below it gave encouragement to additional industrial growth. In 1976 little remained of the agricultural trade center which had characterized the community between 1870 and 1930. The Central State Hospital (formerly

The G.M. & A.C. commandant and cadet officers, 1895.
sitting, l. to r.: James Brown, Lieut. A. B. Scott, Bernard Hawkins;
standing: l., Millard Little, r., Robert Whitfield

the Asylum), had approximately 5,000 employees, and eighteen manufacturing plants employed a total of more than 3,000 people. The town and its immediate environs now exceeded 25,000 inhabitants. The Georgia Youth Development Center and the state women's prison had been added to the town's long list of institutions.

The expansion of the girls' college had exceeded the expectations of its early sponsors. The granting of degrees began in 1921, and the college afterwards survived four name changes. By 1976 it had become Georgia College, a coeducational, multipurpose institution enrolling more than 3,600 students and granting a number of master's degrees. Its library, housed in one of the college's thirty-odd buildings, contained over 100,000 volumes. Such courses as industrial arts had given way to sophisticated instruction in business and in public administration, as well as paramedical courses and a strong array of liberal studies, all pursuing the college's original purpose of fulfilling the needs of a new social and economic order.

Just three blocks away the Georgia Military College stood more as a symbol of the Old South and of the town's more remote past. In 1976 it was under the leadership of Major General (Ret.) Eugene A. Salet. For almost a full century it had commanded a high degree of loyalty and support from the community even while remaining a drain on the town's limited financial resources. Over the years it had maintained a stable enrollment which averaged 500 cadets. It provided these students a high quality of military education and served the community well in other respects. Among its alumni were the distinguished chemist, Charles H. Herty, Congressman Carl Vinson, and Willie J. Usery, Jr., who became the secretary of labor in President Gerald Ford's cabinet. Carl Vinson was the congressional representative of his district for half a century, serving as House Chairman of the Naval Affairs Committee in the United States Congress from 1931 to the end of World War II and later presiding as Chairman of the Armed Services Committee. In these positions Vinson guided to its final passage what was perhaps the largest outlay of military appropriations in the history of the world. An article in a national periodical in 1951 stated that while Soviet military might was centered in the Kremlin, America's military power might be pin-pointed at Milledgeville, Georgia, which at that time had a population of only 9,000.[83] Even though exaggerated, this statement was indeed well-deserved recognition for the small community which had struggled so long and valiantly for more than commonplace identity.

Notes

ABBREVIATIONS

CU	Confederate Union
FU	Federal Union
GA	Georgia Argus
GDAH	Georgia Department of Archives and History
Georgia Laws	Acts of the General Assembly of the State of Georgia
GJ	Georgia Journal
GS	Georgia Statesman
NA	National Archives
Official Records	The War of the Rebellion: A Compilation of the Official Records of the Union and Confederate Armies
Senate Journal	Journal of the Senate of the State of Georgia
S&P	Statesman and Patriot
SR	Southern Recorder
UR	Union Recorder

CHAPTER ONE

1. Correspondence Relative to the Public Deposits, *American State Papers* (38 vols., Washington, 1832–1861): *Indian Affairs*, I, 81–82.

2. Ray H. Mattison, "The Creek Trading House—From Colerain to Fort Hawkins," *Georgia Historical Quarterly*, XXX (Sept. 1946), 169–183.

3. George Sibbald, *Notes and Observations on the Pine Lands of Georgia ...* (Augusta, 1801), 61.

4. Leola Selman Beeson, *History Stories of Milledgeville and Baldwin County* (Macon, 1943), 8.

5. David Benedict, *General History of the Baptist Denomination* (2 vols., Boston, 1813), II, 532; Robert Watkins and George Watkins, *Digest of the Laws of Georgia ... to 1798* (Philadelphia, 1800), 445.

6. *American State Papers: Indian Affairs*, I, 368.

7. Jackson to the Secretary of War, May 1, 1798, pp. 170–175; Jackson to

Thomas King, July 23, 1798, p. 239; Jackson to Ben Hawkins, July 21, 1798, p. 226—all in Governor's Letter Book, 1798, Georgia Department of Archives and History (hereafter abbreviated GDAH), Atlanta.

8. Jackson to Judge Carnes, March 8, 1798, in Governor's Letter Book, 1798, pp. 116–117, GDAH.

9. *American State Papers: Indian Affairs*, I, 407–409.

10. *Ibid.*, 482–483.

11. *Ibid.*, 484; Louise Frederick Hays, *Hero of Hornet's Nest* (New York, 1946), 257.

12. *American State Papers: Foreign Relations*, I, 482–483.

13. *American State Papers: Indian Affairs*, I, 482–483.

14. See the map of Milledgeville drawn by Daniel Sturges in 1808 (hereafter cited as Sturges Map), in the Surveyor General Office, Atlanta.

15. *American State Papers: Indian Affairs*, I, 497–498.

16. Beeson, *Stories*, 10.

17. John R. Swanton, *The Indians of the Southeastern United States*, Smithsonian Bull. 137 (Washington, 1946), 165, 181; Beeson, *Stories*, 7.

18. John H. Goff, "Some Major Indian Trading Paths Across the Georgia Piedmont," *Georgia Mineral Newsletter*, VI (Winter 1953), 122–131.

19. *Federal Union* (Milledgeville), April 3, 1872 (Hereafter cited as *FU*).

20. Mark Van Doren, ed., *The Travels of William Bartram*, (New York, 1928), 363–364; William Bartram, *Travels Through North and South Carolina, Georgia, East and West Florida, the Cherokee Country* . . . (Philadelphia, 1791), 377–378, 458–459.

21. Beeson, *Stories*, 120; Albert James Pickett, *History of Alabama and Incidentally of Georgia and Mississippi* . . . (Birmingham, 1962), 498.

22. Francis Paul Prucha, *A Guide to the Military Posts of the United States* (Madison, 1964), 74, 116.

23. Mattison, "Creek Trading House," 169–170.

24. Military Book Number One, 1800–1802, War Office, p. 111, Record Group 94. National Archives (hereafter cited as NA).

25. *FU*, April 3, 1872.

26. James Ripley Jacobs, *The Beginning of the United States Army, 1783–1812* (Princeton, 1947), 80.

27. *FU*, July 9, 1867.

28. Mattison, "Creek Trading House," 177.

29. Miscellaneous File, Fort Wilkinson, Sept. 17, 1803, Report of Freights from Philadelphia to Darien, Record Group 94, NA.

30. Mattison, "Creek Trading House," 180.

31. Passports Issued by the Governors of Georgia, 1785–1820; Governor's Letter Book, 1802–1809, pp. 206–207—both in GDAH; *American State Papers: Indian Affairs*, I, 651; Augustin S. Clayton, *A Compilation of the Laws of the State of Georgia* . . . (Augusta, 1812), 701–703 (hereafter cited as Clayton, *Compilations*).

32. Clayton, *Compilations*, 705–708.

33. John Ragan Map of District Number One, Aug. 7, 1804, Surveyor General

Office; John Clark, *Considerations on the Purity of the Principles of William H. Crawford* . . . (Augusta, 1819), 146.

34. John H. Goff, "Short Studies of Georgia Place Names," *Georgia Mineral Newsletter*, XVI (Fall 1964), 70–71.

35. *American State Papers: Indian Affairs*, I, 417; Travis E. Smith, "A History of the Milledgeville Baptist Church" (a manuscript in private possession), 15 (hereafter cited as T. E. Smith, "Baptist Church"); John H. Goff, "Short Studies of Georgia Place Names," *Georgia Mineral Newsletter*, XIII (Fall 1960), 129.

36. Clayton, *Compilations*, 100, 107, 357–359, 363.

37. Daniel Sturges, Instructions to Levin Wales, Esq., for Dividing the Counties of Wilkinson and Baldwin . . . 21st Feby., 1804, GDAH (hereafter cited as Sturges Manuscript).

38. See the original land map of Washington County (1785) in the Surveyor General Office, Atlanta.

39. Clayton, *Compilations*, 101–107.

40. Sturges Manuscript, 1–3, 5–6.

41. Levin Wales, Map of District Number Two, Baldwin County, in the Surveyor General Office, Atlanta; John H. Goff, "Edward Lloyd Thomas, Surveyor," *Emory University Quarterly*, XVIII (Summer 1962), 108ff.

42. *Acts of the General Assembly of the State of Georgia*, 1803 (Louisville, 1804), 4–14 (hereafter cited as *Georgia Laws*, with the appropriate year in which the laws were enacted); *Union Recorder* (Milledgeville), Aug. 17, 1930 (hereafter cited as *UR*); Beeson, *Stories*, 29.

43. Clayton, *Compilations*, 100–107.

44. *Georgia Laws* (1804), 29; *ibid.* (Extra Session, 1806), 3–14.

45. *Ibid.* (1805), 51, (1807), 3; Clayton, *Compilations*, 79–281.

46. Clayton, *Compilations*, 296; *Georgia Laws* (1806), 15.

47. Clayton, *Compilations*, 356, 486, 487; *The Milledgeville Times*, Jan. 18, 1941; *Georgia Journal* (Milledgeville), Sept. 2, 1812, Aug. 10, 1814 (hereafter cited as *GJ*).

48. Clayton, *Compilations*, 357–359.

CHAPTER TWO

1. *Georgia Laws* (Extra Session, 1803), 14.

2. John Clark to John Milledge, Sept. 27, 1804, in John Milledge, Correspondence, GDAH; Clayton, *Compilations*, 107.

3. See Carlton Welborn's map of Milledgeville made in 1804, in the Surveyor General Office, Atlanta; Sturges Map, GDAH.

4. Clayton, *Compilations*, 362.

5. *UR*, Sept. 25, 1877.

6. *Journal of the Senate of the State of Georgia* . . . *1805* (Augusta, 1805), 13 (hereafter cited as *Senate Journal* with appropriate date).

7. *UR*, June 18, 1873.

8. *Ibid.*, May 17, 1881.

9. *Ibid.*, Sept. 25, 1877; *Senate Journal* (1805), 13; Clayton, *Compilations*, 196; *Georgia Laws* (1805), 48, (1809), 93.

10. Clayton, *Compilations*, 322–326, 621, 624, 625; *Georgia Laws* (1806), 32.

11. Clayton, *Compilations*, 361, 365, 390; *Georgia Laws* (1807), 11.

12. Executive Minutes, 1816–1817, p. 91, GDAH; Clayton, *Compilations*, 623–625.

13. *Georgia Laws* (1810), 62–68.

14. *UR*, July 9, 1887.

15. Clayton, *Compilations*, 265; *Georgia Laws* (1805), 33.

16. John Herbert and A. M. Devereaux to Governor Jared Irwin, June 25, 1807, in Irwin, Correspondence, GDAH; Executive Minutes, Jan. 1, 1811, to Sept. 30, 1812, p. 247, GDAH; Clayton, *Compilations*, 400; Beeson, *Stories*, 55.

17. Clayton, *Compilations*, 698–699; Beeson, *Stories*, 34; *Statesman and Patriot* (Milledgeville), July 5, 1828 (hereafter cited as *S & P*).

18. Recommendations to Governor Lumpkin, Feb. 23, 1833, GDAH; William D. Jarrett to Governor George R. Gilmer, Feb. 9, 1830, GDAH; *Southern Recorder* (Milledgeville), Feb. 26, 1834 (hereafter cited as *SR*).

19. *The Reflector* (Milledgeville), Sept. 29, 1818.

20. *FU*, Nov. 3, 1835.

21. *Senate Journal* (1811), 10; *Georgia Laws* (1810), 72; *GJ*, May 8, 1811; A. M. Devereaux to Governor B. B. Mitchell, Aug. 28, 1811, GDAH.

22. Sturges's map, approved by the commissioners on Sept. 3, 1808, shows the location of eight springs in the town and six shoals on the Oconee River five of which were below the town. Also shown are the eighty-four four-acre residential squares and four twenty-acre public squares.

23. *GJ*, July 24, 1810, Feb. 28, May 1, 1811; Thomas Fitch, Journal, 1809, a manuscript journal in private possession, a copy of which is in the library of Georgia College, Milledgeville.

24. This map, sketched by Daniel Mulford in 1809, was enclosed in a letter to Levi Mulford dated July 6. It is cited hereafter as the Mulford Map. It is part of the widely scattered Mulford-Fitch correspondence, several items of which are in the Yale University Library. Other items are in private possession but have been transcribed and are now in the library at Georgia College, Milledgeville.

25. Beeson, *Stories*, 56–57.

26. Clayton, *Compilations*, 571; Executive Minutes, Dec. 26, 1809, GDAH.

27. *UR*, May 21, 1889; Leola Selman Beeson, *One Hundred Years of the Old Governor's Mansion* (Macon, 1938), 2–3.

28. Beeson, *Stories*, 62.

29. *UR*, Nov. 5, 1889.

30. Lucius Q. C. Lamar, *A Compilation of the Laws of the State of Georgia* [*1810–1819*] . . . (Augusta, 1821), 968 (hereafter cited as Lamar, *A Compilation*); Clayton, *Compilations*, 390–391; *Georgia Laws* (1807), 69 *et passim*; Beeson, *Stories*, 156.

31. T. E. Smith, "Baptist Church," 7.

32. George G. Smith, *The Life and Letters of James Osgood Andrew* . . . (Mobile, 1883), 59 (hereafter cited as G. G. Smith, *James O. Andrew*).

33. Benedict, *General History of the Baptist Denomination*, II, 352; Watkins, *Digest*, 445.

34. Minutes, Island Creek Baptist Church, 1806, in private possession; T. E. Smith, "Baptist Church," 2.

35. Smith, "Baptist Church," 7.

36. *Ibid.*, 8; Record of the Commissioners of the City of Milledgeville, June 15, 1814 (hereafter cited as Record of Commissioners). These records, in possession of the city clerk of Milledgeville, cover the period of municipal government from 1811 to 1836; microfilm copies are available in GDAH Drawer 200, Box 10, Roll 3291.

37. T. E. Smith, "Baptist Church," 10, 26.

38. *Ibid.*, 34; *S & P*, Jan. 28, 1828.

39. T. E. Smith, "Baptist Church," 34–38.

40. *UR*, July 19, 1887.

41. *SR*, Oct. 21, 1823.

42. *UR*, Nov. 4, 1874, July 19, 1887.

43. *GJ*, Nov. 12, 1809, Sept. 2, 1812; *UR*, Nov. 4, 1874.

44. *The Milledgeville Intelligencer*, Nov. 22, 1808.

45. *GJ*, Aug. 29, 1910.

46. *Ibid.*, Dec. 5, 1810.

47. *Ibid.*, July 17, 1811; *SR*, No. 7, 1820.

48. *GJ*, Jan. 1, 1812.

49. *SR*, Oct. 21, 1823.

50. *Ibid.*, Sept. 21, 1824; *GJ*, Oct. 9, 1816, Sept. 21, 1824, May 14, 1834.

51. *SR*, Sept. 21, 1814, May 14, 1834, May 23, 1837, Oct. 16, 1838, Nov. 18, 1858.

52. *S & P*, March 24, 1828.

53. *FU*, May 12, 1835; Adiel Sherwood, *A Gazeteer of Georgia, 1829* (Philadelphia, 1829), 133–136; *UR*, Nov. 5, 1889.

54. James Silk Buckingham, *The Slave States of America* (2 vols., London, 1842), I, 189, 190–191.

55. Garnett Andrews, *Reminiscences of an Old Georgia Lawyer* (Atlanta, 1870), 24.

56. *SR*, June 22, Feb. 24, 1824.

57. Sir Charles Lyell, *A Second Visit to the United States of North America* (2 vols., London, 1850), II, 189.

58. *Georgia Laws* (1837), 112, 266; *ibid.*, (1849–50), 174; Clayton, *Compilations*, 107, 209, 265, 322.

59. *SR*, March 7, 1820, July 8, 1823.

60. Record of Commissioners, 1804–1807 (m.p.), City Hall.

61. Mulford Map, Georgia College Library, Milledgeville.

62. *GJ*, March 12, 1827; *UR*, May 1, 1883.

63. *Georgia Argus* (Milledgeville), Jan. 10, 1810.

64. *FU*, May 29, 1872.

65. Lamar, *A Compilation*, 772.

66. *Senate Journal* (1811), 12; *Georgia Argus*, June 13, 1810.

67. *SR*, Oct. 8, 1822; *GJ*, May 25, 1814; Buckingham, *Slave States*, I, 233.

68. Daniel Mulford to Levi Mulford, July 6, 1809, in Fitch-Mulford Correspondence, Yale University Library.

69. *GJ*, Oct. 27, 1813, Aug. 10, 1810; *Georgia Laws* (1835), 266; *ibid.*, (1837), 112; *ibid.*, (1859–50), 174; *UR*, May 17, 1881.

70. Buckingham, *Slave States*, I, 233.

71. *SR*, Feb. 24, 1835.

72. *FU*, June 7, 1832.

73. *SR*, Aug. 27, 1822.

74. Thomas Fitch to Daniel Mulford, Jan. 28, 1809, and March 30, 1810, Fitch-Mulford Correspondence, Yale University Library.

75. E. Merton Coulter, "Scull Shoals: An Extinct Georgia Manufacturing and Farming Community," *Georgia Historical Quarterly*, XLVIII (March 1964), 34–35, 59–60; *Georgia Laws* (1805), 44, 45; *ibid.*, (1808), 30; *GJ*, Feb. 16, 1814.

76. *Georgia Statesman* (Milledgeville), April 26, 1827 (hereafter cited as *GS*); *S & P*, Nov. 29, 1829.

77. *SR*, Feb. 28, 1820.

78. *Ibid.*, March 21, Feb. 22, 1820, May 1, 1821.

79. *GJ*, Jan. 10, 1816; *SR*, Feb. 22, 1820.

80. Adiel Sherwood, *A Gazeteer of Georgia, 1827* (Washington, 1837), 201; *SR*, Oct. 28, 1823, Nov. 26, 1824, Aug. 25, 1831; Hawes, Mitchel, and Collins (Darien, Ga.) to T. Parker, March 1, 1835, GDAH; *FU*, Feb. 13, 1838.

81. *S&P*, May 19, 1828; *GJ*, Dec. 12, 1810; D. B. Warden, *A Statistical, Political and Historical Account of the United States* (3 vols., Edinburgh, 1819), II, 466.

82. *FU*, Feb. 22, 1831; Census of Baldwin County, Slave Inhabitants of Baldwin County in 1830, p. 26, Georgia College Library.

83. *GJ*, May 4, 1814, and Nov. 29, 1815.

84. Warren Grice, *Georgia Through Two Centuries*, ed. E. Merton Coulter (3 vols., New York, 1966), I, 444, 445.

85. *FU*, July 11, 1865; *S & P*, Jan. 7, 1828.

86. *UR*, May 1, 1883.

87. *GJ*, June 28, 1815.

88. Ulrich B. Phillips, "Historical Notes of Milledgeville, Georgia," *The Gulf States Historical Magazine*, Nov. 1903, p. 171; Census of Baldwin County, 1820, microfilm, Georgia College Library.

89. Sherwood, *Gazeteer of Georgia*, (1829), 19; *UR*, May 1, 1883.

90. Phillips, "Historical Notes," 164–165; *SR*, Oct. 22, 1822.

91. *GJ*, Nov. 23, 1814, Feb. 8, 1815.

92. *S & P*, July 23, 1827; *UR*, March 11, 1884.

93. *SR*, Jan. 9, 1844.

94. *GJ*, Oct. 31, 1809.

95. T. E. Smith, "Baptist Church," 13.

96. *GJ*, Jan. 6, 1814; T. E. Smith, "Baptist Church," 11.

97. T. E. Smith, "Baptist Church," 12.

98. Anna Maria Green Cook, *History of Baldwin County, Georgia* (Anderson, S. C., 1925), 404–411.

99. *Ibid.*, 384–386.

100. *UR*, Sept. 16, 1919.

101. Philip Graham, *The Life and Poems of Mirabeau B. Lamar* (Chapel Hill, 1938), 29; Edward Mayes, *Lucius Q. C. Lamar: His Life, Times and Speeches* (Nashville, 1896), 15–17.

102. Wirt Armstead Cate, *Lucius Q. C. Lamar: Secession and Reunion* (Chapel Hill, 1935), 14; *UR*, July 14, 1896.

103. Tax Returns, 1832, Records of Baldwin County, Baldwin County Courthouse.

104. Cook, *Baldwin County*, 381; Will of Zachariah Lamar, Will Book B (1842), 40–45, Records of Baldwin County, Baldwin County Courthouse.

105. T. E. Smith, "Baptist Church," 15.

106. *SR*, April 26, May 3, 1836.

107. Louis T. Griffith and John E. Talmadge, *Georgia Journalism, 1763–1950* (Athens, 1951), 50; *FU*, Feb. 15, 1831.

108. *GJ*, Nov. 28, 1810; *FU*, March 29, 1872; Cook, *Baldwin County*, 310.

109. *SR*, Dec. 16, 1823.

110. Cook, *Baldwin County*, 347; *FU*, Oct. 25, 1853.

111. Nelle Womack Hines, *A Treasure Album of Milledgeville and Baldwin County, Georgia* (Macon, 1949), 37.

112. *UR*, Sept. 27, 1887.

113. Cook, *Baldwin County*, 424–425; Hines, *A Treasure Album*, 41.

114. Joseph Gaston Baillie Bullock, *A History and Genealogy of the Family of Baillie of Dunain* (Green Bay, Wis., 1898), 8–9, 70–71; Cook, *Baldwin County*, 360–365.

115. James C. Bonner, "Tustunnugee Hutkee and Creek Factionalism on the Georgia-Alabama Frontier," *The Alabama Review*, April 1957, pp. 118–120; James C. Bonner, "William McIntosh," in *Georgians in Profile*, ed. Horace Montgomery (Athens, 1958), 114–193.

116. *GJ*, May 12, 1811.

117. *SR*, June 25, 1861; Cook, *Baldwin County*, 330–332.

118. *GJ*, June 28, 1815.

119. *SR*, Oct. 7, 1823.

120. *S & P*, Feb. 11, July 19, 1828; *UR*, July 23, 1889.

121. Sherwood, *Gazeteer of Georgia* (1829), 135–136; Phillips, "Historical Notes," 1–11; *S & P*, July 12, 1828.

122. *UR*, July 25, 1893.

123. Mrs. Anne Royall, *Southern Tour; or Second Series of the Black Book* . . . (3 vols., Washington, 1830–31), II, 112–113.

124. *GS*, March 16, 1827.

CHAPTER THREE

1. *UR*, March 11, 1884.

2. *GJ*, July 12, Aug. 9, Sept. 6, 1815.

3. *Ibid.*, Dec. 20, 1816.

4. *GJ*, Sept. 25, 1816.

5. Lamar, *A Compilation*, 85.

6. Milton Sidney Heath, *Constructive Liberalism: The Role of the State in the Economic Development of Georgia* (Cambridge, Mass., 1954), 83.

7. *Ibid.*, 184, 186.

8. Lamar, *A Compilation*, 85.

9. *SR*, June 23, 1885; *Standard of Union* (Milledgeville), Jan. 1, 1841.

10. *SR*, July 23, 1844; *FU*, Nov. 5, 1839.

11. *FU*, Oct. 16, 1830, Oct. 4, 1832.

12. *Ibid.*, June 6, 1832, Sept. 20, 1836; *Georgia Laws* (1836), 53; Minutes of the City Council of Milledgeville, Aug. 4, 1853 (hereafter cited as Minutes of City Council). These records, which begin with the year 1837 and run continuously from that date, are in the possession of the Milledgeville City Clerk; microfilm copies are in GDAH, Drawer 9, Boxes 75 and 76.

13. *GJ*, Nov. 23, Dec. 21, 1814; *UR*, Jan. 18, 1881.

14. *SR*, No. 3, 1821; E. Merton Coulter, *A Short History of Georgia* (Chapel Hill, 1933), 228.

15. *UR*, Dec. 28, 1880; Beeson, *Stories*, 61.

16. *SR*, Aug. 20, Sept. 17, Oct. 15, 1822.

17. *S & P*, Jan. 7, 1828.

18. *GJ*, Sept. 4, 27, 1815.

19. *UR*, Jan. 18, 1881.

20. Karl Bernhard, *Travels Through North America During the Years 1825 and 1826* (2 vols., Philadelphia, 1828), II, 20.

21. James C. Bonner, "The Georgia Penitentiary at Milledgeville, 1817–1874," *Georgia Historical Quarterly*, LV (Fall 1971).

22. *Report of the Principal Keeper of the Georgia Penitentiary, 1872–1873* (Atlanta, 1873), 16–17.

23. *Ibid.*, 14; *Georgia Laws* (1831), 70.

24. *GJ*, Oct. 27, 1813; *SR*, Feb. 21, 1821; John Clark, *Considerations on the Purity of Principles of William H. Crawford . . .* (Augusta, 1819), 130–138.

25. *GJ*, Dec. 13, 1815; *SR*, Nov. 13, 1821.

26. *GJ*, May 18, 1814.

27. *UR*, Jan. 23, 1883, June 30, 1896.

28. *Ibid.*, Dec. 28, 1880; William Henry Sparks, *The Memories of Fifty Years . . .* (Macon, 1882), 128–130.

29. *UR*, Dec. 28, Jan. 11, 1881; Bernhard, *Travels*, II, 19.

30. *Ibid*, II, 20.

31. *GS*, April 16, 1827.

32. Record of Commissioners, Feb. 12, 1830; *FU*, July 10, Aug. 7, 1830; Ira

Berlin, "After Nat Turner: Letters from the North," *Journal of Negro History*, LV (April 1970), 144.

33. *FU*, July 17, 1830.

34. *Ibid.*, Aug. 25, Dec. 29, 1831, Jan. 19, 1832; *SR*, Jan. 5, 1832.

35. *SR*, Dec. 8, 1831.

36. *Ibid.*, Dec. 22, 1831, Jan. 5, 1832; *FU*, Dec. 29, 1831, Jan. 5, 1832.

37. *FU*, April 11, 1837; *UR*, Feb. 15, 1881; *FU*, Dec. 31, 1867.

38. James L. Harrison, *Biographical Directory of the American Congress, 1774–1849* (Washington, 1950), 1048. Howell Cobb to Mrs. Cobb, July 9, 1852, in the Cobb-Erwin-Lamar Papers, University of Georgia Library; *FU*, Jan. 31, 1834.

39. *FU*, Dec. 4, 11, 1833; *S & P*, June 14, 1828; *FU*, Aug. 1, 1835, Dec. 6, 1836.

40. *S & P*, June 21, 1828; *GJ*, June 16, 1828.

41. *UR*, March 25, 1879; *The Floridian*, June 12, 1841; *Florida State Sentinel*, Feb. 18, 1842; *FU*, Jan. 7, 1840.

42. *UR*, March 5, 1879; Franklin M. Garrett, *Atlanta and Environs* (New York, 1954), 958–959.

43. *The Reflector* (Milledgeville), Aug. 8, 29, Sept. 1, 1818.

44. *GJ*, Feb. 28, 1811, Dec. 1, 1813, Jan. 25, 1815.

45. *Ibid.*, Sept. 2, Dec. 12, 1812, April 6, 1814.

46. *SR*, May 18, 1824; *GJ*, April 24, 1811, April 15, 1813 (Supplement), Jan. 10, 1816.

47. *GJ*, Oct. 26, 1819; *SR*, July 10, 1830.

48. L. W. Richardson, "Templeton Reid, Early Coin-Maker," *Georgia Magazine*, May 1971, p. 5; *GA*, Aug. 10, 1813; *SR*, July 24, 1830.

49. *GJ*, Dec. 12, 1810, Dec. 13, 1815; *SR*, June 21, 1820.

50. *SR*, May 24, 1825.

51. *GA*, Jan. 16, Feb. 20, 1810.

52. *Ibid.*, Jan. 16, 1810; *SR*, Nov. 21, 1820.

53. *GA*, March 27, 1810.

54. *UR*, Feb. 13, 1883; Howell Cobb to Mrs. Cobb, Oct. 25, 1853, in the Cobb-Erwin-Lamar Papers, University of Georgia Library.

55. Retailer's Bonds, Feb., 1831–Jan., 1863, in Records of Baldwin County, Baldwin County Courthouse; *SR*, Nov. 20, 1820, May 18, 1824.

56. *The Reflector*, Sept. 29, 1818; *CU*, Oct. 27, 1813, Jan. 10, 1816; *SR*, Nov. 21, 1820, May 18, 1824.

57. *GA*, Sept. 9, 1810; *GJ*, Sept. 5, 12, 1810.

58. *GJ*, May 10, 1815.

59. *The Reflector*, Nov. 24, 1818; *SR*, Feb. 15, 1820; *S & P*, Oct. 15, 1827.

60. *GJ*, Dec. 1, 1813, March 24, Dec. 13, 1815; *SR*, May 18, 1824.

61. *SR*, May 16, 1820.

62. *UR*, Jan. 11, 1881, Jan. 3, 1888, Feb. 14, 1899; Charlotte Adams Ford, "The Public Career of Tomlinson Fort, M. D." (M.A. thesis, University of Georgia, 1964), 20.

63. Beeson, *Stories*, 45.

64. *Ibid.*, 43.

65. *SR*, March 21, 1820.

66. *GA*, March 6, 1810.

67. Kate Hayes Fort, *Memoirs of the Fort and Fannin Families* (Chattanooga, 1905), 35; *SR*, May 12, 1835.

68. Bernhard, *Travels*, II, 20.

69. *Milledgeville Intelligencer*, Nov. 22, 1808; Minutes of City Council, Oct. 22, 1853, City Hall.

CHAPTER FOUR

1. *UR*, May 26, 1891.

2. *Ibid.*, Feb. 13, 1883.

3. Executive Minutes, 1811–1812, GDAH; *GJ*, Sept. 25, 1816.

4. *FU*, Jan. 25, 1831.

5. *UR*, April 20, 1883.

6. *SR*, Dec. 28, 1847; Nelson Tift Diary, p. 61, in the Tift Papers, University of Georgia Library.

7. Tift Diary, Nov. 14, 20, 1841.

8. *Ibid.*, Nov. 21, 23, 1841.

9. James A. Bryan to Katherine H. Bryan, Dec. 12, 1840, James A. Bryan Letters, in private possession.

10. *Senate Journal* (1833), 21, (1836), 10, (1841), 6; *UR*, March 11, 1884, Sept. 6, 1890.

11. Clayton, *Compilations*, 40, 347, 659; Lamar, *A Compilation*, 47, 50, 54, 56, 58, 61, 64, 65, 67, 69, 99; *Georgia Laws* (1835), 17; *The Reflector*, Dec. 15, 1818.

12. *UR*, April 17, 1883.

13. *S & P*, Nov. 12, 1827, Oct. 4, 1828; *GS*, April 9, 1827.

14. *UR*, Oct. 11, 1887.

15. *SR*, Dec. 5, 1820, Jan. 29, 1834.

16. *GJ*, Oct. 26, 1819; *SR*, Dec. 20, 1832.

17. *The Reflector*, March 24, 1818; *SR*, Jan. 10, May 30, 1837, Jan. 2, 1838.

18. *S & P*, April 7, 1828.

19. Daniel Mulford to Levi Mulford, July 6, 1809, in Fitch-Mulford Correspondence, Yale University Library.

20. *GA*, July 11, 1810.

21. *GJ*, June 16, 1813, July 6, 1814; July 11, 1820, July 10, 1821; *The Reflector*, June 30, 1818.

22. *UR*, March 11, 1854.

23. *S & P*, July 19, 1828; *FU*, July 11, 1837.

24. *FU*, July 7, 1840.

25. *SR*, July 7, 1857.

26. Griffith and Talmadge, *Georgia Journalism*, 50; Beeson, *Stories*, 36.

27. Beeson, *Stories*, 37; *SR*, Aug. 27, 1834.

28. *SR*, March 1, 1832, July 1, 1845.

29. *Ibid.*, Jan. 16, Feb. 20, March 12, 26, 1844.

30. G. C. Witherspoon to Howell Cobb, Aug. 19, 1851; Carlisle P. B. Martin to Governor Cobb, Sept. 21, 1851; and C. A. L. Lamar to Cobb, Nov. 12, 1851—all in the Cobb-Erwin-Lamar Papers, University of Georgia Library.

31. William B. Mitchell to Cobb, Oct. 8, 1851, in *ibid.*

32. Clayton, *Compilations*, 40; Daniel Mulford, Notes on Journey to Georgia, October, 1808, and Thomas Fitch to Daniel Mulford, July 20, 1810, in Fitch-Mulford Correspondence, Yale University Library.

33. Daniel Mulford to Levi Mulford, Nov. 15, 1808, Jan. 10, 1809, and Daniel Mulford to Mrs. John Crane, July 22, 1809, in Fitch-Mulford Correspondence, Yale University Library.

34. *GJ*, April 5, 1815 (Supplement).

35. *GJ*, Feb. 12, 1814, Oct. 26, 1819; *GA*, April 10, 1810; *SR*, Feb. 15, 1820.

36. Phillips, "Historical Notes," 163; *S & P*, April 5, 1828; Governor Joseph E. Brown to Dr. J. C. McReynolds, Jan. 30, 1863, Hargrett Collection, University of Georgia Library.

37. William G. Roberts, "Tomlinson Fort of Milledgeville, Georgia," *Journal of the History of Medicine and Allied Sciences*, XXIII (April 1968), 132.

38. *S & P*, Jan. 4, 1828.

39. Roberts, "Tomlinson Fort," 132–136.

40. *Ibid.*, 139, 142, 146, 151; George R. Gilmer, *Sketches of Some of the First Settlers of Upper Georgia* . . . (New York, 1855), 160.

41. Peter G. Crawford, "History of the Milledgeville State Hospital" (a typescript dated at Augusta in 1955), 1–5, 8, 23, Georgia College Library.

42. Roberts, "Tomlinson Fort," 138–139.

43. *FU*, Jan. 14, April 28, June 2, July 1, 1835; *SR*, May 5, 12, 1835.

44. John P. Fort, *A Memorial and Personal Reminiscences* (New York, 1918), 54, 57; *FU*, May 5, 12, 1835.

45. Minutes of City Council, Jan. 31, 1842, Feb. 14, 1863, City Hall.

46. Tomlinson Fort, *A Dissertation on the Practice of Medicine Containing an Account of the Causes, Symptoms and Treatment of Diseases* . . . (Milledgeville, 1849), 501; Roberts, "Tomlinson Fort," 146.

47. *SR*, Sept. 10, 1822; Roberts, "Tomlinson Fort," 137.

48. *FU*, Nov. 13, 1849.

49. Roberts, "Tomlinson Fort," 137.

50. George G. Smith, Jr., *The History of Methodism in Georgia and Florida from 1785 to 1865* (Macon, 1877), 106–116.

51. *Ibid.*, 106–110; Alfred M. Pierce, *A History of Methodism in Georgia* . . . (Atlanta, 1956), 86, 96, 263.

52. George White, *Historical Collections of Georgia* . . . (Savannah, 1849), 268; G. G. Smith, Methodism, 516–518.

53. G. G. Smith, *Methodism*, 151, 218.

54. *Ibid.*, 218, 264.

55. *Ibid.*, 117; James C. Bonner, ed., "Journal of a Mission to Georgia in 1827," *Georgia Historical Quarterly*, XLIV (March 1960), 6–7.

56. G. G. Smith, *Methodism*, 153; Daniel Mulford to Mrs. John Crane, July 22, 1809, Fitch-Mulford Correspondence, Yale University Library.

57. G. G. Smith, *Methodism*, 109.

58. John Lambert, *Travels Through Canada and the United States of North America in the Years, 1806, 1807 and 1808* (2 vols., London, 1814), II, 271.

59. *Ibid.*, II, 272; G. G. Smith, *Methodism*, 234; *SR*, Sept. 19, 1826.

60. *S & P*, Oct. 18, 1828.

61. *SR*, March 7, 1820.

62. Lambert, *Travels*, II, 269.

63. T. E. Smith, "Baptist Church," 42, 49, 74.

64. *Ibid.*, 18, 31; *SR*, Jan. 13, 1824; *Atlanta Journal*, Mar. 10, 1933.

65. Beeson, *Stories*, 60; T. E. Smith, "Baptist Church," 18, 20.

66. T. E. Smith, "Baptist Church," 39, 49.

67. Iverson L. Brooks, "The True State of the Church in Georgia," in *S & P*, Sept. 6, 1828.

68. T. E. Smith, "Baptist Church," 24.

69. Basil Manly, Sr., to Iverson L. Brooks, Aug. 10, 1824, Iverson L. Brooks Letters, in private possession.

70. Diary of James Barrow, Dec. 28, 1805, Jan. 7, 1819, Barrow-McKinley Papers, University of Georgia Library.

71. T. E. Smith, "Baptist Church," 35.

72. *SR*, Dec. 24, 1844, Nov. 19, 1861, April 21, 1863; *FU*, Jan. 8, 1867; Records of the St. Stephen's Parish, Milledgeville, Georgia, 1–2; *Georgia Laws* (1841), 42.

73. Allen P. Tankersley, *College Life at Old Oglethorpe* (Athens, 1951), 1–11.

74. *The Reflector*, Sept. 29, 1818; *GJ*, Dec. 13, 1818.

75. *GJ*, March 11, 1812, Aug. 31, 1814; *SR*, June 3, 1822, Aug. 21, 1838.

76. *UR*, April 28, 1885.

77. Phillips, "Historical Notes," 164; Mulford Map; Minutes of City Council, June 18, 1840, City Hall.

78. *UR*, May 19, 1885.

79. *SR*, Aug. 11, 1835.

80. Beeson, *Stories*, 101–102.

81. *GA*, Feb. 27, 1910; *GJ*, Dec. 19, 1809, Aug. 1, 1810, May 18, 1814, Dec. 2, 1812.

82. *GJ*, Aug. 14, 1816; James C. Bonner, ed., *The Journal of a Milledgeville Girl, 1861–1867* (Athens, 1964), 1–3.

83. *GJ*, Oct. 9, 1816; *SR*, Jan. 8, 1822.

84. *GJ*, Dec. 4, 1821, Aug. 5, 1822; John A. Cuthbert, *Digest of all the Laws and Resolutions Now in Force in the State of Georgia on the Subject of Public Education and Free Schools* (Milledgeville, 1832), 10, 31, 32, 34.

85. *Georgia Laws* (1822), 52, 105, 120, 205, 206 (1823), 31, 222.

86. Cuthbert, *Digest*, 10, 31–34; William C. Dawson, *Compilation of the Laws of the State of Georgia* (Milledgeville, 1831), 15–16 (hereafter cited as Dawson, *Laws*).

87. *FU*, Sept. 4, 1830; Minutes, Board of Trustees, University of Georgia, 1817–1859 (3 vols.), II, 224, 241; University of Georgia Library; Cuthbert, *Digest*, 184.

88. Beeson, *Stories*, 160–62; *S & P*, May 10, 1828; Cuthbert, *Digest*, 31, 32.

89. Return of the State and Condition of the Baldwin County Academy . . . [November, 1833] To His Excellency the Governor of Georgia, GDAH; Baldwin County School Records (GDAH record group 12, series 4); Report of the Baldwin County Poor School Fund, 1831; *ibid.*, Statement of the Funds of Baldwin County Academy, 1831; *ibid.*, Poor Schools, 1824–1836, 1838–1845.

90. *S & P*, May 18, 1828.

91. *Ibid.*, June 21, Dec. 27, 1828.

92. *SR*, Nov. 10, Dec. 22, 1831, June 7, 1832.

93. *Ibid.*, Feb. 12, 1832, Dec. 22, 1835.

94. *Ibid.*, Jan. 5, 1832.

95. *Ibid.*, Dec. 20, 1832; *UR*, July 5, 1932.

96. *SR*, Dec. 2, 1834; *FU*, Dec. 24, 1834; William J. Northen, "Carlisle Pollock Beman," in *Men of Mark in Georgia* (7 vols., Atlanta, 1906–1912), II, 95.

97. *UR*, Feb. 7, 1893.

98. *Ibid.*, March 7, 21. May 9, 1893.

99. *Ibid.*, August 15, 1893.

100. *SR*, Nov. 5, 1834; *UR*, March 7, 1893.

101. *UR*, May 9, 30, 1893.

102. Tankersley, *Old Oglethorpe*, 7–19; Charles Wallace Howard, *An Appeal in Behalf of Oglethorpe University* (Augusta, 1835), 3; *SR*, Jan. 10, 1837.

CHAPTER FIVE

1. *GJ*, Sept. 20, 1815.

2. *Ibid.*, Dec. 23, 1814.

3. Phillips, "Historical Notes," 169.

4. *GJ*, July 17, 1816; *Milledgeville News*, Jan. 31, 1913; *S & P*, Feb. 11, 1828.

5. Record of Commissioners, Dec. 29, 1820; GDAH; *GS*, May 10, 1815, Jan. 16, 1827.

6. *FU*, March 1, 1852; *SR*, Feb. 5, 1834, Sept. 17, 1835, May 5, 1840.

7. Minutes of City Council, Dec. 9, 1846, Dec. 22, 1851, City Hall.

8. *Ibid.* Nov. 1, 1839, Oct. 7, 1848, Dec. 5, 1850.

9. *Ibid.*, (1860), 133–137.

10. *Ibid.*, Nov. 1, 1837; Record of Commissioners, May 13, 1815, GDAH; *GJ*, May 10, 1815.

11. Record of Commissioners, Sept. 31, 1828, GDAH; *SR*, Feb. 2, 1832; *FU*, Feb. 22, 1831.

12. Executive Minutes, 1816–1817, p. 204, GDAH; Minutes of City Council, Feb. 6, 1845, City Hall.

13. *SR*, Oct. 21, 1823, Nov. 24, 1831; Record of Commissioners, June 11, 1822, GDAH; *FU*, Nov. 24, 1831; Augustin H. Hansell, Memoirs (an unpublished typescript, *ca.* 1905, in the Georgia College Library.

14. Minutes of City Council, Feb. 6, 1845, City Hall; Record of Commissioners, March 11, 1830, GDAH; *SR*, June 12, 1833; *FU*, June 20, 1837; Record of Commissioners, Dec. 29, 1820.

15. Minutes of City Council, Apr. 8, 1854, City Hall; *SR*, Apr. 28, 1854.

16. Record of Commissioners, Feb. 12, 1829, GDAH; Minutes of City Council, Nov. 1, 1839, June 26, 1840, Oct. 18, 1854, Aug. 19, 1859, Feb. 13, 1850, City Hall.

17. Record of Commissioners, Jan. 13, 1815, July 24, 1818, GDAH.

18. *Ibid*, Jan. 26, 1813, June 25, 1825.

19. *GJ*, March 20, 1816; *SR*, March 18, 1823.

20. Record of Commissioners, Feb. 28, 1813, March 16, 22, 1823, GDAH.

21. *Ibid.*, Feb. 12, 1829; *SR*, Jan. 27, 1824; *S & P*, June 7, 1828.

22. *FU*, Nov. 20, 1833.

23. *SR*, Nov. 10, 1831; *UR*, Feb. 27, 1883; Charles H. Nelson, Principal Keeper, to Governor George W. Crawford, Nov. 10, 1843, Penitentiary Records, GDAH.

24. Governor Cobb to Mrs. Cobb, Oct. 25, 1853, Cobb-Erwin-Lamar Papers, University of Georgia Library.

25. *GA*, April 24, Sept. 12, 1810; *SR*, Aug. 13, 1839; Minutes of City Council Dec. 20, 1838, Jan. 9, 1847, Jan. 1, 1851, City Hall; Record of Commissioners, Sept. 11, 1813, GDAH.

26. *SR*, April 23, 1839; *FU*, June 30, 1837; Minutes of City Council Jan. 7, Nov. 11, 1861, City Hall; *UR*, July 22, 29, 1890, June 16, 1891.

27. Minutes of City Council, Aug. 1, 1850, City Hall.

28. *Ibid.*, June 17, 1858.

29. *Ibid.*, Oct. 8, 1841.

30. *Ibid.*, Jan. 12, 13, 1847, Mar. 4, 1858.

31. *Ibid.*, June 16, 1838; Phillips, "Historical Notes," 164.

32. Phillips, "Historical Notes," 164; Record of Commissioners, Feb. 8, 1813, GDAH; Minutes of City Council, July 15, 1861. City Hall; *SR*, Aug. 13, 1861; Grand Jury Indictments, March 26, 1819, Baldwin County Courthouse.

33. *GJ*, July 19, 1815; Minutes of City Council, Dec. 24, 1860, City Hall.

34. *GA*, Jan. 30, 1810.

35. Phillips, "Historical Notes," 163, 164; Record of Commissioners, Sept. 8, 1813, Feb. 2, 1825, GDAH.

36. *Sixth Census of the United States ... 1840* (Washington, 1841), 231–233; *SR*, Nov. 3, 1840.

37. Minutes of City Council, Nov. 4, 1858, City Hall.

38. Conveyance deed dated Dec. 8, 1831, Tomlinson Fort Papers, Emory University Library.

39. *UR*, July 2, 1901.

40. *GJ*, Sept. 18, 1811.

41. Will of Zachariah Lamar (codicil), May 2, 1832, Will Book B, 1832, Baldwin County Courthouse.

42. *GA*, Feb. 27, Nov. 28, 1810; *The Reflector*, Sept. 29, 1818.

43. *SR*, March 7, 1820, July 24, 1821, Oct. 21, 1823.

44. *Ibid.*, July 24, 1821; *GJ*, Dec. 13, 1815; April 27, May 4, 1814.

45. *SR*, March 14, 1820.

46. *Ibid.*, Oct. 4, 1832; *GJ*, Oct. 26, 1819.

47. Record of Commissioners, Feb. 15, Mar. 4, 1813, May 13, 1815, GDAH; Minutes of City Council, Aug. 31, 1843, Dec. 19, 1839, Sept. 18, 1841, Oct. 8, 1854, May 20, 1859, City Hall; Phillips, "Historical Notes," 186.

48. Minutes of City Council, Dec. 19, 1837, Dec. 8, 1856, City Hall.

49. Phillips, "Historical Notes," 169–170.

50. Record of Commissioners, Jan. 6, July 14, 1813, Jan. 8, 1825, May 10, 1813, July 24, 1817, Sept. 4, 1820, City Hall.

51. *Ibid.*, Feb. 21, 1823, Feb. 12, 1825.

52. *Ibid.*, Sept. 13, 15, 1831.

53. *Ibid.*, Sept. 11, 1813, April 22, 1831.

54. Phillips, "Historical Notes," 166; Record of Commissioners, Sept. 15, 1831, GDAH.

55. Minutes of the Inferior Court of Baldwin County (1812–1826), Nov. 8, 1816, Feb. 12, 1819, April 14, 1815, Jan. 3, 1822, Nov. 1, Dec. 1, 1825, March 15, 1825, Baldwin County Courthouse; James Barrow, Diary, Feb. 21, 1819.

56. Minutes of the Inferior Court (1812–1826), Jan. 9, 1815, April 5, Oct. 1, 1821.

57. *SR*, March 7, 1820.

58. Minute Book C, 286, 289, Early County Courthouse, Blakely.

59. Joseph C. G. Kennedy, *Agriculture in the United States in 1860* . . . (Washington, 1864), 22, 23; Census of Baldwin County, Schedule I: Free Inhabitants of Baldwin County in 1860, and Schedule II: Slave Inhabitants of Baldwin County in 1860, Georgia College Library.

60. Phillips, "Historical Notes," 169; James C. Bonner, "Profile of a Late Ante-Bellum Community," *American Historical Review*, XLIX (July 1944), 674.

CHAPTER SIX

1. Milledgeville Tax Digest (1859–1867), Digest for 1860, pp. 200–204, City Hall.

2. Census of Baldwin County, Schedule II: Slave Inhabitants in 1860, Georgia College Library.

3. *Sixth Census of the United States* . . . (Washington, 1841), 232–33; John P. Fort, *A Memorial and Personal Reminiscence* (New York, 1918), 72; *UR*, Sept. 25, 1883; *SR*, Nov. 9, 1858.

4. Nelle Womack Hines, *A Treasure Album of Milledgeville and Baldwin County, Georgia* (Macon, 1949), 45.

5. *UR*, Oct. 9, 1930; Census of Baldwin County, Schedule IV, Census of Agriculture in 1860, Georgia College Library.

6. *SR*, Feb. 19, 1834; Census of Baldwin County, Schedule IV, Census of Agriculture in 1860, Georgia College Library.

7. *SR*, Jan. 15, 1834; *FU*, Jan. 22, 1834; *UR*, June 6, 1893.

8. *SR*, March 31, 1840.

9. *South Countryman*, Nov. 17, 1863; *SR*, Sept. 15, 1863.

10. *SR*, March 15, 1858, Jan. 10, 1865; Census of Baldwin County, Schedule IV, Census of Agriculture in 1860, Georgia College Library.

11. *SR*, Sept. 18, 1838, Dec. 21, 1841; *UR*, July 10, 1930.

12. *SR*, June 11, 1834; *UR*, Aug. 20, 1889.

13. *FU*, July 17, 1830, Feb. 1, 1831, June 28, 1832; *SR*, July 7, 1831, June 28, 1832.

14. Mrs. David Ferguson, Scrapbook, p. 15, in private possession; *UR*, Aug. 20, 29, 1899.

15. *UR*, July 6, 1873, July 6, 1939, June 29, 1949.

16. *SR*, Nov. 1, 1859, Jan. 5, 1861; *FU*, Oct. 13, 1868; *UR*, June 29, 1945.

17. H. A. Norris to Governor William Schley, May 13, 1836, Telamon Cuyler Collection, University of Georgia Library.

18. *SR*, April 5, 1836, Jan. 10, 1837.

19. Beeson, *Stories*, 66–67.

20. Mrs. Frederick Fuller Hurlburt, Farmington, Connecticut, to James C. Bonner, June 27, 1966.

21. Governor's Letter Book (1835–1840), p. 195, GDAH.

22. Cook, Lane, Corning and Company to Timothy Porter, Sept. 21, 1837, in GDAH; Memorandum entitled "Passage" in Governor's Letter Book (1835–1840).

23. *SR*, April 24, 1838, April 4, 1840, Nov. 10, 1857; *FU*, Nov. 5, 1839.

24. Governor Schley to Henry Parsons, April 6, 1836, in Governor's Letter Book (1835–1840), p. 64.

25. *GJ*, Nov. 12, 1839; *SR*, April 24, 1860; Lyell, *Second Visit*, II, 23.

26. W. N. Mitchette to Howell Cobb, Oct. 14, 1851, Cobb-Erwin-Lamar Papers, University of Georgia Library.

27. *SR*, Jan. 5, 1858; Lyell, *Second Visit*, II, 23.

28. Sidney Andrews, *The South Since the War* . . . (Boston, 1866), 240; G. H. Stueckrath, "Milledgeville, the Capital of Georgia," *DeBow's Review*, III (Jan. 1860), 110; *SR*, Dec. 20, 1859.

29. *Ibid.*, Feb. 9, 1848.

30. *SR*, Jan. 12, 1841; *UR*, Oct. 5, 1866; Lyell, *Second Visit*, II, 17; *SR*, Oct. 19, 1847, Jan. 2, 1844.

31. *SR*, Sept. 12, 1851.

32. *Ibid.*, Sept. 24, 1850, Feb. 15, 1853.

33. *Ibid.*, Aug. 30, 1853, March 10, 1857, May 8, 1860.

34. *Ibid.*, Sept. 1, 1857, June 1, Oct. 9, 1858, Oct. 8, 1859.

35. *Ibid.*, Feb. 14, 1854, Oct. 8, 1859.

36. *Ibid.*, Dec. 21, 1847, Feb. 29, 1848.

37. *Ibid.*, Jan. 11, 1848; Minutes of City Council, Feb. 17, 1859, p. 105, City Hall.

38. Minutes of City Council, Nov. 4, 1858, Jan. 6, 1859, City Hall; *SR*, Dec. 6, 1853.

39. *SR*, April 28, 1854, Oct. 9, Nov. 13, Nov. 20, 1855, Nov. 4, 1856, May 10, 1857, May 1, 1960.

40. *Ibid.*, Nov. 2, 1858, Oct. 16, 1860.

41. *Ibid.*, Feb. 14, 1854.

42. *Ibid.*, Oct. 30, 1855.

43. *Ibid*, Nov. 6, 1855.

44. *Ibid.*, Dec. 8, 1855; *Georgia Laws* (1855–56), 18; *ibid.*, (1857), 21.

45. *SR*, Oct. 13, 1857; *UR*, Aug. 21, 1883.

46. *Manufactures of the United States in 1860* (Washington, 1865), 61; *UR*, Aug. 12, 1902; Joseph C. G. Kennedy, *Agriculture in the United States*, 22, 23.

47. *SR*, March 1, June 1, 1858, March 1, Nov. 23, 1859; *UR*, March 8, 1892, Jan. 2, 1924; *FU*, June 14, 1870.

CHAPTER SEVEN

1. Governor Charles J. McDonald to Mrs. W. F. Weems, May 7, 1843, in private possession; *GJ*, Nov. 12, 1839; Beeson, *Stories*, 163, 164.

2. *UR*, Aug. 21, 1883; Lyell, *Second Visit*, II, 19, 20.

3. Hiram Buckner to Howell Cobb, Sept. 20, 1851, in Cobb-Erwin-Lamar Papers, University of Georgia Library.

4. Robert E. Martin to Howell Cobb, Sept. 20, 1851, in *ibid.*; *UR*, Sept. 16, 1884.

5. Howell Cobb to Mrs. Cobb, Sept. 20, 1852; Mrs. Cobb to John A. Cobb, July 23, 1852—both in Cobb-Erwin-Lamar Papers, University of Georgia Library.

6. *SR*, Sept. 10, 1861.

7. John E. Simpson, *Howell Cobb: The Politics of Ambition* (Chicago, 1973), 19.

8. *Ibid.*, 115, 130.

9. *Ibid.*, 27.

10. *SR*, Dec. 23, 1851.

11. Receipts, Dec. 1, 1851, Jan. 5, 1853, May 1, 1854, in Cobb-Erwin-Lamar Papers, University of Georgia Library.

12. C. A. L. Lamar to Governor Cobb, Dec. 8, 1851; H. H. Prince to Governor Cobb, Dec. 1, 1851; John Basil Lamar to Cobb, Dec. 4, 1851—all in *ibid.*

13. *UR*, Sept. 16, 1884; Howell Cobb, Jr., to John A. Cobb, April 10, 1853, in Cobb-Erwin-Lamar Papers, University of Georgia Library.

14. Mrs. Howell Cobb to Governor Cobb, Oct. 29, 1853, in Cobb-Erwin-Lamar Papers, University of Georgia Library. *SR*, Dec. 23, 1851.

15. O. H. Prince to John Basil Lamar, Oct. 12, 1852, in Cobb-Erwin-Lamar Papers, University of Georgia Library.

16. Simpson, *Howell Cobb*, 46.

17. Mrs. Howell Cobb to John Cobb, Jan. 15, 1853; Mrs. Cobb to John Basil Lamar, April 7, 1853; M. M. McDonald to Mrs. Cobb, July 27, 1852; Tomlinson Fort to Governor Cobb, July 27, 1853; Wilkes Flagg to John Basil Lamar, Dec. 12 1853—all in the Cobb-Erwin-Lamar Papers, University of Georgia Library.

18. Mrs. Cobb to John Basil Lamar, April 7, 1852; M. M. McDonald to Mrs. Cobb, July 27, 1852; John A. Cobb to Mrs. Cobb, July 24, 1852; John A. Cobb to Howell Cobb, Jr., July 13, 1852—all in *ibid.*

19. Lamar Cobb to John A. Cobb, April 5, 1853; Howell Cobb to John A. Cobb, Feb. 7, 1853—all in *ibid.*

20. John A. Cobb to Governor Cobb, June 10, 1853, *ibid.*

21. Horace Montgomery, *Johnny Cobb: Confederate Aristocrat* (Athens, 1964), 36, 37.

22. *UR*, July 3, 1883.

23. Beeson, *One Hundred Years*, 28, 29; Sue Fort to Sister, Dec. 5, 1855, in the Tomlinson Fort Papers, Emory University Library.

24. *UR*, Sept. 2, 1884, Oct. 4, 1887.

25. *Ibid.*, Sept. 2, 1884.

26. *FU*, Dec. 13, 1853.

27. Sue Fort to Sister, Dec. 8, 1855, Tomlinson Fort Papers, Emory University Library.

28. *Ibid.*

29. Beeson, *One Hundred Years*, 37.

30. *SR*, Dec. 18, 1855, Sept. 1, 1857; *FU*, Nov. 15, 1853, Dec. 6, 1859.

31. Sue Fort to Sister, Dec. 5, 1855, Tomlinson Fort Papers, Emory University Library.

32. Mrs. Joseph E. Brown to Mrs. Mary L. Grisham, Nov. 8, 1857, in the Hargrett Collection, University of Georgia Library.

33. *FU*, Dec. 4, 1866.

34. *SR*, Nov. 30, 1858; Mrs. Joseph E. Brown to Mother, Nov. 29, 1858, Hargrett Collection, University of Georgia Library.

35. *UR*, Dec. 4, 1894; Herbert Fielder, *A Sketch of the Life and Times . . . of Joseph E. Brown* (Springfield, 1883), 99.

36. Lucy Barrow Cobb to John A. Cobb, July 19, 1864; Lucy to John A. Cobb, July 30, 1864—both in Cobb-Erwin-Lamar Papers, University of Georgia Library.

37. *SR*, Dec. 24, 1861, Aug. 3, 1864; Governor Brown to J. P. Reed, Dec. 17, 1861; Hargrett Collection, University of Georgia Library; *FU*, July 26, 1864; *Confederate Union*, Aug. 9, 1864 (hereafter cited as *CU*).

38. *SR*, April 14, 1863; Joseph E. Brown, Tax Returns for 1860 (Box 1, Folder 6), Hargrett Collection, University of Georgia Library; Report of the Committee . . . on the Financial Operations of the State . . . (Milledgeville, 1866), 1585, 1593 (a typescript in the Hargrett Collection).

39. Statement by Mrs. Joseph E. Brown, November, 1857 (Box 1, Folder 14),

Hargrett Collection; Governor Brown to James L. Seward, June 19, 1863, in *ibid.*;
Governor Brown to W. H. Hunt, June 21, 1858, in *ibid.*

40. Governor Brown to Daniel Grambling, April 5, 1858, in *ibid.*

41. Governor Brown to Mrs. Richard M. Orme, Aug. 7, 1865, in *ibid.*

CHAPTER EIGHT

1. Census of Baldwin County, Schedule II: Slave Inhabitants in 1860, Georgia
College Library.

2. *SR*, Oct. 9, 1860.

3. Minutes of the City Council, Jan. 7, 1861, City Hall; *SR*, Feb. 26, 1861.

4. Thomas Conn Bryan, *Confederate Georgia* (Athens, 1953), 2; *SR*, Jan. 18,
1861; Mary Nisbet to Mrs. Mary Jones, Jan. 17, 1861, quoted in Robert M. Myers,
Children of Pride (New Haven, 1972), 642.

5. Sara Fort Milton, "Woman's Work in the South in the Sixties," in *UR*, Aug.
14, 1930.

6. Beeson, *Stories*, 50; Bryan, *Confederate Georgia*, 10; *SR*, Feb. 26, 1861.

7. Bonner, *Journal of a Milledgeville Girl*, 8–9; *UR*, Jan. 19, 1875.

8. Martha Lou Fort to Tomlinson Fort, Jr., Jan. 13, 1861; Tomlinson Fort to
George Fort, Feb. 21, 1862—both in Tomlinson Fort Papers, Emory University
Library.

9. Martha Lou Fort to George Fort, Dec. 21, 1861, in *ibid.*

10. Martha Lou Fort to Tomlinson Fort, Jr., June 13, 1861, in *ibid.*

11. John P. Fort to Mother, Nov. 24, 1861, in *ibid.*

12. *SR*, July 2, Sept. 3, 1861, Jan. 12, 1862; *CU*, Dec. 16, 1862.

13. *UR*, Aug. 14, 1930; Byran, *Confederate Georgia*, 24–25.

14. Beeson, *Stories*, 167; *CU*, Oct. 14, 1862; John Basil Lamar to Howell Cobb,
Dec. 4, 1861, Cobb-Erwin-Lamar Papers, University of Georgia Library.

15. *SR*, Jan. 17, 1865; *CU*, July 5, 1864.

16. *SR*, March 1, 1859.

17. *Ibid.*, Nov. 25, 1862, Oct 4, 1864; *CU*, May 3, Oct. 4, 1864.

18. Minutes of the City Council, Sept. 21, 1860, City Hall; *SR*, Sept. 29, 1863.

19. *SR*, Aug. 9, Sept. 12, 1854.

20. *CU*, May 10, 1864.

21. Bonner, *Journal of a Milledgeville Girl*, 42, 43, 47, 59, 62, 64, 71, 83.

22. "Reminiscences of Confederate Soldiers," II, 166, GDAH.

23. Lucy B. Cobb to John Cobb, March 5, 1865, in Cobb-Erwin-Lamar Papers,
University of Georgia Library; Bryan, *Confederate Georgia*, 191.

24. *SR*, June 14, 1864.

25. *Ibid.*, Sept. 10, 1861, Sept. 8, 1863; Minutes of the City Council, Nov. 11,
1861, City Hall; *CU*, Jan. 13, 1864.

26. Executive Minutes, April 10, 1863, GDAH; *CU*, March 31, 1863; *UR*, May
19, 1875.

27. *CU*, March 31, 1863; *UR*, May 19, 1875.

28. *SR*, May 14, 1850, Nov. 5, 1851, Oct. 16, 1860; *Georgia Laws* (1859), 4, 63, 377, 385, 395.

29. *SR*, Nov. 8, 1859; *Georgia Laws* (1859), 11, 63, 377, 385, 395.

30. *Baldwin Blues Act of Incorporation and Company Regulations* (Milledgeville, 1857), 1–3; Simpson, *Howell Cobb*, 166–170; *SR*, April 2, 1861.

31. *SR*, Feb. 26, 1861.

32. Executive Minutes, 1860–1866, 256, GDAH; *SR*, June 17, 1862.

33. *SR*, Sept. 17, Nov. 5, 1861, Jan. 21, March 18, July 28, 1862, July 28, Sept. 15, 1863; *CU*, Sept. 22, 1863.

34. A fairly complete roster of Georgia's Confederate soldiers may be found in Lillian Henderson, *Roster of the Confederate Soldiers of Georgia, 1861–1865* (5 vols., Hapeville, 1960). The book is unindexed, but each company roster is given in alphabetical order.

35. *SR*, Oct. 9, 1860; Tankersley, *Old Oglethorpe*, 102; *UR*, Oct. 12, 1897.

36. *SR*, March 15, 1858, June 4, Nov. 5, 1861; Allie Goodwin Myrick Bowden, *The Story of the Myricks* (Macon, 1952), 61, 63.

37. *SR*, Oct. 9, 1860, June 4, 26, 1861.

38. *UR*, Dec. 12, 1878.

39. *SR*, April 30, 1861; *UR*, Dec. 6, 1878.

40. *SR*, May 30, Sept. 30, 1862, Feb. 10, July 14, 1863, May 24, 1864; *CU*, July 1, Sept. 8, 1863, May 10, 1864.

41. *FU*, Nov. 21, 1865; *CU*, May 9, 1865; Henderson, *Roster of Confederate Soldiers*, I, 614–623; *UR*, Sept. 26, 1899.

42. *SR*, July 30, Aug. 6, 1861.

43. *Ibid.*, March 11, 1862.

44. *Ibid.*, Aug. 27, Oct. 5, 1861.

45. Minutes of the City Council, Nov. 29, 1861, City Hall; *SR*, Dec. 3, 1861, Jan. 14, July 8, Sept. 2, 1862.

46. *SR*, Aug. 19, 1862.

47. *Ibid.*, Sept. 16, 1862.

48. *Ibid.*, April 18, 1862; *FU*, March 27, Nov. 6, 1866.

49. *SR*, Feb. 16, 1864.

50. *SR*, Aug. 19, Sept. 16, 1862, July 21, 1863; *UR*, May 22, 1911.

51. *SR*, Aug. 19, 1862; *UR*, July 2, 1901, Nov. 15, 1904.

52. *SR*, Jan. 14, 1862; *UR*, Aug 10, 1897, July 8, 1901.

53. Tankersley, *Old Oglethorpe*, 115; Beeson, *Stories*, 103.

54. *CU*, June 25, Aug. 15, 1854, March 14, 1865; *SR*, April 15, 1865.

55. Henderson, *Roster of the Confederate Soldiers of Georgia*, IV, 881; Beeson, *Stories*, 149, 153.

56. *SR*, Aug. 29, 1865; *UR*, July 2, 1901.

57. *SR*, July 9, Sept. 7, 1861, Oct. 27, 1863.

58. *Ibid.*, July 30, 1861, Nov. 25, 1862, Dec. 1, 1863; *UR*, Nov. 19, 1895.

59. *CU*, Nov. 4, 1862.

60. *Ibid.*, Feb. 17, 1863; *SR*, Aug. 18, 1863, Dec. 23, 1862.

61. Randolph Spalding to Cousin, Dec. 25, 1889, in the Barrow-McKinley Papers; *CU*, April 11, 1865; *SR*, Aug. 11, 1863.

62. Henderson, *Roster of the Confederate Soldiers of Georgia*, V, 994; *UR*, Sept. 26, 1899.

63. *FU*, March 28, 1868.

64. Ezra G. Warner, *Generals in Gray* (Baton Rouge, 1959), 304; Martha Thomas to James C. Bonner, July 1, 1970; *UR*, June 13, 1863; Clement A. Evans, ed., *Confederate Military History* . . . (12 vols., Atlanta, 1899), VI, 443.

65. Henry W. Thomas, *History of the Doles-Cook Brigade, Army of Northern Virginia, C. S. A.* (Atlanta, 1903), 44–49; Census of Baldwin County: Schedule I: Free Inhabitants in 1860, Georgia College Library; Will Book B, 127, and Appraisements, 1827–1850, p. 441, both in Records of Baldwin County, Baldwin County Courthouse.

66. *SR*, July 30, 1861, May 6, 1862; Warner, *Generals in Gray*, 14; *CU*, Jan. 30, 1864.

67. Douglas S. Freeman, *Lee's Lieutenants* (3 vols., New York, 1944), II, 558–59; *The War of the Rebellion: A Compilation of the Official Records of the Union and Confederate Armies* (128 vols., Washington, 1880–1901), Series I, Pt. II, Vol. XIX, 684, 699 (hereafter cited as *Official Records*); Warner, *Generals in Gray*, 74; *CU*, Jan. 7, 1864.

68. *SR*, May 12, 1863; *UR*, Feb. 21, 1899, March 31, 1903; *Official Records*, Ser. I, Pt. II, Vol. XXVII, 555, 581–583, 922, 1059.

69. Freeman, *Lee's Lieutenants*, III, 395–400; *Official Records*, Ser. I, Pt. II, Vol. XIX, 684, 699.

70. *CU*, June 7, 1864; *UR*, Oct. 5, 1909; *Richmond Whig*, June 6, 1864.

71. *SR*, June 14, 1864; *CU*, June 14, 1864.

72. *UR*, May 11, 1886; *Directory of Milledgeville* (Macon, 1878–79), 25. Marriages, 1852–1869; Deed Book "R," p. 512; Deed Book "M," pp. 388–89; Mortgages, p. 580—all in Records of Baldwin County, Baldwin County Courthouse.

CHAPTER NINE

1. *Official Records*, Ser. I, Pt. II, Vol. XXXVIII, 915; *FU*, July 26, 1864.

2. *Official Records*, Ser. I, Pt. II, Vol. XXXVIII, 926.

3. Guy C. McKinely, Memoirs, July 9, 1930, p. 11 (a typescript in private possession; a copy is in the Georgia College Library); *FU*, Aug. 9, 1864.

4. *FU*, Aug. 9, 16, 1864.

5. Lucy B. Cobb to husband, July 29, 1864, Cobb-Erwin-Lamar Papers, University of Georgia Library.

6. *SR*, Aug. 3, 1864.

7. Executive Minutes, 1860–1866, Aug. 6, 1864, p. 697, GDAH; *SR*, Aug. 23, 1864.

8. Minutes, Board of Trustees of Oglethorpe College and High School, May,

1864, p. 40 (in private possession); F. W. Capers to Samuel K. Talmadge, May 24, 1864, Barrow-McKinley Papers, University of Georgia Library.

9. Lynwood M. Holland, "Georgia Military Institute: The West Point of Georgia, 1851–1864," *Georgia Historical Quarterly*, XLIII (September 1959), 222–247; *CU*, Aug. 15, Nov. 8, 1864.

10. *FU*, Aug. 9, 1864.

11. *SR*, Feb. 22, 1839; Beeson, *Stories*, 135; *SR*, July 30, 1861.

12. John Hammond Papers, Micro 226, Item 848, GDAH; George A. Gordon to James A. Seddon, April 20, 1864, and John Hammond to Sister, July 7, 1864 (in private possession).

13. *SR*, Aug. 23, 30, 1864; *CU*, Aug. 15, 1864.

14. *SR*, Dec. 20, 1864; McKinley, Memoirs, 4, Georgia College Library.

15. *Official Records*, Ser. III, Vol. V, 394–395, 400, 411, 412.

16. Henry Hitchcock, *Marching With Sherman* (New Haven, 1927), 30; George S. Bradley, *The Star Corps* (Milwaukee, 1865), 189.

17. Stephen F. Fleharty, *Our Regiment* (Chicago, 1865), 114; Samuel Toombs, *Reminscences of the War* (Orange, N. J., 1868), 177–178.

18. William T. Sherman, *Memoirs of General W. T. Sherman* (4th ed., 2 vols., New York, 1889), II, 185; Hitchcock, *Marching With Sherman*, 85; Henry J. Aten, *History of the Eighty-Fifth Regiment, Illinois Volunteer Infantry* (Hiawatha, Kansas, 1901), 111.

19. "Reminiscences of Samuel H. Griswold," quoted from *The Jones County News* (Gray, Georgia), Nov. 9, 1908; George W. Nichols, *The Story of the Great March* (New York, 1865), 60, 61; *CU*, April 11, 1865.

20. Sherman, *Memoirs*, II, 186–187; David Lester, Plantation Record Book (in private possession).

21. James M. Folsom, *Heroes and Martyrs of Georgia* (Macon, 1864), 155; *Official Records*, Ser. I, Vol. XLIV, 1; *Milledgeville News*, Dec. 28, 1921.

22. For a more detailed discussion of Snelling's career, see James C. Bonner, "David R. Snelling: A Study in Defection and Desertion in the Civil War," *Georgia Review*, X (Fall 1956).

23. Edwin E. Bryant, *History of the Third Regiment of Wisconsin Volunteer Infantry* (Madison, 1891), 277–292; *UR*, May 10, 1910 (quoting *The Evening Dispatch*, Columbus, Ohio).

24. *SR*, Dec. 20, 1864; *UR*, Nov. 8, 1902.

25. Bradley, *Star Corps*, 192.

26. Mrs. David Ferguson, Scrapbook (in private possession); Beeson, *Stories*, 164; *SR*, Dec. 20, 1864; Fleharty, *Our Regiment*, 114; James Austin Connolly, "Diary," *Transactions of the Illinois State Historical Society . . . 1928* (Springfield, 1928).

27. *CU*, Dec. 3, 13, 1864; *Macon Telegraph*, Nov. 25, 1864; Beeson, *Stories*, 81.

28. Terrell J. Barksdale to Josephine Barksdale Hubert, Dec. 16, 1864, in private possession.

29. "Reminiscences of Samuel H. Griswold," *The Jones County News*, May 7, 1908.

30. Bonner, *Journal of a Milledgeville Girl*, 63.

31. Deed Book O, 429, Records of Baldwin County, Baldwin County Courthouse; Bryan, *Confederate Georgia*, 169; *SR*, Dec. 20, 1864; Nichols, *The Story of the Great March*, 57.

32. Beeson, *Stories*, 167; *UR*, Sept. 5, 1930.

33. McKinley, Memoirs, 5, 8, 10, Georgia College Library.

34. Connolly, "Diary," 610.

35. Fleharty, *Our Regiment*, 114, 115.

36. *Ibid.*, 116.

37. John J. Hight, *History of the Fifty-Eighth Regiment of Indiana Volunteer Infantry* (Princeton, Ind., 1895), 426.

38. Anne Brantley Hargroves to James C. Bonner, Sept. 13, 1945; Record and Pension Office, No. 1206624, War Department Records, National Archives.

39. James Harrison Wilson, *Under the Old Flag* (2 vols., New York, 1912), I, 369–373; Samuel M. Bowman and Richard B. Irwin, *Sherman and His Campaigns* (Cincinnati, 1865), 200; *FU*, Dec. 22, 1868.

40. Eliza F. Andrews, *The War-time Journal of a Georgia Girl, 1864–1865* (New York, 1908), 32–40.

41. Alexander C. Walker to Governor Brown, Dec. 8, 1864, Joseph E. Brown Papers, Duke University Library.

42. *Macon Telegraph*, Dec. 3, 1864; *SR*, Jan. 3, 1865; *CU*, Jan. 3, 1865.

43. *Macon Telegraph*, Nov. 25, 1865; *CU*, Dec. 27, 1864.

44. *CU*, Dec. 27, 1864; M. C. Fulton to Mrs. Joseph E. Brown, Aug. 18, 1865, Hargrett Collection, University of Georgia Library.

45. Governor Brown to H. H. Tucker, May 14, 1869, in the Hargrett Collection.

46. J. T. Headley, *Grant and Sherman: Their Campaigns and Generals* (New York, 1865), 197–200; Executive Minutes, 1860–1866, Dec. 7, 1864, GDAH; Mrs. Joseph E. Brown to parents, March 13, 1865, Hargrett Collection; *CU*, Jan. 3, 1865.

47. Mrs. Brown to parents, March 13, April 27, 1865, Hargrett Collection.

48. Nancy D. Brown to Mrs. Joseph E. Brown, May 25, 1865, in *ibid.*

49. *SR*, Jan. 3, Feb. 14, 1865.

50. Eliza F. Andrews, *War-time Journal*, 155–63; *SR*, Jan. 10, 1865.

51. John Hammond to mother, Jan. 14, 1865, in private possession.

52. *UR*, Jan. 23, 1894.

53. *SR*, May 9, 1865.

54. *Ibid.*, May 2, 1865.

55. Executive Minutes, 1860–1866, May 7, 1865, GDAH; Mrs. Joseph E. Brown to parents, April 27, 1865; Nancy D. Brown to Mrs. Joseph E. Brown, May 25, 1865—both in Hargrett Collection.

56. Executive Minutes, 1860–1866, May 9, 1865, p. 783, GDAH.

CHAPTER TEN

1. *FU*, July 15, 1865; M. C. Fulton to Mrs. Joseph E. Brown, Aug. 18, 1865, in the Hargrett Collection, University of Georgia Library.

2. Joseph E. Brown to President Andrew Johnson, July 15, 1865, Hargrett Collection.

3. *FU*, Dec. 19, 1865.

4. *Ibid.*, Aug. 22, Sept. 19, 1865, Nov. 29, 1870: Mrs. Brown to Mary T. Brown, June 1, 1865, Hargrett Collection.

5. *Senate Journal* (1865), 77; GDAH: *FU*, Jan. 26, April 17, Aug. 14, Oct. 19, 1866.

6. *FU*, Aug. 22, 1865, Sept. 4, 1866; John Hammond to Grandmother, Oct. 20, 1865, John Hammond Papers, GDAH:

7. Minutes of the City Council, Aug. 18, 1865; *CU*, May 9, 1865; *FU*, Sept. 12, 1865, May 25, 1869.

8. *SR*, Oct. 17, 1865.

9. Minutes of the City Council, Aug. 18, 1865, City Hall; *FU*, Sept. 4, 1866; *UR*, Oct. 1, 1878.

10. *FU*, Feb. 26, 1867, Feb. 25, 1868.

11. John Hammond to Grandmother, Oct. 20, 1865, John Hammond Papers, GDAH; Mrs. Joseph E. Brown to Mary T. Brown, June 1, 1865, Hargrett Collection.

12. *FU*, July 25, Sept. 12, 1865.

13. Adolph E. Meyer, *An Educational History of the American People* (New York, 1957), 212, 213; *FU* April 9, 1867.

14. Records of the Bureau of Refugees, Freedmen, and Abandoned Lands, 1865–1872 (hereafter cited as Freedmen's Bureau Records), Dec. 14, 1865, March 1, 1868, M. R. Bell to Captain N. S. Hill, Jan. 14, 1868 (see also entries under dates of Dec. 28, 1867, Feb. 10 and Aug. 1, 1868), Record Group 105, National Archives, Washington, D. C. (records for activities in Georgia are in Box 86); *UR*, Sept. 11, 1900.

15. M. R. Bell to Capt. N. S. Hill, Jan. 14, 1868, "Letters Sent," 46, 47, 126, 132, Freedmen's Bureau Records; *UR*, Jan. 8, 1878.

16. "Cases Tried," Milledgeville, Georgia, 1867, pp. 29, 30, 32, Freedmen's Bureau Records.

17. M. R. Bell to Gen. O. O. Howard, Jan. 11, 1868; Howard to Bell, n.d., Freedmen's Bureau Records.

18. "Baldwin County Contracts," 1867, pp. 1–7, Freedmen's Bureau Records.

19. "Baldwin County Apprentices," Jan., 1866–Dec., 1872, Freedmen's Bureau Records.

20. General Tillson to T. W. White, Jan. 14, 1866, Freedmen's Bureau Records.

21. "Cases Tried," 1867, pp. 28, 32; "Contracts," 1866; entries dated Dec. 28, 1867, and Feb 10, 1868, Freedmen's Bureau Records.

22. Asena Wells to M. R. Bell, May 15, 1868, "Letters Received," Freedmen's Bureau Records.

23. Christopher Bradley to M. R. Bell, June 26, 1868, Freedmen's Bureau Records.

24. "Reports and Miscellaneous Correspondence," Feb. 4, 1866; "The Tucker Case," entries of Feb. 26, March 2, 12, 1866, March 12, 1868; M. R. Bell to Capt. N. S. Hill, Feb. 11, March 12, May 5, 1868, Freedmen's Bureau Records.

25. *FU*, Jan. 1, March 12, June 4, Aug. 27, 1867, Jan. 7, 1868; John R. Lewis, *First Annual Report of the State School Commissioner* . . . (Atlanta, 1871), 20.

26. *FU*, Feb. 5, May 14, 1867, Oct. 13, 1868; "Letters Sent," 1867, pp. 116, 119, 132, Freedmen's Bureau Records.

27. Asbury Catchings to M. R. Bell, April 1, 1868, Freedmen's Bureau Records.

28. Minute Book, Court of Ordinary, Baldwin County, 1877, pp. 154–160, *ibid.*, 1892, p. 18, Baldwin County Courthouse.

29. *UR*, Nov. 5, 1873, July 2, 1901.

30. *FU*, Dec. 29, 1868.

31. *Ibid.*, Jan. 12, 1869, Feb. 21, 1871.

32. *Ibid.*, July 5, 19, 1871.

33. *SR*, March 24, 1868, July 18, 1871; *FU*, March 6, April 3, 1866, June 8, 1867, Aug. 9, 30, Nov. 8, 1871.

34. *FU*, March 9, 1867, March 31, 1868, May 2, 1871; Beeson, *Stories*, 166–167.

35. *FU*, May 11, 1864.

36. *Ibid.*, March 31, 1868, Jan. 31, Sept. 20, 1871.

37. *Ibid.*, Jan. 2, 1866.

38. *SR*, Dec. 5, 1865; Nov. 20, 1866; June 4, 1867; *FU*, Nov. 6, 1866; *UR*, July 17, 1888.

39. *Georgia Laws* (1866), 10; *SR*, June 4, Oct. 29, 1867.

40. *FU*, Jan. 23, March 6, April 7, 1866, May 19, 1867, Aug. 11, 1868; *SR*, Nov. 20, 1866.

41. "Report of Special Committee of Senate to Visit and Examine the Public Buildings at Milledgeville," a manuscript dated Sept. 2, 1868, in GDAH; *FU*, April 2, 1867.

42. *FU*, Oct. 0, 1866, March 19, 1867.

43. *Ibid.*, April 30, 1867.

44. *Ibid.*, July 2, Nov. 5, 1867; James C. Bonner, "Legislative Apportionment and County Unit Voting in Georgia Since 1777," *Georgia Historical Quarterly*, XLVII (Dec. 1963), 155–60.

45. *SR*, Oct. 29, Dec. 17, 1867; *FU*, Sept. 4, Nov. 5, 1867, Feb. 11, 1868.

46. *Ibid.*, Nov. 5, 1867, Jan. 7, 1868.

47. *Ibid.*, Dec. 31, 1867.

48. Pioneer Citizens Society of Atlanta, *History of Atlanta* (Atlanta, 1902), 362; Franklin M. Garrett, *Atlanta and Environs: A Chronicle of its People and Events* (3 vols., New York, 1954), II; Wallace P. Reed, *History of Atlanta, Georgia* (Syracuse, N. Y., 1889), pt. I, pp. 218–222; Thomas H. Martin, *Atlanta and its Builders* (2 vols., Atlanta, 1902), II, 32, 33.

49. *FU*, June 3, 1868.

50. *SR*, Oct. 29, 1867. For a statement by responsible Milledgeville citizens declaring that no conspiracy existed to increase hotel rates and to refuse Negro delegates as guests, see *FU*, Aug. 25, Sept. 1, 1868.

51. Quoted in the Augusta *Daily Constitutionalist*, Dec. 20, 1867.

52. *FU*, Dec. 31, 1867.

53. *Ibid.*, Jan. 28, 1868.

54. Garrett, *Atlanta*, pt. I, 772–775.

55. Executive Minutes, 1866–1870, pp. 113, 115, GDAH.

56. Olive H. Shadgett, "Charles Jones Jenkins, Jr.," in Horace Montgomery, ed., *Georgians in Profile* (Athens, 1958), 220–241.

57. *UR*, March 17, 1891; *FU*, Feb. 4, 1868.

58. *FU*, Oct. 12, 1869; "Letters Sent, 1868," p. 631 in Records of the Third Military District, 1867–1869, NA.

59. Marion Ruger Norcross, "Notes on the Ruger Family" (in private possession); Bryant, *History of the Third Regiment*, 401; "Letters Sent, 1868," p. 631, in Records of the Third Military District, NA; *SR*, March 10, 1868.

60. General Orders No. 91, Third Military Disrict, quoted in *FU*, July 7, 1868; *FU*, July 14, 1868; *Georgia Laws* (1866), 155, (1865–1866), 156.

61. James C. Bonner, "The Georgia Penitentiary at Milledgeville, 1817–1874," *Georgia Historical Quarterly*, LV (Fall 1971), 303.

62. *FU*, June 21, July 14, 1868.

63. *Ibid.*, March 17, 24, April 14, May 2, 26, 1868; Garrett, *Atlanta*, pt. I, 776.

64. *FU*, Jan. 26, Feb. 2, 1869; Martin, *Atlanta and its Builders*, II, 55–57; *UR*, June 4, 1873.

65. *FU*, April 14, 28, May 5, 19, July 28, 1868.

66. *Ibid.*, May 5, 12, 1868.

67. *Ibid.*, Sept. 15, June 23, 1868; Minutes of the City Council, July 1, 1868, City Hall.

68. *UR*, Oct. 28, 1902.

69. *FU*, July 21, Oct. 6, 1868; Garrett, *Atlanta*, I, 786.

70. Minutes of the City Council, 1865–1868, pp. 340–376, City Hall; *FU*, June 23, 1868.

71. *Gainesville Eagle*, Aug. 9, 1904; George L. Jones, "The Political Career of Henry Patillo Farrow, Georgia Republican, 1864–1904" (master's thesis, University of Georgia, 1966), 5, 6, 10, 11; *FU*, June 23, July 7, 28, Aug. 11, 1868.

72. Garrett, *Atlanta*, p. I, 787; *FU*, Feb. 2, 1869; C. P. Crawford, "Memorandum to Governor James Smith," in miscellaneous collections of the Crawford family, in private possession.

73. Garrett, *Atlanta*, pt. I, 774; *FU*, May 11, 1869.

74. *Atlanta Constitution*, Jan. 13, 1869; *FU*, Jan. 16, Feb. 2, July 6, 1869.

75. *The Atlanta Tribune*, quoted in *UR*, Dec. 25, 1877; *UR*, Feb. 18, 1874, Feb. 6, 1877; *FU*, June 8, 1869.

76. *FU*, May 31, Aug. 2, 9, 23, 30, 1870; *SR*, Aug. 23, 1870.

77. Garrett, *Atlanta*, pt. I, 787; *FU*, Aug. 30, Sept. 20, 1870.

78. *FU*, June 7, 14, 1870.

79. *Ibid.*, Nov. 1, 1870; *SR*, Nov. 1, 1870.

80. *FU*, Nov. 9, 1869, Aug. 2, Sept. 6, 1870.

81. *FU*, Feb. 2, 1869, Nov. 1, 1870; Garrett, *Atlanta*, pt. I, 384.

82. *FU*, Sept. 29, 1868, Feb. 2, 9, 23, Mar. 30, Nov. 16, 1869, Aug 6, 1870, Sept. 13, Oct. 11, Nov. 22, 1871; *Augusta Chronicle*, quoted in *FU*, March 2, 1869; *Macon Telegraph*, Feb. 20, 1869.

83. *FU*, May 7, 1873.

84. *FU*, Feb. 2, 1867, March 3, 1868.

85. *UR*, Nov. 26, 1874; *FU*, Oct. 12, 26, 1869, June 7, 1870; Minutes of the Trustees, Oglethorpe College and High School, Nov., 1869, p. 42.

86. *UR*, July 23, 1873; *FU*, Nov. 1, 1871.

87. Garrett, *Atlanta*, pt. I, 771; *FU*, Oct. 4, 1871, Feb. 7, 1872.

88. *FU*, Sept. 20, 1871, March 27, 1872; *UR*, March 4, 1874.

89. *UR*, Oct. 1, 1873.

90. *Ibid.*, Feb. 4, 11, 1874.

91. *FU*, Sept. 20, 1870.

92. *Ibid.*, Nov. 20, 1877; *The Daily Constitutionalist*, July 15, Nov. 17, 1877.

93. *UR*, Nov. 27, 1872, May 30, 1874, March 23, 1875, Feb. 5, 1884, April 20, 1886.

94. *UR*, April 3, Oct. 9, 1877.

95. *The Daily Constitutionalist*, Dec. 2, 1877; *UR*, Dec. 11, 1877; Martin, *Atlanta and its Builders*, II, 82.

96. *UR*, Dec. 11, 1877.

97. Census of Baldwin County, 1870, Georgia College Library; *SR*, June 20, 1870.

CHAPTER ELEVEN

1. *UR*, Dec. 1, 1891.

2. *Ibid.*, Mar. 13, 1872; *UR*, Feb. 12, 1907.

3. *FU*, Aug. 21, 1872, Nov. 26, 1876, Mar. 15, 1890, Nov. 22, 1892, March 24, 1896.

4. *UR*, June 9, 1898, Nov. 23, 1909; *FU*, Feb. 1, 1870, March 28, 1871; *UR*, Sept. 16, 1890, Jan. 3, 1899.

5. *Milledgeville News*, Nov. 27, 1918; *UR*, Sept. 11, 1894, Aug. 18, 1925.

6. *UR*, May 30, 1923.

7. *Ibid.*, June 11, 1873, Feb. 18, 1874.

8. Census of Baldwin County: Schedule II, Slave Inhabitants in 1860, Georgia College Library; Register of Free Persons of Color in Baldwin County, 1832–1864, Book A in Box 64, Drawer 139, GDAH. *UR*, June 14, 1898.

9. *UR*, June 14, 1898.

10. *Ibid.*, May 31, 1887.

11. *Report of the Principal Keeper of the Georgia Penitentiary, 1874* (Savannah, 1875), 4, 9; *UR*, Aug. 24, 1875.

12. *UR*, Dec. 2, 1874, Jan. 4, 1876.

13. *Ibid.*, Feb. 4, 1879.

14. *Ibid.*, Oct. 15, 1885, July 6, 1886.

15. *Ibid.*, Feb. 12, 1873.

16. *Ibid.*, Sept. 3, 1873, Oct. 7, 1890, Oct. 29, 1901.

17. *Ibid.*, April 12, 1898.

18. *Ibid.*, Aug. 24, 1892.

19. *Georgia Laws* (1870), 57, 49, 61.

20. Gustavus J. Orr, *Fifth Annual Report of the State School Commissioner of Georgia* . . . (Savannah, 1876), 86–94; *ibid.* (1877), 5; *UR*, Sept. 3, 1873, April 8, 15, 1874, April 18, 1876.

21. *UR*, April 19, 1882, April 20, 1886.

22. *Ibid.*, June 17, 1879.

23. *FU*, Nov. 15, 1871; Gustavus J. Orr, *Annual Report of the State School Commissioner to the General Assembly of the State of Georgia* (1885–86), 7. See also annual reports of state school commissioners J. S. Hooks (for 1887–88), p. 19, and W. B. Merritt (for 1905), p. 58.

24. *FU*, Sept. 9, 1871, Jan. 17, 1872; *UR*, June 15, 1875, May 10, 1899.

25. *FU*, June 21, 1871, Aug. 9, 16, 1871.

26. *Ibid.*, May 8, 1872.

27. *UR*, Sept. 11, 1872.

28. *SR*, June 27, Aug. 15, 29, Sept. 5, 1871; *FU*, May 8, 1872.

29. *UR*, Aug. 6, 20, 1878; Broadside, *Middle Georgia College*, Oct. 3, 1878, in private possession; *UR*, Jan. 13, 1880; G. J. Orr, *Annual Report* (1880), 79.

30. *Georgia Laws*, (1878–79), 91, 92.

31. *UR*, Oct. 28, 1879, Oct. 23, 1881, June 28, 1886; *Georgia Laws* (1878–79), 95, 96.

32. *UR*, Nov. 19, 1889.

33. *Georgia Laws* (1889), 85; *UR*, Dec. 18, 1888.

34. *UR*, Jan. 22, 1889, April 19, 1898, Nov. 13, 1900, Jan. 2, 1909.

35. *Ibid.*, June 30, 1885, June 14, August 3, 1892, June 27, 1893, Jan. 9, 1894.

36. *Ibid.*, Jan, 4, 1890, Aug. 24, Oct. 12, 1894, May 28, 1895, Aug. 24 1897.

37. *Ibid.*, Jan. 16, 1894, May 28, 1895.

38. *Georgia Laws* (1899), 85; *UR*, April 10, 1930.

39. Daniel H. Hill to Naomi J. Williams, June 27, 1887, in private possession of the author; Henry Kyd Douglas, *I Rode With Stonewall* (Chapel Hill, 1940), 212.

40. *UR*, March 9, 1889.

41. *Ibid.*, Sept. 14, 1880, Jan. 25, June 30, 1885, Oct. 5, 1886. Aug. 12, 1887; *Official Records*, Ser. I, Vol. XXI, 64.

42. *UR*, June 18, Aug. 6, Oct. 1, 1889.

43. *Ibid.*, Aug. 30, 1889, June 14, 1892.

44. *Ibid.*, Oct. 20, 1885, Oct. 5, 1886, April 7, 1891.

45. *Ibid.*, Nov. 12, 1889.

46. *Ibid.*, Oct. 8, Nov. 5, 12, 19, 1889; *Georgia Laws* (1888–1889), II, 10.

47. Lottie H. Curl, "The History of the Georgia State College for Women" 1–29

(master's thesis, George Peabody College for Teachers, 1921); *UR*, Dec. 17, 1889.

48. *UR*, Dec. 17, 1889, March 18, 1890, Aug. 27, 1895.

49. *Ibid.*, Nov. 11, 1890, Aug. 25, 1891, Oct. 20, 1896.

50. *Ibid.*, June 9, 1891.

51. Published in *Annual Report of the American Historical Association for . . . 1908* (Washington, 1909), I, 133–43.

52. *UR*, June 28, Nov. 8, 1892, June 11, 1901, June 6, 1905.

53. *Ibid.*, June 14, 1898; *Snapshots* (Milledgeville, 1904), I, 12.

54. *UR*, April 6, 1897, June 11, 25, July 1, Oct. 22, 1901.

55. *UR*, July 13, 1880, July 13, 1886, June 26, 1888.

56. *Ibid.*, April 24, 1894.

57. *Ibid.*, Dec. 29, 1891, Dec. 31, 1901.

58. *Ibid.*, Jan. 25, 1898, Aug. 16, 1904.

59. *Ibid.*, Sept. 9, 1902.

60. *Ibid.*, Oct. 18, 1898.

61. *Ibid.*, April 16, 1895; *The Brown Book* (Milledgeville, 1910), 77.

62. *UR*, March 8, 1892, Nov. 9, 1897; John F. Stegeman, *The Ghosts of Herty Field* (Athens, 1966), 40.

63. *UR*, May 11, 1892, April 13, 1897.

64. *The Milledgeville News*, April 4, 1913.

65. *UR*, Feb. 26, 1884.

66. Beeson, *Stories*, 78, *UR*, Aug. 13, 1873, June 8, 1898, June 2, 1908, April 23, 1912.

67. *UR*, June 16, 1891.

68. John D. Toomey, "History of the Catholic Church in Milledgeville" (April 1953), 1–6, a manuscript in private possession; *UR*, Dec. 3, 1889.

69. *UR*, Jan. 30, 1887, Oct. 30, 1888, Dec. 3, May 9, 1893; Toomey, "Catholic Church," 4.

70. *UR*, Feb. 4, 1874, Jan. 20, 1880, April 26, 1881, Dec. 3, 1889, Nov. 11, 1890.

71. Minutes of City Council, Jan. 10, 1876, City Hall; *UR*, Nov. 1, 1881, Dec. 5, 1883, July 25, 1893; *FU*, Feb. 18, 1868.

72. *UR*, May 24, 1881, May 21, 1890.

73. *Ibid.*, Sept. 24, 1889, Jan. 14, 1890; *The Milledgeville News*, June 29, 1917; *UR*, Sept. 7, Nov. 23, Dec. 6, 1875, April 20, 1886, May 9, 1916.

74. *UR*, March 23, 1875, Feb. 5, 1884, Sept. 7, 1886, Dec. 13, 1887.

75. *FU*, July 2, 1887; *UR*, May 26, 1873, June 6, 1874, Aug. 22, Dec. 13, 1887.

76. *UR*, Feb. 11, March 4, Apr. 1, June 17, July 15, 1879, Jan. 3, 1888, June 11, Oct. 15, 1889.

77. *Ibid.*, March 4, 1879, Feb. 13, 1894.

78. *FU*, Aug. 16, 1871, Feb. 15, May 3, 1892; *UR*, Jan. 13, 1889, Feb. 6, 1907, Aug. 8, 1911.

79. *UR*, Aug. 4, 1888, Aug. 18, 1927, April 13, 1885, Jan. 18, May 9, 1886, Oct. 27, Nov. 17, 1891, June 27, 1892, Feb. 28, June 6, July 4, Nov. 21, 1893,

July 21, 1896; *The Milledgeville News*, Nov. 28, 1913.

80. *Southern Progress*, April, 1897, p. 6; *UR*, July 8, 1890, Feb. 12, 1895, Feb. 11, 1901, March 8, 1904, Mar. 24, 1908, May 18, 1915, Aug. 18, 1927, Feb. 9, 1928.

81. *UR*, Aug. 2, 1887, Oct. 27, 1891, Jan. 10, 1893.

82. *Ibid.*, June 12, 1898, Feb. 4, 1899, Feb. 10, 1903, Jan. 3. Aug. 22, 1911, March 9, 1922.

83. Beverly Smith, "He Makes the Generals Listen," *The Saturday Evening Post*, March 10, 1951, p. 120.

Bibliography

I. ARTICLES AND MASTER'S THESES

Berlin, Ira. "After Nat Turner: Letters From the North." *Journal of Negro History*, LV (April 1970).

Bonner, James C. "David R. Snelling: A Study in Defection and Desertion in the Civil War." *Georgia Review*, X (Fall 1956).

———. "The Georgia Penitentiary at Milledgeville, 1817–1874." *Georgia Historical Quarterly*, LV (Fall 1971).

———, ed. "Journal of a Mission to Georgia in 1827." *Georgia Historical Quarterly*, XLIV (March 1960).

———. "Profile of a Late Ante-Bellum Community." *American Historical Review*, XLIX (July 1944).

———. "Tustunnuggee Hutkee and Creek Factionalism on the Georgia-Alabama Frontier." *The Alabama Review*, April 1957.

———. "William McIntosh." In *Georgians in Profile*, ed. Horace Montgomery. Athens: The University of Georgia Press, 1958.

Brooks, Iverson L. "The True State of the [Baptist] Church in Georgia." *Statesman and Patriot*, Sept. 26, 1828.

Connolly, Major James A. "Diary." *Transactions of the Illinois State Historical Society . . . 1928*. Springfield, 1928.

Coulter, E. Merton. "Scull Shoals: An Extinct Georgia Manufacturing and Farming Community." *Georgia Historical Quarterly*, XLVIII (March 1964).

Curl, Lottie H. "The History of the Georgia State College for Women." M.A. thesis, George Peabody College for Teachers, 1931.

Ford, Charlotte Adams. "The Public Career of Tomlinson Fort." M.A. thesis, University of Georgia, 1964.

Goff. John H. "Edward Lloyd Thomas, Surveyor." *Emory University Quarterly*, XVIII (Summer 1962).

———. "Short Studies of Georgia Place Names." *Georgia Mineral Newsletter*, XIII (Fall 1960) and XVI (Fall 1964).

———. "Some Major Indian Trading Paths Across the Georgia Piedmont." *Georgia Mineral Newsletter*, VI (Winter 1953).

Griswold, Samuel. "Reminiscences of Samuel H. Griswold." *Jones County News* (Gray, Ga.), Nov. 9, 1908.

Holland, Lynwood M. "Georgia Military Institute: The West Point of Georgia, 1851–1864." *Georgia Historical Quarterly*, XLIII (Sept. 1959).

Jones, George L. "The Political Career of Henry Patillo Farrow, Georgia Republican, 1864–1904." M.A. thesis, University of Georgia, 1966.

Mattison, Ray H. "The Creek Trading House—From Colerain to Fort Hawkins." *Georgia Historical Quarterly*, XXX (Sept. 1946).

Milton, Sara Fort. "Women's Work in the South in the Sixties." *Union-Recorder*, Aug. 14, 1930.

Northen, William J. "Carlisle Pollock Beman." In *Men of Mark in Georgia*. 7 vols. Atlanta: 1906–1912.

Phillips, Ulrich B. "Historical Notes of Milledgeville, Georgia." *The Gulf States Magazine*, November 1903.

Richardson, L. W. "Templeton Reid, Early Coin-Maker." *Georgia Magazine*, May 1971.

Roberts, William G. "Tomlinson Fort of Milledgeville, Georgia." *Journal of the History of Medicine and Allied Sciences*, XXIII (April 1968).

Shadgett, Olive H. "Charles Jones Jenkins, Jr." In *Georgians in Profile*, ed. Horace Montgomery. Athens: The University of Georgia Press, 1958.

Smith, Beverly. "He Makes the Generals Listen." *Saturday Evening Post*, March 10, 1951.

Sonstein, Larry. "A History of the Baldwin Blues." M.A. thesis, Georgia College, 1976.

Stueckrath, G. H. "Milledgeville, the Capital of Georgia." *DeBow's Review*, III (Jan. 1860).

II. BOOKS

Andrews, Eliza F. *The War-time Journal of a Georgia Girl, 1864–1865*. New York: Appleton. 1908.

Andrews, Garnett. *Reminiscences of an Old Georgia Lawyer*. Atlanta: Franklin, 1870.

Andrews, Sidney. *The South Since the War as Shown by Fourteen Weeks of Travel in Georgia and the Carolinas*. Boston: Tichner and Fields, 1866.

Aten, Henry J. *History of the Eighty-Fifth Regiment, Illinois Volunteer Infantry*. Hiawatha, Kansas: Regimental Association, 1901.

Bartram, William. *Travels Through North and South Carolina, Georgia, East and West Florida, the Cherokee Country.* . . . Philadelphia: James and Johnson. 1791.

Beeson, Leola Selman. *History Stories of Milledgeville and Baldwin County, Georgia*. Macon: J. W. Burke, 1943.

———. *The One Hundred Years of the Old Governor's Mansion*. Macon: J. W. Burke, 1938.

Benedict, David. *General History of the Baptist Denomination*. 2 vols. Boston: Lincoln and Edwards, 1813.

Bernhard, Karl. *Travels Through North America During the Years 1825 and 1826*. 2 vols. Philadelphia: Carey, Lee and Carey, 1828.

Bonner, James C., ed. *The Journal of a Milledgeville Girl, 1861–1867*. Athens: The

University of Georgia Press, 1974. The original manuscript is in the University of Georgia Library and is catalogued under "The Journal of Anna Maria Green."

Bowden, Allie Goodwin Myrick. *The Story of the Myricks*. Macon: J. W. Burke, 1952.

Bowman, Samuel M., and Irwin, Richard B. *Sherman and His Campaigns*. Cincinnati: C. F. Vorst, 1865.

Bradley, George S. *The Star Corps*. Milwaukee: Jermain and Brightman, 1865.

Bryan, Thomas Conn. *Confederate Georgia*. Athens: The University of Georgia Press, 1953.

Bryant, Edwin E. *History of the Third Regiment of Wisconsin Volunteer Infantry*. Madison: Veteran Association, 1891.

Buckingham, James Silk. *The Slave States of America*. 2 vols. London: Paris Fisher Son and Co., 1842.

Bullock, Joseph Gaston Baillie. *A History and Genealogy of the Family of Baillie of Dunain*. Green Bay, Wisc.: Gazette Printers, 1898.

Cate, Wirt Armstead. *Lucius Q. C. Lamar: Secession and Reunion*. Chapel Hill: The University of North Carolina Press, 1935.

Clark, John. *Considerations on the Purity of the Principles of William H. Crawford. . . .* Augusta: Georgia Advertizer, 1819.

Cook, Anna Maria Green. *History of Baldwin County, Georgia*. Anderson, S. C.: Key-Hearn, 1925.

Coulter, E. Merton. *A Short History of Georgia*. Chapel Hill: University of North Carolina, 1933.

Evans, Clement A., ed. *Confederate Military History*. 12 vols. Atlanta: Confederate Publishing Co., 1899.

Fielder, Herbert. *A Sketch of the Life and Times and Speeches of Joseph E. Brown*. Springfield, Mass.: Springfield Printing Co., 1883.

Fleharty, Stephen F. *Our Regiment*. Chicago: Brewster and Hanscom, 1865.

Folsom, James M. *Heroes and Martyrs of Georgia*. Macon: Burke, Boykin and Co., 1864.

Fort, John P. *A Memorial and Personal Reminiscence*. New York: Knickerbocker, 1910.

Fort, Kate Haynes. *Memoirs of the Fort and Fannin Families*. Chattanooga: McGowan and Cooke, 1905.

Fort, Tomlinson. *A Dissertation on the Practice of Medicine Containing an Account of the Causes, Symptoms, and Treatment of Diseases. . . .* Milledgeville: Federal Union, 1849.

Freeman, Douglas S. *Lee's Lieutenants*. 3 vols. New York: Scribners, 1944.

Garrett, Franklin M. *Atlanta and Environs: A Chronicle of Its People and Events*. New York: Lewis Publishing Co., 1954.

[Gilmer, George R.] *Sketches of Some of the First Settlers of Upper Georgia, of the Cherokees, and of the Author*. New York: D. Appleton and Co., 1855.

Graham, Philip. *The Life and Poems of Mirabeau B. Lamar*. Chapel Hill: University of North Carolina Press, 1938.

Grice, Warren. *Georgia Through Two Centuries.* Edited by E. Merton Coulter. 3 vols. New York: Lewis Historical Publishing Co., 1966.

Griffith, Louis T., and Talmadge, John E. *Georgia Journalism, 1763–1950.* Athens: University of Georgia Press, 1951.

Hays, Louise Frederick. *Hero of Hornet's Nest: A Biography of Elijah Clarke, 1733 to 1799.* New York: Stratford Press, 1946.

Headley, J. T. *Grant and Sherman: Their Campaigns and Generals.* New York: E. B. Treat, 1865.

Heath, Milton Sidney. *Constructive Liberalism: The Role of the State in the Economic Development of Georgia.* Cambridge, Mass.: Harvard University Press, 1954.

Hight, John J. *History of the Fifty-Eighth Regiment of Indiana Volunteer Infantry.* Princeton, Ind.: Clarion, 1895.

Hines, Nelle Womack. *A Treasure Album of Milledgeville and Baldwin County, Georgia.* Macon: J. W. Burke, 1949.

Hitchcock, Henry. *Marching With Sherman.* New Haven: Yale University Press, 1927.

Howard, Charles Wallace. *An Appeal in Behalf of Ogelthorpe University.* Augusta, 1835.

Jacobs, James Ripley. *The Beginning of the United States Army, 1783–1812.* Princeton: Princeton University Press, 1947.

Kennedy, Joseph C. G. *Agriculture in the United States in 1860.* . . . Washington: Government Printing Office, 1864.

Lamar, Lucius Q. C. *A Compilation of the Laws of the State of Georgia [1810–1819].* . . . Augusta: T. S. Hannon, 1821.

Lambert, John. *Travels Through Canada and the United States of North America in the Years 1806, 1807 and 1808.* 2 vols. London: Craddock and Joy, 1814.

Lewis, John R. *First Annual Report of the State School Commissioner.* . . . Atlanta: New Era Steam Press, 1871.

Lyell, Sir Charles. *A Second Visit to the United States of North America.* 2 vols. New York: Harper, 1850.

Manufactures of the United States in 1860. Washington: Government Printing Office, 1865.

Martin, Thomas H. *Atlanta and its Builders.* 2 vols. Atlanta: Century Memorial Publishing Co., 1902.

Mayes, Edward. *Lucius Q. C. Lamar; His Life, Times, and Speeches, 1825–1893.* Nashville: Methodist Publishing Co., 1896.

Meyer, Adolph E. *An Educational History of the American People.* New York: McGraw-Hill, 1957.

Montgomery, Horace, ed. *Georgians in Profile.* Athens: The University of Georgia Press, 1958.

———. *Johnny Cobb: Confederate Aristocrat.* Athens: The University of Georgia Press, 1958.

Myers, Robert M. *Children of Pride.* New Haven: Yale University Press, 1972.

Nichols, George W. *The Story of the Great March.* New York: Harper, 1865.

Orr, Gustavus J. *Fifth Annual Report of the State School Commissioner of Georgia.* . . . Savannah: State Printer, 1876.

Pickett, Albert James. *History of Alabama and Incidentally of Georgia and Mississippi, from the Earliest Period.* Charleston: Walker and James, 1851; reprint, Birmingham: Birmingham Book and Magazine Co., 1962.

Pierce, Alfred M. *A History of Methodism in Georgia, Feb. 5, 1736–June 24, 1955.* Atlanta: North Georgia Conference Historical Society, 1956.

Pioneer Citizens. *History of Atlanta, 1833–1902.* Atlanta, 1902.

Prucha, Frances Paul. *A Guide to the Military Posts of the United States.* Madison: State Historical Society of Wisconsin, 1964.

Reed, Wallace R. *History of Atlanta, Georgia.* . . . Syracuse: D. Mason, 1899.

Register, Alvaretta Kenan. *The Kenan Family and Some Allied Families.* Statesboro: Kenan Print Shop, 1967.

Report of the Principal Keeper of the Georgia Penitentiary . . . , 1872–73, 1874. Atlanta: State Printer, 1873, 1874.

Report of the Trustees, Superintendent and Resident Physician of the Lunatic Asylum of the State of Georgia . . . , 1861, 1863, 1875. Milledgeville: Boughton, Nisbet, Barnes and Moore, 1861, 1863, 1875.

Royall, Mrs. Anne Newport. *Southern Tour; or Second Series of the Black Book.* . . . 3 vols. Washington: The Author, 1830–1831.

Sherman, William T. *Memoirs of General William T. Sherman.* 2 vols. New York: D. Appleton, 1876; 4th ed., 1889.

Sherwood, Adiel. *A Gazeteer of Georgia, 1827.* Charleston: W. Riley, 1827.

————. *A Gazeteer of Georgia, 1829.* Philadelphia: Martin and Boden, 1829.

Sibbald, George. *Notes and Observations on the Pine Lands of Georgia.* Augusta: William J. Bunce, 1801.

Simpson, John E. *Howell Cobb: The Politics of Ambition.* Chicago: The Adams Press, 1973.

Sixth Census of the United States . . . *1840.* Washington: Blair and Rives, 1841.

Smith, George G. *The History of Methodism in Georgia and Florida from 1785 to 1865.* Macon: J. W. Burke, 1877.

————. *The Life and Letters of James Osgood Andrews, Bishop of the Methodist Episcopal Church, South.* Macon: J. W. Burke, 1883.

Sparks, William Henry. *The Memories of Fifty Years.* . . . Macon: J. W. Burke, 1882.

Stegeman, John F. *The Ghosts of Herty Field.* Athens: The University of Georgia Press, 1966.

Swanton, John R. *The Indians of the Southeastern United States.* Smithsonian Institution, Bulletin 137, Bureau of American Ethnology. Washington: Government Printing Office, 1946.

Tankersley, Allen P. *College Life at Old Oglethorpe.* Athens: The University of Georgia Press, 1951.

Thomas, Henry W. *History of the Doles-Cook Brigade, Army of Northern Virginia, C. S. A.* Atlanta: Franklin Printing Co., 1903.

Toombs, Samuel. *Reminiscences of the War.* Orange, N. J.: Journal Printing Office, 1878.

Van Doren. Mark, ed. *The Travels of William Bartram.* New York: Dover, 1928.

The War of the Rebellion: A Compilation of the Official Records of the Union and

Confederate Armies. 128 vols. and index. Washington: Government Printing Office, 1880–1901.

Warden, D. B. *A Statistical, Political and Historical Account of the United States.* . . . 3 vols. Edinburgh: A. Constable, 1819.

Warner, Ezra J. *General in Gray.* Baton Rouge: The Louisiana University Press, 1959.

Watkins, Robert, and Watkins, George. *Digest of the Laws of Georgia . . . to 1798.* Philadelphia: R. Aitken, 1800.

White, George. *Historical Collections of Georgia: Containing the Most Interesting Facts, Traditions, Biographical Sketches, Anecdotes, Etc.* New York: Pudney and Russell. 1854.

Wilson, James Harrison. *Under the Old Flag.* 2 vols. New York: Appleton, 1912.

III. MANUSCRIPTS, OFFICIAL AND UNOFFICIAL

A. In Georgia Department of Archives and History, Atlanta

Baldwin County School Records, 1831–1845. Record Group 12, Series 4.

Executive Minutes, 1809, Jan. 1, 1811–Sept. 30, 1812; *ibid.*, 1816–1817;·*ibid.*, 1860–1866: *ibid.*, 1866–1870.

Governor's Letter Book, 1798; *ibid.*, 1802–1809; *ibid.*, pt. 1, 1840–1855.

Hammond, John. Papers, 1860–1866. Micro 226, item 848.

Irwin, Jared. Correspondence, 1806–1809.

Milledge, John. Correspondence, 1804.

Passports Issued by the Governors of Georgia, 1785–1820.

Penitentiary Records, 1817–1878.

Register of Free Persons of Color in Baldwin County, 1832–1864. Book A, Box 64, Drawer 139.

"Reminiscences of Confederate Soldiers." Vol. II. Typescript.

Report of Special Committee of Senate to Visit and Examine the Public Buildings of Milledgeville, Sept. 2, 1868.

Sturges, Daniel. Instructions to Levin Wales, Esq., for Dividing the Counties of Wilkinson and Baldwin . . . 21st Feby., 1804.

B. In City Hall, Milledgeville

Minutes of the City Council of Milledgeville, 1837–1976. Office of the City Clerk. (Microfilm copies available in GDAH, Drawer 9, Boxes 75 and 76.)

Record of the Commissioners of the City of Milledgeville, 1804–1807; *ibid.*, 1811–1836. Office of the City Clerk. (Microfilm copies available in GDAH, Drawer 200, Box 10, Roll 3291.)

Tax Digest, City of Milledgeville, 1859–1867.

C. In County Archives of Georgia

Appraisements, 1827–50. Office of Probate Court. Baldwin County Courthouse.

Crawford, Joel. Will. Office of Probate Court. Early County Courthouse, Blakely.

Deed Books M, O, and R. Office of the Clerk of Superior Court. Baldwin County Courthouse.

Grand Jury Indictments, March 28, 1819. Office of Probate Court. Baldwin County Courthouse.

Marriages, 1852. Office of Probate Court. Baldwin County Courthouse.

Minute Book C. Office of Clerk of Superior Court. Early County Courthouse, Blakely.

Minutes of Inferior Court, 1812–1826. Office of Probate Court. Baldwin County Courthouse.

Mortgages, n.d. Office of Probate Court. Baldwin County Courthouse.

Retailer's Bonds, Feb., 1831–Jan. 1863. Office of Probate Court. Baldwin County Courthouse.

Tax Returns, 1832. Office of Probate Court. Baldwin County Courthouse.

Will Book B, 1832. Office of Probate Court. Baldwin County Courthouse.

D. In Libraries and in Private Possession

Barksdale-Hubert Letters. In private possession.

Barrow-McKinley Papers. University of Georgia Library, Athens.

Brooks, Iverson L. Letters. Typescript copy. In private possession.

Brown, Joseph E. Papers. Duke University Library, Durham, N. C.

Bryan, James A. Letters. In private possession.

Census of Baldwin County. Schedule I, Free Inhabitants in 1860 (microfilm). Georgia College Library, Milledgeville.

———. Schedule II, Slave Inhabitants in 1860 (microfilm). Georgia College Library, Milledgeville.

———. Schedule IV, Census of Agriculture in 1860 (microfilm). Georgia College Library, Milledgeville.

———. Slave Inhabitants of Baldwin County in 1830 (typescript). Georgia College Library, Milledgeville.

Cobb-Erwin-Lamar Papers. University of Georgia Library, Athens.

Crawford, Peter G. "History of the Milledgeville State Hospital." Typescript, 1955. Georgia College Library.

Telamon Cuylor Collection. University of Georgia Library, Athens.

Ferguson, Mrs. David. Scrapbook. In private possession.

Fitch, Thomas. Journal, 1809. Original manuscript in private possession. Copy in Georgia College Library.

Fitch-Mulford Correspondence, 1809–1810. Yale University Library, New Haven, Conn.

Fort, Tomlinson. Papers. Emory University Library, Atlanta.

Hansell, Augustin Harris. Memoirs, ca. 1905. Typescript in Southern History Collection. University of North Carolina, Chapel Hill, N.C.

Hargrett Collection. University of Georgia Library, Athens.

Lester, David. Plantation Record Book. In private possession.

McKinley, Guy C. Memoirs, 1930. Typescript in private possession. Copy in Georgia College Library, Milledgeville.

Minutes, Board of Trustees of Oglethorpe College and High School, May 1864. In private possession.

Minutes, Board of Trustees, University of Georgia, 1817–1859. 3 vols. University of Georgia Library, Athens.

Minutes of Island Creek Baptist Church. In private possession.

Mulford, Daniel. Correspondence, 1809. Georgia College Library, Milledgeville.

Norcross, Marion Ruger. Notes on the Ruger Family. In private possession.

Records of the Saint Stephen's Episcopal Church. Typescript copy. In private possession.

Smith, Travis E. "A History of the Milledgeville Baptist Church," 1975. Typescript copy. In private possession.

Tift, Nelson. Papers, University of Georgia Library, Athens.

Toomey, John D. "History of the [Milledgeville] Catholic Church." Typescript, 1953.

Vinton, John R. Journal, Jan. 29—July 30, 1827. Duke University Library, Durham, N.C.

E. In the National Archives, Washington, D. C.

Military Book Number One, 1800–1802. War Office Records. Record Group 94.

Miscellaneous File. Fort Wilkinson, Report of Freights from Philadelphia to Darien, Sept. 17, 1803. Record Group 94.

Records of the Bureau of Refugees, Freedmen, and Abandoned Lands (Georgia), 1865–1872. Record Group 105.

Record and Pension Office, No. 1206624. War Department Records.

Records of the Third Military District. 1867–1869.

IV. MAPS

Frobell, B. W. Map of Milledgeville and the Right Bank of the Oconee River from a Survey by Dr. Mitchell [1866]. Surveyor General Department, Atlanta.

Mulford, Daniel, Map of Milledgeville, 1809. Georgia College Library, Milledgeville.

Original Land Map of Washington County [1785]. Surveyor General Department, Atlanta.

Ragan, John. Map of District Number One [Baldwin County], Aug. 7, 1804. Surveyor General Department, Atlanta.

Sturges, Daniel. Map of Milledgeville, 1805. Surveyor General Department, Atlanta.

Wales, Levin. Map of District Number Two, Baldwin County [1804] Surveyor General Department, Atlanta.

Welborn, Carlton. Map of Milledgeville, 1804. Surveyor General Department, Atlanta.

V. NEWSPAPERS AND
MISCELLANEOUS PUBLICATIONS

Atlanta Constitution, 1869. Atlanta.

Atlanta Journal, 1933. Atlanta.

Atlanta Tribune, 1877. Atlanta.

Baldwin Blues Act of Incorporation and Company Regulations, 1857.

Brown Book, 1910. Yearbook of Georgia Normal and Industrial College.

Confederate Union, 1862–1865. Milledgeville.

Daily Constitutionalist, 1867, 1877. Augusta.

Evening Dispatch, 1868. Columbus, Ohio.

Federal Union, 1830–1862, 1865–1872. Milledgeville.

Floridian, 1841. Tallahassee, Fla.

Florida State Sentinel, 1842. Tallahassee, Fla.

Gainesville Eagle, 1904. Gainesville, Ga.

Georgia Argus, 1810–1813. Milledgeville.

Georgia Journal, 1809–1824, 1827, 1834, 1839. Milledgeville.

Georgia Statesman, 1827–1829. Milledgeville.

Macon Telegraph, 1864, 1865, 1869. Macon.

Middle Georgia College. Broadside dated Oct. 3, 1878. Milledgeville.

Milledgeville Chronicle, 1889. Milledgeville.

Milledgeville Daily Times, 1937–1942. Milledgeville.

Milledgeville Enquirer, 1889. Milledgeville.

Milledgeville Intelligencer, 1808. Milledgeville.

Milledgeville News, 1895, 1913–1918. Milledgeville.

Milledgeville Times, 1941. Milledgeville.

Richmond Whig, 1864. Richmond, Va.

The Reflector, 1818. Milledgeville.

Snapshots, vol. 1, 1904. Georgia Normal and Industrial College.

South Countryman, 1863. Agricultural journal. Marietta.

Southern Progress, 1897. Milledgeville.

Southern Recorder, 1820–1872. Milledgeville.

Standard of Union, 1841. Milledgeville.

Statesman and Patriot, 1827–1829. Milledgeville.

Union-Recorder, 1872–1904, 1909, 1923–1930. Milledgeville. This paper was called *Union and Recorder* from 1872 to 1879.

VI. PRINTED PUBLIC DOCUMENTS

Acts of the General Assembly of the State of Georgia . . . , 1803, 1804–1810, 1822, 1835–1837, 1841, 1849–1850, 1855–1856, 1859, 1866, 1870, 1876–1879, 1889. Before 1868 these acts were published by state printers at Milledgeville; after that date they were produced by state printers in Atlanta and Savannah. Publication occurred annually from 1803 to 1841, biennially from 1850 to 1857, and annually thereafter except for the years 1878–79 and 1889–91.

Annual Report, American Historical Association . . . *1908*. 2 vols. Washington: Government Printing Office, 1909.

Clayton, Augustin S. *A Compilation of the Laws of the State of Georgia.* . . . Augusta: Adams and Durckinck, 1812.

Correspondence Relative to the Public Deposits. *American State Papers, Documents, Legislative and Executive of the Congress of the United States*. 38 vols. Washington: Gales and Seaton, 1832–1861.

Cuthbert, John A. *Digest of all the Laws and Resolutions Now in Force in the State of Georgia on the Subject of Public Education and Free Schools*. Milledgeville: Polhill and Cuthbert, 1832.

Dawson, William C., *Compilation of the Laws of the State of Georgia.* . . . *Milledgeville: Grantland and Orme, 1831*.

Directory of [the Residents of] Milledgeville (1878–1879). Macon: Seifert and Smith, 1878.

Harrison, James L., *Biographical Directory of the American Congress, 1774– 1849.* . . . Washington: Government Printing Office, 1950.

Henderson, Lillian. *Roster of the Confederate Soldiers of Georgia, 1861–1865*. 5 vols. Hapeville: Longino and Porter, 1959–1960.

Journal of the Senate of the State of Georgia . . . , 1805, 1810, 1811, 1833, 1836, 1841, 1865. These items were issued annually by state printers in Augusta and Milledgeville.

Index

Kenan, Augustus H., 39, 78, 95, 117, 128, 156, 202
Kenan, Buck, 116
Kenan, Dicey, 212
Kenan, Lewis H., 165, 169, 211–12
Kenan, Michael J., 39, 92
Kenan, Judge Owen H., 60
Kenan, Thomas Holmes, 38, 172
Kidd, S. J., 158
Kiddock, Davis, 98
Kilpatrick, Gen. Hugh Judson, 183, 192–93
Kimball, Hannibal I., 226
Kimberly, Anson, 51

Lafayette, Gen. Marquis de, 77, 78
Lafayette Hall, 27, 28, 127
Lamar, Andrew J., 40
Lamar, James, 14
Lamar, Jeremiah, 40
Lamar, John Basil, 39, 40, 140, 145
Lamar, Lucius Quintus Cincinnatus, 39, 63, 117
Lamar, Mary Ann, 40
Lamar, Mirabeau B., 39
Lamar, Zachariah, 27, 36, 39, 48, 114
Lanier, Clifford, 170
Lanier, Sidney, 164, 170
Lankford, Lillie, 119
Lataste, Lucien, 98
Lataste, Victor, 99
Law, William, 57
Le Conte, Dr. Joseph, 44
Leikens, George T., 127
Lester, David, 184, 186
Lewis, John W., 151
Lewis, Robert H., 245
Lewis, William, 36
Lincoln, Gen. Benjamin, 2
Locke, Abner, 37
Lockerley Hall, 123
Love, Lt. James T., 8
Lucas, John, 27
Lumpkin, Joseph Henry, 41, 57
Lumpkin, Gov. Wilson, 74, 90, 97, 113
Lunceford, Enoch, 26
Lyell, Sir Charles, 140
Lynes, J. Colton, 244

McAdoo, William Gibbs, Sr., 233

McAdoo, William Gibbs, Jr., 234
McComb, Mary C., 135
McComb, Robert, 28, 63, 123
McDonald, Gov. Charles J., 51, 72, 130, 139
McDonald, Elizabeth, 44
McDuff, Daniel, 114
McGehee, John, 119
McGehee, Nathan, 46
McGillivray, Alexander, 2
McIntosh, Barbara, 43
McIntosh, Chilly, 43
McIntosh, Croesy, 43, 86
McIntosh, Jane, 43
McIntosh, John, 43
McIntosh, Nancy, 207
McIntosh, Capt. William, 43
McIntosh, Chief William, 43, 86
McKinley, Andrews, 38
McKinley, Archibald C., 38, 172, 181
McKinley, Guy C., 38
McKinley, William, Sr., 38, 126, 178, 239, 240
McKinley, William, Jr., 38, 178
Mahon, Jackson, 63
Malcom, John, 73
Manly, Basil, 91
Marlow, Bill, 237
Marlow (Marlor), John, 37
Marlow, Sam, 108
Masonic Hall, 126–27
Mapp, Frances B., 181
Martin, Carlisle P. B., 79
Mathews, Gov. George, 7
Meacham, Henry, 37
Meade, Gen. George H., 220
Meek, Samuel M., 86
Mercer, Jesse, 53, 90
Methodists, 24, 85, 86
Mickeljohn, Andrew J., 168
Middle Georgia Military and Agricultural College, 240–44; becomes Georgia Military College, 257
Midway, 100
Miles, John, 37
Miles, Thomas, 37
Milledge, Gov. John, 17
Milledgeville: Indian trails and trading paths near site of, 8–12; Indian trade, 10–11, 59, 64; surveyed, 17; early houses, 18; water